Lecture Notes in Computer Science 16072

Founding Editors

Gerhard Goos
Juris Hartmanis

Editorial Board Members

Elisa Bertino, *Purdue University, West Lafayette, IN, USA*
Wen Gao, *Peking University, Beijing, China*
Bernhard Steffen, *TU Dortmund University, Dortmund, Germany*
Moti Yung, *Columbia University, New York, NY, USA*

The series Lecture Notes in Computer Science (LNCS), including its subseries Lecture Notes in Artificial Intelligence (LNAI) and Lecture Notes in Bioinformatics (LNBI), has established itself as a medium for the publication of new developments in computer science and information technology research, teaching, and education.

LNCS enjoys close cooperation with the computer science R & D community, the series counts many renowned academics among its volume editors and paper authors, and collaborates with prestigious societies. Its mission is to serve this international community by providing an invaluable service, mainly focused on the publication of conference and workshop proceedings and postproceedings. LNCS commenced publication in 1973.

Walter Senn · Marcello Sanguineti ·
Ausra Saudargiene · Igor V. Tetko ·
Alessandro E. P. Villa · Viktor Jirsa ·
Yoshua Bengio
Editors

Artificial Neural Networks and Machine Learning

ICANN 2025 International Workshops and Special Sessions

34th International Conference on Artificial Neural Networks
Kaunas, Lithuania, September 9–12, 2025
Proceedings, Part V

Editors
Walter Senn
University of Bern
Bern, Switzerland

Ausra Saudargiene
Vytautas Magnus University
Kaunas, Lithuania

Alessandro E. P. Villa
University of Lausanne
Lausanne, Switzerland

Yoshua Bengio
Université de Montréal
Montréal, QC, Canada

Marcello Sanguineti
University of Genoa
Genoa, Italy

Igor V. Tetko
Helmholtz Zentrum München
Neuherberg, Germany

Viktor Jirsa
Aix-Marseille Université
Marseille, France

ISSN 0302-9743 ISSN 1611-3349 (electronic)
Lecture Notes in Computer Science
ISBN 978-3-032-04551-5 ISBN 978-3-032-04552-2 (eBook)
https://doi.org/10.1007/978-3-032-04552-2

© The Editor(s) (if applicable) and The Author(s), under exclusive license
to Springer Nature Switzerland AG 2026, corrected publication 2026

This work is subject to copyright. All rights are solely and exclusively licensed by the Publisher, whether the whole or part of the material is concerned, specifically the rights of translation, reprinting, reuse of illustrations, recitation, broadcasting, reproduction on microfilms or in any other physical way, and transmission or information storage and retrieval, electronic adaptation, computer software, or by similar or dissimilar methodology now known or hereafter developed.
The use of general descriptive names, registered names, trademarks, service marks, etc. in this publication does not imply, even in the absence of a specific statement, that such names are exempt from the relevant protective laws and regulations and therefore free for general use.
The publisher, the authors and the editors are safe to assume that the advice and information in this book are believed to be true and accurate at the date of publication. Neither the publisher nor the authors or the editors give a warranty, expressed or implied, with respect to the material contained herein or for any errors or omissions that may have been made. The publisher remains neutral with regard to jurisdictional claims in published maps and institutional affiliations.

This Springer imprint is published by the registered company Springer Nature Switzerland AG
The registered company address is: Gewerbestrasse 11, 6330 Cham, Switzerland

If disposing of this product, please recycle the paper.

Preface

The 34th International Conference on Artificial Neural Networks (ICANN 2025) was held in Kaunas, Lithuania, from September 9 to 12, 2025.

The International Conference on Artificial Neural Networks (ICANN) serves as a global platform for presenting the latest breakthroughs in artificial intelligence, neural networks, deep learning, and brain-inspired computing. Organized annually by the European Neural Network Society (ENNS), ICANN has, since its inception in 1992, evolved into one of Europe's most prestigious conferences at the intersection of Artificial Intelligence and Neuroscience. It offers researchers, practitioners, and industry professionals a unique opportunity to share innovations, discuss theoretical advances, and explore practical applications of neural computation. The conference strongly values the synergy between theoretical progress and impactful real-world applications, and actively encourages contributions that demonstrate how artificial neural networks are being used to address pressing societal and technological challenges.

We received 375 submissions for the main research track. The research track accepted 170 papers (45%). In addition, there were 42 papers submitted to workshops and special sessions, which were mainly invited contributions (of which 29 were accepted). Each paper was assigned three reviewers, although due to availability and completion rates, an average of 2.2 reviews per paper was obtained, totaling 807 reviews. The review process followed a double-blind peer-review model, and area chairs oversaw quality and fairness. The papers submitted to the main research track were presented over two days. Additionally, one day was devoted to tutorials and one day to workshops.

The General Co-chairs of ICANN 2025 were distinguished experts in the fields of Artificial Intelligence and Neuroscience:

- Yoshua Bengio (Université de Montréal, Canada) is one of the world's leaders in Artificial Intelligence and Deep Learning, the most cited computer scientist worldwide, the recipient of the 2018 A.M. Turing Award, considered to be the "Nobel prize of computing". He is Co-President and Scientific Director of LawZero, a nonprofit organization committed to advancing research and developing technical solutions for safe-by-design AI systems, the Founder and Scientific Advisor of Mila and a Canada CIFAR AI Chair.
- Viktor Jirsa (Aix-Marseille Université, France; EBRAINS Chief Science Officer) is renowned for his fundamental work in theoretical neuroscience, and for open-source simulation platform The Virtual Brain, used to build personalised brain models for epilepsy surgery and other brain disorders. He served as a lead investigator in the EU Flagship Human Brain Project and its successor infrastructure EBRAINS (European Brain REsearch INfrastructureS). Jirsa's contributions have been recognised with numerous honours, including the Human Brain Project Innovation Prize (2021).

The conference featured five keynote talks spanning a wide spectrum of topics, reflecting both emerging scientific challenges and the growing convergence of theoretical insights, real-world applications, and ethical considerations in AI and neuroscience. These talks addressed the frontiers of generative models, causality, brain simulation, ethics, and efficient deep learning, showcasing the diverse landscape ICANN 2025 aimed to represent:

- Bernhard Schölkopf (Max Planck Institute for Intelligent Systems, Tübingen, Germany): *AI Extracting Causality*
- Viktor Jirsa (Aix-Marseille University, France): *Virtual Brain Twins for Health and Disease*
- Gintarė Karolina Džiugaitė (DeepMind, USA): *On Memorization and Unlearning*
- Emmanuel Bengio (McGill University; Recursion/Valence Labs, Canada): *AI and Generative Models*
- Christiane Woopen (University of Bonn, Germany): *Ethics in AI, Neuroscience, Digital Twins, and Consciousness Research Neuroscience and AI for a Flourishing Life*
- Alessio Micheli (University of Pisa, Italy): *A Journey through Efficient Deep Learning on Graphs*

The invited speakers covered topics at the intersection of neuroscience and artificial intelligence such as neuromorphic computing, biophysical modeling, engineering network-based brain therapies, AI oversight, and reasoning-capable robotics in the physical world:

- Mihai Petrovici (NeuroTMA Lab, University of Bern, Switzerland): *Teacher Propagation Through Space, Time and the Brain*
- Mehmet Fatih Yanik (ETH Zürich, Switzerland): *Engineering Brain Activity Patterns for Therapeutics*
- Michael Deistler (Machine Learning in Science, University of Tübingen, Germany): *Building Mechanistic Models of Neural Computations with Simulation-based Machine Learning*
- Ameya Pandurang Prabh (Tübingen AI Center, University of Tübingen, Germany): *Scalable Strategies for AI Oversight of AI - Progress, Pitfalls and Path Forward*
- Ignas Budvytis (Resilient Robotics, UK): *Embodied Reasoning in the Physical World*

Participants had the exclusive opportunity to attend the public Panel Discussion 'Where Does AI Lead To? Opportunities and Risks', where the leading experts Yoshua Bengio, Viktor Jirsa, Christiane Woopen, Gintarė Karolina Džiugaitė, and Bernhard Schölkopf addressed the interaction between AI and Neuroscience, ethical challenges, AI's impact on human identity, and questions about the safe and responsible development of AI.

The ICANN 2025 Organizing Committee committed itself to supporting Diversity and Inclusion within the Artificial Intelligence and Neuroscience communities. As part of this commitment, ICANN 2025 awarded two scholarships of €1000 and €500 to early-career researchers from developing countries and/or underrepresented communities in science and technology. These scholarships were intended to support travel and accommodation costs, helping recipients attend the conference, present their research, and become active members of the ICANN community.

By enabling broader participation, ICANN 2025 continued efforts towards fostering a more inclusive and representative research environment, encouraging the exchange of ideas across cultures, disciplines, and career stages.

We extend our sincere thanks to all the authors, workshop and tutorial organizers, and participants whose scientific contributions and engagement made ICANN 2025 such a dynamic and inspiring event. Crafting a rich and interdisciplinary program would not have been possible without the dedication and significant commitment of the area chairs, the program committee led by Walter Senn (University of Bern, Switzerland) and the organizing committee, especially Ausra Saudargiene (Lithuanian University of Health Sciences/Vytautas Magnus University, Lithuania) and Linas Petkevičius (Vilnius University, Artificial Intelligence Association of Lithuania). We are also deeply grateful to the many volunteers and session chairs, whose behind-the-scenes work ensured the smooth running of the conference, as well as to all reviewers.

We thank Springer for their continued collaboration in publishing the conference proceedings, and Microsoft for providing access to the CMT conference management system and offering technical assistance throughout the organization process.

We deeply appreciate the ongoing support and guidance of the European Neural Network Society (ENNS), whose leadership and vision continue to shape the ICANN community.

September 2025

Ausra Saudargiene
Walter Senn
Igor V. Tetko
Alessandro E. P. Villa
Marcello Sanguineti
Viktor Jirsa
Yoshua Bengio

Organization

General Chairs

Yoshua Bengio — Université de Montréal, Canada
Viktor Jirsa — Aix-Marseille Université, France

Program Committee

Walter Senn (Chair) — University of Bern, Switzerland
Marcello Sanguineti — University of Genova, Italy
Igor V. Tetko — Helmholtz Munich, Germany and BIGCHEM GmbH, Germany
Alessandro E. P. Villa — University of Lausanne, Switzerland
Ausra Saudargiene — Lithuanian University of Health Sciences/Vytautas Magnus University, Lithuania

Honorary Chairs

Vera Kurkova — Czech Academy of Sciences, Czech Republic
Alessandro E. P. Villa — University of Lausanne, Switzerland
Stefan Wermter — University of Hamburg, Germany

Communication Committee

Sebastian Otte — University of Lübeck, Germany
Kristína Malinovská — Comenius University in Bratislava, Slovakia

Local Organizing Committee

Ausra Saudargiene — Lithuanian University of Health Sciences/Vytautas Magnus University, Lithuania
Linas Petkevičius — Vilnius University, Lithuania

Workshop, Tutorials and Special Session Chairs

Povilas Daniusis	Vytautas Magnus University, Lithuania
Dalius Matuzevičius	VilniusTech, Lithuania

Diversity and Inclusion Chair

Kamilė Dementavičiūtė — Vinted, Lithuania

ICANN Steering Committee

Stefan Wermter	University of Hamburg, Germany
Angelo Cangelosi	University of Manchester, UK
Igor Farkaš	Comenius University in Bratislava, Slovakia
Christina Jayne	Teesside University, UK
Matthias Kerzel	University of Hamburg, Germany
Alessandra Lintas	University of Lausanne, Switzerland
Kristína Malinovská	Comenius University in Bratislava, Slovakia
Jaakko Peltonen	Tampere University, Finland
Brigitte Quenet	ESPCI Paris, France
Roseli Wedemann	Rio de Janeiro State University, Brazil
Sebastian Otte	University of Lübeck, Germany
Ausra Saudargiene	Lithuanian University of Health Sciences/Vytautas Magnus University, Lithuania

Keynote Talks Abstracts

Virtual Brain Twins for Health and Disease

Viktor Jirsa

Institut de Neurosciences des Systèmes (INS), Aix-Marseille Université (AMU), France

Abstract. In the past twenty years, we have made significant progress in creating digital models of an individual's brain, so called virtual brain twins. By combining brain imaging data with mathematical models, we can predict outcomes more accurately than using each method separately. Our approach has helped us understand normal brain states, their operation and conditions like healthy aging, dementia and schizophrenia. We illustrate the virtual brain workflow along the example of drug resistant epilepsy, the so-called Virtual Epileptic Patient (VEP): we reconstruct the connectome of an epileptic patient using DTI and co-register other potential imaging data from the same individual (anatomical MRI, computer tomography (CT)). Each brain region is represented by neural population models, which are derived using mean field techniques from statistical physics expressing ensemble activity via collective variables. Subsets of brain regions generating seizures in patients with refractory partial epilepsy are referred to as the epileptogenic zone (EZ). During a seizure, paroxysmal activity is not restricted to the EZ, but may recruit other healthy brain regions and propagate activity through large brain networks. The identification of the EZ is crucial for the success of neurosurgery and presents one of the historically difficult questions in clinical neuroscience. The application of Bayesian inference and model inversion, in particular Hamiltonian Monte Carlo, allows the estimation of the patient's EZ, including estimates of confidence and diagnostics of performance of the inference. In summary, the Virtual Brain Twin augments the value of empirical data by completing missing data, allowing clinical hypothesis testing and optimizing treatment strategies for the individual patient. Virtual Brain Twins are part of the European infrastructure called EBRAINS, which supports researchers worldwide in digital neuroscience.

Biography. Viktor Jirsa, PhD, is Director of the Inserm Institut de Neurosciences des Systèmes (INS U1106) at Aix-Marseille Université and Director of Research (DRCE) at CNRS in Marseille, France. Trained in theoretical physics and applied mathematics (PhD 1996), he pioneered large-scale brain-network models that combine biologically grounded neural dynamics with individual connectomes, establishing a mathematical framework now central to network science in medicine. He is the scientific architect of the open-source simulation platform The Virtual Brain and served as a lead investigator in the EU Flagship Human Brain Project and its successor infrastructure EBRAINS, driving clinical translation of personalised brain models for epilepsy surgery and other disorders. Jirsa's contributions have been recognised with numerous honours, including the Human Brain Project Innovation Prize (2021).

Causal Representations, World Models and Digital Twins

Bernhard Schölkopf[1,2]

[1] Max Planck Institute for Intelligent Systems & ELLIS Institute Tübingen, Germany
[2] Professor at ETH, Zürich, Switzerland

Abstract. Research on understanding and building artificially intelligent systems has moved from symbolic approaches to statistical learning, and is now beginning to study interventional models relying on concepts of causality. Some of the hard open problems of machine learning and AI are intrinsically related to causality, and progress may require advances in our understanding of how to model and infer causality from data, as well as conceptual progress on what constitutes a causal representation and a causal world model. I will present basic concepts and thoughts, as well some applications to astronomy.

Biography. Bernhard Schölkopf's studies machine learning and causal inference, with applications to fields ranging from astronomy to biomedicine, computational photography, music and robotics. Originally trained in physics and mathematics, he earned a Ph.D. in computer science in 1997 and became a Max Planck director in 2001. His awards include the ACM AAAI Allen Newell Award, the BBVA Foundation Frontiers of Knowledge Award, the Leibniz Award, and the Royal Society Milner Award. He is a Professor at ETH Zurich, a Fellow of the ACM and of the CIFAR Program "Learning in Machines and Brains", and a member of the German Academy of Sciences. He helped start the MLSS series of Machine Learning Summer Schools, the ELLIS society, and the Journal of Machine Learning Research, an early development in open access and today the field's flagship journal. In 2023, he founded the ELLIS Institute Tübingen, and acts as its scientific director.

On Memorization and Unlearning

Gintarė Karolina Džiugaitė

Google DeepMind, USA

Abstract. Deep learning models exhibit a complex interplay between memorization and generalization. This talk will begin by exploring the ubiquitous nature of memorization, drawing on prior work on "data diets", example difficulty, pruning, and other empirical evidence. But is memorization essential for generalization? Our recent theoretical work suggests that eliminating it entirely may not be feasible. Instead, I will discuss strategies to mitigate unwanted memorization by focusing on better data curation and efficient unlearning mechanisms. Additionally, I will examine the potential of pruning techniques to selectively remove memorized examples and explore their impact on factual recall versus in-context learning.

Biography. Gintarė is a senior research scientist at Google DeepMind, based in Toronto, an adjunct professor in the McGill University School of Computer Science, and an associate industry member of Mila, the Quebec AI Institute. Prior to joining Google, Gintarė led the Trustworthy AI program at Element AI/ServiceNow, and obtained her Ph.D. in machine learning from the University of Cambridge, under the supervision of Zoubin Ghahramani. Gintarė was recognized as a Rising Star in Machine Learning by the University of Maryland program in 2019. Her research combines theoretical and empirical approaches to understanding deep learning, with a focus on generalization, memorization, unlearning, and network compression.

AI and Generative Models

Emmanuel Bengio

McGill University; Recursion/Valence Labs, Montreal, Canada

Abstract. In this talk I will share some recent progress on training energy-based generative models using the GFlowNet framework and applying them to scientific problems, as well as speculate on the bigger picture; using GFNs to be good Bayesians, and create models that reason about their environment, concluding with an open discussion of next steps and open problems.

Biography. Emmanuel Bengio is a senior ML Scientist at Valence Labs @ Recursion, working on GFlowNet and drug discovery from Mila, Montreal, Canada. He is mainly interested in Machine Learning, especially Deep Learning and Reinforcement Learning and mixing both. Lately, he has been working at the intersection of ML and drug design using the new GFlowNet framework.

Ethics in AI, Neuroscience, Digital Twins, and Consciousness Research Neuroscience and AI for a Flourishing Life

Christiane Woopen

Heinrich Hertz Professor at the University of Bonn, Germany

Abstract. Neuroscience and artificial intelligence are rapidly advancing fields that combine remarkable scientific progress with ambitious visions for the future. At the same time, they face deep conceptual disagreements, ethical concerns, and dystopian anxieties. Their findings—and the methodological innovations they employ, such as digital twins—raise complex ethical questions concerning autonomy, justice, privacy, and sustainability. Moreover, they are grounded in contested assumptions about the brain and its significance for personal identity and agency. These debates inevitably lead to broader philosophical questions about the nature of human beings and their potential distinctiveness within the continuum of life and consciousness. This lecture examines the ethical implications of these interrelated developments and levels of thought, and it argues for the relevance of human flourishing as a guiding ethical principle in addressing them.

Biography. Christiane Woopen is Heinrich Hertz Professor for Life Ethics at the University of Bonn and founding director of the Center for Life Ethics since October 2021. In addition to leading national and international research projects on ethics in digital technologies, sciences and health she is involved in policy advice, including as Chair of the German Ethics Council (2012–2016), as President of the Global Summit of National Ethics Councils (2014–2016), as a member of the UNESCO International Bioethics Committee until 2017, as Co-speaker of the German Data Ethics Commission (2018–2019), and as Chair of the European Group on Ethics in Science and New Technologies (EGE, 2017–2021). Woopen is a member of several academies of sciences (NRW, BBAW, Academia Europaea, National Academy of Medicine in Mexico) and was awarded the Order of Merit of the State of North Rhine-Westphalia as well as the Federal Cross of Merit 1st Class.

A Journey Through Efficient Deep Learning on Graphs

Alessio Micheli

Head of the Computational Intelligence and Machine Learning Group, Department of Computer Science, University of Pisa, Italy

Abstract. Although the investigation on learning in structured domains started in the late 1990s, recently deep learning for graphs has attracted tremendous research interest and increasing attention for applications. Indeed, graphs are powerful and flexible tools for representing relationships among data at different levels of abstraction. Unsurprisingly, the range of applications includes many fields, including biology, chemistry, network science, computer vision, natural languages and many others. On the other hand, extending the data domain to graphs opens new challenges for the field of deep learning, particularly regarding efficiency, which is related to the important aspect of environmental sustainability. The talk will very briefly introduce the area of deep learning for graphs, with a focus on its origins. We will then move on to discuss advanced topics and current open issues by providing an overview of recent progress in my research group. We will pay particular attention to efficiency, the interplay between model depth and learning complex data representations, and explainability on graphs.

Biography. Alessio Micheli is Full Professor at the Department of Computer Science of the University of Pisa, where he is the head and scientific coordinator of the Computational Intelligence & Machine Learning Group (CIML), part of the CAIRNE.eu Research Network. His research interests include machine learning, neural networks, deep learning, learning in structured domains (sequence, tree, and graph data), recurrent and recursive neural networks, reservoir computing, and probabilistic and kernel-based learning for non-vectorial data, with a particular focus and pioneering works on efficient neural networks for learning from graphs. Micheli is the national coordinator of the "Italian Working group on Machine Learning and Data Mining" of the Italian Association for Artificial Intelligence and he has been co-founder/chair of the IEEE CIS Task Force on Reservoir Computing. He is an elected member of the Executive Committee of the European Neural Network Society – ENNS. He serves as an Associate Editor for Neural Networks and IEEE Transactions on Neural Networks and Learning Systems.

Teacher Propagation Through Space, Time and the Brain

Mihai Petrovici

NeuroTMA Lab, University of Bern, Switzerland

Abstract. Whether biological or artificial, intelligence ultimately boils down to the ability of physical substrates to perform (complex) computations efficiently. Which algorithms can "run" on the dynamics of a given substrate? And conversely, which substrates should we build to implement our algorithms of choice? In my talk, I will discuss variants of these questions that are inspired by recent insights from neurobiology and recent developments in neuromorphic engineering. In particular, I will address several challenges of credit assignment in physical neuronal networks and show how they can be met with rigorous math and creative physics.

Biography. Already since my earliest days as an aspiring physicist, I have worked in several fields that are marked by emergent phenomena arising from complex interactions, from high-multiplicity particle collisions to ultracold glasses and, ultimately, neuromorphic systems. It is this "science of complexity" that continues to intrigue and inspire me. Following my PhD with Karlheinz Meier at Heidelberg University, I moved to the University of Bern, where I am now leading the Neuro-inspired Theory, Modeling and Applications (NeuroTMA) Lab.

I believe there is much to learn from brains about cognition, but taking steps beyond biology may well be warranted when building physical substrates for artificial intelligence – there are good reasons for airplanes not to flap their wings. Therefore, in our group, we combine knowledge and methods from a variety of fields - neuroscience, mathematics, physics, machine learning and microelectronics - to understand biological intelligence and extract its key features for subsequent implementation in silico.

Engineering Brain Activity Patterns for Therapeutics

Mehmet Fatih Yanik

ETH Zurich, Chair of Neurotechnology Laboratories, NSC Study Director, Co-director of Institute of Neuroinformatics, ETH Artificial Intelligence Center

Abstract. Brain networks are disrupted in numerous disorders. I will first show how aberrant brain-wide activity patterns can be corrected by targeting distinct network motifs with multiple neuromodulators using a vertebrate model of human epilepsy and autism. This systematic approach rescues behavior unlike any other. Next, I will present two technologies to realize such network corrections in humans: (1) Biocompatible ultraflexible tentacle electrodes that allow single-neuron-resolution network recordings simultaneously from many brain areas, where we can track inter-areal neuronal ensembles year long, and we are currently starting the first human acute recordings. (2) AU-FUS technology that allows us to non-invasively deliver drugs/RNA to specific brain circuits with 1,300x enhanced focal concentration with millimeter precision across the BBB; we are performing the first pre-clinical large animal studies. I will show how targeting dorsal ACC reduces chronic anxiety without motor side effects.

Biography. Yanik received his BS and MS in Engineering and Physics at MIT in 2000, and PhD in Computational and Applied Physics at Stanford in 2006. He completed brief postdoctoral work in Stanford Bioengineering and Neurosurgery. He subsequently served as Assistant (2006) and later as Associate Professor (2009) till his tenure at MIT. He is currently a professor at ETH Zurich in the Institute for Neuroinformatics. His studies are recognized by a NIH Director's Pioneer Award, NIH Director's New Innovator Award, NIH Transformative Research Award, ERC Consolidator Award, SNSF (ERC) Advanced, Bridge Discovery Award, Packard Award in Engineering and Science, Alfred Sloan Award in Neuroscience, NIH Eureka Award, NSF Career Award, Silicon Valley's Innovator's Challenge Award, Technology Review Magazine's "World's top 35 innovators under age 35", and Junior Chamber International's "Outstanding Young Person", among others. His work has been highlighted by The Economist, BBC, Popular Mechanics, Nature, Guardian, ABC, Boston Globe, Scientific American, MIT Technology Review, The Scientist, National Geographic, Blick, and others.

Building Mechanistic Models of Neural Computations with Simulation-Based Machine Learning

Michael Deistler

Machine Learning in Science, University of Tübingen, Germany

Abstract. A central challenge in neuroscience is that many properties of neural systems cannot be measured exactly. This limits our understanding of these systems and our ability to build simulations that match experimental recordings or predict neural responses to unseen stimuli. Inference allows scientists to identify parameters—the properties that cannot be measured exactly—such that biophysical simulations are consistent with experimental measurements of neural activity.

I will present machine learning-based inference methods for biophysical simulations in neuroscience. While the focus is on neuroscience, the methods are broadly applicable. First, I will discuss simulation-based Bayesian inference using neural networks. Second, I will introduce differentiable simulation as a powerful approach for parameter inference in large-scale biophysical models. This allows us to directly optimize parameters using gradient-based methods, even in morphologically detailed models of single cells or networks—overcoming the scalability barriers of previous approaches.

Together, these results demonstrate how machine learning opens new possibilities for constructing and fitting biophysical simulations in neuroscience, helping to bridge the gap between experimental data and mechanistic understanding.

Biography. My research lies at the intersection of machine learning and science. I build inference methods that enable the tuning of mechanistic simulators to match empirical measurements. I have a particular focus on biophysical simulations in neuroscience, where I develop machine learning methods to build large-scale and data-driven models of biological intelligence.

Scalable Strategies for AI Oversight of AI - Progress, Pitfalls and Path Forward

Ameya Pandurang Prabh

Tübingen AI Center, University of Tübingen, Germany

Abstract. As foundation models scale, the aspiration of "AI providing oversight for AI" is becoming practical reality. Recent advances, including large-language-model (LLM) judges that auto-grade outputs and weak-to-strong pipelines where smaller models critique larger ones, demonstrate that automated oversight can effectively augment limited human supervision. However, new evidence exposes a critical flaw: great models increasingly think alike. We show that model errors become more correlated as capabilities improve. The similarity that drives high accuracy also biases LLM judges towards models resembling themselves, and weak-to-strong training becomes less effective as supervisors and students share similar blind spots. This talk outlines a research agenda and practical engineering solutions to maintain trustworthy automated supervision despite model convergence.

Biography. Ameya Prabhu is a postdoctoral researcher at the Tübingen AI Center, hosted by Matthias Bethge. His work focuses on data-centric methodologies, scalable lifelong benchmarks, and oversight mechanisms for foundation models. He earned his PhD at the University of Oxford under the guidance of Adel Bibi and Philip Torr, studying foundations of continual learning, machine unlearning, and lifelong model benchmarking. His current research interests are centered around developing Scientist AI (also known as STEM AI), inspired by the vision of Yoshua Bengio and Evan Hubinger. Specifically, he is working towards creating large language models (LLMs) as non-agentic cognitive systems that explain observed data through generating theories, rather than imitating or pleasing humans. His goal is to build powerful, trustworthy AI systems designed explicitly for safe, sandboxed exploration of STEM problems, without external human modeling or intervention.

Embodied Reasoning in the Physical World

Ignas Budvytis

Resilient Robotics, Cambridge, UK

Abstract. Robotics has recently experienced several significant breakthroughs in various capabilities, including improvements in 3D shape estimation and re-rendering algorithms, open-world perception, video generation-based world models, and solving complex manipulation tasks via imitation learning. However, widespread adoption of generalist robotic systems in the physical world still requires further research breakthroughs. In particular, safely interacting with humans, adapting to changes in tasks or environments, and efficiently learning from human feedback remain critical challenges. All these capabilities rely on embodied reasoning—the ability to understand one's own form factor, action space, and impact on the operating environment. This talk aims to examine AI reasoning from its origins to recent advancements, providing inspiration for novel embodied reasoning systems while highlighting past pitfalls. The presentation reviews early contributions by Turing, McCarthy, and Hayes, and discusses challenges such as the framing problem. Additionally, it covers key milestones in neurosymbolic AI, early visual reasoning, and current efforts in embodied reasoning, including multi-modal foundational models and agentic AI reasoning frameworks. The talk concludes with a brief overview of remaining challenges and future directions for systems that reason effectively in the physical world.

Biography. Ignas Budvytis is an independent researcher and former academic specialising in computer vision, machine learning, and robotics. He is dedicated to developing advanced technologies that enhance how machines perceive and interpret the world. Ignas holds a Bachelor's degree in Computer Science and a PhD in Computer Vision from the University of Cambridge. He recently served as an Assistant Professor of Computer Vision and Robotics in the Department of Engineering at the University of Cambridge.

Contents – Part V

2nd AI in Drug Discovery (AIDD) Workshop

Early-Stage Discovery in the Era of Hard-To-Drug Targets and Giga-Scale Chemical Spaces 3
   Dmitri Kireev

Comparative Analysis of Chemical Structure String Representations for Neural Machine Translation 6
   Kohulan Rajan, Achim Zielesny, and Christoph Steinbeck

ADMETrix: ADMET-Driven De Novo Molecular Generation 15
   Nikolaos Mourdoukoutas, Aigli Korfiati, and Vassilis Pitsikalis

Dimension-Augmented Anisotropy in Graph Neural Diffusion 29
   Tatiana Sycheva, Maxim Beketov, and Ivan Smolyar

Uni-Mol Docking V2: Towards Realistic and Accurate Binding Pose Prediction 34
   Eric Alcaide, Zhifeng Gao, Guolin Ke, Yaqi Li, Linfeng Zhang, Hang Zheng, and Gengmo Zhou

MolEncoder: Improved Masked Language Modeling for Molecules 42
   Fabian P. Krüger, Nicklas Österbacka, Mikhail Kabeshov, Ola Engkvist, and Igor Tetko

Consensus Prediction of Chemical Reactions with OCHEM-R Platform 45
   Igor V. Tetko, Guillaume Godin, Kevin M. Jablonka, Adrian Mirza, and Luc Patiny

Special Session: Neural Networks for Graphs and Beyond

HeNCler: Node Clustering in Heterophilous Graphs via Learned Asymmetric Similarity 55
   Sonny Achten, Zander Op de Beeck, Francesco Tonin, Volkan Cevher, and Johan A. K. Suykens

Visualization and Analysis of the Loss Landscape in Graph Neural Networks 69
   Samir Moustafa, Lorenz Kummer, Simon Fetzel, Nils M. Kriege, and Wilfried N. Gansterer

Special Session: Neurorobotics

Pointing-Guided Target Estimation via Transformer-Based Attention 85
  Luca Müller, Hassan Ali, Philipp Allgeuer, Lukáš Gajdošech, and Stefan Wermter

Keypoint-Based Diffusion for Robotic Motion Planning on the NICOL Robot 98
  Lennart Clasmeier, Jan-Gerrit Habekost, Connor Gäde, Philipp Allgeuer, and Stefan Wermter

Real-Time Syllable Recognition in LIBRAS Using Deep Learning for Human-Robot Interaction 111
  Joelmir Ramos, Nadia Nedjah, and Paulo Victor Rorigues de Carvalho

Generating and Customizing Robotic Arm Trajectories Using Neural Networks 124
  Andrej Lúčny, Matilde Antonj, Carlo Mazzola, Hana Hornáčková, and Igor Farkaš

Robotic Calibration Based on Haptic Feedback Improves Sim-to-Real Transfer 136
  Juraj Gavura, Michal Vavrečka, Igor Farkaš, and Connor Gäde

Towards Bio-inspired Robotic Trajectory Planning via Self-supervised RNN 149
  Miroslav Cibula, Kristína Malinovská, and Matthias Kerzel

3rd International Workshop on Reservoir Computing

Impact of Plasticity-Based Reservoir Adaptation on Spectral Radius and Performance of ESNs 163
  Franziska Weber, Lluís Belanche-Muñoz, and Andreas Maier

Benchmarking Nonlinear Readouts in Linear Reservoir Networks 176
  Giacomo Lagomarsini, Andrea Ceni, and Claudio Gallicchio

Investigating Time-Scales in Deep Echo State Networks for Natural Language Processing 188
  Corrado Baccheschi, Alessandro Bondielli, Alessandro Lenci, Alessio Micheli, Lucia Passaro, Marco Podda, and Domenico Tortorella

A Spectral Interpretation of Redundancy in a Graph Reservoir 201
  Anna Bison and Alessandro Sperduti

Shaping Attractor Landscapes in Boolean Liquid State Machines via STDP
and Global Plasticity 213
    Jérémie Cabessa and Alessandro E. P. Villa

Correction to: ADMETrix: ADMET-Driven De Novo Molecular
Generation C1
    Nikolaos Mourdoukoutas, Aigli Korfiati, and Vassilis Pitsikalis

Abstracts from Workshops and Special Sessions

A Cost-Effective Deep-Learning Method for Extraction of Single
and Multi-stage Organic Synthesis Procedures 227
    Mantas Vaškevičius and Jurgita Kapočiūtė-Dzikienė

MARCUS: A Multimodal AI Platform for Chemical Structure Extraction
and Analysis from Scientific Literature 230
    Kohulan Rajan, Viktor Weißenborn, Laurin Lederer, Achim Zielesny,
    and Christoph Steinbeck

Interpreting Graph Neural Networks with Myerson Values
for Cheminformatics Approaches 232
    Samuel K. R. Homberg, Malte L. Modlich, Marlon Becker, Janosch
    Menke, Garrett M. Morris, Benjamin Risse, and Oliver Koch

Protein Content-Based Microbial Representations Improve Predictions
of Antimicrobial Activity 235
    Roberto Olayo-Alarcon, Daniele Pugno, and Christian L. Müller

Guided Molecular Generation Through Logical Constraints 238
    Emma Meneghini, Paolo Frazzetto, and Nicolò Navarin

Towards an Investigation of Over-Squashing in Temporal Graph Neural
Networks 241
    Domenico Tortorella and Alessio Micheli

The Impact of Readout Strategies on the Memory Capacity of Reservoir
Networks 244
    Denis Kleyko and Martin Nilsson

ResLens: A Visualisation, Optimisation and Descriptive Toolkit
for Designing Deep Echo State Networks 247
    Robert Clarke

Author Index 249

2nd AI in Drug Discovery (AIDD) Workshop

2nd AI in Drug Discovery (AIDD) Workshop

The 2nd Workshop on AI in Drug Discovery (https://e-nns.org/icann2025/aidd) was held within the 34th International Conference on Artificial Neural Networks (ICANN 2025) in Kaunas, Lithuania on September 11th. It collected cutting-edge contributions in the rapidly evolving field of AI-driven drug discovery. Eleven articles were presented during the workshop including one keynote, eight oral reports and two posters.

The contributed articles included different topics covering new platforms for early stage discovery: a platform for difficult drug discovery targets (FRASE-bot) was presented as keynote lecture by Kireev, a reaction retrosynthesis prediction platform (OCHEM-R) by Tetko et al. and the MARCUS platform for chemical structure extraction from literature, an Absorption, Distribution, Metabolism, Excretion, and Toxicity (ADMET)-driven de novo generation (ADMETrix) platform was introduced by Mourdoukoutas et al. Rajan et al. had two presentations: an investigation into the efficiency of different SMILES representations for neural network translation and prediction SMILES to and from IUPAC names. A novel eXplainable AI (XAI) approaches for interpretation of Graph Neural Networks (GNN) using Myerson values was reported by Homberg et al. Sycheva et al. reported studies on the use of Graph Anisotropic Diffusion (GAD) to improve prediction of molecular properties using GNNs. The use of proteome-based representations of bacterial species was shown to improve microbe-specific predictions of antimicrobial activity by Olayo-Alarcon et al. Uni-Mol Docking V2 was developed to provide realistic and accurate binding pose predictions by Alcaide et al. The MolEncoder architecture, which was developed by Krüger et al., after exploration of different settings of masked language models, provided high performance for molecular properties predictions thus making it one of SOT algorithms in the field.

The workshop successfully reached its general aim of bringing together machine learning experts, computational chemists and cheminformatics working on the development and application of ML in chemistry and environmental health. The authors of articles/abstracts of the AIDD workshop were invited to submit their full articles to the special issue of Digital Discovery https://blogs.rsc.org/dd/2025/04/04/ with deadline of December 2025. The workshop was partially supported by the Marie Skłodowska-Curie Actions (MSCA) Doctoral Network European Industrial Doctorate "Explainable AI for Molecules" (AiChemist https://aichemist.eu).

Keynote: Dmitri Kireev, *Department of Chemistry, University of Missouri, USA*

Organizers

Igor V. Tetko	Helmholtz Munich, Germany
Djork-Arné Clevert	Pfizer Worldwide Research Development and Medical, Berlin, Germany
Katya Ahmad	Helmholtz Munich, Germany

Program Committee

Igor V. Tetko	Helmholtz Munich, Germany
Djork-Arné Clevert	Pfizer Worldwide Research Development and Medical, Berlin, Germany
Marco Bertolini	Pfizer Worldwide Research Development and Medical, Berlin, Germany
Peter B. R. Hartog	ETH Zurich, Switzerland
Jie Xia	Institute of Materia Medica, Chinese Academy of Medical Sciences and Peking Union Medical College, China

Early-Stage Discovery in the Era of Hard-To-Drug Targets and Giga-Scale Chemical Spaces

Dmitri Kireev[✉]

Department of Chemistry, University of Missouri, Columbia, MO 65211, USA
`dmitri.kireev@missouri.edu`

Abstract. As lead discovery increasingly targets hard-to-drug proteins, the expansion of chemical space presents unprecedented opportunities for hit identification – yet scalable, effective technologies to exploit these vast spaces remain underdeveloped. We describe recent advances to our FRASE-based hit-finding platform (FRASE-bot), including integration of an AI-powered 3D pharmacophore screening across multi-billion-compound libraries, a Hit-Triage Pretrained Transformer (Hit-TPT), and alchemical binding free energy (ABFE) simulations. We also introduce emerging strategies for leveraging phenotypic data to support both hit identification and lead optimization. The platform's utility is demonstrated across several case studies, including our winning entries in CACHE Challenges #1 and #2.

Keywords: Drug Discovery · Hit finding · Ultra-large chemical spaces · Structure-based approach · Machine learning · Physics-based methods

1 Introduction

Artificial intelligence (AI) has been heralded as a transformative force in drug discovery, promising to accelerate timelines, reduce costs, and uncover novel therapeutic avenues. This optimism has fueled significant investments and the emergence of numerous AI-focused biotech firms. However, recent developments have tempered expectations. Notably, several pioneering AI companies – BenevolentAI, Recursion Pharmaceuticals, and Exscientia – faced setbacks with their clinical trials. These instances underscore the complexities inherent in drug development and suggest that AI, while powerful, is not a panacea [1–3].

The initial wave of AI applications in drug discovery often involved adapting models from other domains, such as natural language processing or image recognition, to biological data without sufficient customization. This approach has sometimes led to models that lack the necessary specificity and interpretability for effective drug development. Consequently, there's a growing recognition that a more nuanced integration of AI is required – one that combines data-driven insights with domain-specific knowledge and traditional methodologies.

In this context, we present progress in our FRASE-based hit-finding platform (FRASE-bot) [4], which embodies a hybrid approach. This platform integrates machine learning (ML)-supported data mining to prefilter billion-scale compound collections, conventional docking techniques, ML-based triage of docking outcomes, and physics-based calculations for ultimate enrichment prior to compound procurement and experimental testing. Through several case studies, including our contributions to CACHE Challenges #1 and #2, we demonstrate the platform's potential in navigating the intricate landscape of modern drug discovery.

2 Objectives

We develop an efficient, scalable computational framework to identify small-molecule binders to "ligand-orphan" targets – those with no known ligands and no discernible binding pockets. The framework must be able to exploit giga-scale compound collections, reduce reliance on brute-force docking, and provide meaningful triage of docking hits.

3 Methodology

FRASE-bot mines available 3D structures of ligand-protein complexes to create a database of FRAgments in Structural Environments (FRASE) [4, 5]. The FRASE database can be screened to identify structural environments similar to those in the target protein and seed the target structure with relevant ligand fragments. FRASE hits are filtered using a graph neural network trained to discriminate native FRASEs from decoy fragment-protein environments – reducing false positives – to retain fragments with the highest likelihood of being native binders. The seeded fragments then inform ultra-large-scale virtual screening of commercially available compounds.

One way to exploit structural knowledge from seeded fragments is to convert them into 3D pharmacophore hypotheses, which can then be used to filter billion-scale commercial compound libraries such as Enamine REAL. However, existing pharmacophore-search algorithms are not fast enough to efficiently process such large databases. To address this limitation, we are developing a contrastive neural network model that maps 3D pharmacophores and ligands into a shared latent space. This enables rapid similarity search over pre-encoded representations of billions of compounds, significantly accelerating the identification of pharmacophore-compatible ligands.

After pharmacophore-based hits are docked and ranked by docking score, thousands of potential binders typically remain, necessitating a reliable method for final hit selection. While we have shown that physics-based approaches, such as alchemical free energy (ABFE) calculations, have demonstrated excellent performance in distinguishing binders from non-binders, they are prohibitively time- and resource-intensive [5]. In principle, machine-learned models for binding free energy (BFE) prediction could serve as an efficient intermediary filter. However, our benchmarking indicates that existing ML-based BFE predictors perform no better than random-number generators in a hit-finding setting [5]. To address this gap, we developed the Hit-Triage Pretrained Transformer (Hit-TPT), a model trained as a binary classifier on DUD-E binder/non-binder data. Hit-TPT employs graph transformer layers followed by a multi-layer perceptron (MLP) to estimate binding likelihood and supports clustering, diversity analysis, and reference-based similarity filtering.

4 Results

The FRASE-bot platform has been validated across multiple ligand-orphan targets:

- CIB1 (Triple-Negative Breast Cancer): Previously intractable to virtual screening. Identified 29 hits (52% hit rate). Lead compound (TR-FRET $IC_{50} = 5$ μM) selectively kills CIB1-dependent cancer cells [4].
- LRRK2-WDR (Parkinson's disease | CACHE Challenge #1): Identified 9 hits, including a lead with SPR $K_D = 3$ μM, active in cellular disease-relevant models [6, 7].
- NSP13 (Broad-spectrum Antivirals | CACHE Challenge #2): Identified 8 hits; antiviral assays in progress.
- Other successful case studies include targets against Alzheimer's (DDX1, IFIH1, DHX58, and PLCγ2) and cancer (NLRC5).

5 Conclusion and Outlook

Our results highlight the need for hybrid strategies in early drug discovery: combining knowledge-driven interaction motifs (FRASEs), large-scale latent-space screening, and rigorous triage. We argue that AI alone is insufficient to overcome the challenges of hard-to-drug targets unless embedded in physically interpretable, modular frameworks.

Next steps include extending our platform toward predictive modeling of phenotypic activity and advancing hit series into lead optimization for neurodegenerative diseases, cancer, and infectious disease.

References

1. Ghislat, G., Hernandez-Hernandez, S., Piyawajanusorn, C., Ballester, P.J.: Data-centric challenges with the application and adoption of artificial intelligence for drug discovery. Expert Opin. Drug Discov. **19**(11), 1297–1307 (2024)
2. Jules, A.: Are we in an AI bubble? Biotech AI startups' value plummet and leads to restructuration [Internet]. LABiotech (2024). Accessed 26 May 2025. https://www.labiotech.eu/trends-news/ai-biotech-bubble/
3. Dunn, A.: After years of hype, the first AI-designed drugs fall short in the clinic [Internet]. Endpoints News (2023). Accessed 26 May 2025. https://endpts.com/first-ai-designed-drugs-fall-short-in-the-clinic-following-years-of-hype/
4. An, Y., et al.: In silico fragment-based discovery of CIB1-directed anti-tumor agents by FRASE-bot. Nat. Commun. **15**(1), 5564 (2024)
5. Wang, X., Hentabli, H., Gautam, S., Mettu, A., Kireev, D.: The last mile problem: a critical assessment of physics-based and AI affinity predictors in early drug discovery. Chemical Science (In revision) (2025)
6. Li, F., et al.: CACHE challenge #1: targeting the WDR domain of LRRK2, a Parkinson's disease associated protein. J. Chem. Inf. Model. 5 November 2024
7. Mettu, A., et al.: Functionally active modulators targeting the LRRK2 WD40 repeat domain identified by FRASE-bot in CACHE Challenge #1. Chem. Sci. **16**(8), 3430–3439 (2025)

Comparative Analysis of Chemical Structure String Representations for Neural Machine Translation

Kohulan Rajan[1], Achim Zielesny[2], and Christoph Steinbeck[1(✉)]

[1] Institute for Inorganic and Analytical Chemistry, Friedrich Schiller University Jena, Lessingstr. 8, 07743 Jena, Germany
christoph.steinbeck@uni-jena.de
[2] Institute for Bioinformatics and Chemoinformatics, Westphalian University of Applied Sciences, August-Schmidt-Ring 10, 45665 Recklinghausen, Germany

Abstract. In this work, we present a comparative analysis of SMILES, DeepSMILES, and SELFIES string representations for chemical structures in neural machine translation tasks in cheminformatics. Using transformer-based models, we systematically evaluated their effectiveness in translating between these representations and the corresponding linguistic IUPAC nomenclature. The experimental results demonstrate comparable performance for all three string representations, with SMILES achieving a marginally higher accuracy (99.30% with stereochemical information, 99.21% without) compared to its alternatives. In scaling experiments with 1, 10, and 50 million compounds, the performance differences remained small, though the performance gap narrowed with larger datasets. These findings suggest that researchers can confidently continue using SMILES for neural machine translation tasks with transformers, which benefits from their extensive support in existing chemical libraries, tools, and databases, rather than adopting newer representations. This work has a significant impact on developing more efficient chemical language models in drug discovery, material science, and chemical database curation.

Keywords: Chemical string representations · Neural machine translation · SMILES · SELFIES · DeepSMILES · Transformer models · Cheminformatics

1 Introduction

Chemical structures can be represented using linear string notations that encode the molecular graphs. Notable examples include the Simplified Molecular Input Line Entry System (SMILES) [1,2] and the International Chemical Identifier (InChI) [3]. These representations were initially developed as human-interpretable and machine readable, facilitating tasks such as database searches and chemical information exchange. Currently, these representations enable computational processing and serve as the foundation for machine translation between chemical notations [4–7]. They also play a significant role in machine learning applications within cheminformatics, where models often require standardised input formats to predict molecular properties or biological activities.

In machine learning applications, there are three prominent string notations which are being widely used. SMILES uses ASCII characters to encode atoms, bonds, and structural features. While human-readable and widely adopted, it has limitations regarding syntactic validity when generated by machine learning models [8]. Alternative representations, such as DeepSMILES [9] and SELFIES [8], have been developed to address these limitations. DeepSMILES [9] modifies SMILES syntax to eliminate the need for matching parentheses and changes the representation of rings. This design aims to reduce syntax errors in sequence models, potentially improving machine generation of valid structures. Meanwhile, SELFIES (Self-Referencing Embedded Strings) implements a self-referencing grammar that guarantees valid molecular graphs for any generated string. In principle, this makes SELFIES ideal for machine learning applications, particularly for generative models.

Determining the optimal string representation for chemical translation tasks is crucial for developing applications that utilise such models. To evaluate performance, we trained models for translation between SMILES, DeepSMILES, SELFIES and the IUPAC nomenclature [10], an extremely elaborate standardised method of unambiguously naming organic chemical compounds. This sequence-to-sequence task provides quantitative metrics for comparing representation effectiveness and requires the models to learn complex patterns in molecular graph representations and linguistic nomenclature rules.

Despite the advantages of newer representations, comparative performance in neural machine translation tasks remains under-explored. This study addresses this gap by evaluating these representations in transformer-based neural networks for translating between chemical structures and nomenclature while also examining how performance scales with increasing training data size.

2 Methods

2.1 Dataset Preparation

For the initial experiment, data was downloaded from the ChEMBL 33 [11] database. For the scaling experiment, data from the PubChem [12] database was utilised. The obtained SDF files from ChEMBL were converted into SMILES strings using the Chemistry Development Kit (CDK) [13]. From PubChem, SMILES strings and IUPAC names were directly downloaded.

The ChEMBL data were filtered to ensure quality and representative coverage. Compounds with molecular weights exceeding 1500 Da were removed. Molecules were restricted to include only C, H, O, N, P, S, F, Cl, Br, I, Se, and B elements. Any compounds containing hydrogen isotopes (D, T), charged groups, or counter ions were systematically excluded from the datasets. Structures containing fewer than 3 or more than 40 bonds were removed during preprocessing. Additionally, molecules exhibiting parsing errors or invalid valences were removed.

For each retained compound, these three string representations were generated:

- SMILES: Generated using the CDK SMILES generator
- DeepSMILES: Converted from SMILES using the DeepSMILES converter
- SELFIES: Converted from SMILES using the SELFIES converter

For the initial experiment, the dataset was split into training (1.5 million molecules) and testing (120,000 molecules) sets using the MaxMin algorithm [17] to ensure diverse structural representation. IUPAC names for this experiment were generated using ChemAxon Molconvert [14] software.

For the scaling experiment, the PubChem dataset was utilised with no filtering applied. Datasets were constructed from PubChem using the MaxMin algorithm to maintain chemical diversity. From 110 million compounds, three dataset tiers were created: large (50 million training/1 million testing), medium (10 million training/1 million testing), and small (1 million training/ 250,000 testing). From the generated SMILES datasets, SELFIES representations were generated for each compound to enable direct comparison between the two formats across different dataset sizes.

2.2 Tokenization Process

SMILES strings were tokenized [5,6] by splitting after every heavy atom (e.g., "C", "N", "O", "Si"); (2) after each open and closed bracket ("(", ")", "[", "]"); (3) after every bond symbol ("=", "#"); and (4) after special characters including ".", "-", "+", ":", ";", "/", "@", "%", and "*". Single-digit numbers were also treated as separate tokens. This approach resulted in 52 unique tokens for SMILES without stereochemistry and 104 tokens with stereochemistry included.

DeepSMILES strings were tokenized in a similar approach to SMILES tokenization, with additional attention to its unique syntax for ring closures. This resulted in 76 unique tokens without stereochemistry and 127 tokens with stereochemistry.

SELFIES strings were tokenized by splitting at closed square brackets ("]") and open square brackets ("["), treating each semantic unit as a distinct token. This yielded 69 unique tokens without stereochemistry and 187 tokens with stereochemistry.

IUPAC names were tokenized using character-level splitting, where each character (including spaces) was treated as a separate token. This approach was selected following experimental evidence by Rajan et al. [6] demonstrating better performance of character-level tokenization compared to rule-based approaches when training with larger datasets.

These tokenization approaches were implemented within the data preprocessing pipeline before model training.

2.3 Model Architecture and Training

A transformer-based neural machine translation model based on the architecture by Vaswani et al. [15] was implemented. The model consisted of 4 transformer layers, 8 attention heads, an embedding dimension of 512, a feed-forward network dimension of 2048 and a dropout rate of 0.1 was used. Models were implemented in Python using Keras and TensorFlow [16] and trained using the version 2.15.0-pjrt.

The model was trained using the Adam optimizer with a custom learning rate scheduler. A Sparse Categorical Cross-Entropy loss function was used to calculate the loss during training. Training occurred on TPU V4-VMs with 128 nodes with a batch size of 6144. Separate models for each string representation, both with and without stereochemical information, were trained and tested.

3 Results and Discussion

3.1 Comparison of Chemical Structure String Representation Performance When Translating to IUPAC Names

The initial experiment utilised the ChEMBL database to evaluate the comparative performance of chemical structure string representations (SMILES, DeepSMILES, and SELFIES). Two parallel tests were conducted – one without stereochemical information and one with full stereochemical information – to assess how effectively each representation handles structural specificity. Six models were trained in total, and their performance was evaluated using test datasets described in the methods section. The test was done by comparing the generated IUPAC names and calculating the average accuracy based on the proportion of identically predicted IUPAC names for each test case.

Table 1. Performance of string representations for translation to IUPAC names

String representation	Without Stereochemistry	With Stereochemistry
SMILES	99.21%	99.30%
DeepSMILES	98.76%	99.03%
SELFIES	98.86%	98.95%

Table 1 presents the comparative performance of the three string representations for translation to IUPAC nomenclature. All three-string representations achieved high accuracy, with SMILES showing slightly superior results to DeepSMILES and SELFIES (differences less than 0.5%). Given these small differences, the results suggest that the established SMILES string representation is the representation of choice for transformer-based translation models.

3.2 IUPAC Names to Chemical String Representation Translation Performance

In this translation experiment, six additional models were trained to convert IUPAC names into SMILES, DeepSMILES, and SELFIES representations. Performance evaluation included both string accuracy and structural validity metrics. The validity of generated structures was assessed by converting all predicted representations to Canonical SMILES (preserving stereochemical information when necessary) and parsing them through the CDK SMILES parser. Structural accuracy was quantified through direct comparison of the predicted structures with reference structures and calculation of Tanimoto similarity indices (from 0, worst, to 1, best) using PubChem fingerprints. Table 2 summarises the results.

Table 2. Performance metrics for IUPAC names to chemical string representation translation

Metrics	SMILES		DeepSMILES		SELFIES	
	Without	With	Without	With	Without	With
Identical Predictions	99.00%	99.10%	99.00%	98.90%	98.00%	98.00%
Valid Structure	99.96%	99.95%	99.98%	99.94%	100.00%	99.99%
Average Tanimoto similarity	0.999	0.999	0.999	0.999	0.998	0.997
Tanimoto 1.0 count	99.70%	99.70%	99.50%	99.50%	98.90%	98.50%

Table 2 demonstrates that SELFIES achieved marginally higher validity rates, while SMILES achieved a slightly better overall performance in exact string matches and structural accuracy as measured by the Tanimoto similarity.

The results show that all three representations perform similarly for neural machine translation of chemical structures, with only small differences in overall accuracy. This finding contrasts with expectations regarding SELFIES, which was designed specifically for machine learning applications yet shows limited measurable advantage over the standard SMILES string representation using a transformer architecture.

The following factors may account for the slightly higher performance of SMILES:

- Representation Efficiency: SMILES uses fewer tokens (52 without stereochemistry) compared to DeepSMILES (76) and SELFIES (69), potentially simplifying the learning task.
- Information Density: SMILES encodes structural information more compactly, with a direct correlation between string length and molecular complexity.

Also, the low number of tokens and shorter overall string lengths could help the transformer to learn the SMILES pattern better compared to DeepSMILES and SELFIES.

In IUPAC nomenclature to chemical string translation, the marginal advantage of SELFIES in producing valid structures (99.99% vs. 99.95% for SMILES) aligns with its design goal of ensuring chemical validity. However, this advantage does not hold for the overall translation accuracy.

When stereochemical information is included, all representations show improved performance, with SMILES again being slightly in front. This suggests that the transformer architecture effectively learns stereochemical patterns across representation types.

3.3 Performance Scaling with Dataset Size

Based on Experiments 3.1 and 3.2, it is evident that using SMILES strings as input yields slightly better overall results, while using SELFIES provides an advantage in obtaining more valid predictions. SELFIES can be easily tokenized as well.

DeepSMILES was excluded from these scaling experiments because preliminary results indicated that its accuracy consistently fell between that of SMILES and SELFIES. Given resource constraints and the clear performance trends established with the two primary representations, the comparison between the standard format (SMILES) and the format specifically designed for machine learning (SELFIES) was conducted.

To further understand and improve upon these findings, along with the increase of dataset size, additional experiments were conducted using both SMILES and SELFIES representations with PubChem data at three different scales: 1 million, 10 million, and 50 million compounds. The results are presented in Table 3.

Table 3. Performance scaling with dataset size using SMILES and SELFIES representations

Train data	SMILES input	SELFIES input
1 million (265,332 test)	83.42%	78.55%
10 million (972,817 test)	92.38%	89.96%
50 million (1,024,000 test)	94.70%	93.23%

The results demonstrate significant performance improvements with increasing dataset size for both representations. For SMILES, the jump from 1 million to 10 million compounds yielded the largest percentage improvement (8.96%), while the increase from 10 million to 50 million compounds produced a smaller but still substantial gain (2.32%). SELFIES showed a similar pattern with improvements of 11.41% and 3.27%, respectively.

The performance difference between SMILES and SELFIES narrowed with larger datasets (from 4.87% at 1 million to 1.47% at 50 million). This convergence suggests that with sufficient training data, the choice of representation becomes less significant, where SELFIES may benefit more from additional training data, though SMILES maintains its slight advantage across all scales tested.

These scaling experiments demonstrate that transformer models benefit substantially from larger datasets, with the most significant gains occurring in the range between 1 million and 50 million training examples.

4 Conclusion

Surprisingly, this study shows that the established SMILES representation for chemical structures performs slightly better in neural machine translation using a transformer architecture than newer string representations. Given the availability of the SMILES representation in existing software libraries, databases, and tools, there is minimal advantage in transitioning to the newer alternatives developed for machine learning applications. The combination of SMILES with transformer-based neural networks achieves the highest accuracy in both forward and reverse translation tasks.

The scaling experiments demonstrate that dataset size has a significant impact on performance, with substantial gains observed when using 10 million training examples and continued improvements with datasets of 50 million scale. This suggests that maximising training data volume is crucial for chemical translation tasks, though with diminishing returns beyond certain thresholds.

These findings can help researchers in the field of cheminformatics to design language models for their research work. They should consider SMILES not only as readily available but also as an adequate representation, especially when translation accuracy is the primary goal, and should prioritise larger training datasets if possible.

Future work will explore whether these findings are a peculiarity of transformer-based architectures or can be generalised to other neural network architectures. In addition, the translation between various chemical representation systems beyond nomenclature will attract attention.

Data Availability

- ChEMBL data downloaded directly from:
  https://doi.org/10.6019/CHEMBL.database.33
- PubChem data downloaded directly from:
  https://ftp.ncbi.nlm.nih.gov/pubchem/Compound/Extras/

Declarations

Acknowledgements. KR acknowledges the research supported with Cloud TPUs from Google's TPU Research Cloud (TRC) for Deep learning model training.

Author contributions. KR initiated the project, developed the software and wrote the paper. AZ and CS supervised the study. All authors read and approved the final manuscript.

Funding. Open Access funding is enabled and organised by Projekt DEAL. This work was funded by the German Research Foundation under project number 239748522 - SFB 1127 ChemBioSys (Project INF).

Ethics Approval and Consent to Participate. Not applicable

Consent for Publication. The authors have given their consent for the work to be published.

Competing Interests. The authors do not have any competing interests to declare.

References

1. Weininger, D.: SMILES, a chemical language and information system. 1. Introduction to methodology and encoding rules. J. Chem. Inf. Comput. Sci. **28**(1), 31–36 (1988). https://doi.org/10.1021/ci00057a005
2. Weininger, D., Weininger, A., Weininger, J.L.: SMILES. 2. Algorithm for generation of unique SMILES notation. J. Chem. Inf. Comput. Sci. **29**(2), 97–101 (1989). https://doi.org/10.1021/ci00062a008
3. Heller, S.R., McNaught, A., Pletnev, I., Stein, S., Tchekhovskoi, D.: InChI, the IUPAC international chemical identifier. J. Cheminformatics **7**(1), 1–34 (2015). https://doi.org/10.1186/s13321-015-0068-4
4. Handsel, J., Matthews, B., Knight, N.J., Coles, S.J.: Translating the InChI: adapting neural machine translation to predict IUPAC names from a chemical identifier. J. Cheminformatics **13**(1), 1–11 (2021). https://doi.org/10.1186/s13321-021-00535-x
5. Rajan, K., Zielesny, A., Steinbeck, C.: STOUT: SMILES to IUPAC names using neural machine translation. J. Cheminformatics **13**(1), 1–14 (2021). https://doi.org/10.1186/s13321-021-00512-4
6. Rajan, K., Zielesny, A., Steinbeck, C.: STOUT V2.0: SMILES to IUPAC name conversion using transformer models. J. Cheminform. **16**, 146 (2024). https://doi.org/10.1186/s13321-024-00941-x
7. Krasnov, L., Khokhlov, I., Fedorov, M.V., Sosnin, S.: Transformer-based artificial neural networks for the conversion between chemical notations. Sci. Rep. **11**, 14798 (2021). https://doi.org/10.1038/s41598-021-94082-y
8. Krenn, M., Häse, F., Nigam, A., Friederich, P., Aspuru-Guzik, A.: Self-referencing embedded strings (SELFIES): a 100% robust molecular string representation. Mach. Learn.: Sci. Technol. **1**, 045024 (2020). https://doi.org/10.1088/2632-2153/aba947
9. O'Boyle, N., Dalke, A.: DeepSMILES: an adaptation of SMILES for use in machine-learning of chemical structures. chemRxiv (2018)
10. Panico, R., Powell, W.H., Richer, J.-C.: A Guide to IUPAC Nomenclature of Organic Compounds, 2nd edn. Blackwell Scientific Publications, Oxford (1993)
11. Gaulton, A., Hersey, A., Nowotka, M., et al.: The ChEMBL database in 2017. Nucleic Acids Res. **45**(D1), D945–D954 (2017). https://doi.org/10.1093/nar/gkw1074
12. Kim, S., Chen, J., Cheng, T., et al.: PubChem 2023 update. Nucleic Acids Res. **51**(D1), D1373–D1380 (2023). https://doi.org/10.1093/nar/gkac956

13. Steinbeck, C., Han, Y., Kuhn, S., Horlacher, O., Luttmann, E., Willighagen, E.: The chemistry development kit (CDK): an open-source java library for chemo- and bioinformatics. J. Chem. Inf. Comput. Sci. **43**(2), 493–500 (2003). https://doi.org/10.1021/ci025584y
14. ChemAxon: MolConvert (2020). https://docs.chemaxon.com/display/lts-lithium/molconvert.md. Accessed 23 Nov 2020
15. Vaswani, A., et al.: Attention is all you need. In: Advances in Neural Information Processing Systems, vol. 30, pp. 5998–6008 (2017)
16. Abadi, M., Agarwal, A., Barham, P., et al.: TensorFlow: large-scale machine learning on heterogeneous systems (2015). arXiv:1603.04467
17. Ashton, M., et al.: Identification of diverse database subsets using property-based and fragment-based molecular descriptions. Quant. Struct. Act. Relatsh. **21**, 598–604 (2002). https://doi.org/10.1002/qsar.200290002

ADMETrix: ADMET-Driven De Novo Molecular Generation

Nikolaos Mourdoukoutas, Aigli Korfiati(✉), and Vassilis Pitsikalis

Deeplab, Athens, Greece
{n.mourdoukoutas,a.korfiati,vpitsik}@deeplab.ai

Abstract. We introduce **ADMETrix**, a de novo drug design framework that combines the generative model REINVENT with ADMET AI, a geometric deep learning architecture for predicting pharmacokinetic and toxicity properties. To our knowledge, this is the first integration enabling real-time generation of small molecules optimized across multiple ADMET endpoints. We evaluate our method in two settings: (i) multi-parameter optimization of ADMET and physicochemical properties, and (ii) scaffold hopping to reduce toxicity while preserving key pharmacophoric features. Using the GuacaMol benchmark, we provide the first systematic evaluation of REINVENT in a multi-objective ADMET context, demonstrating its advantages in generating drug-like, biologically relevant molecules. The code is available at https://github.com/n-mourdou/ADMETrix.

Keywords: de novo generation · ADMET optimization · scaffold-hopping

1 Introduction

The vast chemical space (up to 10^{60} molecules [1]) offers enormous potential for drug discovery, yet only about 10^8 molecules have been synthesized [2]. Ensuring that newly generated molecules meet critical ADMET (Absorption, Distribution, Metabolism, Excretion, and Toxicity) criteria remains challenging, as over 94% of candidate compounds fail these benchmarks [3]. Consequently, robust generative models are needed to navigate this largely uncharted space effectively.

Although de novo molecular generation promises novel structures beyond traditional libraries, optimizing complex ADMET properties adds significant complexity. Early works like REINVENT [4] and ORGAN [5] optimized general drug-likeness metrics such as QED, but focused on isolated properties without integrating multiple, diverse ADMET constraints.

Here, we introduce **ADMETrix**, a framework that unites a state-of-the-art generative model with high-fidelity ADMET predictions in a single system. Our method couples REINVENT with an AI-based ADMET model for real-time, multi-parameter optimization of classical drug-likeness properties and key pharmacokinetic/toxicological endpoints. We benchmark this system in two scenarios: (i) designing molecules from scratch under stringent ADMET and physico-chemical requirements, and (ii) performing scaffold hopping to enhance toxicity profiles of existing leads. Experimental results, featuring new metrics not previously reported for REINVENT, highlight the advantages of our approach. Overall, our work aims to streamline early-stage drug discovery by moving beyond single-property optimization to tackle comprehensive ADMET profiles.

2 Related Work

De novo drug design can be broadly categorized into target-agnostic and target-aware approaches. Target-agnostic methods generate novel small molecules with desired properties, either from scratch or by refining a seed molecule's properties. Target-aware approaches add macromolecular constraints, such as binding affinity for specific pockets. Both typically pair a generative model, which proposes molecules, with an optimization method that refines properties of interest.

Seminal research includes REINVENT and ORGAN [4,5], both of which leverage SMILES representations of molecules and employ the REINVENT optimization algorithm [6]. They differ in their generative backbone: REINVENT uses a recurrent neural network (RNN) [7], whereas ORGAN employs a generative adversarial network [8]. Later methods explored architectures like variational autoencoders [9] and diffusion models [15], spanning 2D molecular graphs to 3D structures.

Most efforts, however, have optimized only a narrow subset of properties. For example, Regression Transformer [10] targets aqueous solubility and reaction yield, while [11,26] focus on logP (a proxy for lipophilicity), drug-likeness (QED), synthetic accessibility, and selected photophysical or electronic properties. Saturn [12] emphasizes QED and logP, whereas MolGAN [13] and MIMOSA [14] optimize QED and penalized logP. Though many frameworks are flexible enough to potentially handle other ADMET properties, no work has comprehensively addressed metabolism, toxicity, or excretion within a single framework.

While current techniques broaden chemical exploration, few, if any, explicitly tackle an entire ADMET suite. Our work addresses this gap by (1) integrating an ADMET-centric objective into the generative process and (2) showing that multi-parameter optimization can reliably identify promising leads early in drug discovery.

3 Method

In this section, we present **ADMETrix**, our integrated de novo molecule generation framework, which combines a generative model with a real-time ADMET prediction module for multi-parameter optimization. We first give an abbreviated overview of each component (Sect. 3.1) and then describe how they are coupled into a single feedback loop with a dedicated scoring function (Sect. 3.2). This modular yet tightly linked design represents our primary methodological contribution, enabling the simultaneous pursuit of novelty, drug-likeness, and favorable ADMET profiles.

3.1 Generative and ADMET Modules

REINVENT. We use REINVENT, an RNN-based model for de novo drug design that applies a policy-gradient approach to molecular generation [16]. It begins from a pre-trained model, trained on a broad subset of ChEMBL [17], and iteratively modifies its generation policy based on a reward function capturing user-defined objectives, such as desired pharmacological or physicochemical properties.

A key feature is how REINVENT computes its *reinforcement-learning objective*. Concretely, each candidate SMILES string S sampled by the model is assigned a reward $R(S)$, which is then used to update the generative agent via a policy-gradient algorithm. In its canonical formulation, the *augmented* negative log-likelihood (Eq. (1)) is defined as (Eq. (1)) $\text{NLL}_{\text{Aug}}(S) = \text{NLL}_{\text{Prior}}(S) - \sigma \cdot R(S)$, where σ is a user-defined scaling factor that sets the relative importance of the property-based reward $R(S)$. The final *loss* is then computed (Eq. (2)) as $\text{loss} = \left(\text{NLL}_{\text{Aug}}(S) - \text{NLL}_{\text{Agent}}(S)\right)^2$.

Here, $\text{NLL}_{\text{Prior}}(S)$ and $\text{NLL}_{\text{Agent}}(S)$ respectively measure the negative log-likelihood under the *prior* and the *agent* models, both of which share the same RNN architecture. The reward $R(S)$ steers the agent toward user-specified objectives. The exact definition of $R(S)$ is user-customizable, typically incorporating diverse criteria (e.g., QSAR, docking scores, or chemical constraints). We will detail how we integrate multi-parameter ADMET scores into the reward in Sect. 3.2.

ADMET AI. For in silico assessment of key pharmacokinetic and toxicity-related endpoints, we integrate ADMET AI, a graph neural network-based model that predicts a wide range of ADMET properties [18]. Trained on 41 ADMET datasets from the Therapeutics Data Commons [19] using a multi-task learning strategy, ADMET AI leverages a Chemprop-RDKit architecture augmented with 200 RDKit-computed [23] physicochemical features. It provides continuous or probabilistic outputs for endpoints such as oral bioavailability, blood-brain barrier permeability, and hepatotoxicity, enabling robust evaluation of diverse drug-like properties.

Moreover, ADMET AI has been extensively benchmarked on the TDC ADMET Leaderboard, where it consistently achieves the highest average rank compared to other models. Its predictions are not only highly accurate but also computationally efficient, delivering results up to 45% faster than competing public ADMET web servers. This combination of robust performance and speed makes ADMET AI a valuable tool in the optimization of molecular properties for drug discovery.

Integration Rationale. Our goal is to create an end-to-end framework where REINVENT's generative engine directly uses ADMET AI's multi-parameter predictions as part of its reward. Specifically, compounds that satisfy multiple ADMET criteria are "steered" toward higher reward values during molecule generation. In the next section, we detail how we embed these property predictions into the final reward function for reinforcement learning.

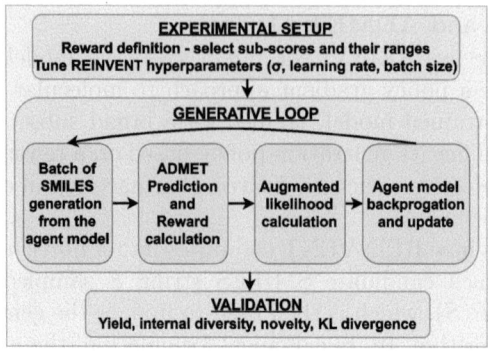

Fig. 1. Schematic of **ADMETrix**.

3.2 Our Integration Strategy

Our main methodological contribution is to embed multi-parameter ADMET AI predictions directly into the generative loop of REINVENT. As described in Sect. 3.1, each sampled SMILES string S is assigned a reward $R(S)$, which is used to compute the augmented likelihood (Eq. (1)) and, ultimately, the loss (Eq. (2)). Here, we define how $R(S)$ captures the *multi-criteria* nature of ADMET optimization.

Multi-parameter ADMET Scoring. Let $\{r_i(S)\}_{i=1}^m$ denote the individual ADMET sub-scores (e.g., toxicity, permeability) from *ADMET AI*, each normalized to the range $[0, 1]$. REINVENT aggregates them into a single reward $R(S)$ using either an arithmetic mean, $R_{\text{arith}}(S) = \frac{\sum_{i=1}^m w_i \cdot r_i(S)}{\sum_{i=1}^m w_i}$, or a geometric mean, $R_{\text{geom}}(S) = \left(\prod_{i=1}^m [r_i(S)]^{w_i}\right)^{\frac{1}{\sum_{i=1}^m w_i}}$. The weights $w_i \geq 0$ indicate the importance of each property. As long as $\sum_{i=1}^m w_i > 0$, both $R_{\text{arith}}(S)$ and $R_{\text{geom}}(S)$ are guaranteed to lie within $[0, 1]$, preserving the normalized range of the individual sub-scores.

Experimental Protocol. Our experimental setup involves defining a specific set of ADMET and physicochemical properties to be optimized, and tuning the hyperparameters of REINVENT accordingly. Specifically, we select properties with reliable predictive accuracy and specify their optimal ranges as input to REINVENT. Hyperparameters of REINVENT such as the reward scaling factor (σ), learning rate, generation batch size, and the number of fine-tuning steps are then tuned, using either a geometric or arithmetic mean for reward aggregation, to maximize the overall reward during training.

Evaluation. We assess the generated molecules using a set of metrics that relate to either target-agnostic or target-aware criteria, depending on the task at hand. In a target-agnostic setting, validation metrics include the reward itself, yield (i.e. the number of unique molecules surpassing a defined threshold), internal diversity, novelty, and distribution alignment metrics such as KL divergence and

Fréchet ChemNet Distance [24]. In target-aware scenarios, additional efficacy-related metrics, such as binding affinity to a target, along with structural features like the number of hydrogen bond donors, acceptors, and specific interactions within the binding site, can be incorporated to ensure that the molecules not only satisfy broad property constraints but also exhibit desired biological activity.

End-to-End Integration. During training, each iteration of *REINVENT* proceeds through five steps: (1) **Batch Generation:** sample a batch of SMILES molecules S from the agent, (2) **ADMET Prediction:** compute $r_i(S)$ for each sampled molecule, (3) **Reward Calculation:** aggregate sub-scores (e.g., geometric mean) to obtain $R(S)$, (4) **Augmented Likelihood:** substitute $R(S)$ into Eq. (1), (5) **Update Agent Model:** compute the loss (Eq. (2)) and backpropagate. **ADMETrix** is depicted in Fig. 1.

This loop continuously biases the generator to propose molecules that meet multiple ADMET criteria while preserving structural novelty. As a result, *REINVENT* converges on designs less likely to fail in later experimental validation, potentially accelerating the early phases of drug discovery.

4 Experiments

We present two case studies demonstrating the performance of **ADMETrix** under different drug-design paradigms. **First**, in the ADMET and physicochemical property optimization scenario, the generative model is tasked with creating novel molecules that balance multiple ADMET endpoints, such as oral bioavailability or toxicity risk, alongside standard drug-likeness descriptors like molecular weight and hydrogen-bond capacity. **Second**, in the scaffold hopping for toxicity reduction case, the goal is to modify a known reference compound to achieve a significantly reduced toxicity profile while preserving essential pharmacophoric features and overall efficacy.

4.1 Optimizing ADMET and Physicochemical Properties

Experimental Setup. ADMET AI provides 50 ADMET properties, but due to reported low accuracy for many of these, we avoided optimizing the less reliable ones. Additionally, properties with inconsistent optimization directions (i.e., sometimes needing minimization and other times maximization) were excluded. We ultimately selected 27 properties that comprehensively cover all ADMET aspects, supplemented by 10 general physicochemical parameters (e.g., molecular weight, topological polar surface area). We conducted a thorough literature review to determine the optimal ranges for each property, which are required inputs for REINVENT.

For REINVENT, we used the arithmetic mean to compute the reward, avoiding numerical underflow and stabilizing fine-tuning. The reward scaling factor (σ), learning rate, batch size, and number of fine-tuning steps were set to 160, 0.0001, 100, and 600, respectively, based on grid-search optimization. All ADMET and physicochemical sub-scores were weighted at 1, except QED (0.6). All random seeds were set to 44.

Fine-Tuning Outcomes. Before assessing the generated molecules, we first confirm that REINVENT has successfully adapted its generative policy. Figure 2 shows the negative log-likelihood (NLL) curves for three components: the agent (blue), the prior (red), and the augmented target (green). The divergence between the agent and prior curves indicates that the model is effectively learning from the reward signal based on ADMET properties. In particular, the decrease in the agent's NLL relative to the prior reflects the model's shift towards generating molecules with improved ADMET profiles. This shift is further validated by the high augmented target values, which incorporate the property-based reward into the likelihood calculation.

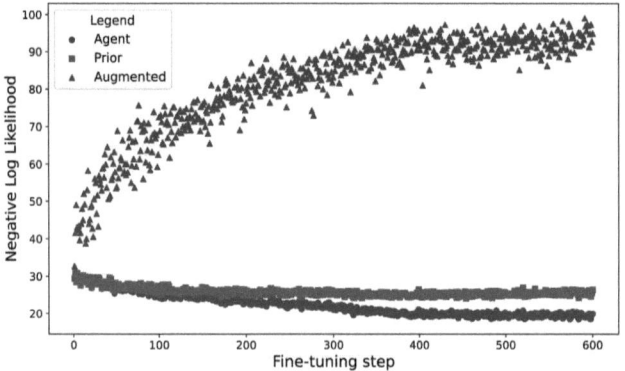

Fig. 2. NLL curves for agent, prior, and augmented during fine-tuning.

Results. In the first experiment, the model successfully generated novel molecules with optimal ADMET profiles. Figure 3 illustrates this, showing five pharmacological properties from ADMET AI that have been selected and plotted for a random subset of REINVENT's training data, serving as an unoptimized baseline, versus an equally sized sample of de novo molecules receiving the highest rewards. We chose a representative mix of absorption, distribution, metabolism, excretion, and toxicity endpoints to reflect the ADMET spectrum. The six panels in Fig. 3 compare these predicted ADMET properties between the original (training) ChEMBL compounds (blue) and the newly generated (de novo) molecules (red), showcasing the clear shift toward more drug-like profiles in the optimized set. Overall, the red histograms show that the de novo molecules have been actively steered by the generative and optimization process toward favorable ADMET property ranges.

Furthermore, we computed the yield [20], defined as the number of unique generated molecules exceeding a reward threshold; internal diversity [21], indicating structural variation among generated molecules (higher values signify greater diversity and lower values suggest mode collapse); and nearest-neighbor similarity [21], measuring resemblance to reference dataset molecules using Tanimoto similarity (0: high novelty, 1: high similarity) and Morgan fingerprints (2048-bit,

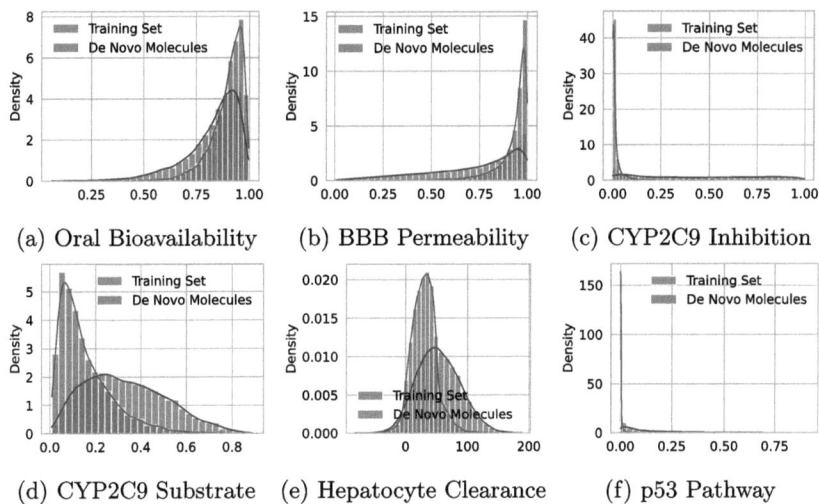

Fig. 3. Selected ADMET properties: absorption (a), distribution (b), metabolism (c, d), excretion (e), and toxicity (f). Blue histograms show the original dataset; red histograms show top de novo molecules. (Color figure online)

radius 2). We report median values and standard deviations across three independent datasets generated with different seeds. **ADMETrix** achieved a yield of 43 ± 6 (threshold = 0.89), internal diversity of 0.8955 ± 0.001, and nearest-neighbor similarity of 0.50 ± 0.007.

Benchmarking REINVENT. To rigorously assess **ADMETrix**, we benchmarked it according to the GuacaMol framework [22], which established a variety of metrics in the field of de novo small molecule generation. Specifically, we evaluated the generated molecules based on their validity (i.e., compliance with RDKit [23] rules), uniqueness and novelty relative to the training set. To assess how well the generated distribution aligns with the training data, we computed the KL divergence over selected physicochemical descriptors and the Fréchet ChemNet Distance (FCD) [24] between the de novo molecules and the training set, where lower values indicate better alignment. Again, we report the median values and standard deviations of these metrics, across three independently generated datasets with different random seeds. To accurately compute novelty and uniqueness, we performed SMILES canonicalization, ensuring that different representations of the same molecule were not mistakenly counted as distinct entities.

The metrics for our method and the benchmarked models are presented in Table 1. Notably, as in [22], KL divergence and FCD have been normalized to the range $[0, 1]$, where higher values indicate better alignment between the generated datasets and the training set. Furthermore, to the best of our knowledge, most of these metrics have not previously been reported for REINVENT in the literature.

REINVENT performs competitively in generating novel, valid, and unique molecules. The relatively low normalized FCD and KL divergence both reflect the deliberate shift in the generated distribution toward drug-like chemical space.

This is a direct result of the optimization constraints imposed during training, which steer the model toward favorable ADMET regions, for instance, maintaining molecular weight below 500 Da and QED values around 0.83 to 0.88. We illustrate this shift in Fig. 4, which compares two representative properties between a random subset of molecules generated by our method and a random subset from REINVENT's original training set.

Overall, **ADMETrix** demonstrates the ability to optimize ADMET properties effectively while maintaining competitive performance against general-purpose generative models, as reflected by the strong validity, uniqueness, and novelty metrics.

Table 1. Comparison of generation metrics across various models.

Model	Novelty	Validity	Uniqueness	FCD	KL
ADMETrix	0.96 ± 0.007	0.99 ± 0.001	0.98 ± 0.0068	0.24 ± 0.02	0.77 ± 0.022
SMILES LSTM [22]	0.912	0.959	**1.000**	**0.913**	0.991
GRAPH MCTS [25]	0.994	**1.000**	**1.000**	0.015	0.522
VAE [26]	0.974	0.870	0.999	0.863	**0.982**
ORGAN [5]	0.687	0.379	0.841	0.000	0.267
AAE [27]	**0.998**	0.822	**1.000**	0.529	0.886

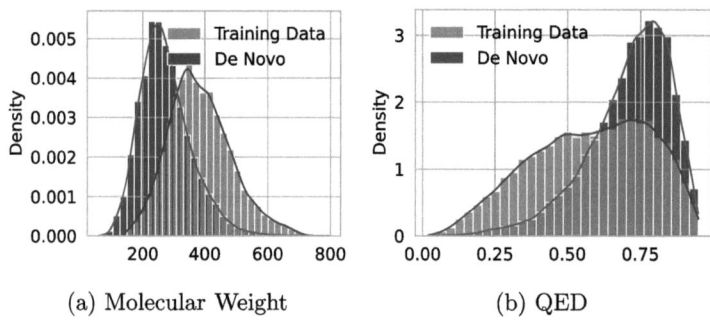

(a) Molecular Weight (b) QED

Fig. 4. Two properties used in the computation of the KL divergence. For the de novo molecules the distributions are shifted toward drug-like ranges, i.e. (a) molecular weight under 500 Da and (b) QED around 0.83–0.88.

4.2 Scaffold Hopping

Scaffold hopping is a common approach in lead optimization [28]. Specifically, the technique involves altering the core structure of a reference compound to create new molecules that are structurally different, while maintaining the overall three-dimensional shape or pharmacophore, with the aim of retaining biological activity against the target protein [28,29]. There have been numerous works, where generative molecular models have been used for this purpose [30–32].

Experimental Setup. To demonstrate the capability of our method in this task, we selected diclofenac, a widely used nonsteroidal anti-inflammatory drug (NSAID) for pain and inflammation management, often prescribed for conditions such as arthritis. It primarily works by inhibiting cyclooxygenase (COX) enzymes to reduce prostaglandin synthesis. Diclofenac is associated with hepatotoxicity, even when administered topically [33]. The hepatotoxicity is linked to diclofenac metabolism, which generates reactive intermediates that contribute to liver damage [34]. ADMET AI predicts a near-certain probability of diclofenac undergoing bioactivation into hepatotoxic metabolites—**drug-induced liver injury (DILI) probability 93%**. Hence, optimizing diclofenac's metabolic profile to minimize the formation of toxic metabolites could improve its safety while maintaining efficacy.

The objective was to minimize the DILI probability while maintaining a moderate Tanimoto similarity to diclofenac. Initially, optimizing solely for these two properties led to undesirable changes in other ADMET characteristics. Consequently, we adopted an iterative approach in which the generated molecules were continuously evaluated for various properties; if any property fell short, it was incorporated into the optimization objective. Tanimoto similarity was computed using Morgan fingerprints via RDKit (2048-bit, radius 2), while all other properties were assessed with ADMET AI. It is important to note that binding-affinity metrics were not included in our analysis. For REINVENT, we opted for the geometric mean, while for the reward scaling factor (σ), learning rate, generation batch size and number of fine-tuning steps the choices were $260, 0.0001, 100$ and 700, respectively. All hyperparameters were tuned via a grid-based approach. All seeds were set to 42.

The final scoring function integrated multiple ADMET properties, each assigned a specific weight to balance their importance. Tanimoto similarity carried the highest weight at 200, followed by DILI probability and mutagenicity predictions, each weighted at 30. Blood-brain barrier penetration, CYP1A2 interaction, CYP2C9 substrate classification, CYP2C9 interaction, CYP2D6 substrate classification, CYP2D6 interaction, CYP3A4 substrate classification, CYP3A4 interaction, and hepatic clearance were all assigned weights of 15. Notably, CYP2C19 interaction and CYP2D6 substrate classification were given slightly higher weights of 25, possibly reflecting their relative importance in this context.

Results. We optimized diclofenac using our method, aiming to reduce its predicted DILI risk while keeping the rest of its profile largely unchanged. Diclofenac already has a strong overall profile, with a quantitative estimate of drug-likeness (QED) score of 0.88.

The de novo top molecule exhibited **a DILI probability of just 7%** - an improvement of 172% over diclofenac - while maintaining a Tanimoto similarity of 38% to the original compound. Its QED decreased slightly to 0.83.

To determine whether diclofenac and the de novo molecule constitute a scaffold-hopping pair, we followed the criteria outlined in [30] and its references.

Specifically, a pair qualifies if the Tanimoto similarity between their Bemis–Murcko scaffolds is less than 60%, and their 3D molecular similarity (SC score), which captures both pharmacophoric features and shape similarity, is greater than 60%. In our case, the Tanimoto similarity between the Bemis–Murcko scaffolds was 20%, while the SC score was 69%, confirming that the pair meets the scaffold-hopping criteria.

To further evaluate the potential of our novel molecule as an alternative to diclofenac, we assessed its binding to the COX-2 enzyme. We used the crystal structure of the COX-2–diclofenac complex (PDB ID: 1PXX) [35] as a reference and performed molecular docking of the de novo molecule using AutoDock Vina [36]. The results confirmed that the molecule successfully bound to the same pocket as diclofenac, with a comparable binding affinity (diclofenac: −7.7 kcal/mol; de novo molecule: −7.3 kcal/mol).

Figure 5 shows an overlay of diclofenac (green) and the de novo designed molecule (yellow), illustrating their similar three-dimensional conformations. Figure 5a highlights the close structural alignment of both ligands, while 5b shows how the de novo molecule occupies the same binding region in the protein pocket. This comparison suggests that the new compound may preserve key interactions essential for activity, potentially offering an alternative with reduced toxicity. Naturally, to validate the functional effect of the de novo compound, further studies, such as molecular dynamics simulations and in vitro testing, are required.

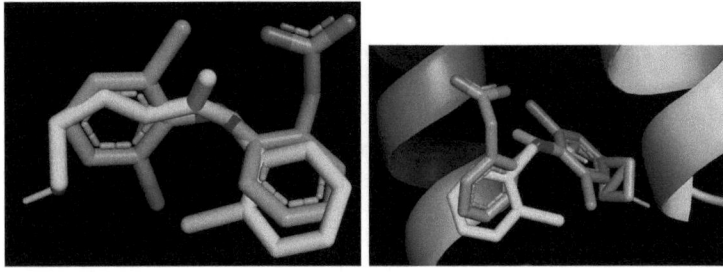

Fig. 5. Scaffold-hopping approach applied to diclofenac, aiming to reduce DILI risk while maintaining COX-2 inhibition. Left: Overlay of diclofenac (green) and the de novo compound (yellow). Right: Both ligands bound in the COX-2 pocket. (Color figure online)

5 Discussion

Our study introduces **ADMETrix**, a rigorously formalized framework that integrates a generative model with an advanced ADMET prediction system, enabling systematic de novo molecular design under complex pharmacokinetic and toxicity constraints. By encoding these constraints into an explicit, multi-objective reward function, **ADMETrix** guides the generation of structurally novel molecules with strong drug-like profiles. This capability is demonstrated through two case studies: one where the model consistently produced 50 novel compounds per run satisfying ADMET and physicochemical criteria, and another where it reduced predicted drug-induced liver injury (DILI) risk from 93% to 7% while preserving pharmacophoric integrity. These results highlight the framework's practical potential for early-stage drug discovery.

Moving forward, we plan to explore latent-variable generative approaches, such as conditional VAEs or diffusion models, that naturally incorporate conditioning on seed molecules and property constraints. This shift could yield more direct and robust control over scaffold transformations and property optimization. Additionally, we aim to expand our scoring function to include binding-affinity predictors, allowing the generation of de novo compounds that not only meet ADMET requirements but also bind effectively to specific targets.

References

1. Polishchuk, P.G., Madzhidov, T.I., Varnek, A.: Estimation of the size of drug-like chemical space based on GDB-17 data. J. Comput. Aided Mol. Des. **27**(8), 675–679 (2013). https://doi.org/10.1007/s10822-013-9672-4
2. Kim, S., et al.: PubChem substance and compound databases. Nucl. Acids Res. **44**(D1), D1202 (2016)
3. Munson, M., et al.: Lead optimization attrition analysis (LOAA): a novel and general methodology for medicinal chemistry. Drug Discov. Today **20**(8), 978–987 (2015)
4. Olivecrona, M., et al.: Molecular de-novo design through deep reinforcement learning. J. Cheminformatics **9**, 1–14 (2017)
5. Guimaraes, G.L., et al.: Objective-reinforced generative adversarial networks (ORGAN) for sequence generation models. arXiv preprint arXiv:1705.10843 (2017)
6. Williams, R.J.: Simple statistical gradient-following algorithms for connectionist reinforcement learning. Mach. Learn. **8**, 229–256 (1992)
7. Rumelhart, D.E., Hinton, G.E., Williams, R.J.: Learning internal representations by error propagation (1985)
8. Goodfellow, I., et al.: Generative adversarial nets. In: Advances in Neural Information Processing Systems, vol. 27 (2014)
9. Jin, W., Barzilay, R., Jaakkola, T.: Junction tree variational autoencoder for molecular graph generation. In: International Conference on Machine Learning. PMLR (2018)
10. Born, J., Manica, M.: Regression transformer enables concurrent sequence regression and generation for molecular language modelling. Nat. Mach. Intell. **5**(4), 432–444 (2023)
11. Lim, J., et al.: Molecular generative model based on conditional variational autoencoder for de novo molecular design. J. Cheminformatics **10**, 1–9 (2018)
12. Guo, J., Philippe, S.: Saturn: sample-efficient generative molecular design using memory manipulation. arXiv preprint arXiv:2405.17066 (2024)
13. De Cao, N., Thomas, K.: MolGAN: an implicit generative model for small molecular graphs. arXiv preprint arXiv:1805.11973 (2018)

14. Fu, T., et al.: Mimosa: multi-constraint molecule sampling for molecule optimization. In: Proceedings of the AAAI Conference on Artificial Intelligence, vol. 35, no. 1 (2021)
15. Vignac, C., et al.: Midi: mixed graph and 3D denoising diffusion for molecule generation. In: Joint European Conference on Machine Learning and Knowledge Discovery in Databases. Springer Nature Switzerland, Cham (2023)
16. Loeffler, H.H., He, J., Tibo, A., et al.: Reinvent 4: modern AI–driven generative molecule design. J. Cheminform. **16**, 20 (2024). https://doi.org/10.1186/s13321-024-00812-5
17. Mendez, D., et al.: ChEMBL: towards direct deposition of bioassay data. Nucl. Acids Res **47**, D930-40 (2019)
18. Swanson, K., et al.: ADMET-AI: a machine learning ADMET platform for evaluation of large-scale chemical libraries. Bioinformatics **40**(7) (2024)
19. Huang, K., et al.: Therapeutics data commons: Machine learning datasets and tasks for drug discovery and development. arXiv preprint arXiv:2102.09548 (2021)
20. Guo, J., Schwaller, P.: Beam enumeration: probabilistic explainability for sample efficient self-conditioned molecular design. arXiv preprint arXiv:2309.13957 (2023)
21. Polykovskiy, D., et al.: Molecular sets (MOSES): a benchmarking platform for molecular generation models. Front. Pharmacol. **11**, 565644 (2020)
22. Brown, N., et al.: GuacaMol: benchmarking models for de novo molecular design. J. Chem. Inf. Model. **59**(3), 1096–1108 (2019)
23. RDKit: Open-source cheminformatics. https://www.rdkit.org
24. Preuer, K., et al.: Fréchet ChemNet distance: a metric for generative models for molecules in drug discovery. J. Chem. Inf. Model. **58**(9), 1736–1741 (2018)
25. Jensen, J.H.: A graph-based genetic algorithm and generative model/Monte Carlo tree search for the exploration of chemical space. Chem. Sci. **10**(12), 3567–3572 (2019)
26. Gómez-Bombarelli, R., et al.: Automatic chemical design using a data-driven continuous representation of molecules. ACS Cent. Sci. **4**(2), 268–276 (2018)
27. Polykovskiy, D., et al.: Entangled conditional adversarial autoencoder for de novo drug discovery. Mol. Pharm. **15**(10), 4398–4405 (2018)
28. Schneider, G., Neidhart, W., Giller, T., Schmid, G.: "Scaffold-Hopping" by topological pharmacophore search: a contribution to virtual screening. Angew. Chem. Int. Ed. Engl. **38**(19), 2894–2896 (1999)
29. Hu, Y., Stumpfe, D., Bajorath, J.: Recent advances in scaffold hopping. J. Med. Chem. **60**(4), 1238–1246 (2017)
30. Zheng, S., Lei, Z., Ai, H., Chen, H., Deng, D., Yang, Y.: Deep scaffold hopping with multimodal transformer neural networks. J. Cheminformatics **13**(1), 1–15 (2021). https://doi.org/10.1186/s13321-021-00565-5
31. Hu, C., et al.: ScaffoldGVAE: scaffold generation and hopping of drug molecules via a variational autoencoder based on multi-view graph neural networks. J. Cheminformatics **15**(1), 91 (2023)
32. Rossen, L., et al.: Scaffold Hopping with Generative Reinforcement Learning (2024)
33. Delungahawatta, T., Pokharel, A., Paz, R., Haas, C.J.: Topical diclofenac-induced hepatotoxicity. J. Community Hosp. Intern. Med. Perspect. **13**(3), 108–112 (2023)
34. Abed Al-Kareem, Z., Aziz, N.D., Ali Zghair, M.: Hepatoprotective effect of coenzyme Q10 in rats with diclofenac toxicity. Arch. Razi Inst. **77**(2), 599–605 (2022)
35. Rowlinson, S.W., et al.: A novel mechanism of cyclooxygenase-2 inhibition involving interactions with Ser-530 and Tyr-385. J. Biol. Chem. **278**(46), 45763–45769 (2003)
36. Eberhardt, J., et al.: AutoDock Vina 1.2.0: new docking methods, expanded force field, and python bindings. J. Chem. Inf. Model. **61**(8), 3891–3898 (2021)

Dimension-Augmented Anisotropy in Graph Neural Diffusion

Tatiana Sycheva[1], Maxim Beketov[2](✉), and Ivan Smolyar[3]

[1] Independent Researcher, Dublin, Ireland
[2] Faculty of Computer Science, HSE University, Moscow, Russia
maxbeketov@outlook.com
[3] EaStCHEM School of Chemistry, University of Edinburgh, Edinburgh, UK

Abstract. We consider Graph Anisotropic Diffusion (GAD), a recently proposed [4] model of graph neural networks, that can be trained to predict desired properties of the graph by performing learnable diffusion of node features on it. In contrast with similar methods, GAD introduces anisotropy of said diffusion by incorporating filters built from the graph's Fiedler vector. In present work we attempt to improve this approach by increasing the dimension of the space in which GAD runs that is, adding filters built from other low-frequency eigenmodes of the graph (eigenvectors of its Laplacian). We report the performance of such "dimension-augmented" GAD in predicting the chemical properties of small organic molecules from the ZINC dataset [5].

Keywords: Graph neural networks · Molecular property prediction · Graph Laplacian

1 Introduction

Graph neural networks (GNNs) (first introduced in [7]) are a family of machine learning models that can be used for all sorts of prediction tasks on graph-structured data [3]. Essentially, GNNs construct a function on the graph that is built from basic building blocks layers, that typically do some form of message-passing (MP) on the graph (an MP layer aggregates – e.g. sums – features of neighboring vertices/edges of the graph, then transforms the result with some nonlinear activation function, and this computation is repeated layer by layer). These layers are parameterized, and these parameters (weights of the GNN) are estimated from the training data sample in such a way that an appropriate loss function of the prediction task is optimized. Even though MP seems limited to only processing information locally at each layer (which suggests considering alternative mechanisms [9]), such GNNs are quite expressive that is, effective at approximating complicated functions on graphs.

Said expressivity of GNNs, however, has its limits: as information is passed through many MP layers, it gets more and more averaged (despite the nonlinearity) this is known as the oversmoothing problem [6]. Among many proposed ways to mitigate oversmoothing is the approach based on Directional Graph Networks (DGNs) [1], where MP is made directional by introducing filters (aggregation weights) from a certain vector field on the graph.

In [4], said directionality was combined with the framework of Graph Neural Diffusion (GRAND) [2] – to result in Graph Anisotropic Diffusion (GAD). In GRAND, node features diffuse over the graph, with diffusion rate being different for each node – that is achieved by making diffusion time a learnable parameter of the GNN layer that evaluates diffusion timesteps. In GAD, this neural diffusion is further extended by introducing anisotropy – prescribing graph edges different values of "thermal conductivity" coefficient. These values are obtained heuristically, from the lowest-frequency eigenvector of the graph Laplacian (Fiedler vector). In present work we propose to further extend this approach by considering more low-frequency eigenvectors to produce more of such (functionally different) anisotropic filters – this can be seen as increasing (augmenting) the dimension in which this neural anisotropic diffusion is happening. We evaluate our modification of GAD model on predicting the chemical properties of small organic molecules from the ZINC dataset [5] and report an improvement in quality compared to original GAD.

2 Proposed Method

Given an undirected graph $G = (V, E)$ with $|V| = n$ vertices (nodes) and $|E| = e$ edges, with $\mathbf{A}$ – its $n \times n$ adjacency matrix, and $\mathbf{D}$ – its (diagonal) degree matrix, (isotropic) diffusion of d node features (d channels of scalar features) forming an $n \times d$ feature matrix $\mathbf{X}$ is given by diffusion equation:

$$\frac{\partial}{\partial t} \mathbf{X}(t) = -\mathbf{D}^{-1} \left(\mathbf{D} - \mathbf{A} \right) \mathbf{X}(t) \tag{1}$$

where t is (diffusion) time and $\mathbf{L} = \mathbf{D} - \mathbf{A}$ is the graph Laplacian matrix. This is a graph analogue of diffusion/heat equation in flat Euclidean space $\partial_t u = \Delta u$ with the Laplace operator being $\Delta = -\mathbf{D}^{-1}\mathbf{L}$.

Complete solution to Equation (1) with initial condition $\mathbf{X}(0)$ is known to be given by matrix exponential $\mathbf{X}(t) = \exp(t\Delta)\,\mathbf{X}(0)$. The idea of Graph Neural Diffusion [2] (following [8]) is essentially to approximate this solution with a GNN by making its layers compute solutions to infinitesimal approximations of (1) forward in (diffusion) time. For one column (channel) $\mathbf{x}$ of the $n \times d$ feature matrix $\mathbf{X}$, such infinitesimal version of (1) reads:

$$\frac{\mathbf{x}(t+\tau) - \mathbf{x}(t)}{\tau} = -\mathbf{D}^{-1}\mathbf{L}\,\mathbf{x}(t+\tau) \tag{2}$$

where τ is the timestep, solving it gives $\mathbf{x}(t+\tau) = (\mathbf{D} + \tau\mathbf{L})^{-1}\,\mathbf{D}\,\mathbf{x}(t)$. This is known as implicit Euler scheme with a backward timestep (function on the RHS of (2) is taken at time $t+\tau$) – which provides certain numerical stability. One layer of Graph Neural Diffusion is thus computing a function parameterized with parameter t

$$h_t(\mathbf{x}) = (\mathbf{D} + t\mathbf{L})^{-1} \mathbf{D} \, \mathbf{x} \qquad (3)$$

on input vector $\mathbf{x}$. Diffusion is "learnable", since t is a learnable parameter (one just needs a differentiable solver to invert $(\mathbf{D} + t\mathbf{L})$) – and each of d channels of the $n \times d$ feature matrix $\mathbf{X}$ diffuses for its own (learned) diffusion time.

With GAD [4] (following [1]) anisotropy (directionality) is introduced into this diffusion process in the following manner. Given the Laplacian matrix $\mathbf{L}$ of the graph, one can find its eigendecomposition. Since the Laplacian is a (symmetric) matrix of form $\mathbf{L} = \mathbf{B}\mathbf{B}^T$ (where $\mathbf{B}$ is the $n \times e$ edge-node incidence matrix), it is positive semidefinite – i.e. its eigenvalues (can be thought of as squared frequencies of graph harmonics) are non-negative real numbers. The eigenvector ϕ corresponding to $\mathbf{L}$'s smallest non-zero eigenvalue plays a very special role in graph theory and is called Fiedler vector.

Given the Fiedler vector ϕ of the input graph, one can define a vector field on the edges of the graph

$$\mathbf{F} = \mathbf{A} \odot \nabla \phi, \qquad (4)$$

where $\odot$ is element wise multiplication, $\mathbf{A}$ is the $n \times n$ adjacency matrix, $\nabla \phi_{ij} = \phi_i - \phi_j$ is the $n \times n$ matrix of gradients of the (scalar field = function on nodes = discrete 0-form) of Fiedler vector components. Note that $\mathbf{F}$ is an antisymmetric matrix (as a vector field = function on oriented edges = discrete 1-form).

With that, as proposed in [1], one can construct two meaningful anisotropic filters:

$$\mathbf{B}_{av} = |\hat{\mathbf{F}}| \quad \text{and} \quad \mathbf{B}_{dx} = \hat{\mathbf{F}} - \mathrm{diag}(\sum_j \hat{\mathbf{F}}_{:,j}) \qquad (5)$$

where $\hat{\mathbf{F}}$ stands for $\mathbf{F}$ after normalizing each row by its L1-norm, $|\cdot|$ denotes the absolute value, subscript : denotes that the corresponding index of a matrix element is not affected by summation. These two filters are applied to input signal vector $\mathbf{x}$ by just matrix-vector multiplication, and, intuitively, $\mathbf{B}_{av}$ provides a smoothing (averaging) of the signal, while $\mathbf{B}_{dx}$ computes its directional derivative – in direction of vector field $\mathbf{F}$.

The proposal of present work is to not limit GAD with only taking the Fiedler vector in (4) for constructing such directional filters, but consider more eigenvectors of $\mathbf{L}$ following ϕ, if ordered by increasing eigenvalue (taking "more low-frequency eigenmodes" of the graph).

On Fig. 1 one can see several such low-frequency eigenmodes of two molecular graphs, with the values of their eigenvector components at the nodes shown in color. The first (a) column shows the Fiedler vectors. Note that higher-frequency eigenvectors in columns (b) and (c) highlight cycles in molecular graphs differently. The intuition behind our proposal is that this augmentation of diffusion with more channel dimensions (in which filters (5) built on such eigenmodes act) – should increase the expressivity of GAD model. Schematically, a layer of our dimension-augmented GAD (DA-GAD) model can be seen on Fig. 2.

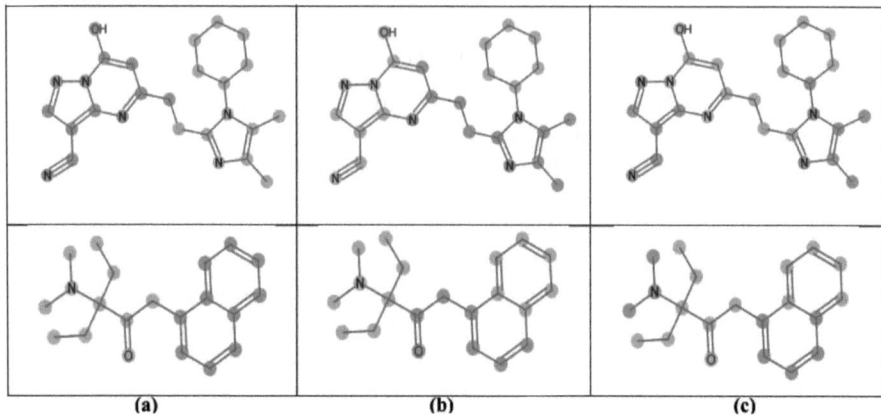

Fig. 1. 3 lowest-frequency eigenmodes of 2 molecular graphs from ZINC dataset.

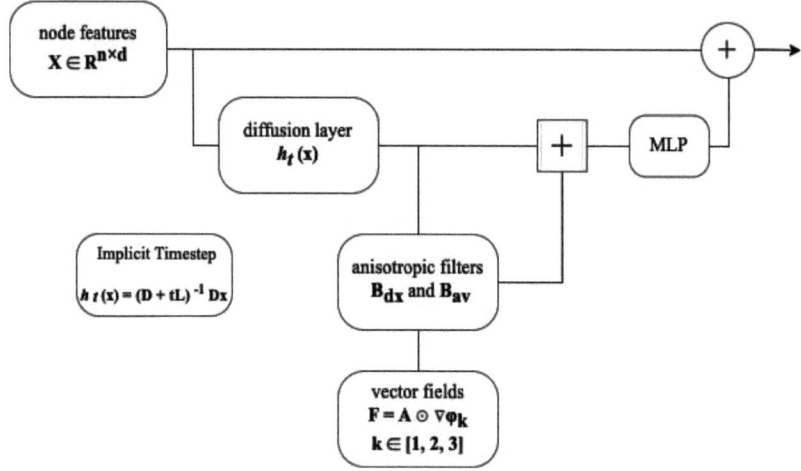

Fig. 2. One layer of dim-augmented GAD.

3 Experimental Results

We've evaluated our proposed architecture on the task of predicting a particular chemical property of small organic molecules from the ZINC dataset [5]. It contains 250K molecular graphs, of 9-37 nodes and 16-84 edges, with node features being (numerically encoded) types of atoms, and edge features being types of bonds. The target variable is constrained solubility (penalised water-octanol partition coefficient), the quality metric of regression is mean absolute error (MAE).

We compare our modification to original GAD in its two variants: GAD-i using the above described implicit Euler scheme, and GAD-s using truncated spectral decomposition of the graph Laplacian to solve the diffusion equation. All models were 4 layers deep, trained for 300 epochs with Adam optimizer with learning rate decaying from 10^{-3} to 10^{-5}.

Our software implementation and all other details are available at: github.com/avdtoto/graph-anisotrophic-diffusion.

Table 1. Results

Model	GAD-i	GAD-s	DA-GAD (2 L eigv-s)
MAE	0.139±0.007	0.140±0.004	**0.127±0.002**

The resulting metrics, as compared to results of [4], are provided in Table 1. We report a $\sim 9\%$ improvement of DA-GAD with 2 low-frequency eigenvectors of the graph Laplacian used for constructing anisotropic filters. For comparison with other contemporary models, see [4] – we note that original GAD is an improvement over most of them.

Acknowledgments. The work of M. Beketov was prepared within the framework of the HSE University Basic Research Program.

Disclosure of Interests. Authors declare no competing interests.

References

1. Beaini, D., Passaro, S., Létourneau, V., Hamilton, W., Corso, G., Liò, P.: Directional graph networks. In: International Conference on Machine Learning, pp. 748–758. PMLR (2021)
2. Chamberlain, B., Rowbottom, J., Gorinova, M.I., Bronstein, M., Webb, S., Rossi, E.: Grand: graph neural diffusion. In: International Conference on Machine Learning, pp. 1407–1418. PMLR (2021)
3. Corso, G., Stark, H., Jegelka, S., Jaakkola, T., Barzilay, R.: Graph neural networks. Nat. Rev. Methods Primers **4**(1), 17 (2024)
4. Elhag, A.A., Corso, G., Stärk, H., Bronstein, M.M.: Graph anisotropic diffusion. arXiv preprint arXiv:2205.00354 (2022)
5. Gómez-Bombarelli, R., et al.: Automatic chemical design using a data-driven continuous representation of molecules. ACS Cent. Sci. **4**(2), 268–276 (2018)
6. Rusch, T.K., Bronstein, M.M., Mishra, S.: A survey on oversmoothing in graph neural networks. arXiv preprint arXiv:2303.10993 (2023)
7. Scarselli, F., Gori, M., Tsoi, A.C., Hagenbuchner, M., Monfardini, G.: The graph neural network model. IEEE Trans. Neural Networks **20**(1), 61–80 (2008)
8. Sharp, N., Attaiki, S., Crane, K., Ovsjanikov, M.: Diffusionnet: discretization agnostic learning on surfaces. ACM Trans. Graph. (TOG) **41**(3), 1–16 (2022)
9. Veličković, P.: Message passing all the way up. arXiv preprint arXiv:2202.11097 (2022)

Uni-Mol Docking V2: Towards Realistic and Accurate Binding Pose Prediction

Eric Alcaide[1,3]($\boxtimes$), Zhifeng Gao[1,2], Guolin Ke[1,2], Yaqi Li[1], Linfeng Zhang[1,2], Hang Zheng[1], and Gengmo Zhou[1]

[1] DP Technology Beijing, Haidian District, Beijing, China
dplc@dp.tech
[2] AI for Science Institute Beijing, Haidian District, Beijing, China
[3] USI, IDSIA, Lugano, Switzerland
https://bohrium.dp.tech/apps/unimoldockingv2

Abstract. In recent years, machine learning (ML) methods have emerged as promising alternatives for molecular docking, offering the potential for high accuracy without incurring prohibitive computational costs. However, recent studies have indicated that these ML models may overfit to quantitative metrics while neglecting the physical constraints inherent in the problem. In this work, we present Uni-Mol Docking V2, which demonstrates a remarkable improvement in performance, accurately predicting the binding poses of 77+% of ligands in the PoseBusters benchmark with an RMSD value of less than 2.0 Å, and 75+% passing all quality checks. This represents a significant increase from the 62% achieved by the previous Uni-Mol Docking model. Notably, our Uni-Mol Docking approach generates chemically accurate predictions, circumventing issues such as chirality inversions and steric clashes that have plagued previous ML models. Furthermore, we observe enhanced performance in terms of high-quality predictions (RMSD values of less than 1.0 Åand 1.5 Å) and physical soundness when Uni-Mol Docking is combined with more physics-based methods like Uni-Dock. Our results represent a significant advancement in the application of artificial intelligence for scientific research, adopting a holistic approach to ligand docking that is well-suited for industrial applications in virtual screening and drug design. The code, data and service for Uni-Mol Docking are publicly available for use and further development in https://github.com/dptech-corp/Uni-Mol.

1 Introduction

The Uni-Mol modelling series [12] described the pretraining of general molecular encoders and showcased their applications in various 2D and 3D downstream tasks such as molecular conformation generation, molecular property prediction and molecular docking. The Uni-Mol paradigm was later extended to quantum property prediction in [6], showcasing the quality and applicability of molecular features learned by the architecture.

In molecular docking, leveraging a pretrained molecular encoder, pretrained pocket encoder and joint pocket-ligand blocks, UniMol Docking achieved superior performance when compared to traditional docking algorithms like Autodock Vina [10] in the CASF-2016 benchmark [8].

Recent work highlighted the need for critical evaluation of physical and chemical plausibility of docked posed by ML models, and showed that despite exhibiting better quantitative metrics such as % of <2.0 Å RMSD, deep learning models did not perform significantly better than traditional docking programs. In that work, UniMol was reported to achieve a 22% <2.0 Å RMSD on the PoseBusters set [3]. However, we attribute this low performance to suboptimal data processing and propose a standard pipeline in this work.

Lately, several works have proposed different approaches to ML docking shortcommings. On the model side, RFAA [5] proposed an all-atom modelling and extended protein folding to proteins, nucleic acids, ions and ligands; DiffDock-pocket [7] and Umol [2] proposed to lower the need for crystal structures by including protein flexibility in the modelling; the latest AlphaFold [9] report followed a similar approach and achieved the highest result on the PoseBusters benchmark, while also showcasing a partial improvement in chemical accuracy (stereochmistry). On the plausibility of results, light postprocessing as an artifact mitigation strategy [1] has been briefly explored, but it did not achieved a complete removal of unplausible results (Fig. 1).

Therefore, this work introduces three main results:

- A reproducible setup for molecular docking for the previously released Uni-Mol Docking, with correct dataset processing and reproducible results, achieving state of the art among publicly available deep-learning based molecular docking in CASF-2016, PoseBusters test set and Astex Diverse Set. Code is made publicly available (See Data & Availability).
- Results from UniMol Docking V2 showcase increased performance on unseen data and achieved the best result to our knowledge on the PoseBusters test set as of November 22, 2023.
- A step change in chemical accuracy of deep learning models, where all the unphysical and chemical issues presented previously for ML models' predictions have been corrected.

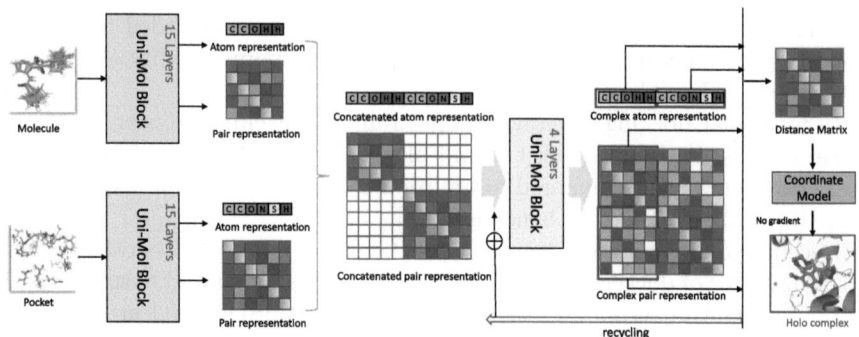

Fig. 1. Framework of Uni-Mol Docking V2

2 Methodlogy

We collect protein-ligand binding data from MOAD [4] for training. The protein data is prepared using a specific pipeline that includes the proper addition of correct hydrogen atoms, protonation information, and completion of missing heavy atoms and residues. We split the data into training and validation sets in a 9:1 ratio randomly. The training of Uni-Mol Docking V2 starts from the pretrained molecular and pocket checkpoints of Uni-Mol, the same as V1. We train the model for 100 epochs on 8 V100 GPUs with a batch size of 64, doubling the size compared to V1.

The UniMol Docking V2 needs the same input as the previous version: a known pocket and the chemical compound to be docked. Based on this, the pocket is taken in cubic format of the ligand size and a margin of 10 Å(similar to existing tools such as AutoDock Vina) and a ligand conformer (which can be provided or automatically built from the ligand smiles using standard cheminformatics tools). The output is a 3D pose of the ligand bound to the protein of interest. By pre-computing pocket features UniMol Docking can be applied to virtual screening scenarios efficiently.

The combination of Uni-Mol Docking and UniDock is tailored for industrial applications and rational drug design use cases, where the binding pocket better characterized. UniDock further allows leveraging information from cofactors and crystalographic waters to further improve accuracy. This setup has been described in a recent preprint [11] As claimed previously, the PoseBusters test set is composed of unseen data for UniMol (both previous and latest V2 version) as that only encompasses selected protein-ligand complexes released until 2019 included, whereas the test set is composed by structures released from 2020 onwards. We report results on both the PoseBusters benchmark set and Astex Diverse benchmark set, as introduced by [3].

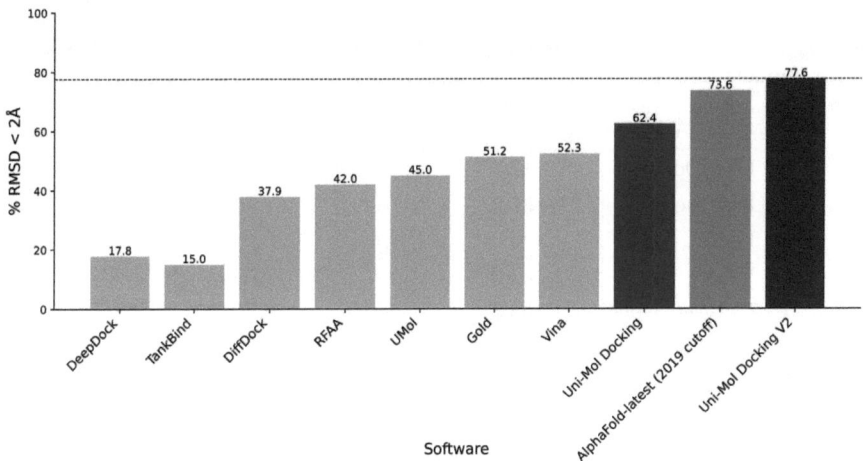

Fig. 2. Performance of different ML docking methods on the PoseBusters test set

3 Results

3.1 Standard Protocol for the Previous Version of Uni-Mol Docking

After following a standardised protocol for inference of the PoseBusters and Astex test sets, the accuracy is substantially higher than that originally reported in the first versions of the preprint in [3]. The % compounds predicted < 2.0 ÅRMSD of the ground truth is above 62%. To our knowledge, this constitutes the best result on the PoseBusters set by an open source model by November 22, 2023. After discussion with [3] authors, we attribute the performance delta to differences in the data ingestion and input generation (the pocket is all atoms <6.0 Åof any ligand heavy atom for this result, but was 8.0 Åin early versions of [3]). The deep learning model architecture and weights are kept the same. To avoid such issues in the future, we make our code available, including a containerized environment, data files and scripts to assemble them, as well as instructions already available on model loading and inference. Although plausibility has not been considered in this result, unphysical artifacts can be mitigated by following strategies such as [1].

3.2 Uni-Mol Docking V2 Results

We present the results obtained by the version of Uni-Mol Docking V2, achieving a staggering 77+% of ligands in the PoseBusters benchmark predicted with < 2.0 ÅRMSD, and 75+% of complexes passing all PoseBusters quality checks. This represents a new state of the art for ML-assisted protein-ligand docking (Table 1 and Fig. 4).

Table 1. Performance on the posebusters and Astex diverse set for different traditional and ML models

< 2.0 Å RMSD(%)	PoseBusters (N = 428)	Astex (N = 85)
DeepDock	17.8	34.12
DiffDock	37.9	71.76
UMol	45	–
Vina	52.3	57.65
Uni-Mol Docking	58.9	82.35
AlphaFold latest	73.6	–
Uni-Mol Docking V2	77.6	95.29

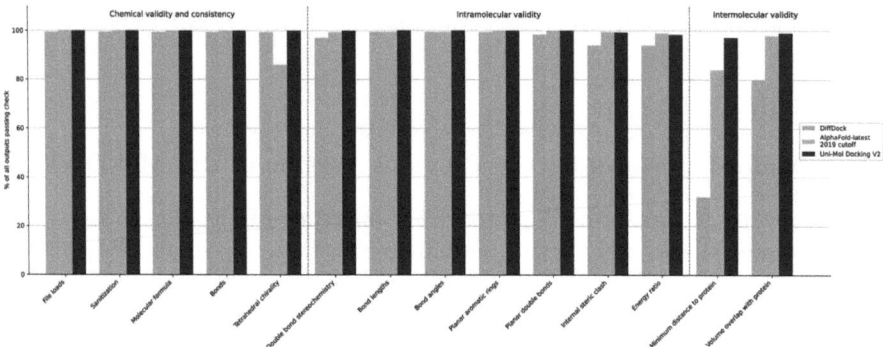

Fig. 3. Comparison of plausibility checks for predictions by DiffDock, AlphaFold latest, and Uni-Mol Docking V2

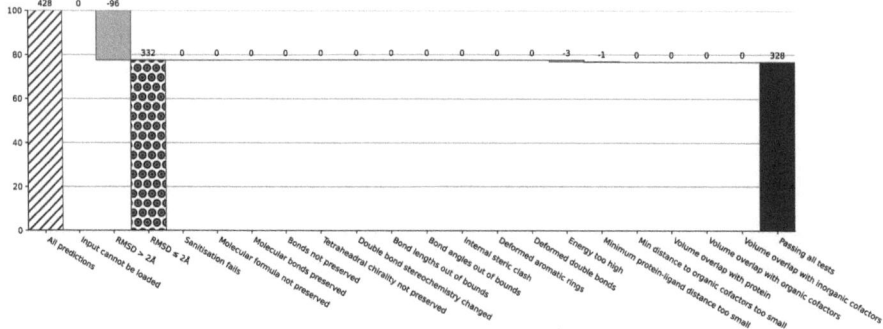

Fig. 4. Waterfall plot showcasing cumulative impact of errors

3.3 Increased Chemical Accuracy

Moreover, we highlight Uni-Mol Docking V2 produces chemically accurate predictions, showcasing no chirality inversions nor steric clashes, unlike previous ML models. All issues presented in [3] have been resolved. 95+% of predictions by Uni-Mol Docking V2 are chemically and physically plausible (as seen in Figs. 2 and 3).

We also report enhanced performance in high-quality predictions (RMSD <1.0 Å and <1.5 Å) and increased physical soundness when Uni-Mol Docking V2 is integrated with physics-based approaches like Uni-Dock. This setup enhances the industrial applications to rational drug design and virtual screening, with higher overall accuracy, reduced risk for overfitting, bigger ratio of high quality predictions, and the integration of additional information of the binding site such as cofactors and crystalographic waters [11].

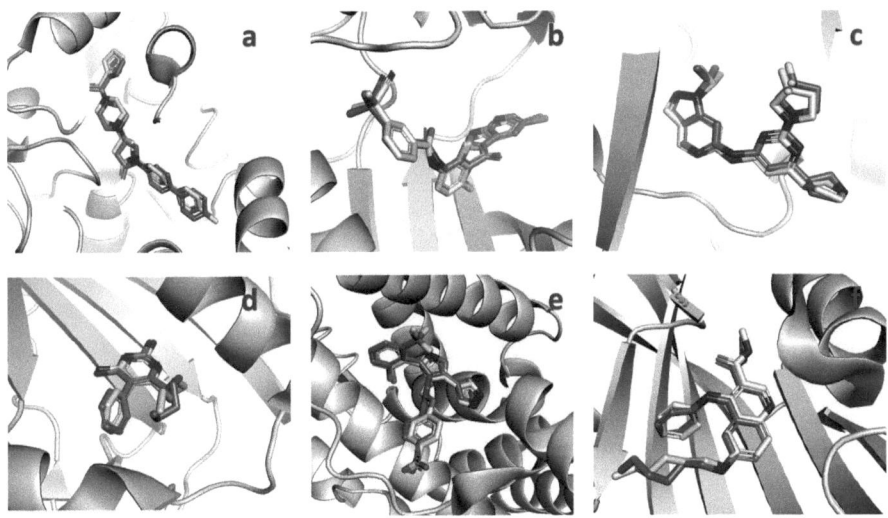

Fig. 5. a: 7PRM, RMSD = 1.11 Å. Inhibition of Monoacylglycerol lipase (MAGL), a key enzyme in the endocannabinoid system, has been proposed as an attractive approach for the treatment of various diseases including neurodegeneration, psychiatric disorders, and cancer; **b**: 8C7Y, RMSD = 0.38 Å. BRAF inhibitors have revolutionized treatment of some cancers such as melanoma, although some undesired effects have been seen, such as the paradoxical hyperactivation of MAPK caused by the ligand-induced dimerization of 1st gen BRAF inhibitors. **c**: 7R9N. RMSD = 0.63 Å. Hematopoietic progenitor kinase 1 (HPK1) is implicated as a negative regulator of T-cell receptor-induced T-cell activation. Inhibition of HPK1 has been shown to increase T-cell antitumor response. **d**: 7XI7, RMSD = 1.25 Å. Novel inhibitors for human dihydrofolate reductase could expand therapeutic options against the parasitic toxoplasmosis infections. **e**: 7NP6, RMSD = 0.54 Å. Inhibition of the nuclear receptor retinoic-acid-receptor-related orphan receptor γt (RORγt) is a promising strategy in the treatment of autoimmune diseases. **f**: 7N03, RMSD = 1.03 Å. MTH1 is a DNA damage control enzyme and potentially synthetic lethal target. Its inhibition could open new avenues in oncologic targeted therapy.

3.4 Case Study

We demonstrate the wide coverage of biochemical space in a wide variety of targets included in the PoseBusters test set with diverse biological functions and of interest in biotechnology, pharmaceutical and medical fields.

4 Conclusion

This latest version of UniMol Docking establishes a new state of the art on the PoseBusters benchmark, surpassing its predecessor, which was the top-performing open-source model to the best of our knowledge at time when it was published. Our findings signify a new frontier in the application of AI for Science in Molecular Docking. This is achieved through a comprehensive approach that addresses the ligand docking problem and rectifies implausible outcomes previously generated by machine learning models. The combination of deep learning methods and physics-based methods improves performance and allows for the incorporation of extra information, making the pipeline more suitable for industrial applications in Virtual Screening and Drug Design (Fig. 5).

Code and Data Availability

All Code and data is available for public, also we provide Uni-Mol Docking V2 service for non-commercial usage:

1. The previous version of Uni-Mol Docking, achieving 62% <2 ÅRMSD on the posebusters set, along with the Posebusters and Astex datasets can be accessed in GitHub via https://github.com/dptech-corp/Uni-Mol/pull/178.
2. Uni-Mol Docking V2, achieving 77.62% <2 Å RMSD on the posebusters set, along with model weight, can be accessed in GitHub via
https://github.com/dptech-corp/Uni-Mol/tree/main/unimol_docking_v2.
3. Uni-Mol Docking V2 service is available as a preliminary demo via https://bohrium.dp.tech/apps/unimoldockingv2.
4. Prepared protein-ligand complex from MOAD is available via https://zenodo.org/records/11191555.

Acknowledgments. Our work is made possible by the dedication and efforts of numerous teams at DP Technology and AI for Science Institute. We would like to acknowledge the support from MLOps Team, PR Team, Drug Discovery Team etc. Contributors (in alphabetical orders).
   - **Eric Alcaide**: Conceptualization, Methodology, Software, Validation, Writing.
   - **Zhifeng Gao**: Supervision, Conceptualization, Methodology, Writing.
   - **Guolin Ke**: Supervision, Project administration, Conceptualization, Methodology.
   - **Yaqi Li**: Data Curation, Investigation, Validation.
   - **Linfeng Zhang**: Supervision, Funding acquisition.
   - **Hang Zheng**: Software, Methodology, Data Curation, Validation.

- **Gengmo Zhou**: Conceptualization, Methodology, Software, Validation, Writing.

This study was also partially funded by the Horizon Europe funding programme under the Marie Skłodowska-Curie Actions Doctoral Networks grant agreement "Explainable AI for Molecules - AiChemist", no. 101120466 (to E.A.) and the Swiss State Secretariat for Education, Research and Innovation (SERI) under contract number 23.00421.

References

1. Alcaide, E., Li, Z., Zheng, H., Gao, Z., Ke, G.: UMD-fit: generating realistic ligand conformations for distance-based deep docking models. In: NeurIPS 2023 Generative AI and Biology (GenBio) Workshop (2023). https://openreview.net/forum?id=BE2hok0lES
2. Bryant, P., Kelkar, A., Guljas, A., Clementi, C., Noé, F.: Structure prediction of protein-ligand complexes from sequence information with Umol. Nat. Commun. **15**(1), 4536 (2024). https://doi.org/10.1038/s41467-024-48837-6
3. Buttenschoen, M., Morris, G.M., Deane, C.M.: Posebusters: AI-based docking methods fail to generate physically valid poses or generalise to novel sequences. Chem. Sci. **15**, 3130–3139 (2024). https://doi.org/10.1039/D3SC04185A
4. Hu, L., Benson, M.L., Smith, R.D., Lerner, M.G., Carlson, H.A.: Binding moad (mother of all databases). Proteins: Struct., Funct., Bioinfor. **60**(3), 333–340 (2005). https://doi.org/10.1002/prot.20512
5. Krishna, R., et al.: Generalized biomolecular modeling and design with rosettafold all-atom. Science **384**(6693), eadl2528 (2024). https://doi.org/10.1126/science.adl2528, https://www.science.org/doi/abs/10.1126/science.adl2528
6. Lu, S., Gao, Z., He, D., Zhang, L., Ke, G.: Data-driven quantum chemical property prediction leveraging 3D conformations with Uni-Mol+. Nat. Commun. **15**(1), 7104 (2024). https://doi.org/10.1038/s41467-024-51321-w
7. Plainer, M., et al.: DiffDock-pocket: diffusion for pocket-level docking with sidechain flexibility (2023). https://neurips.cc/virtual/2023/77419
8. Su, M., et al.: Comparative assessment of scoring functions: the casf-2016 update. J. Chem. Inf. Model. **59**(2), 895–913 (2018). https://doi.org/10.1021/acs.jcim.8b00545
9. Team, I.L., Team, G.D.A.: A glimpse of the next generation of alphafold. https://storage.googleapis.com/deepmind-media/DeepMind.com/Blog/a-glimpse-of-the-next-generation-of-alphafold/alphafold_latest_oct2023.pdf
10. Trott, O., Olson, A.J.: Autodock vina: improving the speed and accuracy of docking with a new scoring function, efficient optimization, and multithreading. J. Comput. Chem. **31**(2), 455–461 (2010). https://doi.org/10.1002/jcc.21334
11. Yang, H., et al.: Synergistic application of molecular docking and machine learning for improved protein-ligand binding pose prediction. Natl. Sci. Open **3**(2), 20230058 (2024). https://doi.org/10.1360/nso/20230058
12. Zhou, G., et al.: Uni-Mol: a universal 3D molecular representation learning framework. In: The Eleventh International Conference on Learning Representations (2023). https://openreview.net/forum?id=6K2RM6wVqKu

MolEncoder: Improved Masked Language Modeling for Molecules

Fabian P. Krüger[1,2,3(✉)], Nicklas Österbacka[1], Mikhail Kabeshov[1], Ola Engkvist[1,4], and Igor Tetko[3]

[1] AstraZeneca R&D, Discovery Sciences, Molecular AI, 431 83 Mölndal, Sweden
[2] TUM School of Computation, Information and Technology, Department of Mathematics, Technical University of Munich, 80333 Munich, Germany
fabian.krueger@tum.de
[3] Helmholtz Munich – German Research Center for Environmental Health (GmbH), Institute of Structural Biology, Molecular Targets and Therapeutics Center, 85764 Neuherberg, Germany
[4] Department of Computer Science and Engineering, Chalmers University of Technology, 412 96 Gothenburg, Sweden

Abstract. Predicting molecular properties is an important challenge in drug discovery. Machine learning methods, particularly those based on transformer architectures, have become increasingly popular for this task by learning molecular representations directly from chemical structure [1,2]. Motivated by progress in natural language processing, many recent approaches apply models of the BERT (Bidirectional Encoder Representations from Transformers) architecture [3] to molecular data using SMILES as the input format [4–9].

In this study, we revisit core design assumptions that originate in natural language processing but are often carried over to molecular tasks without modification. We explore how variations in masking strategies, pretraining dataset size, and model size influence downstream performance in molecular property prediction.

Our findings suggest that common practices inherited from natural language processing do not always yield optimal results in this setting. In particular, we observe that increasing the masking ratio can lead to significant improvements, while scaling up the model or dataset size results in stagnating gains despite higher computational cost (Fig. 1). Building on these observations, we develop MolEncoder, a BERT-style model that achieves improved performance on standard benchmarks while remaining more efficient than existing approaches.

These insights highlight meaningful differences between molecular and textual learning settings. By identifying design choices better suited to chemical data, we aim to support more effective and efficient model development for researchers working in drug discovery and related fields.

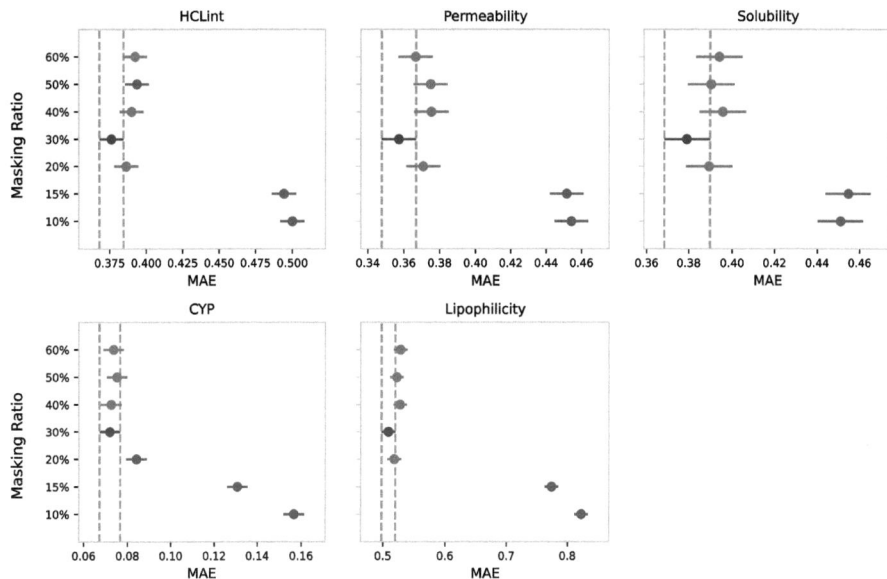

Fig. 1. While prior work used masking ratios of 15% [5–12], we show here that using higher masking ratios significantly improves the mean absolute error (MAE) for five molecular property prediction tasks [13–15]. Error bars show 95% confidence intervals reflecting how well we can distinguish models given the variability from data splitting and fine-tuning across cross-validation folds. Confidence intervals and color coding are based on pairwise Tukey's HSD post hoc tests after a repeated measure ANOVA. Non-overlapping intervals visually reflect statistically significant differences as determined by this procedure. The best-performing model (lowest mean MAE over 5×5 CV) is shown in blue. Models not significantly different from the best are shown in gray; significantly worse models are shown in red. (Color figure online)

Acknowledgments. This study was funded by the Horizon Europe funding programme under the Marie Skłodowska-Curie Actions Doctoral Networks grant agreement "Explainable AI for Molecules - AiChemist", no. 101120466.

References

1. Mak, K.K., Wong, Y.H., Pichika, M.R.: Artificial intelligence in drug discovery and development. Drug Discovery and Evaluation: Safety and Pharmacokinetic Assays, pp. 1461–1498 (2024)
2. Muratov, E.N., et al.: Qsar without borders. Chem. Soc. Rev. **49**(11), 3525–3564 (2020)
3. Devlin, J., Chang, M.W., Lee, K., Toutanova, K.: BERT: pre-training of deep bidirectional transformers for language understanding. In: Proceedings of the 2019 Conference of the North American Chapter of the Association for Computational Linguistics: Human Language Technologies, Volume 1 (Long and Short Papers), pp. 4171–4186 (2019)

4. Weininger, D.: Smiles, a chemical language and information system. 1. Introduction to methodology and encoding rules. J. Chem. Inf. Comput. Sci. **28**(1), 31–36 (1988)
5. Wang, S., Guo, Y., Wang, Y., Sun, H., Huang, J.: Smiles-BERT: large scale unsupervised pre-training for molecular property prediction. In: Proceedings of the 10th ACM International Conference on Bioinformatics, Computational Biology and Health Informatics, pp. 429–436. Association for Computing Machinery, New York, NY, USA (2019)
6. Li, J., Jiang, X.: Mol-BERT: an effective molecular representation with BERT for molecular property prediction. Wirel. Commun. Mob. Comput. **2021**(7181815), 1–7 (2021)
7. Kim, H., Lee, J., Ahn, S., Lee, J.R.: A merged molecular representation learning for molecular properties prediction with a web-based service. Sci. Rep. **11**, 17955 (2021)
8. Ahmad, W., Simon, E., Chithrananda, S., Grand, G., Ramsundar, B.: Chemberta-2: towards chemical foundation models. arXiv preprint arXiv:2209.01712 (2022)
9. Ross, J., Belgodere, B., Chenthamarakshan, V., Padhi, I., Mroueh, Y., Das, P.: Large-scale chemical language representations capture molecular structure and properties. Nat. Mach. Intell. **4**(12), 1256–1264 (2022)
10. Liu, Y., Zhang, R., Li, T., Jiang, J., Ma, J., Wang, P.: Molrope-BERT: an enhanced molecular representation with rotary position embedding for molecular property prediction. J. Mol. Graph. Model. **118**, 108344 (2022)
11. Fabian, B., et al.: Molecular representation learning with language models and domain-relevant auxiliary tasks. arXiv:2011.13230 (2020)
12. Zhang, X.C., et al.: Mg-BERT: leveraging unsupervised atomic representation learning for molecular property prediction. Briefings Bioinform. (2021)
13. Fang, C., et al.: Prospective validation of machine learning algorithms for absorption, distribution, metabolism, and excretion prediction: an industrial perspective. J. Chem. Inf. Model. **63**(11), 3263–3274 (2023)
14. Fluetsch, A., Trunzer, M., Gerebtzoff, G., Rodríguez-Pérez, R.: Deep learning models compared to experimental variability for the prediction of cyp3a4 time-dependent inhibition. Chem. Res. Toxicol. **37**(4), 549–560 (2024)
15. Zdrazil, B., et al.: The chembl database in 2023: a drug discovery platform spanning multiple bioactivity data types and time periods. Nucleic Acids Res. **52**(D1), D1180–D1192 (2024)

Consensus Prediction of Chemical Reactions with OCHEM-R Platform

Igor V. Tetko[1,2(✉)], Guillaume Godin[3], Kevin M. Jablonka[4,5,6], Adrian Mirza[4,6], and Luc Patiny[7]

[1] BIGCHEM GmbH, 85716 Unterschleißheim, Germany
itetko@vcclab.org
[2] Institute of Structural Biology, Molecular Targets and Therapeutics Center, Helmholtz Munich - Deutsches Forschungszentrum Für Gesundheit Und Umwelt (GmbH), 86764 Neuherberg, Germany
[3] Osmo Labs, PBC, 450 E 29Th Street, New York, NY, USA
[4] Laboratory of Organic and Macromolecular Chemistry (IOMC), Friedrich Schiller University Jena, Humboldtstrasse 10, 07743 Jena, Germany
[5] Center for Energy and Environmental Chemistry Jena (CEEC Jena), Friedrich Schiller University Jena, Philosophenweg 7a, 07743 Jena, Germany
[6] Helmholtz Institute for Polymers in Energy Applications Jena (HIPOLE Jena), Lessingstrasse 12-14, 07743 Jena, Germany
[7] Zakodium Sàrl, Lonay, Vaud, Switzerland

Abstract. Here we describe the OCHEM-R platform, developed to propose chemical pathways based on a consensus prediction of retrosynthetic pathways using eight different methods. The developed software allows users to visualize predicted reactions and identify similar reactions using retrieval augmented generation (RAG) . The platform is publicly available at https://ochem.eu.

Keywords: Multistep Reaction prediction · Pathway visualization · LLM · reaction explanation

1 Introduction

Prediction of chemical reactions is a very important yet challenging area of research in chemistry. Despite advances in the prediction of single step retrosynthesis [1–11], the prediction of multistep pathways remains a significant challenge due to ambiguities in the selection of possible precursors at each retrosynthesis step [12, 13]. Researchers have identified two key factors contributing to these limitations: the lack of negative data representing unsuccessful or partially successful reactions and the multiplication of errors when predicting multi-step reactions [13]. We also think that the current retrosynthesis methods do not have strategic multistep thinking, which is how the synthesis is performed by humans. However, the inclusion of such global goals is still to be developed.

The consensus modeling approach (also known as query by committee) has proven its advantages in many different fields, including chemistry, and this approach was the basis the models that led to the most accurate predictions in, e.g., the Kaggle solubility challenge [14] and ToxCast toxicity [15] predictions or recent Tox24 challenge [16–18]. We have noticed that different retrosynthesis prediction approaches, which are based on templates (MHNreact) [10], graph neural networks (LocalRetro) [5] or Transformer models (ChemFormer) [3], frequently provide predictions that tend to be different and not correlated [13]. By harvesting the most accurate predictions from different approaches to predict the individual steps in a retrosynthesis, one can significantly improve the accuracy of models and also better estimate the confidence of predictions to prioritize multistep reaction pathways. To debug the model and aid the chemist in pathway selection, an intuitive visualization was also critically important. The selection of pathways could further be improved if the chemist is provided with additional context, such as similar reactions from the literature. These considerations were behind development of the OCHEM-R platform, which is an extension of the popular On-line Chemical Database and Modelling Environment Platform [19] for prediction of chemical reactions.

2 Methods

Initial analysis of the available retrosynthesis prediction methods (see Table 1) allowed us to identify eight methods that had high reported accuracies according to the results of benchmarking on public datasets.

One of the technical difficulties associated with using consensus approaches for reaction prediction is the necessity of integrating different retrosynthesis methods, each of which requires its own settings and (frequently incompatible) Python environments. Also, the prediction of pathways using different methods requires considerable computational resources. In this respect the OCHEM platform, which uses Java for networking, execution of individual modules and frontend, allows straightforward integration and allows execution of individual methods on different computers.

The top-1 accuracies of retrosynthesis predictions (which were about 60%) were much lower than those of direct synthesis predictions (>92%). Therefore, we used two methods AT and TTL to verify whether predicted reactants could be used to produce the initial compound. If both methods failed to do this, the proposed splitting of the compound into these reactants was considered incorrect.

We supposed that predictions made using different methods are not correlated. Thus, the same reactants simultaneously proposed by several methods were reinforced and obtained a higher likelihood score. For each retrosynthesis prediction method we considered maximum n top predictions made by the method, which were used in consensus scoring (n was an adjustable parameter, taking one of two values, 5 or 10).

Our algorithm enumerated all paths and identified the shortest ones leading to each particular reactant. A probability of reactions along pathways to reach each reactant was calculated. The reactants with the highest probability scores were selected for the next step of retrosynthesis prediction (expansion step). After the expansion, the scores for each reactant were recalculated. If a reactant existed in the database of building blocks, or if its size was less than the number of predefined atoms (MinimumAtoms), the path leading to it was considered partially resolved and this reactant was named as building block (i.e., a potentially purchasable starting material) and was excluded from any further

Table 1. Performances of single-step individual retrosynthesis methods on USPTO-50k dataset [20, 21].

Abbreviation	Description	top-1	top-5	top-10	ref
AT	Transformer pretrained on 2 M SMILES with bidirectional random augmentation (SMILES-to-SMILES translation)	53.5	81.0	85.7	[2]
Chem Former	BART-style denoising Transformer pretrained on 100 M SMILES for generative and predictive chemistry task	54.3	62.3	63	[3]
Edit Retro	Iterative, non-autoregressive SMILES editing Transformer that applies string-level edits (insertions, deletions, reordering) to generate reactants	60.8	86.2	90.3	[4]
Local Retro	Template-based retrosynthesis: uses graph neural networks to predict local atom/bond templates at centers, combined with global reactivity attention	53.4	81	85.7	[5]
UAlign	Template-free graph-to-sequence model: GNN encoder + Transformer decoder with unsupervised SMILES alignment to reuse unchanged substructures during reactant generation	53.5	84.6	90.5	[6]
TTL	Triple Transformer Loop: flags reactive sites, then proceeds through three Transformers sequentially: reaction center prediction, reagent prediction, and forward reaction validation	na	na	na	[7]
T5	Adapts T5's Text-to-Text transformer to chemistry ("T5Chem"/"MolT5"), framing diverse chemical tasks (forward/reverse reaction prediction, yield estimation, captioning) as unified text generation	53.8	76.7	na	[8]
Ring Breaker	Neural model specialized in predicting ring-forming or ring-breaking retrosynthetic disconnections, trained with multiple ring-centric labels for use in CASP systems	na	na	na	[9]

analysis. Otherwise, the reactant was considered as an intermediate and was considered for expansion on the next step. If all intermediate reactants leading to a building block were resolved, the pathway was considered to be resolved. The calculations were run for MaxSteps and typically required about one to two hours depending on the complexity of molecules. If the number of enumerated reactions was larger than MaxResolved, calculations were stopped. The algorithm returned MaxPathways of non-redundant pathways with the highest scores, which were deduplicated by considering the largest fragments in each pathway. The main difficulty was in combinatorial explosion of enumerated pathways and the need to store them in memory of the computer for analysis. For some molecules about 100GB of CPU memory was required to store enumerated pathways.

The predicted pathways were cached in a database, which allowed efficient recalculation of pathways with slightly different settings of the algorithm.

The following main parameters were used to control reaction predictions:

- MaxSteps (7–10) - number of steps for retrosynthesis prediction
- MaxPathways (100) - number of detected non-redundant pathways returned by program
- MaxResolved (10,000,000) - maximum number of enumerated pathways to stop further analysis
- MinimumAtoms (8) - minimum number of atoms in reactant to be considered for retrosynthesis

The other settings include a path to a file containing building blocks, the algorithms used for retrosynthesis and direct synthesis (validation of retrosynthesis).

2.1 Visualization of Reactions

We developed an interactive front-end, building upon the open-source visualizer project (https://github.com/NPellet/visualizer) to facilitate the exploration of neural network-based reaction retrosynthesis results. This browser-based interface enables chemists to:

- Visualize retrosynthetic pathways as interactive graphs.
- Access calculated metrics such as industrial scores.
- Review relevant literature references and reaction examples.
- Rapidly assess the quality and feasibility of proposed synthetic routes.

The platform requires no installations and operates entirely within a web browser, streamlining access and enhancing usability for researchers. Its modular design allows for flexible configuration and integration of new visualization modules, supporting efficient and intuitive analysis of complex retrosynthetic data (Fig. 1).

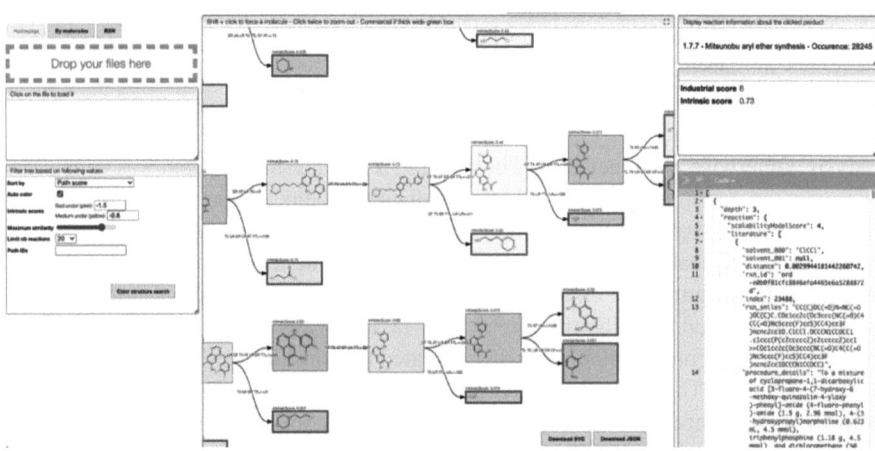

Fig. 1. Example of visualization of pathways. The pathways are shown as trees and can dynamically be filtered. Clicking on an element of the tree will reveal more details.

2.2 Interpretation of Reaction Predictions

To contextualize the reaction predictions, we retrieve literature data using retrieval augmented generation (RAG). For this, we embedded the RXNSMILES of the Open Reaction Database (ORD)[22] using the chemical reaction fingerprints RXNFPs [23] and stored those embeddings in a vector built with FAISS [24]. In addition, we define prototype reactions with scalability factors. By measuring the cosine similarity to those embeddings, we can compute an assessment of the scalability of the queried reaction as a weighted average.

2.3 Implementation and Availability

The OCHEM-R platform is available at https://ochem.eu. Registered OCHEM users can submit their molecules, which, after validation by the administrators, will be predicted by the platform. The submitted molecules and predicted pathways were only viewable by the users that submitted them. The open access version is implemented as an extension of openOCHEM [25], and is publicly available at https://github.com/openochem/ochem-r.

3 Results: Example of Resolved Pathways

A number of synthesized compounds from our partners V.P. Kukhar Institute of Bioorganic Chemistry and Petrochemistry (IBOPC) of the National Academy of Sciences of Ukraine were provided to us for retrosynthesis prediction https://ochem.eu/static/retro.do. Most of the compounds were featured in their recent article [26], which was published after USPTO data were released. An estimation of retrosynthetic pathways was made by a resident expert in chemical synthesis at IBOPC. In general, they found good agreement between the predicted reactions and reactions known in the literature. However, in some cases, OCHEM-R incorrectly proposed reactants. Specifically, it was prone to propose non-selective reactions which could occur at several positions within the main reactant as well as sometimes have issues with protecting/deprotecting groups. Further development of the system is required to address this issue.

4 Discussion

The OCHEM-R platform is targeted towards consensus prediction of chemical pathways for easy integration and prediction of multistep reaction predictions. Its modular structure allows for easy extension to include novel reaction prediction methods or specification of different cost functions to select pathways, e.g. for converged retrosynthesis planning [27], and can be sped up (current analysis takes about one-two hours per molecule) with approaches developed for batch retrosynthesis predictions [28] or other techniques [29]. Due to its modular structure, OCHEM-R can be readily configured to run on different (CPU/GPU, Linux/Mac) architectures, which support respective reaction prediction methods. The current individual implementations of reaction methods are based on original publications and we did not retrain any of the models on the same dataset. Following recent progress in transformer based fine-tuning using LLM approaches [30, 31], we expect that individual models and overall performance of the model will be significantly improved with additional adjustment of weights within the models. Other possible improvements also include prioritisation of reactions based on predicted yield - a task which, however, still remains difficult to solve [32].

Acknowledgement. This study was partially funded by the European Union's Horizon 2020 research and innovation programme under the Marie Skłodowska-Curie Actions grant agreement "Advanced machine learning for Innovative Drug Discovery (AIDD, https://ai-dd.eu)" No. 956832 and Horizon Europe Marie Skłodowska-Curie Actions Doctoral Network grant agreement No. 101120466 "Explainable AI for Molecules" (AiChemist, https://aichemist.eu). We thank Adil Kabylda, Alexandre Tkatchenko and Leonardo Medrano Sandonas for their contribution to OCHEM-R platform development. We also thank Katya Ahmad for her remarks and suggestions and Marina Kachaeva for her feedback about the quality of reaction prediction. In addition, we thank Boris Bulgakov, Ivan Vilotijević, and Lucas Gregor for their feedback on the predictions. The work of KMJ was supported by the Carl Zeiss Stiftung. The work of AM was supported by the Helmholtz Foundation Model initiative of the Helmholtz Association.

References

1. Karpov, P., Godin, G., Tetko, I.V.: A transformer model for retrosynthesis. In: Proceedings of the Artificial Neural Networks and Machine Learning – ICANN 2019: Workshop and Special Sessions; Tetko, I.V., Kůrková, V., Karpov, P., Theis, F., (eds.); Springer International Publishing: Cham, pp. 817–830 (2019). https://doi.org/10.1007/978-3-030-30493-5_78
2. Tetko, I.V., Karpov, P., Van Deursen, R., Godin, G.: State-of-the-art augmented NLP transformer models for direct and single-step retrosynthesis. Nat. Commun. **11**, 5575 (2020). https://doi.org/10.1038/s41467-020-19266-y
3. Irwin, R., Dimitriadis, S., He, J., Bjerrum, E.J.: Chemformer: a pre-trained transformer for computational chemistry. Mach. Learn. Sci. Technol. **3**, 015022 (2022). https://doi.org/10.1088/2632-2153/ac3ffb
4. Han, Y., et al.: Retrosynthesis prediction with an iterative string editing model. Nat. Commun. **15**, 6404 (2024). https://doi.org/10.1038/s41467-024-50617-1
5. Chen, S., Jung, Y.: Deep retrosynthetic reaction prediction using local reactivity and global attention. JACS Au **1**, 1612–1620 (2021). https://doi.org/10.1021/jacsau.1c00246
6. Zeng, K., et al.: Ualign: pushing the limit of template-free retrosynthesis prediction with unsupervised SMILES alignment. J. Cheminformatics **16**, 80 (2024). https://doi.org/10.1186/s13321-024-00877-2
7. Kreutter, D., Reymond, J.-L.: Chemoenzymatic multistep retrosynthesis with transformer loops. Chem. Sci. **15**, 18031–18047 (2024). https://doi.org/10.1039/d4sc02408g
8. Sagawa, T., Kojima, R.: ReactionT5: A Large-Scale Pre-Trained Model towards Application of Limited Reaction Data. *ArXiv E-Prints* (2023). arXiv:2311.06708, https://doi.org/10.48550/arXiv.2311.06708
9. Thakkar, A., Selmi, N., Reymond, J.-L., Engkvist, O., Bjerrum, E.J.: "Ring breaker": neural network driven synthesis prediction of the ring system chemical space. J. Med. Chem. **63**, 8791–8808 (2020). https://doi.org/10.1021/acs.jmedchem.9b01919
10. Seidl, P., et al.: Improving few- and zero-shot reaction template prediction using modern hopfield networks. J. Chem. Inf. Model. **62**, 2111–2120 (2022). https://doi.org/10.1021/acs.jcim.1c01065

11. Schwaller, P., et al.: Predicting retrosynthetic pathways using transformer-based models and a hyper-graph exploration strategy. Chem. Sci. **11**, 3316–3325 (2020). https://doi.org/10.1039/C9SC05704H
12. Hassen, A.K., Torren-Peraire, P., Genheden, S., Verhoeven, J., Preuss, M., Tetko, I.V.: Mind the Retrosynthesis Gap: Bridging the Divide between Single-Step and Multi-Step Retrosynthesis Prediction *ArXiv E-Prints*(2022). arXiv:2212.11809, https://doi.org/10.48550/arXiv.2212.11809
13. Torren-Peraire, P., et al.: Models Matter: the impact of single-step retrosynthesis on synthesis planning. Digit. Discov. **3**, 558–572 (2024). https://doi.org/10.1039/D3DD00252G
14. Hunklinger, A., Hartog, P., Šícho, M., Godin, G., Tetko, I.V.: The openOCHEM consensus model is the best-performing open-source predictive model in the first EUOS/SLAS joint compound solubility challenge. SLAS Discov. **29**, 100144 (2024). https://doi.org/10.1016/j.slasd.2024.01.005
15. Novotarskyi, S., Abdelaziz, A., Sushko, Y., Körner, R., Vogt, J., Tetko, I.V.: ToxCast EPA in vitro to in vivo challenge: insight into the rank-i model. Chem. Res. Toxicol. **29**, 768–775 (2016). https://doi.org/10.1021/acs.chemrestox.5b00481
16. Eytcheson, S.A., Tetko, I.V.: Which Modern AI Methods Provide Accurate Predictions of Toxicological Endpoints? Analysis of Tox24 Challenge Results. Chem. Res. Toxicol. (2025). https://doi.org/10.1021/acs.chemrestox.5c00273
17. Makarov, D.M., Ksenofontov, A.A., Budkov, Y.A.: Consensus modeling for predicting chemical binding to transthyretin as the winning solution of the tox24 challenge. Chem. Res. Toxicol. **38**, 392–399 (2025). https://doi.org/10.1021/acs.chemrestox.4c00421
18. Cirino, T., et al.: Consensus modeling strategies for predicting transthyretin binding affinity from tox24 challenge data. Chem. Res. Toxicol. **38**, 1061–1071 (2025). https://doi.org/10.1021/acs.chemrestox.5c00018
19. Sushko, I., et al.: Online chemical modeling environment (OCHEM): web platform for data storage, model development and publishing of chemical information. J. Comput. Aided Mol. Des. **25**, 533–554 (2011). https://doi.org/10.1007/s10822-011-9440-2
20. Lowe, D.M.: Extraction of Chemical Structures and Reactions from the Literature. PhD Thesis, Apollo - University of Cambridge Repository (2012)
21. Liu, B., et al.: Retrosynthetic reaction prediction using neural sequence-to-sequence models. ACS Cent. Sci. **3**, 1103–1113 (2017). https://doi.org/10.1021/acscentsci.7b00303
22. Kearnes, S.M., et al.: The open reaction database. J. Am. Chem. Soc. **143**, 18820–18826 (2021). https://doi.org/10.1021/jacs.1c09820
23. Schwaller, P., et al.: Mapping the space of chemical reactions using attention-based neural networks. Nat. Mach. Intell. **3**, 144–152 (2021). https://doi.org/10.1038/s42256-020-00284-w
24. Douze, M., et al.: The Faiss Library. *ArXiv E-Prints* (2024). arXiv:2401.08281, https://doi.org/10.48550/arXiv.2401.08281
25. openochem Open OCHEM -- AI Models for Drug Discovery and Environmental Chemistry (2022)
26. Kachaeva, M.V., Pilyo, S.G., Demydchuk, B.A., Prokopenko, V.M., Zhirnov, V.V., Brovarets, V.S.: 4-Cyano-1,3-oxazole-5-sulfonamides as novel promising anticancer lead compounds. Int. J. Curr. Res. **10**, 69410–69425 (2018)
27. Torren-Peraire, P., Verhoeven, J., Herman, D., Ceulemans, H., Tetko, I.V., Wegner, J.K.: Improving route development using convergent retrosynthesis planning. J. Cheminformatics **17**, 26 (2025). https://doi.org/10.1186/s13321-025-00953-1
28. Andronov, M., Andronova, N., Wand, M., Schmidhuber, J., Clevert, D.-A.: Accelerating the inference of string generation-based chemical reaction models for industrial applications. J. Cheminformatics **17**, 31 (2025). https://doi.org/10.1186/s13321-025-00974-w

29. Hartog, P.B.R., Westerlund, A.M., Tetko, I.V., Genheden, S.: Investigations into the efficiency of computer-aided synthesis planning. J. Chem. Inf. Model. **65**, 1771–1781 (2025). https://doi.org/10.1021/acs.jcim.4c01821
30. Hu, E.J., et al.: LoRA: low-rank adaptation of large language models. In Proceedings of the International Conference on Learning Representations (2022)
31. Pratap, S., Aranha, A.R., Kumar, D., Malhotra, G., Iyer, A.P.N.: The fine art of fine-tuning: a structured review of advanced llm fine-tuning techniques. Nat. Lang. Process. J. **11**, 100144 (2025). https://doi.org/10.1016/j.nlp.2025.100144
32. Voinarovska, V., Kabeshov, M., Dudenko, D., Genheden, S., Tetko, I.V.: When yield prediction does not yield prediction: an overview of the current challenges. J. Chem. Inf. Model. **64**, 42–56 (2024). https://doi.org/10.1021/acs.jcim.3c01524

Special Session: Neural Networks for Graphs and Beyond

Special Session: Neural Networks for Graphs and Beyond

Graphs play a crucial role in different fields in modeling complex structures composed of entities and their relationships, including dynamic domains where these relationships can evolve over time. Neural models on graphs enable adaptive solutions for a wide range of learning tasks on graph data, avoiding the need for hand-engineered features or domain-specific knowledge. This capability has driven significant progress in applying machine learning to graph-based problems across various research fields (chemistry, bioinformatics, social and data sciences, etc.). As a result, the design, optimization, and analysis of these graph-based learning models have become central to cutting-edge research, while also presenting a range of open challenges that continue to shape the field's future directions. This special session at ICANN 2025 aims to bring together cutting-edge research and new ideas in neural networks and machine learning models for graphs.

Organizers

Alessio Micheli	University of Pisa, Italy
Benoit Gaüzère	INSA Rouen Normandie, France
Domenico Tortorella	University of Pisa, Italy
Filippo Maria Bianchi	UiT the Arctic University of Norway
Luca Pasa	University of Padova, Italy
Nicolò Navarin	University of Padova, Italy
Vincenzo Carletti	University of Salerno, Italy

HeNCler: Node Clustering in Heterophilous Graphs via Learned Asymmetric Similarity

Sonny Achten[1]( ), Zander Op de Beeck[1], Francesco Tonin[2],
Volkan Cevher[2], and Johan A. K. Suykens[1]

[1] ESAT-STADIUS, KU Leuven, Leuven, Belgium
{sonny.achten,zander.opdebeeck,johan.suykens}@kuleuven.be
[2] LIONS, EPFL, Lausanne, Switzerland
{francesco.tonin,volkan.cevher}@epfl.ch

Abstract. Clustering nodes in heterophilous graphs is challenging as traditional methods assume that effective clustering is characterized by high intra-cluster and low inter-cluster connectivity. To address this, we introduce HeNCler—a novel approach for **He**terophilous **N**ode **Cl**ust**er**ing. HeNCler *learns* a similarity graph by optimizing a clustering-specific objective based on weighted kernel singular value decomposition Our approach enables spectral clustering on an *asymmetric* similarity graph, providing flexibility for both directed and undirected graphs. By solving the primal problem directly, our method overcomes the computational difficulties of traditional adjacency partitioning-based approaches. Experimental results show that HeNCler significantly improves node clustering performance in heterophilous graph settings, highlighting the advantage of its asymmetric graph-learning framework.

Keywords: Heterophily · Clustering · Kernel SVD

1 Introduction

Graph neural networks (GNNs) have substantially advanced machine learning applications to graph-structured data by effectively propagating node attributes end-to-end. Typically, GNNs rely on the assumption of homophily, where nodes with similar labels are more likely to be connected [29]. The homophily assumption holds in contexts such as social networks and citation graphs. It underlies the effectiveness of message-passing GNNs like GCN [14] in tasks such as node classification and graph prediction. In homophilous graphs, local feature aggregation reinforces meaningful representations through neighborhood smoothing.

In heterophilous graphs, such as web or transaction networks, connected nodes often differ in labels, making local aggregation less effective. This requires capturing long-range dependencies by learning edge importance [3,8], which is more feasible in supervised tasks due to label guidance.

Our work specifically targets attributed node clustering in a fully unsupervised setting, where neither labels nor external guidance are available—necessitating the use of unsupervised or self-supervised learning strategies. For instance, auto-encoder type models [15] are primarily focused on node representation learning rather than clustering, making them less suited for directly improving cluster-ability. Various self-supervised, contrastive learning techniques [12,27] enhance node representation learning in homophilous settings only. At the same time, other self-supervised methods have been developed to handle heterophilous graphs [5,26]. However, these methods are designed for the general node representation learning task and lack a clustering objective.

Existing node clustering methods [4,6,25] often rely on proximity-based objectives or partitioning of the adjacency matrix, assuming that effective clustering aligns with high intra-cluster and low inter-cluster similarity—a premise often invalid in heterophilous graphs. Moreover, these methods are typically limited to undirected graphs, disregarding valuable asymmetric information.

This paper introduces HeNCler, a novel approach for node clustering in heterophilous graphs, illustrated in Fig. 1. Existing work overlooks the asymmetric relationships in heterophilous graphs. HeNCler addresses this by using weighted kernel singular value decomposition (wKSVD) to induce a learned asymmetric similarity graph for both directed and undirected graphs. The dual problem of wKSVD aligns with asymmetric kernel spectral clustering, enabling the interpretation of similarities without homophily. By solving the primal problem directly, HeNCler overcomes computational difficulties and shows superior performance in node clustering tasks within heterophilous graphs.

Our contributions in this work can be summarized as follows:

- We introduce HeNCler, a kernel spectral biclustering framework designed to *learn* an induced *asymmetric* similarity graph suited for node clustering of heterophilous graphs, applicable to both directed and undirected graphs.
- We develop a primal-dual framework for a generic weighted kernel singular value decomposition (wKSVD) model.
- We show that the dual wKSVD formulation allows for biclustering of bipartite/asymmetric graphs, while we employ a computationally feasible implementation in the primal wKSVD formulation.
- We further generalize our approach with trainable feature mappings, using node and edge decoders, such that the similarity matrix to cluster is learned.
- We train HeNCler in the primal setting and demonstrate its superior performance on the node clustering task for heterophilous attributed graphs.
- Our implementation and supplementary materials are available on GitHub: https://github.com/sonnyachten/HeNCler/.

2 Preliminaries and Related Work

We use lowercase symbols (e.g., x) for scalars, lowercase bold (e.g., $\boldsymbol{x}$) for vectors and uppercase bold (e.g., $\boldsymbol{X}$) for matrices. A single entry of a matrix is

Node Clustering in Heterophilous Graphs via Learned Asymmetric Similarity   57

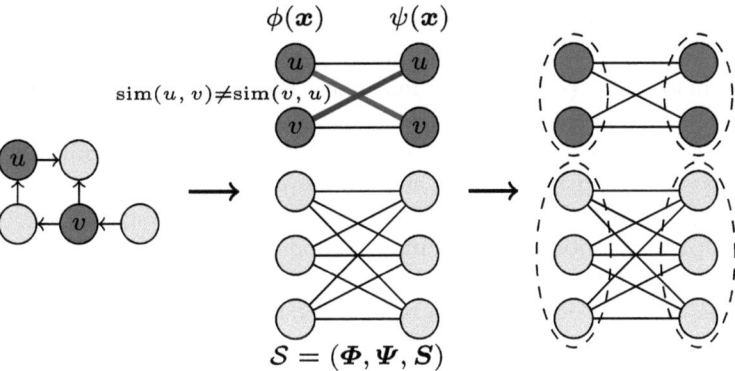

Fig. 1. HeNCler Overview. Starting from a heterophilous (directed) graph, where similar nodes are far apart (left), HeNCler learns two sets of node representations, $\{\phi(\boldsymbol{x}_v)\}_{v\in\mathcal{V}}$ and $\{\psi(\boldsymbol{x}_v)\}_{v\in\mathcal{V}}$, forming a bipartite graph $\mathcal{S}$ (middle), where the similarity between nodes is defined as $S_{uv} = \text{sim}(u,v) = \phi(\boldsymbol{x}_u)^\top \psi(\boldsymbol{x}_v)$. The clustering objective brings related nodes closer in the learned graph, and clusters are then identified using spectral biclustering through wKSVD (right).

represented by X_{ij}. $\phi(\cdot)$ denotes a mapping and $\boldsymbol{\phi}_v = \phi(\boldsymbol{x}_v)$ represents the mapping of node v in the induced feature space. We represent a graph $\mathcal{G}$ by its vertices (i.e., nodes) $\mathcal{V}$ and edges $\mathcal{E}$, $\mathcal{G} = (\mathcal{V}, \mathcal{E})$, or by its node feature matrix and adjacency matrix $\mathcal{G} = (\boldsymbol{X}, \boldsymbol{A})$. For a bipartite graph, we have $\mathcal{G} = (\mathcal{I}, \mathcal{J}, \mathcal{E})$ or $\mathcal{G} = (\boldsymbol{X}_\mathcal{I}, \boldsymbol{X}_\mathcal{J}, \boldsymbol{S})$ where S_{ij} is the edge weight between nodes $i \in \mathcal{I}$ and $j \in \mathcal{J}$. Note that $\boldsymbol{S}$ is generally asymmetric and rectangular, and that the adjacency matrix of the bipartite graph is given by $\boldsymbol{A} = \begin{bmatrix} \boldsymbol{0} & \boldsymbol{S} \\ \boldsymbol{S}^\top & \boldsymbol{0} \end{bmatrix}$.

Kernel singular value decomposition (KSVD) [22] allows for non-linear extensions of the SVD problem and can be applied on data structures such as row and column features, directed graphs, and/or can exploit asymmetric similarity information such as conditional probabilities [13]. Interestingly, KSVD often outperforms the similar, though symmetric, kernel principal component analysis model on tasks where asymmetry is not immediately apparent [13,24].

Spectral clustering generalizations have been proposed in many settings. Spectral graph biclustering [7] formulates the spectral clustering problem of a bipartite graph $\mathcal{G} = (\mathcal{I}, \mathcal{J}, \boldsymbol{S})$ and shows the equivalence with the SVD of the normalized matrix $\boldsymbol{S}_n = \boldsymbol{D}_1^{-1/2} \boldsymbol{S} \boldsymbol{D}_2^{-1/2}$, where $D_{1,ii} = \sum_j S_{ij}$ and $D_{2,jj} = \sum_i S_{ij}$. Cluster assignments for nodes $\mathcal{I}$ and nodes $\mathcal{J}$ can be inferred from the left and right singular vectors respectively. Further, kernel spectral clustering (KSC) [2] proposes a weighted kernel principal component analysis in which the dual formulation corresponds to the random walks interpretation of the spectral clustering problem. KSC and the aforementioned spectral biclustering formulation lack asymmetry and a primal formulation respectively, which are limitations that our model addresses.

Restricted kernel machines (RKM) [23] possess primal and dual model formulations, based on the concept of conjugate feature duality. It is an energy-based framework for (deep) kernel machines. RKMs encompasses many model classes, including classification, regression, kernel principal component analysis, and KSVD, and allows deep kernel learning and deep kernel learning on graphs [1]. One possibility of representing feature maps in RKMs is by means of deep neural networks, e.g., for unsupervised representation learning [16].

Homophilous node clustering methods such as MinCutPool [4] and DMoN [25] introduce unsupervised loss functions in a graph neural network framework. MinCutPool employs a relaxed version of the minimal cut objective applied to the adjacency matrix, while DMoN optimizes the modularity score of clustering assignments with respect to the graph structure. Both methods rely on partitioning the adjacency matrix and inherently assume strong homophily. Moreover, due to their theoretical foundations, these losses are restricted to undirected graphs. Beyond adjacency partitioning, self-supervised and contrastive learning techniques have also been proposed [6,12,27]. These approaches typically use graph proximity as a supervision signal, again assuming a degree of homophily. For instance, S^3GC [6] leverages random walk co-occurrences to infer proximity-based similarities.

Heterophilous node clustering methods predominantly rely on contrastive or self-supervised techniques that are less dependent on local proximity. HoLe [11] addresses unsupervised graph structure learning by iteratively rewiring the graph using intermediate clustering results. This process increases effective homophily, thereby improving clustering performance on moderately heterophilous graphs. SparseGAD [10] sparsifies graph structures to effectively reduce noise from irrelevant edges and enhance the detection of closely related nodes. In contrast, methods like ours aim to learn an entirely new similarity graph, which is particularly valuable for strongly heterophilous settings. Other approaches, such as HGRL [5], employ self-supervised learning by using graph augmentation strategies to capture global and higher-order structural patterns. MUSE [28] builds semantic and contextual views for contrastive learning, integrating multi-view representations through a learned fusion controller.

While adjacency partitioning-based methods have shown strong theoretical and empirical performance on homophilous graphs, they do not extend naturally to heterophilous or directed settings. Conversely, self-supervised clustering approaches, though flexible, often lack explicit clustering objectives and/or still implicitly depend on homophily. In the following section, we introduce HeNCler, which bridges these gaps.

3 Method

Model Motivation. Our approach employs an RKM auto-encoder framework, which has been shown to be effective in unsupervised representation learning by jointly optimizing feature mappings and projection matrices within a kernel-based setting [16]. We propose a weighted KSVD (wKSVD) loss that employs double feature mappings to learn an asymmetric similarity matrix. This *learned* similarity alleviates the homophily assumption by capturing long-range dependencies and enables the modeling of *asymmetric* relationships—making it particularly well-suited for directed graphs. Even in undirected graphs, this asymmetry can capture nuanced relational patterns. In fact, many graphs treated as undirected are inherently directed (e.g., citation networks). Modeling such asymmetries has been shown to be beneficial [13,24]. Additionally, the wKSVD loss admits a spectral graph biclustering interpretation, offering further theoretical insight. We first introduce the general wKSVD framework, followed by our HeNCler model, which operates in the primal setting and jointly learns the feature mappings in an end-to-end manner.

3.1 Kernel Spectral Biclustering with Asymmetric Similarities

Consider a dataset with two input sources $\{x_i\}_{i=1}^n$ and $\{z_j\}_{j=1}^m$, on which we want to define an unsupervised learning task. To this end, we introduce a weighted kernel singular value decomposition model (wKSVD), starting from the following primal optimization problem, which is a weighted variant of the KSVD formulation:

$$\min_{U,V,e,r} J \triangleq \mathrm{Tr}(U^\top V) - \frac{1}{2}\sum_{i=1}^n w_{1,i} e_i^\top \Sigma^{-1} e_i - \frac{1}{2}\sum_{j=1}^m w_{2,j} r_j^\top \Sigma^{-1} r_j$$

$$\text{s.t. } \{e_i = U^\top \phi(x_i), \forall i=1,\ldots,n; \quad r_j = V^\top \psi(z_j), \forall j=1,\ldots,m\}, \quad (1)$$

with projection matrices $U, V \in \mathbb{R}^{d_f \times s}$; strictly positive weighting scalars $w_{1,i}, w_{2,j}$; latent variables $e_i, r_j \in \mathbb{R}^s$; diagonal and positive definite hyperparameter matrix $\Sigma \in \mathbb{R}^{s \times s}$; and centered feature maps $\phi(\cdot) : \mathbb{R}^{d_x} \mapsto \mathbb{R}^{d_f}$ and $\psi(\cdot) : \mathbb{R}^{d_z} \mapsto \mathbb{R}^{d_f}$. Details on centering of the feature maps are provided in the supplementary materials. The following derivation shows the equivalence with the spectral biclustering problem.

Proposition 1. *The solution to the primal problem (1) can be obtained by solving the singular value decomposition of*

$$W_1^{1/2} S W_2^{1/2} = H_e \Sigma H_r^\top, \quad (2)$$

where W_1 and W_2 are diagonal matrices such that $W_{1,ii} = w_{1,i}$ and $W_{2,jj} = w_{2,j}$, $S = \Phi \Psi^\top$ is an asymmetric similarity matrix where $S_{ij} = \phi(x_i)^\top \psi(z_j)$, $\Phi = [\phi(x_1)\ldots\phi(x_n)]^\top$, $\Psi = [\psi(z_1)\ldots\psi(z_m)]^\top$, and where $H_e = [h_{e_1}\ldots h_{e_n}]^\top$, and $H_r = [h_{r_1}\ldots h_{r_m}]^\top$ are the left and right singular vectors respectively; and by applying $r_j = \Sigma h_{r_j}/\sqrt{w_{2,j}}$ and $e_i = \Sigma h_{e_i}/\sqrt{w_{1,i}}$.

Proof. We now introduce dual variables h_{e_i} and h_{r_j} using a specific instance of the FenchelYoung inequality [19]:

$$\frac{1}{2} w_{1,i} e_i^\top \Sigma^{-1} e_i + \frac{1}{2} h_{e_i}^\top \Sigma h_{e_i} \geq \sqrt{w_{1,i}}\, e_i^\top h_{e_i},$$

$$\frac{1}{2} w_{2,j} r_j^\top \Sigma^{-1} r_j + \frac{1}{2} h_{r_j}^\top \Sigma h_{r_j} \geq \sqrt{w_{2,j}}\, r_j^\top h_{r_j}, \quad (3)$$

$\forall e_i, r_j, h_{e_i}, h_{r_j} \in \mathbb{R}^s$; $\forall w_{1,i}, w_{2,j} \in \mathbb{R}_{>0}$; and $\forall \Sigma \in \mathbb{R}_{\succ 0}^{s \times s}$.[1]

By substituting the constraints of (1) and inequalities (3) into the objective function of (1), we obtain an objective in primal and dual variables as an upper bound on the primal objective $\bar{J} \geq J$:

$$\min_{U,V,h_e,h_r} \bar{J} \triangleq \text{Tr}(U^\top V) - \sum_{i=1}^{n} \sqrt{w_{1,i}}\, \phi(x_i)^\top U h_{e_i} + \frac{1}{2} \sum_{i=1}^{n} h_{e_i}^\top \Sigma h_{e_i}$$
$$- \sum_{j=1}^{m} \sqrt{w_{2,j}}\, \psi(z_j)^\top V h_{r_j} + \frac{1}{2} \sum_{j=1}^{m} h_{r_j}^\top \Sigma h_{r_j}. \qquad (4)$$

Next, we formulate the stationarity conditions of problem (4):

$$\frac{\partial \bar{J}}{\partial V} = 0 \Rightarrow U = \sum_{j=1}^{m} \sqrt{w_{2,j}}\, \psi(z_j) h_{r_j}^\top, \quad \frac{\partial \bar{J}}{\partial h_{e_i}} = 0 \Rightarrow \Sigma h_{e_i} = \sqrt{w_{1,i}}\, U^\top \phi(x_i),$$
$$\frac{\partial \bar{J}}{\partial U} = 0 \Rightarrow V = \sum_{i=1}^{n} \sqrt{w_{1,i}}\, \phi(x_i) h_{e_i}^\top, \quad \frac{\partial \bar{J}}{\partial h_{r_j}} = 0 \Rightarrow \Sigma h_{r_j} = \sqrt{w_{2,j}}\, V^\top \psi(z_j), \qquad (5)$$

from which we then eliminate the primal variables U and V. This yields:

$$\begin{bmatrix} 0 & W_1^{1/2} S W_2^{1/2} \\ W_2^{1/2} S^\top W_1^{1/2} & 0 \end{bmatrix} \begin{bmatrix} H_e \\ H_r \end{bmatrix} = \begin{bmatrix} H_e \\ H_r \end{bmatrix} \Sigma, \qquad (6)$$

where $\mathbf{0}$ is an all-zeros matrix. The above eigenvalue problem is equivalent with (2), and the stationarity conditions (5) provide the relationships between primal and dual variables, which concludes the proof. □

We have thus shown the connection between the primal (1) and dual formulation (2). Similarly to the KSVD framework, the wKSVD framework can be used for learning with asymmetric kernel functions and/or rectangular data sources. The spectral biclustering problem can now easily be obtained by choosing the weights $w_{1,i}$ and $w_{2,j}$ appropriately.

Corollary 1. *Given Proposition 1, and by choosing W_1 and W_2 to equal $D_1^{-1/2}$ and $D_2^{-1/2}$, where $D_{1,ii} = \sum_j S_{ij}$ and $D_{2,jj} = \sum_i S_{ij}$, we obtain the random walk interpretation $D_1^{-1/2} S D_2^{-1/2} = H_e \Sigma H_r^\top$ of the spectral graph bipartitioning problem for the bipartite graph $\mathcal{S} = (\Phi, \Psi, S)$.*

Moreover, the wKSVD framework is more general as, on the one hand, one can use a given similarity matrix (e.g. adjacency matrix of a graph) or (asymmetric) kernel function in the dual, or, on the other hand, one can choose to use explicitly defined (deep) feature maps in both primal or dual.

---

[1] Refer to the supplementary materials for verification of these inequalities.

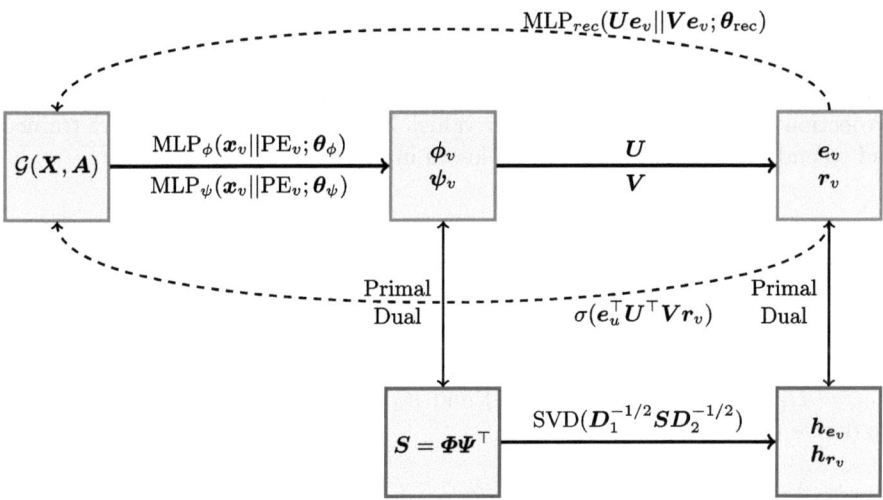

Fig. 2. The HeNCler model. HeNCler operates in the primal setting (top of the figure in red) and uses a double multilayer perceptron (MLP) to map node representations into a feature space. The obtained representations ϕ_v and ψ_v are then projected into a latent space, yielding e_v and r_v respectively. The wKSVD loss ensures that these latent representations correspond to the dual equivalent (bottom of the figure in blue) i.e., a biclustering of the asymmetric similarity graph defined by S. The node and edge reconstructions (dashed arrows) aid in the feature map learning. (Color figure online)

3.2 The HeNCler Model

HeNCler employs the wKSVD framework in a graph setting, where the dataset is a node set $\mathcal{V}$ and where the asymmetry arises from employing two different mappings that operate on the nodes given the entire graph $\mathcal{G} = (\boldsymbol{X}, \boldsymbol{A})$. Our approach is visualized in Fig. 2.

In the preceding subsection, we showed that the primal wKSVD formulation (1) has an equivalent dual problem corresponding to the graph bipartitioning problem. This equivalence holds when $w_{1,i}$ and $w_{2,j}$ are chosen to equal the square root of the inverse of the out-degree and in-degree of a similarity graph $\mathcal{S}$ respectively. The similarity graph $\mathcal{S}$ depends on the feature mappings $\phi(\cdot)$ and $\psi(\cdot)$, which for our method not only depend on the node of interest, but also on the rest of the input graph and the learnable parameters. The mappings for a node v thus become $\phi(\boldsymbol{x}_v, \mathcal{G}; \boldsymbol{\theta}_\phi)$ and $\psi(\boldsymbol{x}_v, \mathcal{G}; \boldsymbol{\theta}_\psi)$ and we will ease these notations to $\phi(\boldsymbol{x}_v)$ and $\psi(\boldsymbol{x}_v)$. The ability of our method to learn these feature mappings is an important aspect of our contribution, as a key motivation is that we need to learn new similarities for clustering heterophilous graphs.

HeNCler's loss function is comprised of three terms: the wKSVD-loss, a node-reconstruction loss, and an edge-reconstruction loss:

$$\mathcal{L}_{\text{wKSVD}}(\boldsymbol{U}, \boldsymbol{V}, \boldsymbol{\Sigma}, \boldsymbol{\theta}_\phi, \boldsymbol{\theta}_\psi) + \mathcal{L}_{\text{NodeRec}}(\boldsymbol{U}, \boldsymbol{V}, \boldsymbol{\theta}_\phi, \boldsymbol{\theta}_\psi, \boldsymbol{\theta}_{\text{rec}}) + \mathcal{L}_{\text{EdgeRec}}(\boldsymbol{U}, \boldsymbol{V}, \boldsymbol{\theta}_\phi, \boldsymbol{\theta}_\psi),$$

where the trainable parameters of the model are in the multilayer perceptron (MLP) feature maps ($\boldsymbol{\theta}_\phi$ and $\boldsymbol{\theta}_\psi$), the MLP node decoder ($\boldsymbol{\theta}_{\text{rec}}$), the $\boldsymbol{U}$ and $\boldsymbol{V}$ projection matrices, and the singular values $\boldsymbol{\Sigma}$. All these parameters are trained end-to-end and we next explain the losses in more detail.

wKSVD-Loss. Instead of solving the SVD in the dual formulation, HeN-Cler leverages the primal formulation (1) of the wKSVD framework for greater computational efficiency. While equation (1) assumes that the feature maps $\phi(\cdot)$ and $\psi(\cdot)$ are fixed, HeNCler utilizes parametric functions $\phi(\cdot; \boldsymbol{\theta}_\phi)$ and $\psi(\cdot; \boldsymbol{\theta}_\psi)$, enabling it to learn new similarities between nodes. By incorporating regularization terms for these functions and defining the weighting scalars as $w_{1,v} = D_{1,vv}^{-1} = 1/\sum_u \phi(\boldsymbol{x}_v)^\top \psi(\boldsymbol{x}_u)$ and $w_{2,v} = D_{2,vv}^{-1} = 1/\sum_u \phi(\boldsymbol{x}_u)^\top \psi(\boldsymbol{x}_v)$, we derive the wKSVD-loss:

$$\mathcal{L}_{\text{wKSVD}} \triangleq -\sum_{v=1}^{|\mathcal{V}|} D_{1,vv}^{-1} \phi(\boldsymbol{x}_v)^\top \boldsymbol{U} \boldsymbol{\Sigma}^{-1} \boldsymbol{U}^\top \phi(\boldsymbol{x}_v) - \sum_{v=1}^{|\mathcal{V}|} D_{2,vv}^{-1} \psi(\boldsymbol{x}_v)^\top \boldsymbol{V} \boldsymbol{\Sigma}^{-1} \boldsymbol{V}^\top \psi(\boldsymbol{x}_v)$$

$$+ \text{Tr}(\boldsymbol{U}^\top \boldsymbol{V}) + \sum_{v=1}^{|\mathcal{V}|} \sqrt{D_{1,vv}^{-1} D_{2,vv}^{-1}} \, \phi(\boldsymbol{x}_v)^\top \psi(\boldsymbol{x}_v). \quad (7)$$

The primal formulation of HeNCler (7) consists of four terms with two distinct objectives. The first two terms promote the weighted variance of the learned node representations $\boldsymbol{e}$ and $\boldsymbol{r}$, encouraging informative embeddings. The third and fourth terms serve as regularizers that enforce asymmetry by penalizing the similarity between $\boldsymbol{U}$ and $\boldsymbol{V}$, and between $\phi(\boldsymbol{x}_v)$ and $\psi(\boldsymbol{x}_v)$, respectively.

For the two feature maps $\phi(\cdot)$ and $\psi(\cdot)$, we employ two MLPs: $\phi(\boldsymbol{x}_v, \mathcal{G}; \boldsymbol{\theta}_\phi) \equiv \text{MLP}_\phi(\boldsymbol{x}_v \| \text{PE}_v; \boldsymbol{\theta}_\phi)$ and $\psi(\boldsymbol{x}_v, \mathcal{G}; \boldsymbol{\theta}_\psi) \equiv \text{MLP}_\psi(\boldsymbol{x}_v \| \text{PE}_v; \boldsymbol{\theta}_\psi)$. We construct a random walks positional encoding (PE) [9] to embed the network's structure and concatenate this encoding with the node attributes. The MLPs have two linear layers with a LeakyReLU activation function in between, followed by a batch normalization layer. The singular values in $\boldsymbol{\Sigma}$ are jointly learned, constrained to lie between 0 and 1, with the additional condition that $\text{Tr}(\boldsymbol{\Sigma}^{-\frac{1}{2}}) = 1$.

Reconstruction Losses. Since the feature maps $\phi(\cdot)$ and $\psi(\cdot)$ need to be learned, an additional loss function beyond the above regularization term is required to effectively optimize the parameters of the MLPs. As the node clustering setting is completely unsupervised, we add a decoder network and a reconstruction loss. This technique has been proven to be effective for unsupervised learning in the RKM-framework [16], as well as for unsupervised node representation learning [21]. For heterophilous graphs, we argue that it is particularly important to also reconstruct node features and not only the graph structure.

For the node reconstruction, we first project the $\boldsymbol{e}$ and $\boldsymbol{r}$ variables back to feature space, concatenate these and then map to input space with another MLP. This MLP has also two layers and a leaky ReLU activation function. The hidden layer size is set to the average of the latent dimension and input dimension. With the mean-squared-error as the associated loss, this gives:

$$\mathcal{L}_{\text{NodeRec}} = \frac{1}{|\mathcal{V}|} \sum_{v \in \mathcal{V}} ||\text{MLP}_{\text{rec}}(\boldsymbol{U}\boldsymbol{e}_v || \boldsymbol{V}\boldsymbol{r}_v; \boldsymbol{\theta}_{\text{rec}}) - \boldsymbol{x}_v||^2.$$

To reconstruct edges, we use a simple dot-product decoder $\sigma(\boldsymbol{e}_u^\top \boldsymbol{U}^\top \boldsymbol{V} \boldsymbol{r}_v)$ where σ is the sigmoid function. By using the $\boldsymbol{e}$ representation for source nodes and $\boldsymbol{r}$ for target nodes, this reconstruction is asymmetric and can reconstruct directed graphs. We use a binary cross-entropy loss:

$$\mathcal{L}_{\text{EdgeRec}} = \frac{1}{|\mathcal{U}|} \sum_{(u,v) \in \mathcal{U}} \text{BCE}(\sigma(\boldsymbol{e}_u^\top \boldsymbol{U}^\top \boldsymbol{V} \boldsymbol{r}_v), \mathcal{E}_{uv}),$$

where $\mathcal{U}$ is a node-tuple set, resampled every epoch, containing $2|\mathcal{V}|$ positive edges from $\mathcal{E}$ and $2|\mathcal{V}|$ negative edges from $\mathcal{E}^C$, and $\mathcal{E}_{uv} \in \{0, 1\}$ indicates whether an edge (u, v) exist: $(u, v) \in \mathcal{E}$.

Constraints and Cluster Assignments. The batch normalization in the MLPs keeps the wKSVD-loss bounded and the constraints on the singular values is enforced by a softmax function. Cluster assignments are obtained by KMeans clustering on the concatenation of learned $\boldsymbol{e}$ and $\boldsymbol{r}$ node representations.

HeNCler jointly learns the wKSVD projection matrices, $\boldsymbol{U}$ and $\boldsymbol{V}$, along with the feature map parameters, $\boldsymbol{\theta}_\phi$ and $\boldsymbol{\theta}_\psi$. The wKSVD loss improves the cluster-ability of the learned similarity graph, ensuring that $\boldsymbol{e}$ and $\boldsymbol{r}$ function as spectral biclustering embeddings. The two distinct feature maps enable asymmetric learning, effectively capturing potential asymmetric relationships in the data, while the reconstruction losses ensure robust and meaningful representation learning.

4 Experiments

Datasets. We assess the performance of HeNCler on heterophilous attributed graphs that are available in literature. We use Texas, Cornell, and Wisconsin [17], which are directed webpage networks where edges encode hyperlinks between pages. Next, we use Chameleon and Squirrel [20], which are undirected Wikipedia webpage networks where edges encode mutual links. We further evaluate our model on three undirected graphs: Roman-Empire, Minesweeper, and Tolokers [18]. These datasets represent, respectively, a graph-structured Wikipedia article, a grid graph inspired by the Minesweeper game, and a crowdsourcing interaction network. More details are provided in the supplementary materials.

Model Selection and Metrics. Model selection in this unsupervised setting is inherently challenging, as the most appropriate evaluation metric depends on the downstream task. Consequently, model selection is beyond the scope of this paper. Instead, we evaluate our model in a task-agnostic manner and ensure a fair comparison with the baselines. We fix the hyperparameter configuration of the models across all datasets. We train for a fixed number of epochs and keep track of the evaluation metrics to report the best observed result. We repeat the training process 10 times and report average best results with standard deviations. We report the normalized mutual information (NMI) and pairwise F1-scores, based on the class labels.

Baselines and Hyperparameters. We compare our model against several methods, including a simple KMeans based on node attributes, adjacency partitioning-based approaches such as MinCutPool [4] and DMoN [25], as well as S^3GC [6], MUSE [28], and HoLe [11], which represent the current state-of-the-art in homophilous and heterophilous node clustering. For HeNCler, we fix the hyperparameters as follows: MLP hidden dimensions 256, output dimensions 128, latent dimension $s = 2 \times$ #classes, learning rate 0.01, and epochs 300. For the baselines, we used their code implementations and the default hyperparameter settings as proposed by the authors. The number of clusters to infer is set to the number of classes for all methods.

Experimental Results. Table 1 presents the experimental results for heterophilous graphs. HeNCler consistently demonstrates superior performance, significantly outperforming the baselines, especially on directed graphs. For undirected graphs, HeNCler also shows strong results, achieving the best performance in 5 out of 10 cases. These results highlight HeNCler's versatility and effectiveness in handling heterophilous graph structures.

Additional experiments are presented in the supplementary materials. We include an ablation study, some experiments on homophilous graphs, a visualization of the learned asymmetries, and a computational complexity analysis.

Discussion. A key motivation behind HeNCler is to learn a new graph representation where nodes belonging to the same cluster are positioned closer together, driven by the clustering objective. This results in spectral biclustering embeddings that exhibit improved cluster-ability. As HeNCler uses KMeans to obtain cluster assignments, the comparisons between HeNCler and KMeans demonstrate that our model enhances the cluster-ability of the node representations relative to the original input features.

The asymmetry in HeNCler eliminates the undirected constraints of traditional adjacency partitioning-based models, enabling superior performance on directed graphs. Furthermore, our ablation study in the supplementary materials shows that, while most of the performance on undirected graphs stems from the graph learning component, HeNCler is able to capture and learn additional meaningful asymmetric information. This capacity to extract valuable asymmetric insights from symmetric data is a common occurrence in KSVD frameworks [13,24]. Importantly, thanks to the added performance boost from asymmetry,

Table 1. Experimental results on heterophilous graphs. We report NMI and F1 scores for 10 runs (mean ± standard deviation), where higher values indicate better performance. The best results for each metric are highlighted in bold. OOM indicates an out-of-memory error on a 16GB GPU.

Dataset		Baselines						Ours
		KMeans	MinCutPool	DMoN	S^3GC	MUSE	HoLe	HeNCler
tex	NMI	4.97±1.00	11.60±2.19	9.06±2.11	11.56±1.46	39.23±4.91	7.51±0.37	**43.65±2.52**
	F1	59.27±0.83	55.26±0.56	47.76±4.79	43.69±2.74	65.96±3.52	35.30±0.44	**71.39±2.16**
corn	NMI	5.42±2.04	17.04±1.61	12.49±2.51	14.48±1.79	38.99±2.73	14.23±0.17	**41.52±4.35**
	F1	52.97±0.24	51.21±5.06	43.83±6.23	33.13±0.83	60.58±3.61	34.64±0.56	**63.40±3.67**
wis	NMI	6.84±4.39	13.38±2.36	12.56±1.23	13.07±0.61	39.71±2.22	11.89±0.42	**47.13±1.76**
	F1	56.16±0.58	55.63±2.96	45.72±7.85	31.71±2.25	58.94±3.09	37.05±0.02	**68.30±2.17**
cha	NMI	0.44±0.11	11.88±1.99	12.87±1.86	15.83±0.26	23.06±0.28	8.76±0.15	**23.89±0.84**
	F1	**53.23±0.07**	50.40±5.65	45.05±4.30	36.51±0.24	52.10±0.48	30.61±0.09	44.14±1.83
squi	NMI	1.40±2.12	6.35±0.32	3.08±0.38	3.83±0.11	8.30±0.23	4.99±0.09	**9.67±0.13**
	F1	54.05±2.72	**55.26±0.57**	49.21±2.74	35.08±0.18	50.07±5.99	28.71±0.36	36.51±2.39
rom	NMI	35.20±1.79	9.97±2.02	13.14±0.53	14.48±0.21	**40.50±0.73**	OOM	36.99±0.61
	F1	37.17±2.12	**42.19±0.26**	22.69±3.91	17.76±0.53	38.34±0.35		35.43±1.07
mine	NMI	0.02±0.02	6.16±2.17	**6.87±2.91**	6.53±0.17	0.06±0.01	6.46±0.07	0.06±0.00
	F1	73.63±3.58	71.76±8.86	70.42±9.47	48.78±0.63	75.77±2.24	63.01±0.13	**76.48±1.56**
tol	NMI	3.04±2.83	6.68±0.98	6.69±0.20	5.99±0.05	6.67±0.55	5.14±0.06	**6.73±0.59**
	F1	65.56±10.49	72.10±10.38	67.87±4.74	59.17±0.27	73.56±1.94	66.35±1.12	**73.66±2.10**

on top of the benefits from similarity learning, HeNCler outperforms state-of-the-art models, even when applied to undirected graphs.

While our experiments focus on benchmark heterophilous graphs, the design of HeNCler makes it a promising candidate for domains characterized by relational asymmetry and weak homophily. For example, in community detection within directed social or communication networks, HeNCler's ability to model asymmetric relationships could help capture influence flows that do not align with node similarity. In recommender systems, HeNCler could be applied to bipartite user-item graphs by using separate feature maps for each node type. This would enable the construction of a learned bipartite similarity graph that aligns user preferences with item characteristics in an unsupervised manner. Similarly, in biological networks such as gene regulatory systems, the model's capacity to handle directed, heterophilous interactions could prove valuable.

5 Conclusion and Future Work

We tackle three limitations of current node clustering algorithms that prevent these methods from effectively clustering nodes in heterophilous graphs: they assume homophily in their loss, they are only defined for undirected graphs and/or they lack a specific focus on clustering.

To this end, we introduce a weighted kernel SVD framework and harness its primal-dual equivalences. HeNCler relies on the dual interpretation for its theoretical motivation, while it benefits from the computational advantages of its implementation in the primal. It learns new similarities, which are asymmetric where necessary, and node embeddings resulting from the spectral biclustering interpretation of these learned similarities. As empirical evidence shows, our approach effectively eliminates the aforementioned limitations, significantly outperforming current state-of-the-art alternatives.

Future work could explore integrating contrastive learning into HeNCler, potentially combining the strengths of both paradigms. Another direction is to investigate cluster assignments in a graph pooling setting (i.e., differentiable graph coarsening), enabling end-to-end training for downstream graph-level tasks. Additionally, applying HeNCler to real-world domains such as recommender systems, biological networks, or directed social graphs–where asymmetric and heterophilous structures naturally occur–would be an important step toward validating its broader applicability.

Acknowledgments. ESAT-STADIUS has received funding from the European Research Council under the European Union's Horizon 2020 research and innovation program/ERC Advanced Grant E-DUALITY (787960). This paper reflects only the authors' views and the Union is not liable for any use that may be made of the contained information. ESAT-STADIUS received funding from the Flemish Government (AI Research Program); iBOF/23/064; KU Leuven C1 project C14/24/103. Johan Suykens and Sonny Achten are also affiliated to Leuven.AI - KU Leuven institute for AI, B-3000, Leuven, Belgium.

LIONS-EPFL was supported by Hasler Foundation Program: Hasler Responsible AI (project number 21043), by the ARO under Grant Number W911NF-24-1-0048, and by the Swiss National Science Foundation (SNSF) under grant number 200021_205011.

Disclosure of Interests. The authors have no competing interests to declare that are relevant to the content of this article.

References

1. Achten, S., Tonin, F., Patrinos, P., Suykens, J.A.K: Unsupervised neighborhood propagation kernel layers for semi-supervised node classification. In: Proceedings of the AAAI Conference on Artificial Intelligence, vol. 38, no. 10, pp. 10766–10774 (2024)
2. Alzate, C., Suykens, J.A.K.: Multiway spectral clustering with out-of-sample extensions through weighted kernel PCA. IEEE Trans. Pattern Anal. Mach. Intell. **32**(2), 335–347 (2010)
3. Bi, W., Du, L., Fu, Q., Wang, Y., Han, S., Zhang, D.: Make heterophilic graphs better fit GNN: a graph rewiring approach. IEEE Trans. Knowl. Data Eng. **36**(12), 8744–8757 (2024)
4. Bianchi, F.M., Grattarola, D., Alippi, C.: Spectral clustering with graph neural networks for graph pooling. In: International Conference on Machine Learning (2020)

5. Chen, J., Zhu, G., Qi, Y., Yuan, C., Huang, Y.: Towards self-supervised learning on graphs with heterophily. In: ACM International Conference on Information & Knowledge Management, pp. 201–211 (2022)
6. Devvrit, F., Sinha, A., Dhillon, I.S, Jain, P.: S3GC: scalable self-supervised graph clustering. In: Advances in Neural Information Processing Systems (2022)
7. Dhillon, I.S.: Co-clustering documents and words using bipartite spectral graph partitioning. In: ACM SIGKDD International Conference on Knowledge Discovery and Data Mining (2001)
8. Dwivedi, V.P., Bresson, X.: A generalization of transformer networks to graphs. In: Methods and Applications, AAAI Workshop on Deep Learning on Graphs (2021)
9. Dwivedi, V.P., Luu, A.T., Laurent, T., Bengio, Y., Bresson, X.: Graph neural networks with learnable structural and positional representations. In: International Conference on Learning Representations (2022)
10. Gong, Z., et al.: Beyond homophily: robust graph anomaly detection via neural sparsification. In: International Joint Conference on Artificial Intelligence (2023)
11. Gu, M., et al.: Homophily-enhanced structure learning for graph clustering. In: Proceedings of the 32nd ACM International Conference on Information and Knowledge Management, pp. 577–586 (2023)
12. Hassani, K., Ahmadi, A.H.K.: Contrastive multi-view representation learning on graphs. In: International Conference on Machine Learning (2020)
13. He, M., He, F., Shi, L., Huang, X., Suykens, J.A.K.: Learning with asymmetric kernels: least squares and feature interpretation. IEEE Trans. Pattern Anal. Mach. Intell. **45**(8), 10044–10054 (2023)
14. Kipf, T.N., Welling, M.: Semi-supervised classification with graph convolutional networks. In: International Conference on Learning Representations (2017)
15. Pan, S., Hu, R., Fung, S.F., Long, G., Jiang, J., Zhang, C.: Learning graph embedding with adversarial training methods. IEEE Trans. Cybern. **50**(6), 2475–2487 (2020)
16. Pandey, A., Fanuel, M., Schreurs, J., Suykens, J.A.K.: Disentangled representation learning and generation with manifold optimization. Neural Comput. **34**(10), 2009–2036 (2022)
17. Pei, H., Wei, B., Chang, K.C.C., Lei, Y., Yang, B.: Geom-GCN: geometric graph convolutional networks. In: International Conference on Learning Representations (2020)
18. Platonov, O., Kuznedelev, D., Diskin, M., Babenko, A., Prokhorenkova, L.: A critical look at the evaluation of GNNs under heterophily: are we really making progress? In: International Conference on Learning Representations (2023)
19. Rockafellar, R.T.: Conjugate Duality and Optimization. SIAM (1974)
20. Rozemberczki, B., Allen, C., Sarkar, R.: Multi-scale attributed node embedding. J. Complex Netw. **9**(1), 1–22 (2021)
21. Sun, D., Li, D., Ding, Z., Zhang, X., Tang, J.: Dual-decoder graph autoencoder for unsupervised graph representation learning. Knowl.-Based Syst. **234**, 107564 (2021)
22. Suykens, J.A.K.: SVD revisited: a new variational principle, compatible feature maps and nonlinear extensions. Appl. Comput. Harmon. Anal. **40**(3), 600–609 (2016)
23. Suykens, J.A.K.: Deep restricted kernel machines using conjugate feature duality. Neural Comput. **29**(8), 2123–2163 (2017)
24. Tao, Q., Tonin, F., Lambert, A., Chen, Y., Patrinos, P., Suykens, J.A.K.: Learning in feature spaces via coupled covariances: asymmetric kernel SVD and Nyström method. In: International Conference on Machine Learning (2024)

25. Tsitsulin, A., Palowitch, J., Perozzi, B., Müller, E.: Graph clustering with graph neural networks. J. Mach. Learn. Res. **24**(127), 1–21 (2023)
26. Xiao, T., Chen, Z., Guo, Z., Zhuang, Z., Wang, S.: Decoupled self-supervised learning for graphs. In: Advances in Neural Information Processing Systems (2022)
27. You, Y., Chen, T., Sui, Y., Chen, T., Wang, Z., Shen, Y.: Graph contrastive learning with augmentations. In: Advances in Neural Information Processing Systems (2020)
28. Yuan, M., Chen, M., Li, X.: MUSE: multi-view contrastive learning for heterophilic graphs. In: ACM International Conference on Information and Knowledge Management, pp. 3094–3103 (2023)
29. Zheng, X., et al.: Graph neural networks for graphs with heterophily: a survey. arXiv:2202.07082 (2024)

Visualization and Analysis of the Loss Landscape in Graph Neural Networks

Samir Moustafa[1,2](✉), Lorenz Kummer[1,2], Simon Fetzel[1],
Nils M. Kriege[1,3], and Wilfried N. Gansterer[1]

[1] Faculty of Computer Science, University of Vienna, Vienna, Austria
{simonf93,nils.kriege,wilfried.gansterer,
samir.moustafa,lorenz.kummer}@univie.ac.at
[2] UniVie Doctoral School Computer Science, University of Vienna, Vienna, Austria
[3] Research Network Data Science, University of Vienna, Vienna, Austria

Abstract. Graph Neural Networks (GNNs) are powerful models for graph-structured data, with broad applications. However, the interplay between GNN parameter optimization, expressivity, and generalization remains poorly understood. We address this by introducing an efficient learnable dimensionality reduction method for visualizing GNN loss landscapes, and by analyzing the effects of over-smoothing, jumping knowledge, quantization, sparsification, and preconditioner on GNN optimization. Our learnable projection method surpasses the state-of-the-art PCA-based approach, enabling accurate reconstruction of high-dimensional parameters with lower memory usage. We further show that architecture, sparsification, and optimizer's preconditioning significantly impact the GNN optimization landscape and their training process and final prediction performance. These insights contribute to developing more efficient designs of GNN architectures and training strategies.

Keywords: Graph Neural Networks · Loss Landscape

1 Introduction

Graph Neural Networks (GNNs) are tailored for graph-structured data and excel in tasks like network analysis, molecular property prediction, and recommendation systems [26]. Compared to Deep Neural Networks (DNNs), they have fewer parameters but higher computational costs due to large input graphs [18,31]. The relationship between GNNs optimization dynamics and graph structure, architectural design, or numerical precision is poorly understood [26].

GNN research has focused chiefly on theoretical expressivity–the ability to distinguish non-isomorphic graphs or structurally distinct nodes [17]. While deeper networks are more expressive, over-smoothing [26] limits practical depth by making node embeddings indistinguishable. Although theoretical expressivity results guarantee the existence of suitable parameters, standard optimization

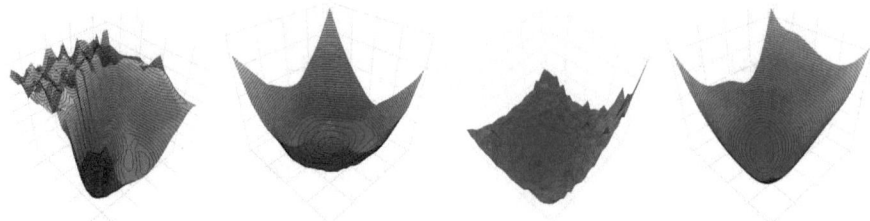

(a) ResNet56 without skip connections (b) ResNet56 with skip connections (c) GCN without jumping knowledge (d) GCN with jumping knowledge

Fig. 1. 3D loss landscapes of ResNet56 on CIFAR-10 [13] and GCN on Cora [5], with and without architectural modifications. Skip connections in ResNet56 yield a smoother landscape, facilitating training, while jumping knowledge in GCN produces a sharper, deeper minimum, allowing fast and reliable convergence.

techniques may fail to recover them, revealing a gap between theory and practice. The interplay among expressivity, generalization, and optimization remains insufficiently understood [17].

Analyzing loss landscapes and training trajectories can illuminate the gap between theoretical and practical GNN behavior, yet it remains underexplored. The loss landscape maps parameters to loss values, offering a geometric view of model behavior, and is typically highly non-convex and complex, particularly under varying data distributions [14]. Understanding the loss landscape yields insights into optimization, generalization, and the stability of learned representations [1]. Loss landscape analysis for GNNs remains unexplored, hindered by challenges inherent to graph-structured data, message passing, and architectural diversity [26]. Recent advancements in GNNs training techniques, aimed at improving generalization [28], reducing inference time [29,31], or optimizing parameters [11], have further complicated the understanding of the GNN loss landscape by obscuring the relationship between model parameters and loss.

This paper addresses this gap and sheds light on the importance and methods of analyzing and visualizing the loss landscape in GNNs.

Contribution of the Paper: Our contributions are threefold: **(1)** We propose a novel learnable projection technique for loss landscape visualization, mapping high-dimensional parameters into 2D and restoring them, while supporting batching for controlling memory usage. **(2)** We provide a comprehensive analysis of GNN training techniques and their effects on the loss landscape, considering over-smoothing [26], jumping knowledge [28], quantization [18], sparsification [29], and optimizer preconditioning [11].

Preliminaries: A *graph* G is a pair (V, E), where V is a finite set of nodes and E is a finite set of edges. Let A denote the adjacency matrix of G with order $|V|$. Each node $v_i \in V$ has an associated feature vector $x_i \in \mathbb{R}^f$, stacked into a matrix $X \in \mathbb{R}^{|V| \times f}$. We consider a classification setting, assuming each node has an expected class, and in total there are C classes, represented by $Y \in \mathbb{R}^{|V| \times C}$.

A GNN is parameterized by θ, defining a function $\mathcal{F}_\theta : (A, X) \to Y$. GNNs employ message passing, where each node aggregates neighbor embeddings, implemented via multiplication of the adjacency matrix A and feature matrix X. At the kth layer, $X^{(k)}$ is computed as $AX^{(k-1)}\theta^{(k)}$, where $X^{(k-1)}$ is the embedding from layer $k - 1$ [26]. Training of a GNN aims to adjust θ so that $\mathcal{F}_\theta(X)$, given G, approximates the target Y. During training, the loss function ε measures the discrepancy between the expected and actual outputs; we use multi-class cross-entropy, though any differentiable loss is applicable. During training, gradients of $\varepsilon(\mathcal{F}_\theta(A, X), Y)$ with respect to θ are computed to update parameters and minimize the error.

A loss landscape visualization depicts how the loss varies with the model parameters. Ideally, a well-fitted model yields a smooth, convex landscape, as shown in Fig. 1b and 1d.

GNN Architectures: This work focuses on three fundamental GNN architectures selected for their pivotal role in the evolution and comprehension of GNNs. Graph Convolution Network (GCN) [12] applies convolution in the spectral domain to capture local graph structures invariant to graph isomorphisms. Graph Attention Network (GAT) [25] utilizes an attention mechanism that allows nodes to weigh their neighbors' influence dynamically, enhancing model flexibility and performance on graph-structured data. Graph Isomorphism Network (GIN) [27] is more powerful in distinguishing different graph structures than GCN and GAT by using a multilayer perceptron (MLP) and a learnable parameter for feature updating, achieving theoretical equivalence with the Weisfeiler-Lehman test. Table 1 presents the mathematical formulations for GCN, GIN, and GAT, detailing aggregation and update functions based on hidden states h_i, output embeddings x_i, neighborhood structures $\mathcal{N}(i)$, and the $\alpha_{ij} = \frac{e_{i,j}}{\sum_{k \in \mathcal{N}(i)} e_{i,k}}$, such that $e_{i,j} = \text{LeakyReLU}\left(a^\top [\theta h_i \| \theta h_j]\right)$, and a is the attention learnable parameter.

Table 1. Standard aggregation and update functions in the kth layer of three GNN architectures: GCN, GAT, and GIN. These functions gather (aggregation) and transform (update) operations by collecting information from each node's neighborhood.

Architecture	Aggregation Function	Update Function
GCN [12]	$h_i^{(k)} = \sum_{j \in \mathcal{N}(i) \cup \{i\}} \frac{1}{\sqrt{d_i d_j}} x_j^{(k-1)}$	$x_i^{(k)} = \text{ReLU}\left(\theta^{(k)} h_i^{(k)}\right)$
GAT [25]	$h_i^{(k)} = \sum_{j \in \mathcal{N}(i) \cup \{i\}} \alpha_{i,j}^{(k)} x_j^{(k-1)}$	$x_i^{(k)} = \text{ReLU}\left(\theta^{(k)} h_i^{(k)}\right)$
GIN [27]	$h_i^{(k)} = \left(1 + \epsilon^{(k)}\right) x_i^{(k-1)} + \sum_{j \in \mathcal{N}(i)} x_j^{(k-1)}$	$x_i^{(k)} = \text{MLP}^{(k)}\left(h_i^{(k)}\right)$

Problem Definition: The loss landscape $L(\theta)$ depends on the architecture, input data, target output, parameters, and error function. Visualizing $L(\theta)$ helps reveal how the error adapts to parameter changes, where $L(\theta)$ reduces to $\varepsilon(\mathcal{F}_\theta(A, X), Y)$ with other factors fixed. This landscape captures the model's error across parameter configurations. Optimization seeks parameters minimizing ε, but is hindered by non-convexity and local minima. Due to the high dimensionality of θ, a full mathematical analysis of $L(\theta)$ is typically intractable.

2 Related Work

In this section, we delve into the definition of the loss landscape, the limitations of GNNs, explore various methods that have been adapted specifically for GNNs, and discuss the prevalent optimization challenges associated with them.

Loss Landscape Visualization: Despite the non-convexity of $L(\theta)$, DNNs often train efficiently by converging to local minima. This raises questions [6] about whether training avoids local minima or if saddle points dominate optimization dynamics. [6] study $L(\lambda, \theta_i + (1-\lambda), \theta^*)$ for $\lambda \in \mathbb{R}$, where θ_i and θ^* are parameters from epoch i and the final training epoch, respectively. They observe elevated loss regions between solutions, consistent with [10]. Visualization techniques include barycentric and bilinear interpolation, and projections along random or PCA directions [14,16]. Moreover, [10] analyzed how optimization trajectories change when the algorithm switches mid-training, typically after loss stagnation. Post-switch trajectories consistently diverge, suggesting optimizers follow distinct paths at saddle points. Loss landscapes remain similar across runs with the same optimizer but different initializations. Despite differing final parameters, loss and accuracy are often comparable–a result also observed in [23], where varying the learning rate led to multiple equally performant optima [7].

Over-Smoothing and Jumping Knowledge: A key challenge in GNN training is over-smoothing, where node embeddings become increasingly similar with depth, diminishing node identity and discriminative power [26]. Over-smoothing occurs as the row of $X^{(l)}$ converges to the same vector as $l \to \infty$ [26]. This can be quantified via similarity or distance measures between rows of $X^{(l)}$.

Jumping Knowledge (JK) mitigates over-smoothing by allowing node representations to aggregate multi-distance neighborhood information across layers. The final representation is given by $X^{(l)} = \phi(X^{(0)}, X^{(1)}, ..., X^{(l-1)})$, where ϕ combines outputs from all previous layers. JK parallels residual connections in CNNs [22], enhancing trainability and addressing vanishing gradients.

Quantization and Sparsification: Quantization lowers memory, computation, and power demands by converting weights or activations to lower-precision formats, enabling efficient deployment at the cost of approximation errors [4]. [31] proposes a GNN-specific method that learns per-node bit-widths based on aggregation values, capturing topological variance. This adds complexity, requiring group-specific learning rates.

Sparsification reduces GNN memory and computation by constructing sparse graphs that retain essential structure. GraphSAINT [29] samples subgraphs to preserve batch connectivity, using normalization and diverse strategies to control bias and variance. Its effectiveness depends critically on sampling quality [26].

Optimization Challenges and Strategies: DNN optimization has shifted focus from local minima, which may support generalization [7], to saddle points as the main challenge [10,20]. Low-error solutions exhibit parameter space symmetry, with local minima often matching global optima in fully connected networks [1,19]. Under conditions like identity mappings or over-parameterization, stochastic gradient descent (SGD) can reach global optima [15,24]. In high dimensions, saddle points prevail, and methods like natural gradient descent (NGD) are effective for escaping them [2]. [11] introduces an information-geometric optimization method for GNNs using NGD, with the Fisher Information Matrix approximated via KFAC to avoid second-order derivatives. This improves efficiency and outperforms ADAM and SGD.

Overall, the unique structural characteristics of GNNs, alongside their phenomena and methodologies, present unexplored dimensions in understanding how they shape the loss landscape and govern optimization trajectories.

3 Methodology

Consider a k-layer graph neural network with parameters $\theta = (\theta^0, \theta^1, \ldots, \theta^k)$, where each θ^i is a vector or matrix. Let $\Theta \in \mathbb{R}^d$ denote the flattened concatenation of all elements in θ, with d as the parameter dimension. The optimized flattened concatenated parameters are denoted $\Theta^* \in \mathbb{R}^d$.

Dimensionality Reduction for Visualization: To visualize the high-dimensional parameter space $\mathbb{R}^d$, dimensionality reduction to 2D is applied using two directions $b^1, b^2 \in \mathbb{R}^d$. The mapping from 2D to $\mathbb{R}^d$ is defined by the function

$$M : \mathbb{R}^2 \to \mathbb{R}^d \text{ with } (x, y) \mapsto \Theta^* + x \cdot b^1 + y \cdot b^2, \qquad (1)$$

where x and y are the visualization's axes. The visualization is then created via

$$\Psi : (x, y) \mapsto L(M(x, y)) \qquad (2)$$

The directions b^1, b^2 can be selected via various methods; one common approach is random initialization [14]. Each direction vector $(b_0, b_1, \ldots, b_d)$ is partitioned into segments $\hat{b}_l = (b_m, \ldots, b_k)$, corresponding to specific network parameters (e.g., weight matrices or bias vectors). These segments are normalized using their magnitude and that of the corresponding optimal parameters $\hat{\Theta}^*_l = (\Theta^*_m, \ldots, \Theta^*_k)$, ensuring each direction is scaled relative to its associated optimized values. This scaling ensures that each direction vector segment matches the magnitude of its corresponding optimal parameter segment. The normalization is formalized as:

$$\hat{b}'_j := \frac{\hat{b}_l}{\|\hat{b}_l\|} \|\hat{\Theta}^*_l\| \tag{3}$$

Normalized random directions allow a more balanced and representative visualization of the high-dimensional parameters.

Visualizing the Optimizer Trajectory: To visualize optimizer trajectories, directions b^1 and b^2 are selected to align with the subspace spanned by parameters Θ_i, $0 \leq i \leq n$, across all n epochs. Using Θ^* as the origin, differences $D_i = \Theta_i - \Theta^*$ form a matrix $D \in \mathbb{R}^{n \times d}$. PCA on the covariance of D yields b^1 and b^2 [16]. However, computing the covariance matrix and its eigenvectors is memory-intensive for large networks [14], despite $n \ll d$ reducing the impact of D itself.

Projection into Visualization Space: To visualize trajectories, a point $p \in \mathbb{R}^d$ must be projected into the 2D visualization space (x, y) by solving:

$$p = \Theta^* + x \cdot b^1 + y \cdot b^2 + r \tag{4}$$

where r is the reconstruction error vector, which should be minimized. Basis pairs can be compared via their reconstruction error r, whereby a smaller r indicates a preferable basis. If the basis vectors b^1, b^2 are orthonormal [14], the dot product can be used to calculate the coordinates as $x = \langle p - \Theta^*, b^1 \rangle$ and $y = \langle p - \Theta^*, b^2 \rangle$. In general, b^1, b^2 are not orthonormal and not orthogonal. Therefore, an underdetermined linear equation system needs to be solved.

$$\begin{pmatrix} b^1 & b^2 \end{pmatrix} \begin{pmatrix} x \\ y \end{pmatrix} = p - \Theta^* \tag{5}$$

The solution only approximates p; the true loss may differ from $\Psi(x, y)$ in Eq. (2). Hence, 2D trajectory visualizations such as contour plots are preferred.

Learnable Projection: We propose a novel dimensionality reduction method, the *learnable projection model*, defined by a matrix $P \in \mathbb{R}^{2 \times d}$, where $P = \begin{pmatrix} b^1 & b^2 \end{pmatrix}^\top$. P defines the projection unambiguously, encodes high-dimensional parameters into 2D, and decodes them back. Given input matrix D from Sect. 3, each point is encoded as $z_i = D_i P^\top \in \mathbb{R}^2$, assuming orthonormal b^1, b^2 (see Sect. 3). Decoding is performed via $z_i P$, equivalent to the mapping function M in Eq. (1).

The learnable projection model is trained to minimize the Euclidean distance between D and zP via Mean Squared Error (MSE), thereby minimizing the reconstruction error r from Eq. (4) and yielding a 2D basis with low projection error. For optimization, the problem is formulated as:

$$\min_{b^1, b^2 \in \mathbb{R}^d} \text{MSE}(D, DP^\top P), \quad D \in \mathbb{R}^{n \times d}, \quad P = \begin{pmatrix} b^1 & b^2 \end{pmatrix}^\top \in \mathbb{R}^{2 \times d}. \tag{6}$$

Table 2. Characteristics of node classification datasets across different domains.

	Cora [5]	Citeseer [5]	Pubmed [21]	OGB-Arxiv [8]	OGB-MAG [8]
Number of Nodes	2,708	3,327	19,717	169,343	1,939,743
Number of Edges	10,556	9,104	88,648	1,166,243	21,111,007
Features per Node	1,433	3,703	500	128	128
Number of Classes	7	6	3	23	349

Simplifying the objective yields an upper bound: minimizing $\|I_d - P^\top P\|_2^2$, where I_d is the $d \times d$ identity matrix. This reformulation shifts the focus to minimizing the squared spectral norm of $I_d - P^\top P$. This formulation relates to the orthogonal Procrustes problem, though it omits explicit dependence on Θ^* and Θ_i encoded in D. The ℓ_1 reconstruction error $\|r\|_1$ enables comparison with PCA-based methods, as both aim to minimize the same error term from Eq. (4), which highlights the effectiveness of our learnable projection relative to PCA, despite both sharing the same objective.

Theoretically, both our approach and PCA aim to minimize the *reconstruction error*, as defined in Eq. 7 from [3]:

$$\min_{V_q} \sum_{i=1}^{N} \| (x_i - \bar{x} - V_q V_q^\top (x_i - \bar{x})) \|^2 \qquad (7)$$

where x_i are the data samples, $\bar{x}$ is the mean and V_q is a matrix consisting of q orthonormal columns. Unlike PCA, which computes V_q via eigenvectors, our approach uses gradient-based optimization, avoiding covariance matrix computation and associated memory overhead. Grouping rows of D into batches enables the learnable projection to train on D_i in a batched manner, reducing memory usage even further.

4 Experimental Setup

This section summarizes the hardware, datasets, and trajectory visualization process, including PCA-based projection [14] and training of our learnable projection method. Experiments[1] were conducted on an Intel Xeon Gold 6130 (64 cores, 256GB RAM, x86_64 architecture). For evaluation and visualization, we used standard benchmark datasets, summarized in Table 2.

Projection Methods Pipelines and Memory Requirements: During training, GNN parameters from each epoch are stored to construct the matrix D and train the learnable projection (Sect. 3). Models are trained for up to 1000 epochs with early stopping, using ADAM (learning rate 0.01, weight decay 0.002). To ensure fair runtime comparison with PCA, our method is evaluated on CPU only, despite

---

[1] Code is available at https://github.com/SamirMoustafa/torch-loss-landscape/.

being GPU capable. PCA is computed via LOBPCG on CPU, and its memory cost grows with model size due to the covariance matrix.

Both methods require the matrix $D \in \mathbb{R}^{n \times d}$, but PCA additionally computes a $d \times d$ covariance matrix, while the learnable projection supports batching with batch size B, operating on $B \times d$ subsets of D. Thus, PCA incurs $\frac{d}{B}$ times the amount of memory compared to the learnable projection.

5 Evaluation and Analysis

Reconstruction error is computed between ground-truth GNN parameters and their reconstructions from the 2D landscape (x, y). It serves as a proxy for how well the learned directions capture training dynamics. Given the difficulty of quantitatively evaluating visualization quality, reconstruction error offers an intuitive assessment metric.

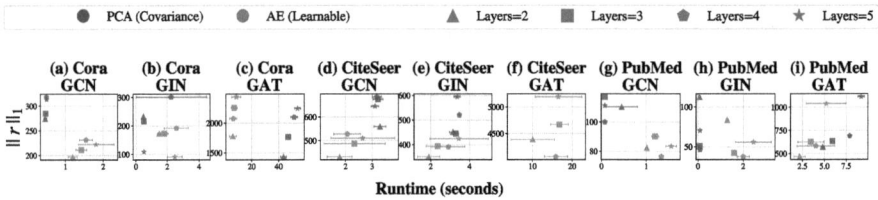

Fig. 2. Reconstruction errors $\|r\|_1$ versus the time taken to compute the projection directions for GNN architectures, respectively, with 2, 3, 4, and 5 layers on different datasets. Points represent the mean of 10 runs, and the line is the standard deviation.

Figure 2 shows mean reconstruction error (y-axis) and runtime (x-axis) for PCA-based projection [14] and our learnable projection, averaged over ten runs. For the GCN model, averaging over the number of layers, the learnable projection consistently lowers reconstruction error but alters runtime: on Cora the mean error drops from 297.67 to 215.46, on CiteSeer the error drops from 640.89 to 489.6, and on PubMed the error drops from 109.68 to 83.12, with GIN showing analogous trends. In contrast, for GAT on Cora, PCA yields slightly better reconstruction error when averaging over the number of layers (1887.09 vs. 2141.08), while the learnable projection reduces runtime from 48.94 seconds to 6.45 seconds (7.6× faster). PCA results for GAT on CiteSeer were omitted (exceeded 256 GB memory) due to the dense graph and GAT's large parameter count.

Impact of Skip Connections and JK on Loss Landscapes: Fig. 1 presents 3D loss landscape visualizations to illustrate the impact of architectural changes. For ResNet56 on CIFAR-10 [22], the landscape without skip connections (Fig. 1a) exhibits multiple local minima and saddle points. In contrast, adding skip connections (Fig. 1b) smooths the landscape, mitigating vanishing gradients and facilitating optimization. Similarly, Jumping Knowledge (JK), analogous to skip connections in GNNs, alters the loss landscape. As shown in Fig. 1d, JK appears to reduce the non-convexity of the GCN loss surface, potentially leading to a smoother optimization landscape. Without JK (Fig. 1c), the surface flattens and is noisy due to over-smoothing [26], obscuring the minimum.

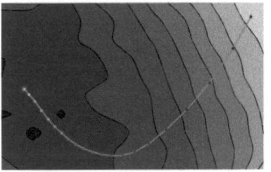
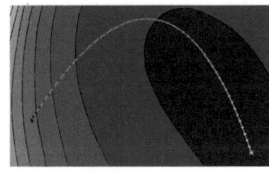
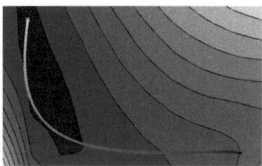

(a) Five-layer GCN training trajectory on the Cora dataset shows the optimizer skipping several local minima.

(b) Training trajectory for an eight-layer GCN with residuals [9] on the OGB-Arxiv dataset.

(c) Trajectory for an 8-layer GAMLP during training on the OGB-MAG dataset.

Fig. 3. Learning trajectories of GNNs shown via the learnable projection method.

Figure 3a illustrates the optimizer trajectory toward Θ^* (marked $\times$), the final optimizer point intended to represent the optimum. However, near this identified final point, at least three local minima exist. This suboptimality arises from over-smoothing: many nodes aggregate similar information during propagation, causing their features to become indistinguishable.

Consequently, the final GNN layer produces identical predictions for these nodes. As a result, different nodes incur the same loss value, creating a flat loss surface near the non-optimal point. This flat region disrupts optimization by having identical gradients, preventing further progress toward the true optimum.

Table 3 shows that increasing GCN depth degrades accuracy and increases loss, with a sharp decline beyond four layers. This supports the observation that deeper architectures induce flatter, non-convex loss landscapes. In the 6-layer case, the optimizer fails to converge to a local minimum, hindering regularization and reducing accuracy. Jumping Knowledge variants can mitigate this degradation. [9] introduces residual connections with an error correlation mechanism that propagates residuals from training to test data. As shown in Fig. 3b, their 8-layer GCN on OGB-Arxiv achieves 73.5% test accuracy with 0.727 loss, converging to a minimum without flat surrounding regions.

Figure 3c visualizes the loss trajectory of an 8-layer Graph Attention Multilayer Perceptron (GAMLP) [30] trained on OGB-MAG. Despite the model and dataset size, the learnable projection effectively visualizes the training process.

Table 3. Mean and standard deviation of loss and accuracy over 10 runs for GCN on Cora.

Layers	Loss ↓	Acc. (%) ↑
2	0.86 ±0.2	81.02 ±0.9
3	**0.85** ±0.2	**81.5** ±1.0
4	0.86 ±0.2	80.1 ±0.9
5	0.88 ±0.2	79.1 ±1.4
6	1.33 ±0.5	77.9 ±2.0

Quantization and Sparsification: While prior work has analyzed the loss landscapes of quantized DNNs across various architectures, no study has, to our knowledge, examined this for quantized GNNs. Addressing this gap, we adopt the state-of-the-art mixed-precision GNN quantization method from [31], which maintains performance across diverse datasets and tasks at both node and graph levels. Figure 4 visualizes the loss landscape of a quantized GAT, chosen for its sensitivity to perturbations in attention parameters. Quantization introduces approximation noise, increasing landscape ruggedness and local minima. Despite this, the optimizer achieves high accuracy, attributed to the method in [31], which uses group-wise learning rates within ADAM. However, this approach requires extensive hyperparameter tuning. Figure 4a and 4c show that, despite bypassing local minima, the model converges to accuracy-maximizing solutions.

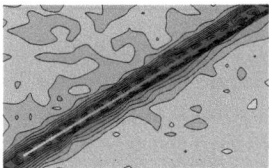
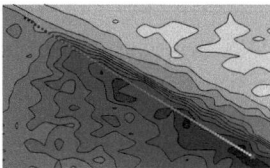
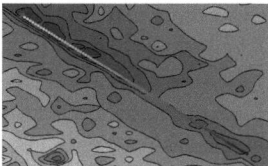

(a) Training on the Cora dataset, yielding a loss of 1.206 and an accuracy rate of 83.6%.

(b) Training on the CiteSeer dataset, yielding a loss of 1.09 and an accuracy rate of 71.8%.

(c) Training on the PubMed dataset, yielding a loss of 0.79 and an accuracy rate of 75.6%.

Fig. 4. Visualizing the training trajectory of a quantized GAT architecture across three different datasets, using our learnable projection method. The trajectory path appears as a straight line due to the bending in the loss landscape and its progression from a significantly far non-optimal point to the optimal point.

Concerning sparsification, as noted in Sect. 2, local minima do not inherently hinder DNN training. In GNNs, graph sparsification can act as regularization, improving generalization and training efficiency by simplifying the graph and encouraging convergence to diverse local minima. We use the GIN architecture, known for matching the expressivity of the Weisfeiler-Lehman test [27], as its performance is highly sensitive to structural changes like sparsification, which can notably increase loss landscape ruggedness. Figure 5b shows the impact of sparsification on the GIN loss landscape for the Cora dataset. Using Graph-SAINT [29], we compare sparsified and non-sparsified training. Sparsification increases the number of local minima, resulting in a more rugged loss landscape.

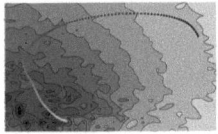 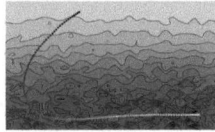 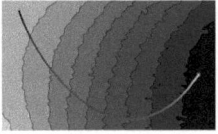 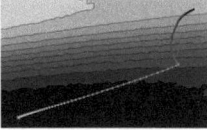

(a) Native and complete graph structure is utilized.   (b) Sparsification randomly omits parts of the graph.   (c) Without preconditioner, and the final loss value is 0.31.   (d) With preconditioner after the 50-th epoch, loss is 0.03.

Fig. 5. Training trajectories for GIN (a, b) and GCN (c, d) architecture during the training on Cora dataset, illustrating the effects of sparsification and preconditioning techniques.

KFAC Preconditioning: As noted in Sect. 2, the KFAC preconditioner enhances optimization by adapting step sizes to local curvature, increasing the likelihood of reaching better minima in fewer iterations. This can lower final loss and improve post-training performance. Figure 5d illustrates the impact of applying the KFAC preconditioner during the final 50 training epochs, compared to early application. This highlights its influence on the optimizer's trajectory. Notably, the pre-KFAC trajectory resembles that in Fig. 5c, indicating consistent behavior prior to preconditioning.

6 Conclusion

We introduced a learnable projection method for visualizing GNN optimization trajectories, which outperformed the PCA-based approach in reconstruction error across most experiments. The negligible runtime increase is offset by lower memory usage, which is proportional to the batch size, enabling our method to scale to larger architectures compared to the PCA-based approach.

We analyzed the effects of over-smoothing, jumping knowledge, quantization, sparsification, and preconditioning on GNN optimization. Each impacts the loss landscape, trajectories, or both. While aligning with DNN findings, our results provide GNN-specific insights, highlighting the role of architectural choices in efficient training. Specifically, we identified that increasing GNN depth exacerbates over-smoothing, yielding flatter, non-convex loss landscapes and reduced performance. Quantization and sparsification introduce ruggedness and additional local minima. Preconditioning effectively alters optimizer trajectories, significantly aiding loss reduction.

In summary, GNN architecture, quantization, sparsification, and preconditioning substantially affect optimization trajectories, underscoring the importance of their careful consideration in GNN design and training.

Acknowledgment. Nils Kriege was supported by the Vienna Science and Technology Fund (WWTF) [10.47379/VRG19009].

References

1. Choromanska, A., Henaff, M., Mathieu, M., Arous, G.B., LeCun, Y.: The loss surfaces of multilayer networks. In: International Conference on Artificial Intelligence and Statistics, pp. 192–204 (2015). https://proceedings.mlr.press/v38/choromanska15.pdf
2. Dauphin, Y., et al.: Identifying and attacking the saddle point problem in high-dimensional non-convex optimization. In: Conference on Neural Information Processing Systems (2014). https://proceedings.neurips.cc/paper_files/paper/2014/file/04192426585542c54b96ba14445be996-Paper.pdf
3. Franklin, J.: The elements of statistical learning: data mining, inference and prediction. Math. Intell. **27**(2), 83–85 (2005). https://doi.org/10.1007/BF02985802
4. Gholami, A., Kim, S., Dong, Z., Yao, Z., Mahoney, M.W., Keutzer, K.: A survey of quantization methods for efficient neural network inference. In: Low-Power Computer Vision, pp. 291–326. Chapman and Hall/CRC (2022). https://doi.org/10.1201/9781003162810-13
5. Giles, L., Bollacker, K., Lawrence, S.: CiteSeer: an automatic citation indexing system. In: ACM International Conference on Digital Libraries (1998). https://doi.org/10.1145/276675.276685
6. Goodfellow, I., Vinyals, O.: Qualitatively characterizing neural network optimization problems. In: International Conference on Learning Representations (2015). https://doi.org/10.48550/arXiv.1412.6544
7. Hochreiter, S., Schmidhuber, J.: Flat minima. Neural Comput. (1997). https://doi.org/10.1162/neco.1997.9.1.1
8. Hu, W., et al.: Open graph benchmark: datasets for machine learning on graphs. In: Conference on Neural Information Processing Systems (2020). https://papers.neurips.cc/paper/2020/file/fb60d411a5c5b72b2e7d3527cfc84fd0-Paper.pdf
9. Huang, Q., He, H., Singh, A., Lim, S., Benson, A.: Combining label propagation and simple models out-performs graph neural networks. In: International Conference on Learning Representations (2021). https://openreview.net/pdf?id=8E1-f3VhX1o
10. Im, D.J., Tao, M., Branson, K.: An empirical analysis of the optimization of deep network loss surfaces. arXiv preprint arXiv:1612.04010 (2016)
11. Izadi, M.R., Fang, Y., Stevenson, R., Lin, L.: Optimization of graph neural networks with natural gradient descent. In: IEEE International Conference on Big Data (Big Data), pp. 171–179. IEEE (2020). https://doi.org/10.1109/bigdata50022.2020.9378063
12. Kipf, T., Welling, M.: Semi-supervised classification with graph convolutional networks. In: International Conference on Learning Representations (2017). https://openreview.net/pdf?id=SJU4ayYgl
13. Krizhevsky, A., Nair, V., Hinton, G.: Canadian Institute for Advanced Research (2009). http://www.cs.toronto.edu/~kriz/cifar.html
14. Li, H., Xu, Z., Taylor, G., Studer, C., Goldstein, T.: Visualizing the loss landscape of neural nets. In: Conference on Neural Information Processing Systems (2018). https://proceedings.neurips.cc/paper_files/paper/2018/file/a41b3bb3e6b050b6c9067c67f663b915-Paper.pdf

15. Li, Y., Yuan, Y.: Convergence analysis of two-layer neural networks with ReLU activation. In: Conference on Neural Information Processing Systems (2017). https://proceedings.neurips.cc/paper_files/paper/2017/file/a96b65a721e561e1e3de768ac819ffbb-Paper.pdf
16. Lorch, E.: Visualizing deep network training trajectories with PCA. In: International Conference on Machine Learning Visualization Workshop (2016)
17. Morris, C., et al.: Weisfeiler and Leman go machine learning: the story so far. J. Mach. Learn. Res. (2023). https://www.jmlr.org/papers/volume24/22-0240/22-0240.pdf
18. Moustafa, S., Kriege, N., Gansterer, W.: Efficient mixed precision quantization in graph neural networks. In: IEEE 41st International Conference on Data Engineering (2025). https://www.computer.org/csdl/proceedings-article/icde/2025/360300e038/26FZCgBUg4U
19. Nguyen, Q., Hein, M.: The loss surface of deep and wide neural networks. In: International Conference on Machine Learning (2017). https://dl.acm.org/doi/10.5555/3305890.3305950
20. Saxe, A., McClelland, J., Ganguli, S.: Exact solutions to the nonlinear dynamics of learning in deep linear neural networks. In: International Conference on Learning Representations (2014). https://openreview.net/forum?id=_wzZwKpTDF_9C
21. Sen, P., Namata, G., Bilgic, M., Getoor, L., Gallagher, B., Eliassi-Rad, T.: Collective classification in network data. AI Mag. **29**(3), 93–93 (2008). https://doi.org/10.1609/aimag.v29i3.2157
22. Shafiq, M., Gu, Z.: Deep residual learning for image recognition: a survey. Appl. Sci. **12**(18), 8972 (2022). https://doi.org/10.3390/app12188972
23. Smith, L., Topin, N.: Exploring loss function topology with cyclical learning rate. arXiv preprint arXiv:1702.04283 (2017)
24. Soltanolkotabi, M., Javanmard, A., Lee, J.D.: Theoretical insights into the optimization landscape of over-parameterized shallow neural networks. IEEE Trans. Inf. Theory **65**(2), 742–769 (2019). https://doi.org/10.1109/tit.2018.2854560
25. Velickovic, P., Cucurull, G., Casanova, A., Romero, A., Liò, P., Bengio, Y.: Graph attention networks. In: International Conference on Learning Representations (2018). https://openreview.net/pdf?id=rJXMpikCZ
26. Wu, L., Cui, P., Pei, J., Zhao, L., Guo, X.: Graph neural networks: foundation, frontiers and applications. In: Proceedings of the 28th ACM SIGKDD Conference on Knowledge Discovery and Data Mining (2022)
27. Xu, K., Hu, W., Leskovec, J., Jegelka, S.: How powerful are graph neural networks? In: International Conference on Learning Representations (2019). https://openreview.net/pdf?id=ryGs6iA5Km
28. Xu, K., Li, C., Tian, Y., Sonobe, T., Kawarabayashi, K., Jegelka, S.: Representation learning on graphs with jumping knowledge networks. In: International Conference on Machine Learning (2018). https://proceedings.mlr.press/v80/xu18c/xu18c.pdf
29. Zeng, H., Zhou, H., Srivastava, A., Kannan, R., Prasanna, V.: GraphSAINT: graph sampling based inductive learning method. In: International Conference on Learning Representations (2020). https://openreview.net/pdf?id=BJe8pkHFwS
30. Zhang, W., et al.: Graph attention multi-layer perceptron. In: Knowledge Discovery and Data Mining (2022). https://dl.acm.org/doi/10.1145/3534678.3539121
31. Zhu, Z.A., et al.: A^2Q: aggregation-aware quantization for graph neural networks. In: International Conference on Learning Representations (2023). https://openreview.net/pdf?id=7L2mgi0TNEP

Special Session: Neurorobotics

Special Session: Neurorobotics

The unique field of neurorobotics aims at bringing together research in machine learning, robotics and bio-inspired artificial intelligence, in particular artificial neural networks. Following the "understanding by building" methodology, cognitive robotics studies cognition by employing human-like neural models of cognitive capacities in robots that enable them to interact with and learn from complex and multimodal environments thus gaining their cognitive abilities. In connection with human-robot interaction (HRI), cognitive modeling represents a way to make robots more considerate and aware of people as well as make their behavior more legible and explainable and make interaction with robots smoother and more efficient promoting advances in HRI. After two successful Neurorobotics special sessions at ICANN 2023 and ICANN 2024, we have successfully held the third edition of this special session at ICANN 2025, organized under the Horizon Europe project TERAIS (https://terais.eu/).

The primary topic of this edition was motion planning and perception of humans as well as robotic motion, providing an intriguing insight into how robots and humans may understand each other to enrich their communication and collaboration and promote better HRI. The comprehension of humans by robots extended from estimating targets of pointing gestures to understanding sign language. The motion planning research focused on producing human-legible as well as bio-inspired self-supervised robot arm trajectories. The topic of cross-modal learning has been addressed in several papers including haptic feedback-aided learning and human-robot collaboration. The synergies of the presented research have fostered fruitful discussions within the session and have given inspiration for future research.

Organizers

Kristína Malinovská	Comenius University Bratislava, Slovakia
Matthias Kerzel	University of Hamburg, Germany
Stefan Wermter	University of Hamburg, Germany
Igor Farkaš	Comenius University Bratislava, Slovakia
Andrej Lúčny	Comenius University Bratislava
Hassan Ali	University of Hamburg, Germany
Omar Eldardeer	Istituto Italiano di Tecnologia, Italy

Pointing-Guided Target Estimation via Transformer-Based Attention

Luca Müller[1]($^{\boxtimes}$)⬤, Hassan Ali[1]⬤, Philipp Allgeuer[1]⬤, Lukáš Gajdošech[2]⬤, and Stefan Wermter[1]⬤

[1] University of Hamburg, Department of Informatics, Knowledge Technology Research Group, Hamburg, Germany
{luca.mueller,hassan.ali,philipp.allgeuer,stefan.wermter}@uni-hamburg.de
[2] Comenius University, Faculty of Mathematics and Informatics, Bratislava, Slovakia
lukas.gajdosech@fmph.uniba.sk

Abstract. Deictic gestures, like pointing, are a fundamental form of non-verbal communication, enabling humans to direct attention to specific objects or locations. This capability is essential in Human-Robot Interaction (HRI), where robots should be able to predict human intent and anticipate appropriate responses. In this work, we propose the **Multi-Modality Inter-TransFormer (MM-ITF)**, a modular architecture to predict objects in a controlled tabletop scenario with the NICOL robot, where humans indicate targets through natural pointing gestures. Leveraging inter-modality attention, MM-ITF maps 2D pointing gestures to object locations, assigns a likelihood score to each, and identifies the most likely target. Our results demonstrate that the method can accurately predict the intended object using monocular RGB data, thus enabling intuitive and accessible human-robot collaboration. To evaluate the performance, we introduce a patch confusion matrix, providing insights into the model's predictions across candidate object locations.
Code available at: https://github.com/lucamuellercode/MMITF

Keywords: Pose-object Matching · Attention-based Feature Fusion · Social Robotics

1 Introduction

The development of robots that collaborate with humans is increasing in various fields like industrial automation, healthcare, and domestic environments. As robots integrate further into society, their ability to react to human intent becomes a critical aspect of effective Human-Robot Interaction (HRI). Deictic gestures, such as pointing, provide a natural and intuitive means for humans to convey intent toward specific objects [16]. Due to the inherent ambiguity in natural language, pointing gestures offer a more precise spatial referral [27], and bypass language barriers [11]. According to Lenz [18], objective pointing enables humans to direct attention to objects within the shared visual field of the pointer and receiver, relying on the pointer's body pose alignment to the intended target. However, predicting a pointing target is challenging due to the need to detect hand poses, estimate direction, and identify the intended object. Traditional methods rely on measuring [4,10,12] or estimating [5] a pointing vector from 3D body representations, requiring costly hardware or extra processing, thus motivating the need for lightweight 2D approaches like ours.

Fig. 1. The participant interacts with the robot, pointing to an object. Objects are represented by centroids, with scores indicating their likelihood of being the target. The probability for the non-pointing case appears in the upper left corner.

The field of Human-Object Interaction (HOI) offers an alternative perspective on pointing gestures, emphasizing contextual relationships in predicting human intentions when interacting with objects. As such, a pointing gesture can be considered a form of HOI in itself. Encoder-decoder transformer architectures are a useful tool to learn the contextual representations of such interactions, producing robust attention maps [3]. Ji et al. extended this by introducing inter-modality attention [13], which fuses information across modalities, thus improving human-object reasoning. In our work, we propose the **Multi-Modality Inter-TransFormer (MM-ITF)**, which is a transformer-based encoder-decoder model that adapts inter-modality attention to capture the relationship between hand pose key points and object locations in a tabletop scenario (Fig. 1). The proposed approach is RGB-based. Thus, it requires no extra equipment, wearable devices, or calibration. Our main contributions are as follows:

1. An **end-to-end transformer model** (Sect. 3.4), using inter-modal attention to predict in a single forward pass whether a human is pointing, and if so, which object is targeted.
2. An **evaluation with a social robot** (Sect. 4.2) in comparison to a 2D baseline in a controlled tabletop scenario, following prior setups [1,2].
3. A **novel patch confusion matrix** (Sect. 4.3), constructed by mapping predicted object locations to discrete image regions, providing a structured visualization of the model's predictions, and supporting interpretability.

2 Related Work

Many traditional approaches estimate a vector to determine a pointing gesture's direction and project it into the scene to predict the target through intersection. This often requires 3D scene representations for precise estimation. Such representations can be obtained using sensors like IMUs [25] and EMG [10], offering high accuracy but requiring calibration and restricting movements. Multi-camera setups [17] and depth sensors [28] can reconstruct 3D human poses, but demand additional hardware and calibration. Moreover, single RGB camera approaches infer depth using models like MiDaS [24] and pose estimators [7,19,20], combining techniques as in [21], where skeleton data and ORB-SLAM [23] were integrated. However, a key challenge in pointing vector estimation is that the key points used to measure the vector–such as the forearm [10], index finger [12], or a vector formed from the nose to the index finger [4]–may not be collinear with the intended target. Approaches, like Bamani et al. [5], address this by learning a pointing vector directly from 2D input, yet their approach relies on multiple models, including depth estimation, arm segmentation, and pretrained pointing estimation with wearable sensor data. Ultimately, these methods determine the target object using geometric rules, typically by computing where the pointing vector intersects a plane in the scene's representation [5,21].

On the other hand, HOI detection localizes humans and objects in a scene and predicts their interactions [3]. Recent approaches leverage transformer-based encoder-decoder architectures [9,15,26,29,31] for end-to-end scene understanding, typically following a three-step strategy. First, a backbone network, like a CNN or DETR [8], extracts visual features. These feature maps are processed by the encoder for visual embedding. Then, the decoder attends to the encoded features using learnable queries representing interaction instances, followed by a simple prediction layer that generates the final HOI output: (human, interaction, object). Further, Ji et al. [13] introduce inter-modality attention by leveraging transformer-based attention to model dependencies between any pair of tokens. This allows human pose features to attend to object features within the encoder, enhancing the embedding and improving the model's ability to capture human-object relationships. In this work, we adopt the encoder-decoder strategy from HOI methods to interpret human pointing gestures in robotic scenarios. By integrating inter-modality attention [13], we model the global scene context using hand pose and object location features, mapping them as hand-object pairs. Our work enables robots to infer human non-verbal pointing cues in a modular architecture, while eliminating the need for predefined geometric rules.

3 Methodology

We propose MM-ITF, an approach designed to predict target objects indicated by pointing gestures, using a multimodal integration of hand poses and object locations. The architecture consists of a pretrained backbone for feature extraction, an encoder to capture global context, and a decoder that maps this context to hand-object pairs. Finally, a prediction layer assigns likelihood scores to each object. In the following, we describe the dataset, robotic platform, and architecture in detail.

3.1 Dataset and Robot Platform

Our work revolves around the Neuro-Inspired COLlaborator (NICOL) [14], earlier shown in Fig. 1, which is a humanoid robotic platform designed to integrate both social interaction and physical collaboration. It features a stereo vision system, articulated arms, and an expressive face for multimodal interaction. The robot is fixed on a tabletop, creating a shared environment for collaboration between humans and the robot. The dataset consists of 30 videos, captured using the fisheye camera embedded in the robot's left eye, showing 18 participants pointing at several objects in a controlled scenario. Each video features ten standard YCB objects [6] on the table, facilitating the scenario's replication. Following the robot's request to point at random objects, each participant performed nine pointing tasks—seven times with a single object and twice bi-manually with two objects simultaneously. In each frame in which pointing occurs, we locate hands and objects as 2D coordinates in the image space using pretrained models, resulting in a dataset of 572 samples with 356 pointing and 216 resting hands, each paired with a list of target objects.

Since transformers require large amounts of training data, we apply data augmentation by modifying the 2D coordinates of hand key points and object locations. Specifically, we introduce mirroring, eight random shifts along both the x- and y-axes, and eight rotations. These transformations are applied jointly to both the hand and the objects within a sample to ensure that the hand continues to point toward the intended target. Additionally, we apply Gaussian noise at four increasing levels to the hand key points and object locations to introduce robustness to minor input variations. The noise is sampled from a zero-mean normal distribution with standard deviations ranging up to 3 pixels and is randomly applied to 30% of the 2D coordinates. The augmented data significantly increased data variability, yielding 2,342,912 augmented samples.

3.2 Feature Extraction and Preprocessing

Our architecture has two input channels: hand pose and object location. Given an input frame, we extract hand key points and object bounding boxes. Also, we derive a third relationship feature, representing the angle between the index finger and each object location.[1] For hand pose estimation, we use MediaPipe [30] to detect 21 landmarks per hand. Each landmark $\mathbf{lm}_i^p$ is a 2D coordinate:

$$\mathcal{P} = \{\mathbf{lm}_i^p\}_{i=1}^{21}, \quad \mathbf{lm}_i^p \in \mathbb{R}^2 \qquad (1)$$

The spatial arrangement of these landmarks captures what we refer to as the *hand configuration*, which encodes information about the hand's position, orientation, and gesture state, i.e., pointing or resting.

---
[1] We use superscripts to denote modalities: p (pose), o (object), and r (relationship).

For object detection, we employ OWLv2 [22], which generates a set of bounding boxes $\{b_i^o\}$, each defined as $(x_{min}, y_{min}, x_{max}, y_{max})$. From these, we compute their *centroids* as the center point of each bounding box, forming the sequence $\{c_i^o\}$, $i \in \{1, \ldots, N_t\}$, where N_t denotes the number of detected objects. To account for cases where no object is being pointed at, we define a non-object token $c_{\text{non-object}} = (-1, -1)$, choosing a value outside the valid image space for a clear distinction. With this token, the final sequence is:

$$\mathcal{O} = \{c_i^o\}_{i=1}^{N_t} \cup \{c_{\text{non-object}}\}, \quad c_i^o, c_{\text{non-object}} \in \mathbb{R}^2 \tag{2}$$

We generate a third feature as the angular alignment between the index finger landmarks and each *centroid*, reflecting the relationship between each hand-object pair. The *finger vector* is defined using the index fingertip and the topmost index finger joint, $\mathbf{v}_{\text{finger}} = \text{lm}_{\text{index\_finger\_tip}}^p - \text{lm}_{\text{index\_finger\_dip}}^p$.[2] For each detected object, we compute the vector from the index fingertip to the object centroid, $\mathbf{v}_{\text{to\_centroid},i} = c_i^o - \text{lm}_{\text{index\_finger\_tip}}^p$, and obtain the angle:

$$\theta_i = \arccos\left(\frac{\mathbf{v}_{\text{finger}} \cdot \mathbf{v}_{\text{to\_centroid},i}}{\|\mathbf{v}_{\text{finger}}\| \cdot \|\mathbf{v}_{\text{to\_centroid},i}\|}\right), \tag{3}$$

This results in the sequence $\{\theta_i^r\}$, $i \in \{1, \ldots, N_t\}$, where N_t denotes the number of objects. Similar to the object location sequence, we account for non-pointing hands by defining a non-relation token $\theta_{\text{non-relation}} = -1$, chosen outside the expected valid range for radians. With this token, the final sequence is:

$$\mathcal{R} = \{\theta_i^r\}_{i=1}^{N_t} \cup \{\theta_{\text{non-relation}}\}, \quad \theta_i^r \in [0, \pi], \quad \theta_{\text{non-relation}} \in \mathbb{R} \tag{4}$$

3.3 Embedding and Positional Encoding

The x- and y-values of the hand and object features are normalized to the interval $[0, 1]$ using the image width W and height H:

$$\tilde{x} = \frac{x}{W}, \quad \tilde{y} = \frac{y}{H} \tag{5}$$

Since relationship, pose, and object inputs have different dimensionalities, we project them to a common embedding space of dimension d_T. All (x, y) inputs, including centroid coordinates and hand landmarks, are embedded independently, with x and y projected to $d_T/2$ dimensions each, and then concatenated. Angles are directly projected to d_T, ensuring a unified representation across all inputs.

For positional encoding, we follow [8, 13] and compute sinusoidal embeddings separately for x and y, concatenating them to form the final representation:

$$\mathcal{PE}(\tilde{x}, \tilde{y}) = \text{concat}(PE(\tilde{x}), PE(\tilde{y})), \tag{6}$$

---

[2] The index_finger_dip is the distal interphalangeal (DIP) joint of the index finger, the first joint below the fingertip.

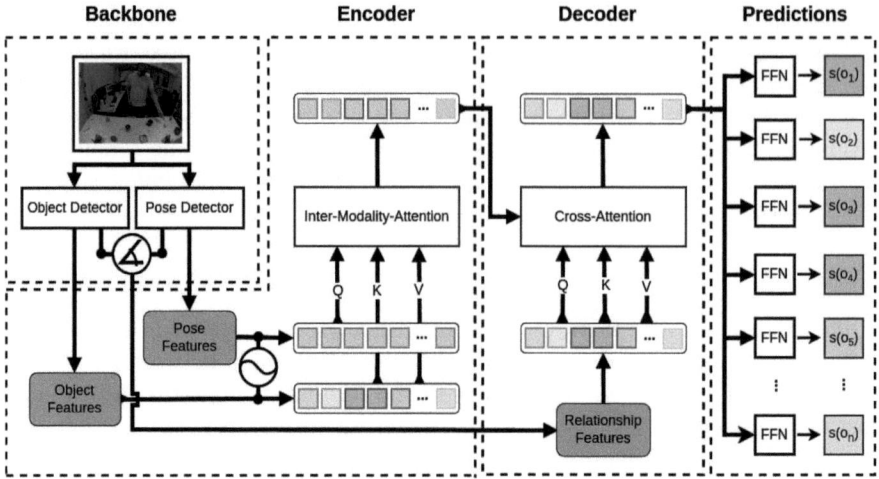

Fig. 2. MM-ITF combines hand pose, object locations, and their angular relationship (∠) to predict pointing targets. The encoder uses hand pose features as queries (Q) and object features as keys (K) and values (V), enabling inter-modality attention to capture global context. The decoder maps this context to hand-object pairs as relationship tokens, and a Feedforward Network (FFN) assigns scores $s(o_i)$ to all objects.

$$PE(*)_{2i} = \sin(*/10000^{2i/d_T}), \tag{7}$$

$$PE(*)_{2i+1} = \cos(*/10000^{2i/d_T}), \tag{8}$$

where $*$ represents either $\tilde{x}$ or $\tilde{y}$. Since angles do not represent positional information in image space, we normalize them to $[0, 2\pi]$, project them directly to d_T, and exclude them from positional encoding. After embedding and encoding, the final transformer input is structured as follows:

$$\mathcal{P}' = \{\mathcal{PE}(W_h \mathbf{lm}_i^p)\}_{i=1}^{21}, \quad W_h \in \mathbb{R}^{d_T \times 2} \tag{9}$$

$$\mathcal{O}' = \{\mathcal{PE}(W_o \mathbf{c}_i^o)\}_{i=1}^{N_t+1}, \quad W_o \in \mathbb{R}^{d_T \times 2} \tag{10}$$

$$\mathcal{R}' = \{W_r \theta_i^r\}_{i=1}^{N_t+1}, \quad W_r \in \mathbb{R}^{d_T \times 1} \tag{11}$$

3.4 Inter-modality Transformer

An overview of the architecture is shown in Fig. 2. Our backbone produces an object sequence $\mathcal{O}'$ and a pose sequence $\mathcal{P}'$ as input to the encoder. In the inter-modality attention block, pose features act as *queries*, attending to object locations, which serve as *keys* and *values*. Each token in the pose sequence aggregates object location information, and the encoder outputs a *pose-object memory* that encodes the global context between the hand and detected objects.

Our decoder processes a sequence of relationship tokens $\mathcal{R}'$, constructed from pose and object location data. These tokens first undergo self-attention before attending, as *queries*, to the *pose-object memory* produced by the encoder. The cross-attention mechanism enables each relationship token to integrate scene-wide information, leveraging the global context captured by the encoder and mapping it to its respective hand-object pair. The decoder outputs a sequence of tokens, each encoding pose-object information for a specific hand-object pair.

The decoder's output sequence is processed by a Feedforward Network (FFN) with a sigmoid activation function, assigning a score to each token. The i-th decoder output token corresponds to the i-th input relationship token, representing a specific hand-object pair. These scores allow ranking the objects, where the model predicts the index j of the token with the highest score. Since each token retains its mapping to the original input relationship tokens, the predicted index identifies the hand-object pair most likely to fulfill the pointing relationship.

We frame our task as binary classification, where each output representation is evaluated based on whether it fulfills the pointing relationship. To optimize this, we use Binary Cross-Entropy (BCE) loss, encouraging the model to assign higher scores to hand-object pairs that align with the pointing relationship while reducing scores for those that do not. Since our goal is to generate scores for every object rather than make a strict binary decision, we do not apply a threshold to separate pointing and non-pointing tokens. Instead, we rank the raw scores, selecting the object with the highest likelihood as the predicted pointing target.

4 Experiments and Evaluation

We evaluate the MM-ITF architecture by comparing different channel configurations. Specifically, we compare a two-modality setup utilizing the hand pose and object location and a three-modality setup consisting of the same modalities in addition to the relationship feature (see Sect. 3.2). Our two-modality setup uses the same architecture described in Fig. 2 where the relationship feature is replaced by the object location as input to the decoder. The results of both modality configurations are compared to a baseline that predicts objects based on proximity to a vector derived from the pointing gesture. In the following, we introduce the baseline, present the results, and conclude with a visual analysis of the model's predictions using a patch confusion matrix.

4.1 Baseline for Evaluation

As baseline, we use a 2D method proposed by Ali et al. [1] to predict objects indicated by pointing hand gestures. This method was applied to the same tabletop scenario with the NICOL robot. It consists of a Multi-layer Perceptron (MLP) that uses hand landmarks to determine whether the user is pointing. The final target objects are predicted based on proximity of the object's centroid to a continuous line that passes through the wrist and index finger key points. We choose this baseline because, similar to our approach, it relies completely on 2D data. Furthermore, its prior application within the same robotic setup ensures a fair and meaningful comparison. The baseline uses the same pretrained models for extracting hand key points and object locations, i.e., MediaPipe and OWLv2.

4.2 Experiment Results

We performed an eight-fold cross-validation, in which we trained eight models for both the baseline gesture classifier and our MM-ITF architecture. The 30 scenes from the dataset (see Sect. 3.1) were split for training, validation, and testing. Each model was trained on 21 scenes and validated on a unique subset of three, ensuring that all scenes were used for validation once, except for six scenes which were held out as a test set. Table 1 summarizes the test results, in which the values reflect the average performance across all models. MM-ITF in the three-modality setup (pose, object, and relationship data) achieves 90% accuracy, slightly above the baseline at 89%, showing that objects indicated by pointing gestures can be learned to a comparable performance without additional geometric post-processing. While the baseline relies on a two-stage geometric approach, our model jointly predicts both the gesture state and target object in a single step. Both methods similarly achieve high Top-2 accuracy, ranking the target object within the top two choices in 96% of cases.

Table 1. Average object prediction results for the baseline method and our proposed MM-ITF architecture, with a two-modality and a three-modality configuration

Model	Accuracy	Precision	Recall	F1-Score	Top-2 Accuracy
Baseline [1]	0.89 ± 0.008	0.84 ± 0.007	0.90 ± 0.012	0.85 ± 0.008	**0.96 ± 0.004**
MM-ITF*	0.71 ± 0.044	0.70 ± 0.037	0.68 ± 0.044	0.67 ± 0.041	0.92 ± 0.014
MM-ITF**	**0.90 ± 0.017**	**0.88 ± 0.019**	**0.92 ± 0.019**	**0.90 ± 0.019**	**0.96 ± 0.008**

* Our model trained with **two modalities** (hand pose and object locations).
** Our model trained with all **three modalities**, including the relationship feature.

Although the MM-ITF two-modality setup (pose and object) reaches only 71% accuracy, it achieves a high Top-2 accuracy of 92%, showing that it learns a meaningful link between the hand pose and object location but struggles to make a fine-grained correct final prediction. This suggests that while the model captures contextual relationships between hand pose and object location, it benefits noticeably from the relationship feature to improve object ranking precision.

Since the baseline selects the nearest object along a continuous line through the wrist and index finger, its predictions are straightforward to interpret. However, we need a confusion matrix to analyze the MM-ITF's performance. A confusion matrix over predicted indices would offer limited insight, as object locations vary across samples, and constructing one based on centroids is impractical due to the extremely large number of possible positions. Therefore, we introduce a method to discretize our architecture's outputs, mapping object centroids to fixed image regions for structured visual analysis.

Fig. 3. A visualization of the performance of our architecture using patches. The table space is divided into evenly sized, non-overlapping patches, and centroids (red dots) are assigned to patches by dividing their x, y coordinates by the patch width and height. The assigned patches are highlighted in purple. (Color figure online)

4.3 Measuring Spatial Understanding

We further evaluate the performance of our architecture by visualizing the predicted objects. The table area in the image space is divided into evenly sized, non-overlapping patches, as illustrated in Fig. 3. Since our model predicts an index corresponding to the object centroid (x, y) in image coordinates, each predicted and ground-truth centroid is mapped to a patch based on its coordinates. This mapping is achieved by dividing the x-coordinate by the patch width and the y-coordinate by the patch height. As a result, the centroid predictions are discretized into predefined image regions, enabling structured spatial analysis through a confusion matrix over patches. Patches with no assigned predictions are filtered out, and row normalization is applied to enhance interpretability.

For a more detailed analysis of our MM-ITF model's output, we construct a patch confusion matrix, which visualizes how predicted object centroid locations align with ground-truth centroids. Assigned patches for predicted centroids are shown along the x-axis, and those for ground-truth centroids along the y-axis. Each entry (i, j) represents how often a ground-truth centroid in patch i is predicted as patch j. Diagonal entries correspond to correct predictions, while off-diagonal values indicate spatial misclassifications. Additionally, the first row and last column of the matrix represent the non-object class, distinguishing non-pointing gestures from those associated with an object.

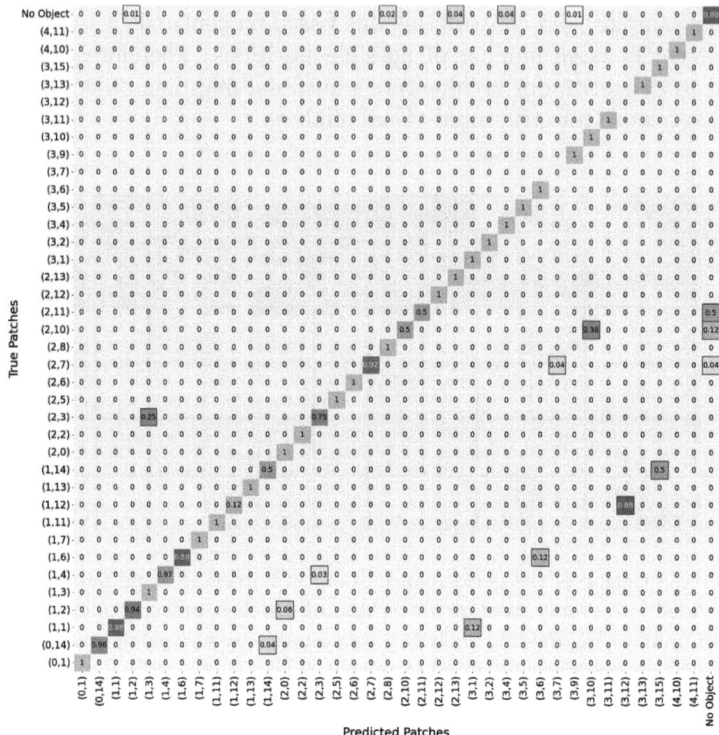

Fig. 4. The patch confusion matrix shows the mapping between predicted and target centroids to discrete regions in image space. Predictions are shown on the x-axis, targets on the y-axis. The first row and last column represent the non-object case.

Examining the confusion matrix (Fig. 4) for the three-modality setup reveals that correct predictions frequently receive high scores, demonstrating the model's ability to distinguish target objects of a pointing gesture, even in close proximity.[3] This suggests that the relationship feature plays a key role in guiding target selection. However, when multiple objects align perfectly with the pointing direction, the model often predicts an object behind the actual target relative to the participant. For example, objects at (1, 12) are misclassified as (3, 12) in 88% of cases, (2, 10) as (3, 10) in 38%, and (1, 14) as (3, 15) in 50% of cases. Together, these findings indicate a strong reliance on hand-object alignment.

Beyond object predictions, the model distinguishes between pointing and non-pointing hands but prioritizes hand location over *hand configuration*. For example, it sometimes predicts no-object for gestures originating from positions typically associated with resting hands, as observed at patch (2, 11). This suggests that hand position outweighs landmark arrangement, reinforcing the model's reliance on hand-object alignment and proximity over hand articulation.

---

[3] The matrix shows average results over eight models; see Sect. 4.2 for details.

The results for the two-modality setup reinforce our findings. The relationship feature improves both target object and gesture state identification, reducing confusion between closely positioned objects and correctly classifying aligned ones. It also helps distinguish pointing gestures from resting hand positions, reducing misclassification as non-pointing. While the two-modality setup reaches a high Top-2 accuracy of 92%, indicating that the model captures general spatial relations, the relationship feature provides crucial guidance for fine-grained distinctions and prevents over-reliance on proximity cues.

5 Conclusion

In this work, we proposed a framework for interpreting human pointing gestures toward objects. Operating purely in 2D, we leveraged the transformer's attention mechanism as a coherence score to map deictic gestures to object locations–without relying on predefined geometric rules, additional equipment, or 3D representations of the shared workspace. Our approach predicts, in a single step, whether a user is pointing and, if so, the most likely target object. This enables a reliable mapping between a deictic gesture and its inferred object, based solely on human pose. By ranking likely target objects, our method serves as a building block for downstream tasks aimed at estimating human intent in collaborative scenarios. In this sense, our work contributes to a robot's social skill set, enabling more intuitive and seamless interaction through the interpretation of pointing gestures. The architecture is modular and extendable, reflecting the multimodal nature of human communication.

While the current setup assumes fixed positions for the camera, table, and participants, future work will explore more dynamic and flexible interaction settings. We also aim to extend the hand features with modalities such as gaze, further enriching the global context between human and object features modeled by the encoder–and, in doing so, expanding the possibilities for humans to effortlessly indicate their intent to a robot.

Acknowledgements. This research was supported by the EU under the Horizon Europe programme (TERAIS, TRAIL), and by the DFG (Crossmodal Learning TRR-169). We thank Matthias Kerzel for his insightful comments that helped improve this manuscript.

Disclosure of Interests. The authors declare that they have no conflict of interest.

References

1. Ali, H., Allgeuer, P., Wermter, S.: Comparing apples to oranges: LLM-powered multimodal intention prediction in an object categorization task. In: ICSR (2024)
2. Allgeuer, P., Ali, H., Wermter, S.: When robots get chatty: grounding multimodal human-robot conversation and collaboration, pp. 306–321. Springer (2024)
3. Antoun, M., Asmar, D.: Human object interaction detection: design and survey. Image Vis. Comput. **130**(C) (2023)

4. Azari, B., Lim, A., Vaughan, R.T.: Commodifying pointing in HRI: simple and fast pointing gesture detection from RGB-D images. In: Conference on Computer and Robot Vision (CRV), pp. 174–180 (2019)
5. Bamani, E., Nissinman, E., Koenigsberg, L., Meir, I., Matalon, Y., Sintov, A.: Recognition and estimation of human finger pointing with an RGB camera for robot directive. arXiv preprint arXiv:2307.02949 (2023)
6. Calli, B., Singh, A., Walsman, A., Srinivasa, S., Abbeel, P., Dollar, A.M.: The YCB object and model set: towards common benchmarks for manipulation research. In: International Conference on Advanced Robotics ICAR, pp. 510–517 (2015)
7. Cao, Z., Hidalgo, G., Simon, T., Wei, S.E., Sheikh, Y.: OpenPose: realtime multi-person 2D pose estimation using part affinity fields. IEEE Trans. Pattern Anal. Mach. Int. **43**(01), 172–186 (2021)
8. Carion, N., Massa, F., Synnaeve, G., Usunier, N., Kirillov, A., Zagoruyko, S.: End-to-End object detection with transformers. In: Vedaldi, A., Bischof, H., Brox, T., Frahm, J.-M. (eds.) ECCV 2020. LNCS, vol. 12346, pp. 213–229. Springer, Cham (2020). https://doi.org/10.1007/978-3-030-58452-8_13
9. Chen, M., Liao, Y., Liu, S., Chen, Z., Wang, F., Qian, C.: Reformulating HOI detection as adaptive set prediction. In: CVPR, pp. 9004–9013 (2021)
10. Haque, F., Nancel, M., Vogel, D.: Myopoint: pointing and clicking using forearm mounted electromyography and inertial motion sensors. In: Proceedings of the 33rd Annual ACM Conference on Human Factors in Computing Systems, pp. 3653–3656. CHI '15, Association for Computing Machinery, NY, USA (2015)
11. Hewe, G.W.: Gesture language in culture contact. In: Sign Language Studies 3, vol. 4, pp. 1–34. Gallaudet University Press (1974)
12. Hu, K., Canavan, S., Yin, L.: Hand pointing estimation for human computer interaction based on two orthogonal-views. In: Proceedings of International Conference on Pattern Recognition, pp. 3760–3763 (2010)
13. Ji, J., Desai, R., Niebles, J.C.: Detecting human-object relationships in videos. In: ICCV, pp. 8106–8116 (2021)
14. Kerzel, M., et al.: NICOL: a neuro-inspired collaborative semi-humanoid robot that bridges social interaction and reliable manipulation. IEEE Access **11** (2023)
15. Kim, B., Lee, J., Kang, J., Kim, E.S., Kim, H.J.: HOTR: end-to-end human-object interaction detection with transformers. In: CVPR, pp. 74–83 (2021)
16. Kita, S. (ed.): Pointing: Where Language, Culture, and Cognition Meet. Lawrence Erlbaum Associates, Mahwah, NJ (2003)
17. Kuramochi, A., Komuro, T.: 3D hand pointing recognition over a wide area using two fisheye cameras, pp. 58–67. Springer (2021)
18. Lenz, F.: Deictic Conceptualisation of Space, Time and Person. John Benjamins (2003)
19. Lugaresi, C., et al.: MediaPipe: a framework for perceiving and processing reality. In: Third Workshop on Computer Vision for AR/VR at IEEE CVPR 2019 (2019)
20. Maji, D., Nagori, S., Mathew, M., Poddar, D.: YOLO-pose: enhancing YOLO for multi person pose estimation using object keypoint similarity loss. In: CVPR Workshops, pp. 2637–2646 (2022)
21. Medeiros, A.C.S., Ratsamee, P., Orlosky, J., Uranishi, Y., Higashida, M., Takemura, H.: 3D pointing gestures as target selection tools: guiding monocular UAVs during window selection in an outdoor environment. ROBOMECH J. **8**(1), 1–19 (2021). https://doi.org/10.1186/s40648-021-00200-w
22. Minderer, M., Gritsenko, A., Houlsby, N.: scaling open-vocabulary object detection. In: Proceedings of the 37th International Conference on Neural Information Processing Systems. NIPS '23, Curran Associates Inc., Red Hook, NY, USA (2023)

23. Mur-Artal, R., Montiel, J.M.M., Tardos, J.D.: ORB-SLAM: a versatile and accurate monocular SLAM system. IEEE Trans. Rob. **31**(5), 1147–1163 (2015)
24. Ranftl, R., Lasinger, K., Hafner, D., Schindler, K., Koltun, V.: Towards robust monocular depth estimation: mixing datasets for zero-shot cross-dataset transfer. IEEE Trans. Pattern Anal. Mach. Int. **44**(03), 1623–1637 (2022)
25. Sikeridis, D., Antonakopoulos, T.: An IMU-based wearable system for automatic pointing during presentations. Image Process. Commun. **21** (2017)
26. Tamura, M., Ohashi, H., Yoshinaga, T.: QPIC: query-based pairwise human-object interaction detection with image-wide contextual information. In: CVPR, pp. 10405–10414 (2021)
27. Tomasello, M.: Origins of Human Communication. MIT Press (2008)
28. Tölgyessy, M., Dekan, M., Duchoň, F., Rodina, J., Hubinský, P., Chovanec, L.: Foundations of visual linear human-robot interaction via pointing gesture navigation. Int. J. Soc. Robot. **9**, 1–15 (2017)
29. Zhang, A., et al.: Mining the benefits of two-stage and one-stage HOI detection. In: Ranzato, M., Beygelzimer, A., Dauphin, Y., Liang, P., Vaughan, J.W. (eds.) Advances in Neural Information Processing Systems, vol. 34, pp. 17209–17220. Curran Associates, Inc. (2021)
30. Zhang, F., et al.: MediaPipe hands: on-device real-time hand tracking. arXiv preprint arXiv:2006.10214 (2020)
31. Zou, C., et al.: End-to-end human object interaction detection with HOI transformer. In: CVPR, pp. 11820–11829 (2021)

Keypoint-Based Diffusion for Robotic Motion Planning on the NICOL Robot

Lennart Clasmeier, Jan-Gerrit Habekost[✉], Connor Gäde[✉], Philipp Allgeuer[✉], and Stefan Wermter[✉]

Knowledge Technology, Department of Informatics, University of Hamburg, Hamburg, Germany
{jan-gerrit.habekost,connor.gaede,philipp.allgeuer, stefan.wermter}@uni-hamburg.de

Abstract. We propose a novel diffusion-based action model for robotic motion planning. Commonly, established numerical planning approaches are used to solve general motion planning problems, but have significant runtime requirements. By leveraging the power of deep learning, we are able to achieve good results in a much smaller runtime by learning from a dataset generated by these planners. While our initial model uses point cloud embeddings in the input to predict keypoint-based joint sequences in its output, we observed in our ablation study that it remained challenging to condition the network on the point cloud embeddings. We identified some biases in our dataset and refined it, which improved the model's performance. Our model, even without the use of the point cloud encodings, outperforms numerical models by an order of magnitude regarding the runtime, while reaching a success rate of up to 90% of collision free solutions on the test set.

Keywords: Motion Planning · Diffusion Networks · Humanoid Robots

1 Introduction

Robotic motion planning is the process of finding a collision-free plan from a start configuration to a goal configuration. With the emergence of robotic agents, which are supposed to act autonomously in changing environments, the safety and adaptability of these machines become a core concern. Numerical motion planning algorithms could help to overcome this task by offering high adaptability to unknown environments, with theoretical guarantees for the optimality and completeness of the plans. These guarantees, however, come at high computational costs, making near real-time applications impossible and rendering these algorithms unfeasible in interactive scenarios. Neural motion planners propose a solution by replacing the lengthy planning process with fast neural inference.

L. Clasmeier and J.-G. Habekost—These authors contributed equally to this work. The authors gratefully acknowledge funding from Horizon Europe under the MSCA grant agreement No 101072488 (TRAIL).

Although recent research in the field shows promising results [2,4,5,26], motion planning remains an open task, since current approaches are specific to robots and environments, and data generation is very costly.

This work proposes and explores a new diffusion-based approach to neural motion planning on the NICOL platform. The model approaches the task of motion planning by learning from a synthetic dataset generated by numeric motion planners to create similar plans. Our initial approach uses point cloud encodings representing the environment at inference time; Ablation experiments reveal that these do not lead to a higher success rate, but slightly decrease the path lengths. By facilitating spatio-temporal diffusion in the joint space of the robot, we are able to generate 16-step action sequences in a single diffusion run. By reducing the plans to keypoint representations, 16 steps are enough to generate a plan in one go, which speeds up the planning time significantly. Further, we apply a batched planning approach, utilizing the parallel inference of the GPU to predict multiple plans for the same task at once, which further stabilized the models' performance and allowed us to reach a 90% success rate of collision free plans on unseen in-distribution data.

2 Related Work

Neural Motion Planning. Early neural approaches utilize bio-inspired topological networks with handcrafted neural dynamics to solve low-dimensional dynamic motion planning problems without any learnable parameters [24]. Ichter et al. [10] introduce a learning sampler that generates candidate configurations for a plan as seed vertices in the data structure of numerical motion planning methods to speed up convergence. Motion planning networks [21], which strongly inspired this work, introduce a behavior-cloning approach by utilizing an MLP-based action predictor and a point cloud encoder to generate trajectories iteratively. We build upon this approach by replacing the MLP action predictor with a diffusion architecture, which has shown promising capabilities in the field of behavior cloning. Motion policy networks [5] are based on a similar behavior cloning approach, but use point cloud-based representations of the robot and the target. Neural MP [4] extends the aforementioned approach by utilizing more diverse scenes and an updated architecture. Khan et al. [15] propose graph neural network to predict critical nodes for an RRT-based motion planner. The more sophisticated GraphMP [26] trains two GNNs. One GNN serves as a neural collision checker and the other predicts a graph in the configuration search space. Both networks are trained truth plans and collision data aggregated from standard methods. CPP Flow [17] utilizes the null space of the IK-Flow inverse kinematics approach to find collision-free joint space trajectories for a given end-effector trajectory. Zhang et al. show how visuo-motor architectures can be used for motion planning of Cartesian robots in 2D and 3D space [25], by predicting a probability map of the robot's position for the next image frame.

Numerical Motion Planning. Robotic motion planning is a well-known problem that is traditionally approached through sampling-based graph search, as done by probabilistic road maps (PRM) [13] and Rapidly-exploring random trees (RRT) [16]. Performance and runtime can be drastically reduced by introducing domain-specific knowledge through heuristics such as A^* [9]. Karaman and Frazzoli [12] show that an adaptive data structure that is extended with new vertices leads to stochastic optimality without increasing the asymptotic runtime. Informed RRT* [6] limits the search space after an initial solution is found to speed-up convergence. BIT* [7] starts the sampling process with a limited search space and grows it over the runtime. AIT* [23] introduces an adaptive heuristic to further reduce the search space and runtime.

Diffusion for Robotic Control. DALL-E-Bot [11] utilizes a diffusion model to create target scene views in a robotic manipulation task. Diffusion Policy [3] introduces diffusion for joint control, using it to generate task-specific robot trajectories conditioned on the robot state and an image encoding of the environment. Diffusion models have proven themselves in behavior cloning by stabilizing the mapping of a single input to multiple equally valid outputs by utilizing the noise space. Therefore, we follow this approach in our work as an action generator. π_0 [1] extends a medium-sized Llama architecture by a diffusion head to train a language-conditioned multi-policy agent. Octo [18] also uses a diffusion head approach for action generation but introduces a multi-modal Octo transformer to generate an embedding for the diffusion head. Spisak et al. [22] explore the capabilities of diffusion for robotic imitation learning by predicting a first-person view of a robot from a third-person view of the same robot, demonstrating the task. Carvalho et al. [2] use a diffusion model as a sampling prior for motion planning, generating plans from noise, without any environmental perception in the input, similar to our ablation study.

3 Approach

We approach the motion planning problem from a behavior-cloning perspective by training a neural network to predict plans from a dataset in a supervised way. The neural architecture is based on the diffusion policy approach, but instead of using image features from an image encoder, we also initially considered the embeddings from a point cloud encoder. The diffusion model uses a start and a goal configuration in the robot's joint space and a point cloud embedding of the scene to generate the next 16 steps along a collision-free path to the goal.

3.1 The NICOL Robot

As a robotic platform, we use the NICOL (Neuro-Inspired COLlaborator) robot [14] in its tabletop setting. NICOL is a robotic platform designed for the application of machine learning algorithms in human-robot interaction and manipulation scenarios. NICOL has two 8-DOF Manipulators with anthropomorphic

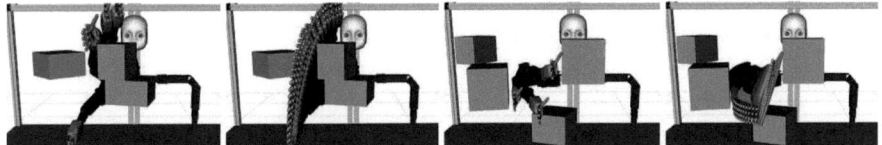

Fig. 1. Example keypoints and fixed step plans from the training dataset

Table 1. The aggregated angular distance of the joints along the plans in radians

Dataset	mean	var	max	min
train	6.63	15.66	79.21	0.06
test	5.36	8.41	20.49	0.38

hands to solve challenging manipulation tasks. The head holds two 4K fisheye cameras; additionally, the robot frame holds multiple depth sensors that scan the workspace from different angles. The torso of the NICOL robot is fixed in a tabletop setting with the arms mounted 40 cm above the tabletop .

3.2 Dataset

Since the plans depend on the robot's layout, we had to create a custom dataset for our scenario. The dataset consists of 5000 scenes with 20 plans, resulting in 100000 plans (Table 1). We use MoveIt to generate ground truth plans in randomly generated scenes with 3 or 4 cuboids of varying sizes. The positions and rotation of the objects are sampled from the Cartesian workspace bounds of the right arm, and spaced at least 30 cm apart. The start and the goal poses for the plans are generated via CycleIK [8] with a fixed side-grasp orientation within the workspace bounds, and rejection sampling is applied to ensure the validity of the poses before planning. For each scene, 20 plans are generated with a planning time of 20 s. We found that shorter planning times led to high failure rates during data generation, due to the numerical planner not finding collision-free plans. The point clouds are generated synthetically by sampling points from the cuboid planes.

In our experiments, we test two different plan representations shown in Fig. 1. In the fixed step size representation, the robot configurations are spread along the path equally. The keypoint representation reduces the plans to the key poses of the motion. The key poses are retrieved by filtering the plans by an acceleration threshold, since a change in acceleration leads to a change in the direction of the motion. The different representations of the plans strongly influence the distribution of the training data and, thereby, the model's behavior.

For each step along the plans, a training sample is created containing this step as the start, the last step of the plan as the goal, and the following 16 configurations as the target, which is padded with the goal.

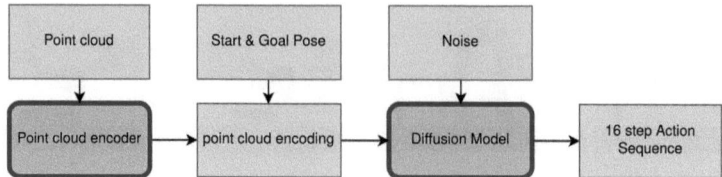

Fig. 2. Neural Architecture: The point clouds of the environment are encoded and concatenated with the start and goal configuration. This vector is used as conditioning of the diffusion model, which generates a 16-step action sequence from a noise vector

3.3 Neural Architecture

The model's architecture consists of a point cloud encoder and a diffusion-based action generator as shown in Fig. 2. The initially hypothesized point cloud embedding is generated from the point cloud encoder and concatenated with the start and end states of the desired plan to create the condition of the diffusion model.

Action Predictor. The action prediction model is based on the diffusion policy implementation from [3]. The CNN-based model uses a noise-predicting Unet that consists of multiple conditional residual blocks. The conditioning is achieved via Feature-wise Linear Modulation (FiLM) [19]. The action predictor generates 16-step action sequences for a given task description consisting of start, goal, and point cloud embedding. To achieve this, the noise-prediction network is used as the gradient field of our training distribution. The noise-prediction network takes a batch of action sequences of the form Bx16x8 as input and outputs a tensor of the same shape. Since we treat the model as a gradient field, the output tensor is the gradient that moves our input vector to low-energy regions. We can apply this gradient to the input to move it closer to the training distribution. At inference time, we start the process from uniformly distributed noise and apply the inverted diffusion process 100 times to get the final output.

Fig. 3. Example output of the auto encoder, input point clouds in the top row and model output in the bottom row

Point Cloud Encoder. The initially pursued, optional point cloud encoder is a simple PointNet [20] based architecture using a stack of three 1D convolutional layers followed by a global max pooling operation to calculate the encodings. The model takes fixed-size point clouds containing 4096 points. The encoder is pre-trained in combination with an MLP decoder as an autoencoder on a task-specific dataset of point clouds. The model is trained on the chamfer distance loss between the generated point cloud and the target point cloud.

Figure 3 shows the testing output of the autoencoder model. Although the recreated point clouds are noisier than the original ones, the model can capture the general geometric information of the point clouds. We decided to use a simple architecture for our approach for multiple reasons. Many modern architectures are designed to combine geometrical information with other features like point color, but since we only use geometrical data, we do not need this kind of capability. Since computation time matters a lot in our approach, we decided to use a fast and time-tested approach for this work.

3.4 Trajectory Generation

Trajectories are generated by the sampling process of the diffusion model. The global condition features are generated by concatenating the start and goal configuration in joint space and the point cloud embedding. The inverse diffusion process is performed on uniformly sampled noise with the given condition to generate the next configurations along the trajectory. The action horizon of the model is set to 16, which allows us to generate 16 steps of the trajectory for a given task description in one forward pass. The generated plans are individually interpolated to a fixed step size, re-scaled, and checked for collision. If the last configuration of the generated trajectory does not reach the target, we continue planning by using the final configuration of the generated plan as the new start configuration.

The neural approach offers batched inference, which can be used for batched trajectory generation. This allows us to generate plans for different scenarios simultaneously or to create multiple plans for the same scenario. In our approach, we are using the latter to increase and stabilize the performance of our model. Since the diffusion process starts from noise, the model is stochastic, and sampling different noise for the same task can result in different outputs.

4 Results

We trained the model on the keypoint plans and the fixed step representation plans and compared the model's behavior. The batched planning approach is successful if at least one plan from the batch reaches the target with a collision-free trajectory. Table 2 lists the success rates of our models on the test dataset. Since our dataset contains many short plans, we report the success rate on the subset of hard trajectories with more than four keypoints separately. We defined the model's success rate as the percentage of test plans the batched planning

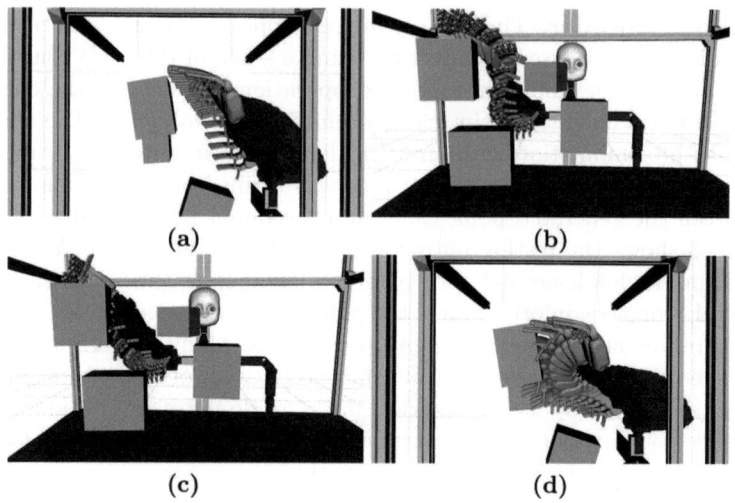

Fig. 4. Example of collision free solutions (a)(b) and colliding solutions (c)(d)

approach can solve successfully. Figure 4 shows example plans generated by the model. While the successful solutions create a nearly optimal motion around one of the obstacles, other plans from the same batch ignore the obstacle. Since this hints at a low effect of the point cloud embeddings on the plan prediction, we conducted an ablation study on the model without the point cloud embeddings. The high amount of short plans in the dataset introduces a strong bias toward direct motion towards the goal configuration in the training data. To test the effect of this, we trained the model on the refined subset of the training plans with more than four keypoints.

4.1 Inference Time

The inference runtime of most diffusion models is higher compared to regression approaches that only require a single forward pass. However, the runtime of numerical methods is magnitudes higher due to extensive collision checking and

Table 2. Overview of model performance

Model	Success rate all	Success rate hard
Fixed step	87.75%	69.86%
Keypoints	90.50%	75.34%
Ablation	88.00%	69.17%
Keypoints refined	91.17%	77.40%
Ablation refined	**92.00%**	**78.67%**

iterative trajectory optimization. During data generation, we fixed the planning time to 20 s to achieve an acceptable success rate of the numerical planner. We report the average runtime for our motion planning architecture as well as the individual ratio of model inference runtime and collision checking runtime in Table 3. The diffusion model has an average runtime of approximately 2 s, showing a very small variance, while the collision check has a runtime of 1 s.

Table 3. Inference time per planning step in seconds (Keypoints)

Time	mean	var	max	min
Full Time	3.02	0.26	4.77	2.06
Inference	1.97	0.01	2.41	1.86
Collision checking	1.05	0.22	2.83	0.09

Table 4. Difference in Plan length to test plans in radians

Model	mean	var	max	min
Fixed step	0.62	0.6	7.2	−7.33
Keypoints	0.5	0.89	5.51	−7.92

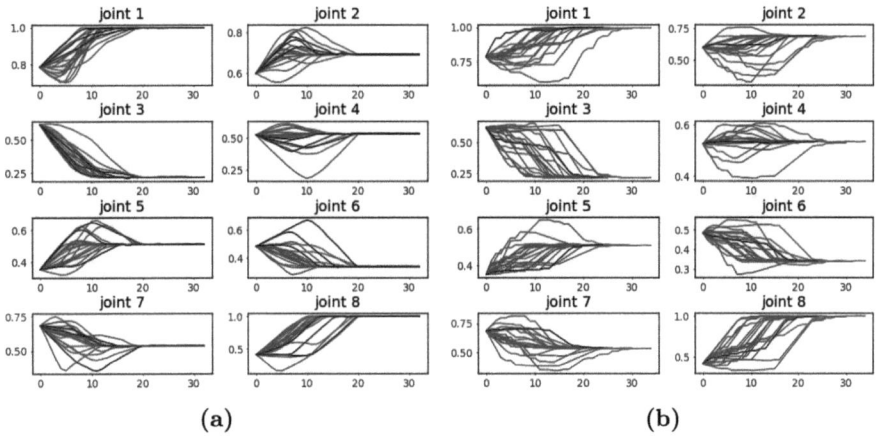

Fig. 5. Batch of plans in normalized joint space. Collision-free plans are marked blue. (a) Fixed step size plans (b) Keypoint plans (Color figure online)

4.2 Fixed-Step and Keypoint Representations

Figure 5 shows example outputs of the two different approaches of plan representation. The fixed-step approach generates smoother trajectories, imitating the smooth trajectories from the training data. The key point trajectories are more jagged since we interpolate linearly between the key points. The key point-based plans are less aligned since some of the plans include extra steps at the start. Overall, the models show similar behavior and explore a similar part of the solution space. As Table 4 shows, fixed step plans tend to be slightly longer, which can be explained by the curve of the trajectories. Since the fixed step size approach usually requires two planning steps to generate the full trajectory, which doubles the overall runtime, we focus further experiments on keypoint trajectories.

4.3 Point Cloud Ablation

The point cloud is removed from the FiLM conditioning for this experiment. We aim to identify biases in the training data and process. We hypothesized that a lack of perception would lead to a decrease in performance since obstacle avoidance requires a representation of the search space. Surprisingly, the ablation model performed equally well compared to the standard model.

The behaviour pattern originates from the batched path sampling process we apply to the stochastic diffusion model so that the model effectively learns to find a variety of paths for the same start and goal pose during training. It has to be noted that NICOL's large redundant configuration space is heavily constrained in this experiment, mainly due to the tabletop setup and the fixed hand orientation. This allows the training to collapse into a limited number of dynamic motion primitives accounting for a high success rate that does not generalize to the set of the most complex test scenes.

Figure 6a and Fig. 6b show the model's performance with and without point clouds after 50 training epochs. Both models have a similar overall success rate of approximately 90% on all plans, with the point cloud-conditioned model showing a better performance on the subset of more difficult plans Table 2. When we analyze the distribution of likelihoods to generate a successful solution after 50 epochs, both distributions look very similar, with the model based on the point cloud encodings having a higher in-batch success rate on the easy trajectories. While the point cloud embeddings did not improve the success rate, they affected the plan length positively, as Table 5 shows.

Table 5. Difference in plan length to test plans in radians

Model	mean	var	max	min
Keypoint	0.5	0.89	5.51	−7.92
Ablation	0.66	0.99	7.94	−5.42

Table 6. Refined dataset: Difference in plan length to test plans in radians

Model	mean	var	max	min
Keypoint	0.74	0.72	3.99	−7.07
Ablation	1.01	1.22	9.04	−7.02

4.4 Refined Training Data

As our experiments have shown, the model learns to solve easy plans with high probability, while struggling with the harder tasks from the test set. Since our dataset is biased towards short trajectories, removing these from the training data should help the model generalize better towards the harder tasks. We can filter the training data for all the plans that move directly towards the target, which we consider easy, and remove them from the training dataset. We define these plans to have four or fewer key points.

Figure 6c and 6d show the behavior of the models with and without point clouds, trained on the refined dataset. Reducing the bias in the training data positively affected the model's performance. A distribution shift toward the middle can be observed by looking at the distribution of likelihoods. While some certainty for the easy plans was lost, the model was able to find collision-free solutions for more of the hard scenarios. It can be seen in Table 2 that the model generalizes to the easy trajectories, even though not being trained on them.

When we examine the plan length metrics (Table 6), we see that all models lost a bit of average plan quality by removing the easy samples from the training data. This lines up with our observations of the distribution of the in-batch success being less concentrated at the extremes.

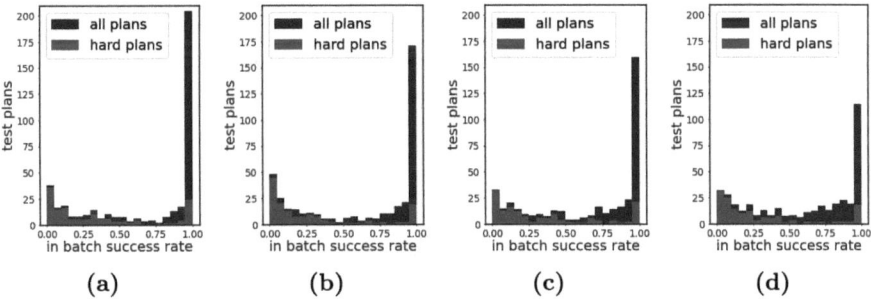

Fig. 6. In batch success rate **(a)** baseline **(b)** ablation **(c)** baseline refined dataset **(d)** ablation refined dataset

5 Discussion

The behavior cloning approach we use does not include collision information in the training loss. The network is merely trained on successful trajectories that are derived from a stochastic algorithm and is thus biased by many factors, such as the planning algorithm, the collision checking algorithm, and the joint limits of the robot. A suitable, differentiable, batched collision checker, which is, to the best of our knowledge, unavailable at this point in time, would pose a new gold standard to enforce point cloud-conditioning in a reinforcement learning-inspired manner. Related work [4,5] shows that the integration of point clouds into action models is 1) successfully possible and 2) crucial for successful deployment in real-world scenarios. The cited approaches generate more realistic scenes, such as household environments, to derive task-specific plans, moving away from the definition of generalized motion planning. In addition, these approaches use larger datasets by an order of magnitude. We identify the fixed end-effector orientation in our data aggregation method as a key issue that can lead to a missing variety of the dataset. Motion Policy Networks [5] use point cloud representations of the robot and the end-effector target in the same latent space as the scene point clouds in combination with the robot state and report a loss of 30% success rate when using only the joint state instead. We identify the robot proprioception via point cloud encodings as the key advantage compared to our approach, which only uses point cloud encodings of the environment.

In the presented approach, we successfully introduce a neural model that generates collision-free trajectories much faster than traditional planners. The results of our point cloud ablation study revealed that the point cloud embeddings in the input, while slightly reducing the average plan length, do not increase the success rate of our model, even though the point cloud auto-encoder we utilize produces meaningful embeddings. The architecture of our ablation study is similar to the approach of Carvalho et al. [2], who observed similar capabilities of diffusion models for motion planning. The simpler architecture does not directly rely on the perception of the robot, bringing the model to a real robot is therefore much easier, since we do not have to accommodate for the shift in the input distribution usually introduced by noisy sensors. The average runtime of our model of 3 s is by an order of magnitude lower compared to the 20s planning time of the PRM* planner, while reaching a success rate of 90% on the test set.

6 Conclusion

In this paper, we introduced a novel diffusion architecture for robotic motion planning. While our approach shows good performance on the test data, the integration of point clouds into the sampling process was still challenging in our experiments, as shown in the ablation study. We suspect various biases in the dataset and the missing proprioception of the robotic agent as the origin of the malfunctioning of the point cloud input, which we are going to investigate further in our future work. By facilitating the batched plan generation capabilities of our model and the use of keypoint-based plans, our approach is an order of magnitude faster than the planning process of numerical solvers as PRM*, while keeping a success rate of 90% on the test data. Combining our approach with a numeric planner as a backup allows us to skip the lengthy planning most of the time at a low constant cost while keeping a high quality of plans in terms of plan length.

References

1. Black, K., et al.: π_0: a vision-language-action flow model for general robot control. arXiv preprint arXiv:2410.24164 (2024)
2. Carvalho, J., Le, A.T., Baierl, M., Koert, D., Peters, J.: Motion planning diffusion: learning and planning of robot motions with diffusion models. In: 2023 IEEE/RSJ Int. Conf. on Intelligent Robots and Systems (IROS), pp. 1916–1923. IEEE (2023)
3. Chi, C., et al.: Diffusion policy: visuomotor policy learning via action diffusion. In: Proceedings of Robotics: Science and Systems (RSS) (2023)

4. Dalal, M., Yang, J., Mendonca, R., Khaky, Y., Salakhutdinov, R., Pathak, D.: Neural MP: a generalist neural motion planner. arXiv preprint arXiv:2409.05864 (2024)
5. Fishman, A., Murali, A., Eppner, C., Peele, B., Boots, B., Fox, D.: Motion policy networks. In: Conference on Robot Learning, pp. 967–977. PMLR (2023)
6. Gammell, J.D., Srinivasa, S.S., Barfoot, T.D.: Informed RRT*: optimal incremental path planning focused through an admissible ellipsoidal heuristic. In: Proceedings of the IEEE/RSJ International Conference on Intelligent Robots and Systems (IROS), vol. 2, pp. 3–1 (2014)
7. Gammell, J.D., Srinivasa, S.S., Barfoot, T.D.: Batch informed trees (BIT*): sampling-based optimal planning via the heuristically guided search of implicit random geometric graphs. In: 2015 IEEE International Conference on Robotics and Automation (ICRA), pp. 3067–3074. IEEE (2015)
8. Habekost, J.G., Strahl, E., Allgeuer, P., Kerzel, M., Wermter, S.: CycleIK: neuro-inspired inverse kinematics. In: Iliadis, L., Papaleonidas, A., Angelov, P., Jayne, C. (eds.) ICANN 2023. LNCS, vol. 14254, pp. 457–470. Springer, Cham (2023). https://doi.org/10.1007/978-3-031-44207-0_38
9. Hart, P.E., Nilsson, N.J., Raphael, B.: A formal basis for the heuristic determination of minimum cost paths. IEEE Trans. Syst. Sci. Cybernet. **4**(2), 100–107 (1968)
10. Ichter, B., Harrison, J., Pavone, M.: Learning sampling distributions for robot motion planning. In: 2018 IEEE International Conference on Robotics and Automation (ICRA), pp. 7087–7094. IEEE (2018)
11. Kapelyukh, I., Vosylius, V., Johns, E.: DALL-E-Bot: introducing web-scale diffusion models to robotics. IEEE Robot. Autom. Lett. **8**(7), 3956–3963 (2023)
12. Karaman, S., Frazzoli, E.: Sampling-based algorithms for optimal motion planning. Int. J. Robot. Res. **30**(7), 846–894 (2011)
13. Kavraki, L., Svestka, P., Latombe, J.C., Overmars, M.: Probabilistic roadmaps for path planning in high-dimensional configuration spaces. IEEE Trans. Robot. Autom. **12**(4), 566–580 (1996)
14. Kerzel, M., et al.: NICOL: a neuro-inspired collaborative semi-humanoid robot that bridges social interaction and reliable manipulation (2023)
15. Khan, A., Ribeiro, A., Kumar, V., Francis, A.G.: Graph neural networks for motion planning. arXiv preprint arXiv:2006.06248 (2020)
16. LaValle, S.: Rapidly-exploring random trees: a new tool for path planning. Research Report 9811 (1998)
17. Morgan, J., Millard, D., Sukhatme, G.S.: CPPFlow: generative inverse kinematics for efficient and robust cartesian path planning. In: 2024 IEEE International Conference on Robotics and Automation (ICRA), pp. 12279–12785. IEEE (2024)
18. Octo Model Team, et al.: Octo: an open-source generalist robot policy. In: Proceedings of Robotics: Science and Systems, Delft, Netherlands (2024)
19. Perez, E., Strub, F., De Vries, H., Dumoulin, V., Courville, A.: Film: visual reasoning with a general conditioning layer. In: Proceedings of the AAAI Conference on Artificial Intelligence, vol. 32 (2018)
20. Qi, C.R., Su, H., Mo, K., Guibas, L.J.: PointNet: deep learning on point sets for 3D classification and segmentation. In: Proceedings of the IEEE Conference on Computer Vision and Pattern Recognition, pp. 652–660 (2017)
21. Qureshi, A.H., Miao, Y., Simeonov, A., Yip, M.C.: Motion planning networks: bridging the gap between learning-based and classical motion planners. IEEE Trans. Rob. **37**(1), 48–66 (2020)

22. Spisak, J., Kerzel, M., Wermter, S.: Diffusing in someone else's shoes: robotic perspective-taking with diffusion. In: 2024 IEEE-RAS 23rd International Conference on Humanoid Robots (Humanoids), pp. 141–148. IEEE (2024)
23. Strub, M.P., Gammell, J.D.: Adaptively informed trees (AIT*): fast asymptotically optimal path planning through adaptive heuristics. In: 2020 IEEE International Conference on Robotics and Automation (ICRA), pp. 3191–3198. IEEE (2020)
24. Yang, S.X., Meng, M.: An efficient neural network approach to dynamic robot motion planning. Neural Netw. **13**(2), 143–148 (2000)
25. Zang, X., Yin, M., Huang, L., Yu, J., Zonouz, S., Yuan, B.: Robot motion planning as video prediction: a spatio-temporal neural network-based motion planner. In: 2022 IEEE/RSJ International Conference on Intelligent Robots and Systems (IROS), pp. 12492–12499 (2022)
26. Zang, X., Yin, M., Xiao, J., Zonouz, S., Yuan, B.: GraphMP: graph neural network-based motion planning with efficient graph search. Adv. Neural. Inf. Process. Syst. **36**, 3131–3142 (2023)

Real-Time Syllable Recognition in LIBRAS Using Deep Learning for Human-Robot Interaction

Joelmir Ramos[1](✉), Nadia Nedjah[2], and Paulo Victor Rorigues de Carvalho[1]

[1] Federal University of Rio de Janeiro (UFRJ), Rio de Janeiro, Brazil
joelmiramos@gmail.com
[2] State University of Rio de Janeiro (UERJ), Rio de Janeiro, Brazil

Abstract. This work presents a real-time syllable-level recognition system for LIBRAS, the Brazilian Sign Language. The system extracts 2D hand landmarks using MediaPipe and a Gaussian Temporal Smoothing technique to reduce frame-wise jitter. Two deep learning models are implemented for classification: a Multilayer Perceptron (MLP) and a Convolutional Neural Network (CNN). A dataset of 27,456 samples covering all 26 LIBRAS syllables was constructed for training and evaluation. Experiments were conducted on both a desktop workstation and a Raspberry Pi 4 to assess classification accuracy and inference latency. The CNN model achieves an average accuracy of 97.4%, with an inference latency of approximately 50 ms on desktop and 195 ms on Raspberry Pi, meeting the typical requirements for Human-Robot Interaction (HRI) systems. Furthermore, the proposed system was successfully deployed on the humanoid robotic platform 14-bis, demonstrating real-time syllable detection in a practical HRI scenario. These results confirm the feasibility of deploying lightweight LIBRAS classifiers on low-cost embedded platforms, enabling inclusive, scalable, and real-time applications in assistive and educational robotics.

Keywords: Sign language recognition · HRI · Gesture classification

1 Introduction

Sign language is a vital form of communication for millions of deaf and hard-of-hearing individuals around the world. In Brazil, LIBRAS is the official sign language and serves as the primary mode of communication for the local deaf community [20]. Despite its importance, social and technological barriers still hinder full communication between signers and non-signers, especially in environments such as schools, hospitals and public services. While many existing sign language recognition systems focus on translating complete words or phrases, the accurate detection of syllables is an underexplored but crucial challenge [10]. In

LIBRAS syllables serve as intermediate units that bridge the gap between isolated signs and full sentences.

Computer vision and deep learning have emerged as powerful tools in the development of gesture recognition systems. Using RGB cameras and frameworks such as MediaPipe, it is possible to track key points on the hands and extract meaningful spatial features. Classification techniques as SVMs and Random Forests, as well as deep learning architectures as RNNs, LSTMs and GCNs [13].

This work presents a real-time visual recognition system for LIBRAS syllables, leveraging 2D hand keypoints extracted using the MediaPipe framework, followed by a Gaussian Temporal Smoothing technique to mitigate frame-wise jitter. Two deep learning models (MLP and CNN) were implemented and comparatively evaluated for classification. The main contributions include the development of a balanced and fully annotated dataset containing over 27,000 samples, the introduction of a temporal smoothing step in the data preprocessing pipeline, and the deployment and testing of the system on low-cost embedded hardware (Raspberry Pi 4).

This work is organized as follows: Sect. 2 presents a review of related work in sign language recognition. Section 3 details the proposed method. Section 4 details the performance evaluation. Section 5 presents the conclusions and outlines directions for future works.

2 Related Works

Sign Language Recognition (SLR) has advanced considerably in recent years, largely driven by the integration of deep learning techniques into human-computer interaction systems [5]. Costa Filho et al. [6] utilized Kinect-based[1] depth maps and k-Nearest Neighbors (kNN) classifiers for hand configuration recognition. De Carvalho et al. [4] proposed a modular architecture integrating YOLO, ResNet, and MLP, achieving reasonable accuracy but with limited real-time performance (4 FPS). Despite their contributions, these approaches were constrained by high computational costs and reliance on depth sensors or segmentation techniques.

Recent landmark-based methods have sought to reduce computational load while enabling real-time execution. Sulaksono et al. [18] combined CNN and LSTM architectures for syllable recognition in the Indonesian Sign System (SIBI), while Putra et al. [16] employed MediaPipe landmarks with Transformer and Seq2Seq-LSTM models for American Sign Language (ASL) translation, demonstrating the benefits of attention mechanisms for sequential modeling.

Several works have focused on enhancing spatio-temporal modeling through advanced deep learning architectures. Miah et al. [12] introduced GmTC, integrating GCNs, CNNs, and MHSA for multi-lingual SLR across datasets such

---

[1] https://developer.microsoft.com/en-us/windows/kinect/.

as ASL, KSL, BSL, JSL, and LSA64. Da Silva et al. [17] proposed a multi-stream I3D-LSTM architecture for LIBRAS recognition achieving 99.8% accuracy. Mukhedkar et al. [14] introduced GLTS, fusing CNNs, SVMs, and NLP modules with RGB and depth data for gesture translation. Within the LIBRAS domain, Alves et al. [2] encoded landmarks into 2D skeleton images for ResNet18 classification, achieving up to 93% accuracy.

Alternative approaches based on sensor data and feature optimization have also emerged. Leiva et al. [11] designed a wearable glove-based system for Pakistan Sign Language (PSL) recognition using SVM and kNNs on a Raspberry Pi 3B, reaching 97% accuracy. Goel et al. [7] introduced AEGWO-Net, combining autoencoders and Grey Wolf Optimization for feature reduction from HOG inputs, achieving 98.4% accuracy. Hasan et al. [9] proposed a multimodal deep learning framework for Bangla Sign Language, fusing pose-based CNN-LSTM-ViT models with audio signals and achieving 94.71% accuracy. Focusing on architectural innovation, Altaher et al. [1] proposed Mamba-based models (ViM and RSM) for ASL alphabet recognition achieving 99.98% accuracy.

Real-time syllable-level LIBRAS recognition on low-cost embedded platforms remains underexplored. This work addresses this gap by proposing a lightweight system optimized for embedded HRI applications.

3 Proposed Method

The proposed method follows a structured pipeline composed of five sequential stages, as illustrated in Fig. 1. First, video frames are continuously acquired from a camera in the Video Capture stage. These frames are then processed by the Hand Landmark Detection stage, which utilizes the pre-trained MediaPipe Hands framework to identify 21 anatomical keypoints on the hand and output their two-dimensional coordinates (x_i, y_i) for $i = 1, \ldots, 21$. In the subsequent Normalization stage, the raw coordinates are translated and scaled relative to the wrist reference point to mitigate the effects of hand position and size variations.

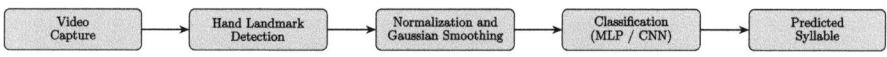

Fig. 1. Block diagram of the proposed LIBRAS syllable classification system

Additionally, to reduce frame-wise jitter inherent in landmark detection, a Gaussian Temporal Smoothing technique is applied over a sliding window of frames, enhancing spatial consistency across time. The resulting smoothed and normalized landmarks are then concatenated into a 42-dimensional feature vector. This vector is passed to the Classification stage, where two alternative deep learning models (MLP or CNN), analyze the input and generate a discrete syllable prediction. Finally, the system outputs the recognized Predicted Syllable, completing the classification pipeline.

3.1 Hand Landmark Extraction

Hand landmark extraction in this study is based on the pre-trained MediaPipe Hands framework, which employs an efficient two-stage pipeline for real-time tracking using only RGB input. In the first stage, a palm detector identifies a bounding box $\mathcal{B} \subset I$ for each hand in the input image $I \in \mathbb{R}^{H \times W \times 3}$ using a single-shot detection (SSD) model optimized for mobile inference. In the second stage, a regression-based hand landmark model processes the cropped region $\mathcal{B}$ and predicts 21 anatomical keypoints $\mathcal{L} = \{(x_i, y_i, z_i) \mid i = 1, \ldots, 21\}$, where (x_i, y_i) represent 2D image coordinates and z_i encodes relative depth with respect to the wrist [21].

Given an input image $I \in \mathbb{R}^{H \times W \times 3}$, the system outputs $\mathcal{L} = \{(x_i, y_i, z_i) \in \mathbb{R}^3 \mid i = 1, \ldots, 21\}$. The landmarks are then translated relative to the wrist (ℓ_0) and normalized by a scale factor s defined as the maximum Euclidean distance from the wrist to the fingertips:

$$s = \max_{i \in \mathcal{T}} \sqrt{(x_i - x_0)^2 + (y_i - y_0)^2}, \quad \mathcal{T} \subset \{4, 8, 12, 16, 20\}. \tag{1}$$

The final normalized coordinates are:

$$(x'_i, y'_i, z'_i) = \left(\frac{x_i - x_0}{s}, \frac{y_i - y_0}{s}, \frac{z_i - z_0}{s} \right). \tag{2}$$

Figure 2 illustrates the configuration of landmarks, which are used to describe the spatial configuration of the hand independently of its absolute position or size in the image. Each sample consists of a time series of (x, y) coordinates associated with the 21 keypoints, extracted from individual video frames.

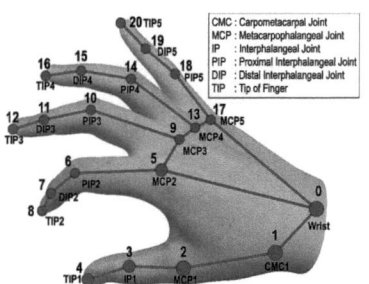

Fig. 2. The twenty one anatomical landmarks detected by MediaPipe hands are illustrated based on a figure from [21]

To improve data quality and reduce the impact of frame-wise jitter inherent in landmark detection, we introduced an additional Gaussian Temporal Smoothing step after the normalization process. Although classification is performed on static frames, we applied Gaussian Temporal Smoothing during both the data preparation stage (before model training) and later during the inference phase to ensure consistency between training and deployment. This dual-stage application aimed to minimize the effect of landmark noise in both learning and operational contexts, especially when running on real-time embedded systems.

For each landmark coordinate (x'_i, y'_i), a one-dimensional Gaussian filter was applied over a sliding window of n consecutive frames along the temporal dimension. This process is mathematically described as:

$$x_i^{\text{smooth}}(t) = \frac{1}{\sqrt{2\pi\sigma^2}} \sum_{k=-n}^{n} x'_i(t+k) \cdot \exp\left(-\frac{k^2}{2\sigma^2}\right), \qquad (3)$$

where $x'_i(t+k)$ represents the normalized coordinate of landmark i at frame $t+k$, and σ is the standard deviation controlling the smoothing strength. A similar formulation was applied to y'_i coordinates.

This temporal smoothing technique reduces high-frequency noise caused by minor detection instabilities between frames, resulting in more stable and consistent landmark trajectories over time. The smoothing was implemented using the *gaussian_filter1d* function from the SciPy Python library. The standard deviation σ was empirically set to 2 after preliminary experiments to balance noise reduction with gesture distinctiveness. For this work, the output is a fixed-length reduced vector $\mathbf{v} \in \mathbb{R}^{42}$ containing all normalized coordinates of the 21 landmarks, where:

$$\mathbf{v} = \left[x_1^{\text{smooth}}, y_1^{\text{smooth}}, \ldots, x_{21}^{\text{smooth}}, y_{21}^{\text{smooth}}\right]. \qquad (4)$$

3.2 Data Acquisition and Preprocessing

The dataset used in this study consists of 27,456 RGB images covering all 26 LIBRAS syllables (AZ), with 1,056 samples per class. Image acquisition was performed using a standard webcam (960 × 540 resolution, 30 FPS) in a controlled indoor environment, with deliberate variation in lighting conditions and camera-to-hand distance. The dataset was collected by a single adult participant performing each syllable multiple times over several sessions, intentionally introducing intra-user variability in hand positioning and orientation. For each captured image, a corresponding 42-dimensional vector of normalized 2D hand landmarks was extracted using the pre-trained MediaPipe Hands framework. The image files follow the naming convention "Letter-Number" and each is stored in a folder corresponding to its target syllable class. The complete dataset, including all images and their associated landmark vectors, is publicly available at the link[2]. Figure 3 presents one example image for each class, overlaid with the detected landmarks. Although data collection involved a single signer, the intentional session-to-session variability aimed to mitigate user-specific overfitting. However, no explicit cross-participant or cross-session validation was performed, which we recognize as a limitation and an opportunity for future work involving a larger and more diverse group of signers.

---

[2] http://drive.google.com/file/d/1eIBZIRvcvPf-jLF0rl_AUE7B6-J2lqIl/view?usp=sharing.

3.3 Classification with Neural Networks

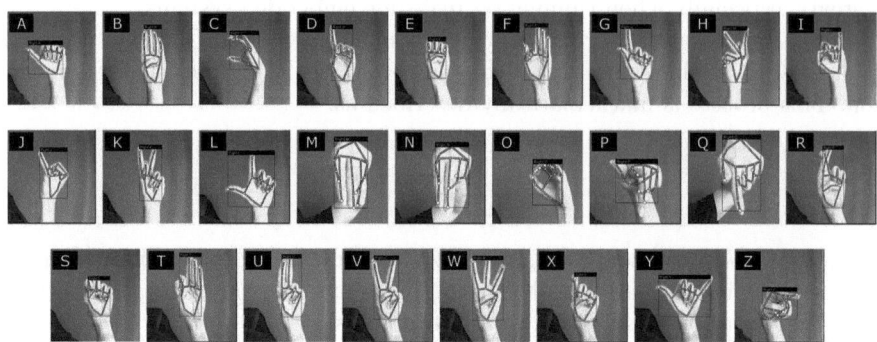

Fig. 3. Classification for each LIBRAS syllable with detected landmarks

To classify hand gestures, two deep learning architectures were implemented and compared: MLP and CNN. Both models were trained using the same set of pre-processed 2D landmark data. The choice of MLP and CNN was motivated by their low computational cost, ease of deployment on embedded platforms, and suitability for small to medium-sized datasets. Given the real-time constraints of the target application and the limited computational resources available on devices like the Raspberry Pi 4, more complex architectures such as Vision Transformers, Graph Convolutional Networks (GCNs), or 3D Convolutional Networks were intentionally avoided due to their higher memory footprint and inference latency. The MLP offers a lightweight baseline model capable of learning from flattened feature vectors, while the CNN, when applied over the reshaped landmark data, provides the ability to capture local spatial patterns between adjacent keypoints without incurring excessive computational overhead. This balance between performance and efficiency makes both models well-suited for real-time, low-latency human-computer interaction scenarios, which is the primary focus of this study.

Multilayer Perceptron (MLP). The MLP model receives as input a flattened and normalized vector of length 42, corresponding to the (x, y) coordinates of the 21 hand landmarks extracted per frame. The architecture consists of three fully connected layers: an input layer with 42 units, followed by two hidden layers with 20 and 10 neurons respectively, each using ReLU activation to introduce non-linearity and enable the learning of complex decision boundaries. Dropout regularization with rates of 0.2 and 0.4 is applied after each hidden layer to mitigate overfitting, given the relatively small input dimensionality and dataset size. The final output layer uses a softmax activation with 26 units, representing the probability distribution over the LIBRAS syllable classes. This simple and lightweight architecture was selected to ensure low inference latency and compatibility with resource-constrained embedded platforms.

Convolutional Neural Network (CNN). To better capture spatial relationships among hand keypoints, a second model was implemented using a 1D CNN. The input data, originally a 42-dimensional vector of 2D landmarks, was reshaped into a two-dimensional array with shape (21, 2), preserving the anatomical order of joints across the hand. The final CNN architecture, selected after grid search optimization, consists of two Conv1D layers with 32 and 64 filters, kernel sizes of 3, each followed by ReLU activations and a MaxPooling1D and GlobalMaxPooling1D layer, respectively. A fully connected dense layer with 64 neurons and dropout regularization follows, ending with a softmax output layer with 26 units for classification. The total number of trainable parameters is 12,282. This design balances model complexity and computational efficiency for real-time deployment on embedded platforms.

To optimize the architecture and training parameters of the neural networks, a grid search strategy was conducted during the training phase using the Keras Tuner framework. This process involves systematically evaluating multiple combinations of key hyperparameters. The final CNN architecture was selected based on the best-performing combination of these hyperparameters, balancing classification accuracy and model complexity.

Although CNNs are traditionally designed for dense spatial data like images, recent studies have demonstrated their effectiveness when applied to structured features such as 2D landmark sequences [15,19]. The sequential organization of landmarks allows the CNN to learn local spatial dependencies between neighboring joints, capturing geometric patterns that MLPs may struggle to model.

A standard 80/20 train-test split is used, with the dataset partitioned at the individual frame level, as each sample corresponds to a static RGB image and its associated 2D landmark vector. Since the dataset does not include continuous video sequences, each frame was treated as an independent sample to minimize the risk of temporal correlation between training and testing sets. Within the 80% training portion, a 5-fold cross-validation procedure was employed for model tuning and hyperparameter optimization. All models were trained using the Adam optimizer and sparse categorical cross-entropy loss function. During training, all models were trained for up to 100 epochs with a batch size of 64, using early stopping and real-time monitoring of validation accuracy to assess generalization performance.

4 Performance Evaluation

To evaluate the performance and efficiency of the proposed method, a series of experiments are conducted focusing on classification accuracy, inference latency and real-time execution viability. All training and preliminary evaluations are performed on a desktop workstation with an Intel Core i7 processor (2.6 GHz), 8 GB of RAM and running Windows 10. To assess deployment feasibility on low-cost embedded platforms, the trained models are deployed on a Raspberry Pi 4, featuring a Quad-Core 64-bit processor at 1.5 GHz and 4 GB of RAM, running the Raspbian OS. This hardware was chosen for its accessibility and common use in educational and robotic applications. The experiments used the dataset described in Sect. 3.2. The neural network models were implemented using the TensorFlow and Keras libraries.

The model performance is evaluated using four standard classification metrics: precision, recall, F1-score, and accuracy. Each metric was analyzed individually for both the MLP and CNN models across all classes in the LIBRAS syllable dataset. Figure 4 presents the per-class accuracy for both models. The CNN consistently outperformed the MLP across nearly all classes, achieving accuracy rates above 95% for most syllables. The letters 'D', 'E', 'P', 'U', 'V' and 'X' presented low accuracy in the MLP model. In particular 'U' and 'V' due to the similarity in the gesture, the 'X' due to similarities with the letters 'D', 'E' and 'S'. And the letter 'R', 'M' and 'N' has finger occlusion that makes it difficult to capture the gesture pattern.

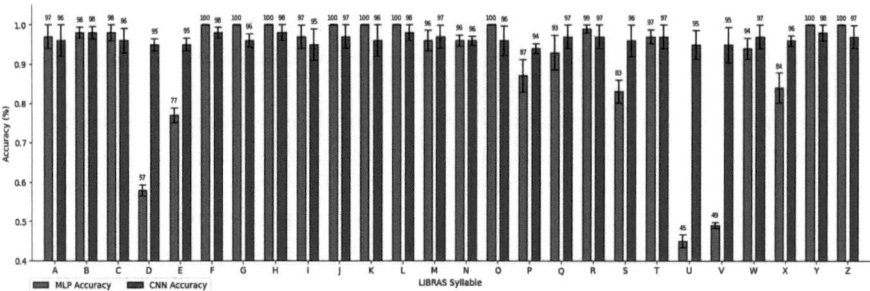

Fig. 4. Accuracy per Class of MLP vs CNN for LIBRAS syllables

Table 1 summarizes the average performance metrics for both models. The performance differences between the MLP and CNN models can be attributed to their respective architectural characteristics. The MLP, operating on a flattened feature vector, struggles to capture local spatial dependencies between hand joint. In contrast, the CNN leverages 1D convolutions over the structured landmark input, enabling it to model local geometric patterns more effectively.

Table 1. Classification performance metrics and corresponding standard deviations for MLP and CNN models

Metric	MLP Mean (%)	MLP Std (%)	CNN Mean (%)	CNN Std (%)
Precision	88.2	1.8	96.4	2.1
Recall	90.1	1.6	97.6	1.4
F1-score	89.6	1.4	96.1	1.2
Accuracy	87.3	2.5	97.4	1.1

To analyze classification performance across LIBRAS syllables, Fig. 5 presents the confusion matrices for both models. The CNN (Fig. 5a) exhibits a stronger diagonal concentration and fewer off-diagonal errors compared to the MLP (Fig. 5b), indicating superior generalization and class-wise accuracy.

In the MLP, the main confusions occurred between visually similar syllables such as 'O' and 'C', 'U' and 'R', and 'V' and 'U', likely due to occlusions and overlapping finger configurations. For the CNN, residual errors were observed primarily between 'U' and 'R', 'V' and 'U', and 'I' and 'Y', reflecting the inherent visual similarity and landmark overlap among these gestures.

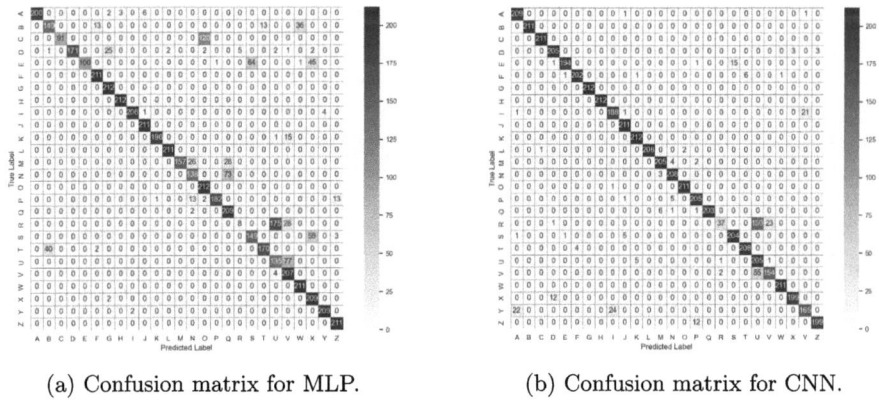

(a) Confusion matrix for MLP.   (b) Confusion matrix for CNN.

Fig. 5. Confusion matrices for the 26 LIBRAS syllables

The latency of the proposed system was measured to assess its feasibility for real-time implementation on both desktop and embedded platforms. On the desktop environment, the CNN consistently achieved lower latency across all classes, with an average inference time of 50.2 ms, compared to 63.0 ms for the MLP. On the Raspberry Pi, latency values increased due to hardware limitations, with the CNN maintaining superior performance, reaching an average latency of 194.9 ms, while the MLP recorded 235.0 ms. Both models remain close to latency thresholds typically considered acceptable for real-time responsiveness in assistive HRI scenarios, where response times below 200 ms are desirable [8]. A detailed comparison of inference latency and standard deviation for both models is presented in Table 2. Minor variations in latency per syllable were observed, which we attribute to runtime fluctuations related to frame-wise landmark detection stability and hardware-related processing jitter. Additionally, caching behavior, background noise, and system resource scheduling on the Raspberry Pi and PC can introduce natural variability in inference timing.

Table 3 provides a comparative overview of existing LIBRAS-related datasets and recognition models. It is important to emphasize that each referenced work was trained and evaluated on its own specific dataset, with differing numbers of

Table 2. Latency for MLP and CNN on PC and Raspberry

Device	Model	Mean (ms)	Std (ms)
PC	MLP	63.0	20.2
PC	CNN	50.2	6.6
Raspberry Pi	MLP	235.0	24.5
Raspberry Pi	CNN	194.9	17.5

classes, data modalities and experimental protocols. For example, in LibrasImages, Costa Filho et al. [6] utilized Kinect-based depth maps and kNN classifiers for hand configuration recognition. Bastos et al. [3] employed handcrafted features such as HOG and Zernike moments combined with neural networks, achieving 96.7% accuracy on a 40-class dataset. The Libras91 dataset [4] was used to train the HandArch deep learning framework, which attained 99% accuracy across 91 classes. These studies do not report experiments related to real-time deployment. For reference purposes only, we also include the classification performance of our MLP and CNN models, which were exclusively trained and evaluated on our own custom dataset consisting of 26 LIBRAS syllables, under the conditions described in Sect. 3.2. This table is not intended as a direct benchmark comparison, but rather as an overview of related LIBRAS recognition efforts using different methodologies and datasets.

Table 3. Comparison with previous work

Study	Class	Sample	Accuracy (%)
LibrasImages [6]	61	12,200	95.0
Bastos [3]	40	9,600	96.7
Libras91 [4]	91	108,896	99.0
This work (MLP)	26	27,456	87.3
This work (CNN)	26	27,456	97.4

To illustrate the performance of the proposed system, demonstration videos for both models are publicly available. A video showcasing the MLP model running on a desktop platform can be accessed in MLP link[3]. Additionally, a demonstration of the CNN model, also running on a desktop under challenging lighting conditions, is available in CNN link[4].

To validate the applicability of the proposed system in real HRI scenarios, the CNN model was deployed on the humanoid robotic platform 14-bis. The 14-bis is a private platform with articulated arms, limbs and head, allowing physical

---
[3] https://youtube.com/shorts/ZmfIluNnjK4?feature=share.
[4] https://youtu.be/bzs4EO0B5NI.

movements and basic gestural interactions. During the experiment, the robot remained in its control station connected to the desktop PC. A human participant performed the syllables 1.6 m away from the robot, under natural lighting and with varying background elements, including full-body visibility. The robot successfully detected the performed syllables in real time, demonstrating the system's robustness against environmental noise and distance variations. Figure 6a shows the 14-bis robot, and Fig. 6b presents an example frame running on the robot. A video demonstration is available at Robot Application link[5].

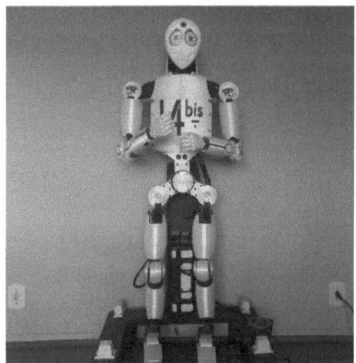
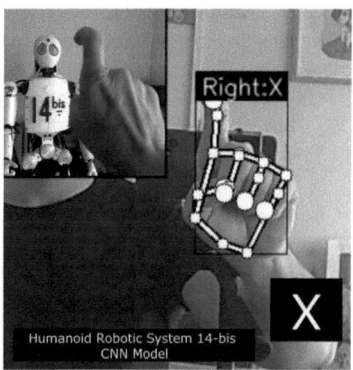

(a) 14-bis humanoid robot   (b) Syllable detection

Fig. 6. Real-time LIBRAS syllable recognition using the 14-bis humanoid robot

5 Conclusion

This work presents a real-time syllable-level recognition system for LIBRAS, combining 2D hand landmark extraction with deep learning-based classification using MLP and CNN architectures. A novel, publicly available dataset of 27,456 samples was created under varied lighting and distance conditions to promote generalization. Experimental results confirm the system's accuracy, low computational cost, and feasibility for deployment on both desktop and Raspberry Pi 4 platforms. The CNN model demonstrated superior performance in both classification and inference latency. Additionally, real-time detection was successfully implemented and tested on the humanoid robot 14-bis, validating the system's applicability to HRI scenarios. We explicitly acknowledge that the current system focuses on static, frame-level recognition without temporal context modeling, a design choice made to meet real-time constraints on embedded hardware. Future work will explore temporal models such as LSTM or Transformer-based architectures to enable continuous sign language recognition and we also intend to expand the dataset by including multiple signers and capturing more diverse environmental conditions to further improve generalization and robustness.

---

[5] https://youtube.com/shorts/riL7Yw-PTkk.

References

1. Altaher, A.S., et al.: Mamba vision models: automated American sign language recognition. Franklin Open, 100224 (2025)
2. Alves, C.E.G., Boldt, F.D.A., Paixão, T.M.: Enhancing Brazilian sign language recognition through skeleton image representation. In: 2024 37th SIBGRAPI Conference on Graphics, Patterns and Images (SIBGRAPI), pp. 1–6. IEEE (2024)
3. Bastos, I.L., Angelo, M.F., Loula, A.C.: Recognition of static gestures applied to Brazilian sign language (LIBRAS). In: SIBGRAPI Conference on Graphics, Patterns and Images, pp. 305–312. IEEE (2015)
4. de Carvalho, G.P., Brandão, A.L., Ferreira, F.T.: HandArch: a deep learning architecture for libras hand configuration recognition. In: Workshop de Visão Computacional (WVC), pp. 19–24. SBC (2021)
5. Cheok, M.J., Omar, Z., Jaward, M.H.: A review of hand gesture and sign language recognition techniques. Int. J. Mach. Learn. Cybern. **10**, 131–153 (2019)
6. Costa Filho, C.F.F., Souza, R.S.d., Santos, J.R.d., Santos, B.L.d., Costa, M.G.F.: A fully automatic method for recognizing hand configurations of Brazilian sign language. Res. Biomed. Eng. **33**(1), 78–89 (2017)
7. Goel, R., Bansal, S., Gupta, K.: Improved feature reduction framework for sign language recognition using autoencoders and adaptive grey wolf optimization. Sci. Rep. **15**(1), 2300 (2025)
8. Goodrich, M.A., Schultz, A.C., et al.: Human–robot interaction: a survey. Found. Trends® Hum.–Comput. Interact. **1**(3), 203–275 (2008)
9. Hasan, A., Hasan Jobayer, M., Abdullah Al Mahmud Pias, M., Alam, T., Khan, R.: Bangla sign language recognition with multimodal deep learning fusion. Eng. Rep. **7**(4), e70139 (2025)
10. Ibrahim, N.B., Zayed, H.H., Selim, M.M.: Advances, challenges and opportunities in continuous sign language recognition. J. Eng. Appl. Sci. **15**(5), 1205–1227 (2020)
11. Leiva, V., Rahman, M.Z.U., Akbar, M.A., Castro, C., Huerta, M., Riaz, M.T.: A real-time intelligent system based on machine-learning methods for improving communication in sign language. IEEE Access (2025)
12. Miah, A.S.M., Hasan, M.A.M., Tomioka, Y., Shin, J.: Hand gesture recognition for multi-culture sign language using graph and general deep learning network. IEEE Open J. Comput. Soc. (2024)
13. Mohamed, A.S., Hassan, N.F., Jamil, A.S.: Real-time hand gesture recognition: a comprehensive review of techniques, applications, and challenges. Cybern. Inf. Technol. **24**(3) (2024)
14. Mukhedkar, M., Deshmukh, D.P., Chaudhari: Efficient development of gesture language translation system using CNN. In: International Conference on Computing Communication and Networking Technologies (ICCCNT), pp. 1–6. IEEE (2024)
15. Priyanka, K., Rithik, R., Jaswanth, C., Rajesh, C.: A fusion of CNN, MLP, and MediaPipe for advanced hand gesture recognition. In: International Conference on Recent Advances in Science and Engineering (ICRASET), pp. 1–5. IEEE (2024)
16. Putra, G.G.S., D'Layla, A.W.C., Wahono: American sign language to text translation using transformer and seq2seq with LSTM. In: International Conference on Technology Innovation and Its Applications (ICTIIA), pp. 1–6. IEEE (2024)
17. da Silva, D.R., de Araújo, T.M.U., do Rêgo, T.G.: A multiple stream architecture for the recognition of signs in Brazilian sign language in the context of health. Multimedia Tools Appl. **83**(7), 19767–19785 (2024)

18. Sulaksono, J., Girinatari, I.A.D., Sudarma, M., Swarmardika: Sibi syllable recognition system with LSTm. In: International Conference on Smart-Green Technology and Information Systems (ICSGTEIS), pp. 94–97. IEEE (2023)
19. Verma, A.R., Singh, G., Meghwal, K., Ramji, B., Dadheech, P.K.: Enhancing sign language detection through mediapipe and convolutional neural networks (CNN). arXiv preprint arXiv:2406.03729 (2024)
20. Xavier, A.N., Agrella, R.P.: Brazilian sign language (LIBRAS). Sign languages of the world: a comparative handbook, pp. 129–158 (2015)
21. Zhang, F., et al.: MediaPipe hands: on-device real-time hand tracking. arXiv preprint arXiv:2006.10214 (2020)

Generating and Customizing Robotic Arm Trajectories Using Neural Networks

Andrej Lúčny[1](✉), Matilde Antonj[2,3], Carlo Mazzola[3], Hana Hornáčková[1], and Igor Farkaš[1]

[1] Faculty of Mathematics, Physics and Informatics, Comenius University Bratislava, Bratislava, Slovakia
{lucny,hornackova52,farkas}@fmph.uniba.sk
[2] DIBRIS, University of Genoa, Genoa, Italy
[3] CONTACT, Italian Institute of Technology, Genoa, Italy
{Carlo.Mazzola,Matilde.Antonj}@iit.it

Abstract. We introduce a neural network approach for generating and customizing the trajectory of a robotic arm, that guarantees precision and repeatability. To highlight the potential of this novel method, we describe the design and implementation of the technique and show its application in an experimental setting of cognitive robotics. In this scenario, the NICO robot was characterized by the ability to point to specific points in space with precise linear movements, increasing the predictability of the robotic action during its interaction with humans. To achieve this goal, the neural network computes the forward kinematics of the robot arm. By integrating it with a generator of joint angles, another neural network was developed and trained on an artificial dataset created from suitable start and end poses of the robotic arm. Through the computation of angular velocities, the robot was characterized by its ability to perform the movement, and the quality of its action was evaluated in terms of shape and accuracy. Thanks to its broad applicability, our approach successfully generates precise trajectories that could be customized in their shape and adapted to different settings. The code is released at https://github.com/andylucny/nico2/tree/main/generate.

Keywords: robotics · kinematics · neural network

1 Introduction

In human–robot interaction (HRI) scenarios, the design of robotic motion must extend beyond efficiency in reaching a goal; it must also support human ability to interpret, predict, and feel safe around robotic actions. When humans and robots share the same physical space, the legibility of robot trajectories – the ease with which a human observer can infer the robot intent [1] – becomes critical for effective, safe, and explainable collaboration. We can characterize legible movement by its distinctiveness, helping observers disambiguate between potential goals based on robot behavior [2].

To study human perception while interacting with robots, it is essential to design the robotic behavior to be repeatable and controllable [3–5]. In this context, we address the problem of generating high-precise and controllable robotic arm trajectories that exhibit given shapes to serve as a foundation for studying human perception of robot legibility. Precision is crucial: subtle inaccuracies or inconsistencies in the generated trajectories could confound human interpretation, undermining the experimental study of legibility. Our work, therefore, aims to provide a method for creating repeatable, controlled motion patterns, enabling systematic investigation of how humans perceive and predict robot movements during embodied interaction. Theoretically, it should be possible to meet our needs with inverse kinematics (IK). However, we finally succeeded with a custom approach due to practical problems, including a lack of the robot model in a suitable format for the framework that matches our accommodated hardware, including the forefinger, combining movement with pointing.

To this end, we propose a neural network-based approach for trajectory generation capable of producing smooth and accurate movements corresponding to predefined shapes. This method constitutes an important step toward developing repeatable and scalable tools to study motion legibility in HRI. Ultimately, it addresses the broader challenges of reducing robot unpredictability and improving interpretability and safety in shared environments [6].

In detail, implementing software for an experiment in cognitive robotics, we faced a problem in calculating the trajectories of a humanoid robot arm moving in line with a forefinger pointing in the direction of the movement to a specified point. This problem we can theoretically solve by any method of IK that we gradually apply for iterative calculation of the arm angles for each point (in 3D) of the line starting from the previous such point and for the orientation vector (roll, pitch, yaw) that is constant along the whole line and corresponds to its direction. Since we aimed to simplify our job as much as possible, we employed a powerful library dedicated to training neural networks (Pytorch).

Forward and inverse kinematics are fundamental concepts in robotics. Forward kinematics (FK) is the computation of the end-effector position and orientation based on known joint parameters, typically using Denavit-Hartenberg convention variant [7]. In contrast, IK addresses the problem of determining the joint parameters required to achieve the target position and orientation of the end effector [8]. This problem is often more complex due to the possibility of multiple solutions, redundancy, and the necessity of holding some given constraints, such as ranges of joint angles. In our case, we also need to follow a given trajectory shape. Analytical solutions exist for simple manipulators, but we must employ iterative methods for more complicated effectors like our robotic arm [9].

Therefore, we have designed the method described in detail below. It benefits from the power of today's tools for training neural networks, is easy to use, and is suitable for controlling the movement of robots along any chosen trajectory. It does not suffer from constraints like the FABRIK algorithm [10,11], and unlike most traditional approaches, it generates a complete trajectory in one step.

Unlike recent approaches based on solving the IK problem using neural networks [12–14], we do not need to leverage large datasets of robot poses and corresponding joint configurations, which is a typical condition for the application of machine learning. In contrast, our method can provide such data. The feedforward neural networks, which are trained to predict joint configurations given a desired position of the end effector, can stem from them. Our method contributes to these approaches since deep learning models solving the inverse kinematics are often trained on synthetic data generated by robot simulation environments. Our method is general and does not depend on a particular type of robot. On the other hand, all the concrete values we employ in our examples are relevant to our humanoid robot NICO [15], developed at the University of Hamburg and slightly improved for our purposes.

2 Method

First, we implement forward kinematics for our robot, which enables us to calculate position and orientation from angles and gradients of angles from the gradients of position and orientation. Then, we incorporate this module into a network, in which training provides us with IK constrained by ranges of angles. Finally, we run this network in parallel for all trajectory points and regularize the poses based on their training so that they not only solve IK for individual trajectory points but also correspond to fluent overall movement.

2.1 Formal Definition of the Problem

Our method requires measuring the start and end poses of the robotic arm (given by joint angles), the shape of the trajectory, and the number of steps to control the motors. The start pose $\boldsymbol{p}^s = (\theta_1^s, \theta_2^s, \ldots, \theta_m^s)$ and the end pose $\boldsymbol{p}^e = (\theta_1^e, \theta_2^e, \ldots, \theta_m^e)$ are tuples of angles; in our particular case, we use $m = 7$ degrees of freedom. From these poses, we calculate the goal start point $\boldsymbol{P}^s = (x_s, y_s, z_s)$ and the goal end point $\boldsymbol{P}^e = (x_e, y_e, z_e)$ by FK described below. We translate the trajectory of the desired shape with these points and divide it into n segments. This division must be accurate enough to assume constant angular velocities for individual motors within one segment. However, the duration of these segments must correspond to our ability to poll the motors via the bus they are connected to. We have to choose n to balance the two requirements.

The division provides us with $n+1$ goal points $\boldsymbol{P}_i^g$, where $\boldsymbol{P}_0^g = \boldsymbol{P}^s$ and $\boldsymbol{P}_n^g = \boldsymbol{P}^e$. When the requested shape is a straight line, the goal points are

$$\boldsymbol{P}_i^g = (x_s + \frac{i}{n}(x_e - x_s), y_s + \frac{i}{n}(y_e - y_s), z_s + \frac{i}{n}(z_e - z_s)) \text{ for } i = 0, 1, \ldots, n \quad (1)$$

However, when the shape is different, we can implement any strategy for their generation, e.g. splines.

In addition, we can derive n goal vectors $\boldsymbol{v}_i^g$ from the $n+1$ goal points as $\boldsymbol{v}_i^g = \boldsymbol{P}_{i+1}^g - \boldsymbol{P}_i^g$ for $i = 0, 1, \ldots, n-1$. All vectors are identical when the trajectory shape is a line; in this case, $\boldsymbol{v}_i = (\boldsymbol{P}^e - \boldsymbol{P}^s)/n$. The method provides us with $n+1$ poses of the robot arm (joint angles) $\{(\theta_1^i, \theta_2^i, \ldots \theta_m^i) \mid i = 0, 1, \ldots, n\}$.

From them, we can easily calculate the corresponding angular velocities that move all the motors during the whole segment, taking T/n ms, where T is the selected duration of the whole movement in milliseconds.

2.2 Neural Network Architecture for Forward Kinematics

We build the FK module from four building blocks:

$$T(x,y,z) = \begin{bmatrix} 1 & 0 & 0 & t_x \\ 0 & 1 & 0 & t_y \\ 0 & 0 & 1 & t_z \\ 0 & 0 & 0 & 1 \end{bmatrix} \quad R_x(\theta) = \begin{bmatrix} 1 & 0 & 0 & 0 \\ 0 & \cos\theta & -\sin\theta & 0 \\ 0 & \sin\theta & \cos\theta & 0 \\ 0 & 0 & 0 & 1 \end{bmatrix}$$

$$R_y(\theta) = \begin{bmatrix} \cos\theta & 0 & -\sin\theta & 0 \\ 0 & 1 & 0 & 0 \\ \sin\theta & 0 & \cos\theta & 0 \\ 0 & 0 & 0 & 1 \end{bmatrix} \quad R_z(\theta) = \begin{bmatrix} \cos\theta & -\sin\theta & 0 & 0 \\ \sin\theta & \cos\theta & 0 & 0 \\ 0 & 0 & 1 & 0 \\ 0 & 0 & 0 & 1 \end{bmatrix}$$

where $T(x,y,z)$ is translation in 3D space, $R_x(\theta), R_y(\theta), R_z(\theta)$ are rotations given by θ around x, y, z axes, respectively.

We can express FK as a product $M_0 \times M_1 \times \ldots \times M_{k-1}$ of such matrices that correspond to our robot mechanics [16,17]. When we project the vector $(0,0,0,1)$ with these transforms, we gradually get points for individual joints in the form of $(x,y,z,1)$; the last of them being the point of the end effector:

$$(x, y, z, 1)^\top = M_{k-1} \times \ldots \times M_1 \times M_0 \times (0, 0, 0, 1)^\top \tag{2}$$

Similarly, when using 3×3 parts of the rotational matrices, we can project the vector $(0,0,1)$ to get joint orientations, including the roll, pitch, and yaw of the end effector.

$$(\text{roll}, \text{pitch}, \text{yaw})^\top = R_{l-1} \times \ldots \times R_1 \times R_0 \times (0, 0, 1)^\top \tag{3}$$

The forward kinematics of the right arm of NICO robot corresponds to

$$\text{FK}(\theta_1, \theta_2, \theta_3, \theta_4, \theta_5, \theta_6, \theta_7) \tag{4}$$
$$= T(0, 5, 19.5) \times R_z(90°) \times R_z(\theta_1) \tag{5}$$
$$\times T(0, -1.5, 2.5) \times R_y(90°) \times R_z(\theta_2) \tag{6}$$
$$\times T(3, 0, 9.5) \times R_x(-90°) \times R_z(-\theta_3) \tag{7}$$
$$\times T(17.5, 0, 0) \times R_x(90°) \times R_z(180°) \times R_z(-\theta_4) \tag{8}$$
$$\times T(10, 0, 0) \times R_y(90°) \times R_z(-\theta_5/2) \tag{9}$$
$$\times T(0, 0, 10) \times R_x(-90°) \times R_z(-90°) \times R_z(\theta_6/4.5 + 10) \tag{10}$$
$$\times T(0, -1, 0) \times T(6, 0, 0) \times R_z(20 + (\theta_7 + 180)/4.5) \tag{11}$$
$$\times T(6, 0, 0) \times R_y(90°) \tag{12}$$

The reference system has its origin $(0,0,0)$ at the base of the robot torso. The x-axis points behind the robot, the y-axis points laterally to its right, and the z-axis is parallel to gravity but pointing upward. Each line above moves the point to the next joint: the first line to *shoulder_z*, the second to *shoulder_y*, the third to *arm_x*, and the next ones to *elbow_y*, *wrist_z*, *wrist_x*, and the last one to *indexfinger_x*. (Angles for the wrist and fingers are measured only in degree-like units, so we must recalculate them to degrees.)

Unlike the traditional approach, we never evaluate the product of all matrices $M_{k-1} \times \ldots \times M_1 \times M_0$ (see Eq. 2). We always multiply the initial vector $(0,0,0,1)^\top$ by matrices one by one: $(M_{k-1} \times \ldots \times (M_1 \times (M_0 \times (0,0,0,1)^\top))\ldots)$. The most important deviation is that the input to this module is not the initial vector but the joint angles θ_j. We apply cosine and sine on them, update the matrices, and output the calculated position and orientation of the end effector. So, though the matrices linearly process vectors, this module is made to be a very nonlinear module of a neural network. Neither parameter of this module is trainable (although it could be within another project). However, we can run it not only in the forward mode that calculates point and orientation from angles but also in the backward mode that calculates angles' gradients upon the deviation of the point and orientation from their goal values. Also, it is essential to implement this module to receive not only a single input but also a batch, as is usual for neural networks.

2.3 Neural Network Architecture for Inverse Kinematics

With the module mentioned above, we can turn the IK problem (finding joint angles for a given 3D point and orientation) into training a neural network consisting of two parts: a generator of angles and the FK module. The generator provides proposals for angles, and the FK transforms them into the corresponding 3D point and orientation. Then, we aim to adjust the generator parameters to decrease the distance between the predicted values and the target.

Since we seek to train a neural network, we must formally define a dataset, while we know only one desired output (the given point and orientation). We can treat this requirement by assigning a formal input to the generator, always 1. We process it by a linear layer of m neurons, each having one weight and no bias, whose weights code the angles.

The primary design challenge for the generator is to operationalise the weights training while preserving the angle ranges. We need to ensure that the angles are within their range, can reach the extreme value, and break away from it as required during training. Clipping the angle values is not a solution due to zero gradients at the extremes. Therefore, first, we generate angles in the form of logits $z_j \in (-\infty, \infty)$, and then we apply a sigmoid and turn them to degrees, considering their range:

$$\theta_j = \theta_j^{\min} + \sigma(z_j)(\theta_j^{\max} - \theta_j^{\min}) \tag{13}$$

If we create a dataset with a single sample of input 1 and output x, y, z, roll, pitch, and yaw, we could train the model until the weights in the linear layer correspond to the proper logits that provide the desired output. Then, we can use the above formula to get the corresponding values in degrees that form the required pose of the robotic arm.

2.4 Neural Network Architecture for Trajectory Generation

If we use this kind of IK for all the goal points, the poses we get will implement a movement that is not fluent enough. We must solicit a global constraint to ensure the generated movement's fluency and make training of all poses in parallel. Nothing is easier within frameworks for training neural networks. We can express the fluency of the generated movement by minimizing angle differences through the generated poses. Implementing parallelization is also simple if the FK module already supports batches. We extend the number of inputs to the linear layer from one to $n+1$ and bypass the summation in its *neurons*, so its output has the shape $(n+1) \times m$. Then, we apply the same formula to keep angles in ranges to the tensor, which turns logits to angles in degrees p_i. In addition, we feed them as a batch into the FK module and get $(n+1)$ points P_i. Finally, we apply a suitable loss function compounded from individual IK problems for each point and the global constraint for the fluency of the trajectory (Fig. 1).

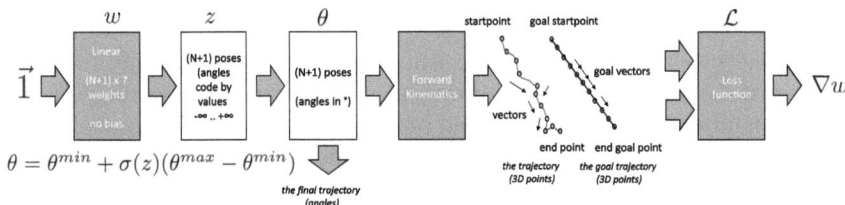

Fig. 1. Schema of the neural network whose training leads to the generation of the robotic arm trajectory

Moreover, we prefer to match the start and end poses as precisely as possible. It is a good practice because these are the only two poses that we specified but also because the purpose of the trajectories can require their exact matching.

As a result, our loss function will combine the following:

- the mean distance between output points $\boldsymbol{P}_i$ and goal points $\boldsymbol{P}_i^g$:
$$\mathcal{L}_0 = \frac{1}{3n+3} \sum_{i=0}^{n} \|\boldsymbol{P}_i - \boldsymbol{P}_i^g\|^2$$
- negative mean of cosines of angles between output orientation vectors $\boldsymbol{v}_i$ and goal vectors $\boldsymbol{v}_i^g$ (in our particular case of the linear shape $\boldsymbol{v}_i^g = (\boldsymbol{P}^e - \boldsymbol{P}^s)/n$):
$$\mathcal{L}_1 = 1 - \frac{1}{n+1} \sum_{i=0}^{n} \frac{\boldsymbol{v}_i^T \boldsymbol{v}_i^g}{\|\boldsymbol{v}_i\| \|\boldsymbol{v}_i^g\|}$$
- distance between the start pose $\boldsymbol{p}^s$ and its prediction $\boldsymbol{p}_0$:
$$\mathcal{L}_2 = \|\boldsymbol{p}^s - \boldsymbol{p}_0\|^2$$

- distance between the end pose p^e and its prediction p_n:
  $\mathcal{L}_3 = \|p^e - p_n\|^2$
- distance between the start point P^s and its prediction P_0:
  $\mathcal{L}_4 = \|P^s - P_0\|^2$
- distance between the end point P^e and its prediction P_n:
  $\mathcal{L}_5 = \|P^e - P_n\|^2$
- mean distance between the consecutive poses
  $\mathcal{L}_6 = \frac{1}{nm} \sum_{i=0}^{n-1} \|p_{i+1} - p_i\|^2$

The overall loss is a weighted sum of these seven losses

$$\mathcal{L} = c_0\mathcal{L}_0 + c_1\mathcal{L}_1 + c_2\mathcal{L}_2 + c_3\mathcal{L}_3 + c_4\mathcal{L}_4 + c_5\mathcal{L}_5 + c_6\mathcal{L}_6 \tag{14}$$

Since we require very exact start and end poses, we put significant weights on the corresponding components of the loss function. Further, we equally weigh the influence of the position and orientation of the end effector. Finally, we assign a low but stable bias to the last component of the loss function that makes changes in angles as regular as possible. Based on experimentation, we have used weights: $c_0 = 1$, $c_1 = 50$, $c_2 = 5$, $c_3 = 100$, $c_4 = 10$, $c_5 = 200$, $c_6 = 1$.

Generating the whole trajectory with one training process requires slightly modifying the dataset for the single IK problem. The dataset again contains a single sample. Its input is a vector of $n + 1$ ones, and the desired output is the vector of the $n + 1$ goal points and orientations. We use Adam optimizer with learning rate 0.1. The initial setup of weights representing logits of angles follows analogical mixtures of the start and end poses as we mix the goal points from the start and endpoint. This training gradually achieves the required shape of the trajectory and improves its fluency. The training transforms an initial trajectory designed in the joint space of the robot to the trajectory of the required shape in the Cartesian space. Therefore, this method retrieves the 3D coordinates that the robot's end effector should assume to follow the required trajectory. We can stop training when the angles do not change enough. We can also stop when the generated trajectory has a sufficient shape. The duration of training varies from seconds to minutes; it depends mainly on the end point and the availability of the sought trajectory.

3 Results

Our method of generating a trajectory for a robotic arm was evaluated to ensure the accuracy of the trajectories and to guarantee the required shape. In the NICO robot we use its seven degrees of freedom: three in the shoulder, one in the elbow, two in the wrist, and one for the forefinger. We divided the trajectory into $n = 50$ segments. As mentioned above, this number is a trade-off between considering the angular velocities constant within one segment (the larger n, the better) and polling motors (the lower n, the better) via the bus to which they are connected. In the case of our application, we connected the motors of the NICO robot via RS485, and it was not easy to balance the two requirements. We had to bypass the more sophisticated Pypot control interface and turn off command confirmation on the motors via the low-level Dynamixel SDK protocol. Only in this way did we achieve $n = 50$, corresponding to 40 ms per segment, polling per 2–4 ms, considering the total requested duration of the movement $T = 2s$. We described FK by the product of 24 translational or rotational matrices depending on the seven angle values (degrees of freedom) (Eq. 4–12).

Following the objectives of the experiment [18], we generated seven trajectories to touch seven selected points on the touchscreen. They started from the same position with the raised arm and provided pointing by the forefinger to the point of touch throughout the movement, except in the starting phase. We recorded the start pose and seven touching poses. The NICO robot enables switching torque off and on and reading the current angles anytime, so managing this is quite comfortable. Training generated the trajectories successfully, as shown in Fig. 2. The number of iterations is provided in Table 1.

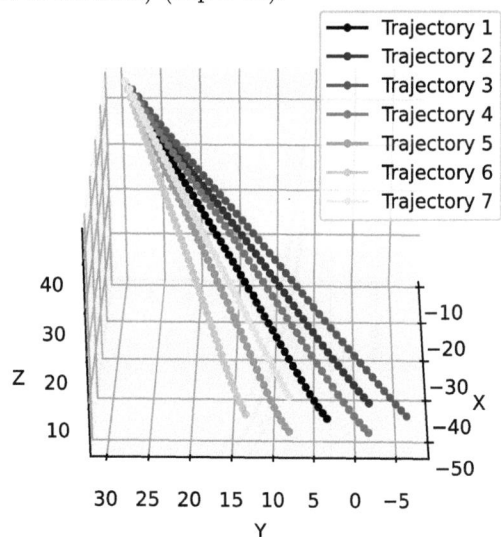

Fig. 2. The generated trajectories (front view). Each trajectory starts at the same start and ends at a different endpoint in the x-y plane. We can see that the trajectories have the required line shape

Since the NICO robot has only one degree of freedom at the elbow, it isn't easy to reach some spots with its arm, namely spots close to the robot. It may be the reason why closer points require a much higher number of iterations.

Table 1. Duration and accuracy of trajectories generation (our method)

Trajectory ID	Iterations	Duration on CPU	Loss	Distance from the line [mm]	Pointing deviation [°]
1	651	9 s	8.83	0.31 ± 0.18	12 ± 11.8
2	2374	29 s	9.82	0.26 ± 0.13	12 ± 12.0
3	374	5 s	7.51	0.28 ± 0.13	11 ± 10.5
4	1153	15 s	9.98	0.38 ± 0.22	11 ± 10.2
5	2224	27 s	9.98	0.40 ± 0.25	12 ± 11.3
6	369	5 s	8.58	0.36 ± 0.26	13 ± 13.1
7	12394	151 s	9.96	0.23 ± 0.23	14 ± 12.1

Evaluation of the quality of the generated trajectories employed the following criteria:

1. The distance of the end effector point from the line and the pointing deviation (the last two columns in Table 1).
2. The distance between the touching point on the surface and the intersection of the linear fit from the end effector to the surface. For each percentage of the trajectory, this distance was computed and evaluated (see Fig. 3).

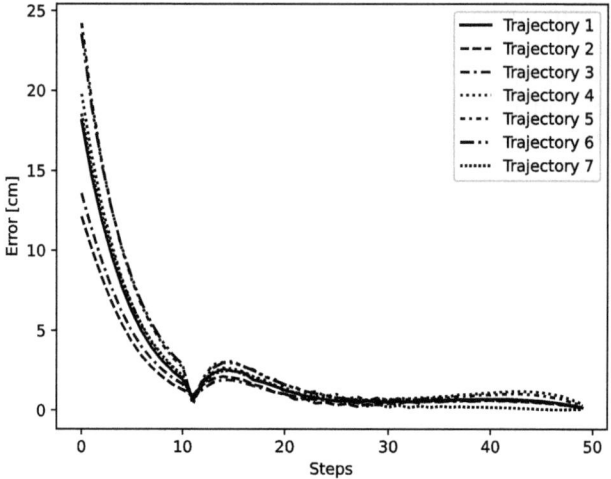

Fig. 3. The pointing error in cm for all trajectories (split into 50 steps). The closer the end effector is to the touching point, the more accurate the pointing is. From the beginning, it takes some time to point with the forefinger, and the fitting (from the last ten values) is less reliable for the first steps. The error has the character of damped oscillations, from which we see the absolute value

While criterion 1. focuses on the trajectory shape, criterion 2. is more specific for our application related to the pointing action. The teaser video is available at https://youtu.be/UIqqin3cJfs.

Examining the impact of the individual parts of our loss function, we have performed the ablation study. Namely, avoiding losses $\mathcal{L}_0$ or $\mathcal{L}_6$ has a devastating effect on the whole movement, while the ablation of loss $\mathcal{L}_1$ moderately affects the pointing behavior. Ablation of $\mathcal{L}_0$ causes the generated trajectory to resemble the linear movement in the angle space; $\mathcal{L}_7$ causes the robot arm to shake. The losses $\mathcal{L}_2$, $\mathcal{L}_3$, $\mathcal{L}_4$, and $\mathcal{L}_5$ are specific to our application, and we could avoid them for applications where exact start and end poses are not crucial.

When we compare our method with traditional inverse kinematics, it is clear that we benefit from the ability to apply more local and global constraints to the trajectory. We have implemented a similar generation based on conventional inverse kinematics. We have selected the touching pose (more important than the start pose) as the initial pose, and we gradually called inverse kinematics for points on the line. We have specified not only the end-effector point, but also its orientation to be the same as the orientation of the line. In this case, trajectory generation is much faster; however, the accuracy of the pointing vector is much worse, and the start pose significantly varies (while it is constant by our method); see Table 2. The fluency of the movement is comparable. As a result, the traditionally generated trajectory is less legible. The teaser video is available at https://youtu.be/PnguzMA5pDo.

Table 2. Accuracy of trajectories generation (the traditional method)

Trajectory ID	Distance from the line [mm]	Pointing deviation [°]	Start point variation [mm]
1	2.84 ± 1.73	65 ± 27.0	5.6
2	3.38 ± 2.09	70 ± 27.4	5.9
3	1.39 ± 0.54	63 ± 33.2	6.9
4	3.02 ± 1.87	59 ± 26.9	5.6
5	2.91 ± 1.66	63 ± 26.6	5.4
6	2.00 ± 1.08	63 ± 30.2	5.5
7	1.52 ± 0.59	70 ± 33.6	6.5

To support the generality of our method, we have also applied it to another task requiring precise control of the robotic arm movement. We have implemented drawing letters in the air. We selected roughly a noncolliding position of the robot arm and projected the shape of a letter to the frontal plane passing through the end of the robot's forefinger. And train our neural network to get the trajectory. After 2000 iterations, we have come to a perfect solution. In this case, we can avoid losses for start and end positions since they are not crucial for this application, and all goal vectors will correspond to the normal vector of the drawing plane. The teaser video is available at https://youtu.be/PsnmP7Kvx8g.

4 Conclusion

This work introduced a novel, data-efficient method for generating robot arm trajectories constrained by desired start and end poses and a specified spatial path. Our approach is based on modern deep learning frameworks, leveraging a differentiable forward kinematics module integrated into a trainable neural network. This setup enables simultaneous inverse kinematics computation across the entire trajectory while maintaining motion fluency and respecting joint range constraints. Crucially, unlike typical learning-based approaches to IK, our method does not require pre-existing datasets. Instead, it could generate such data for a given set of trajectory shapes.

We demonstrated the utility of our method in a cognitive robotics experiment requiring human-interpretable robotic motion. Using the NICO humanoid robot, we successfully generated precise and smooth pointing trajectories, ensuring consistent start poses and exact endpoint accuracy, providing a new, efficient method of trajectory generation to customize and generate precise movements for the robot's arm. The results confirmed both the practicality and generality of our approach, with trajectory generation converging within a reasonable time and the resulting motions fulfilling the task-specific requirements.

Our method presents an accessible and flexible alternative for trajectory generation in robotics. Its independence from large datasets, ability to enforce movement fluency, and ease of integration into standard neural network workflows make it a compelling tool for various applications, from human–robot interaction studies to general-purpose robotic control. Future work will include speeding up the method for real-time applications and integrating it with vision and reasoning models.

Acknowledgments. This work was supported by Horizon Europe project TERAIS, no. 101079338. A.L. and I.F. were also supported by the Slovak Grant Agency for Science, project VEGA 1/0373/23.

References

1. Mazzola, C., Ali, H., Malinovská, K., Farkaš, I.: An interaction-centered approach to robot trustworthiness: building justified trust via mutual understanding (2025, Under review)
2. Dragan, A.D., Lee, K.C., Srinivasa, S.S.: Legibility and predictability of robot motion. In: ACM/IEEE International Conference on Human-Robot Interaction, pp. 301–308 (2013). https://doi.org/10.1109/HRI.2013.6483603
3. Sciutti, A., Sandini, G.: Interacting with robots to investigate the bases of social interaction. IEEE Trans. Neural Syst. Rehabil. Eng. **25**(12), 2295–2304 (2017). https://doi.org/10.1109/TNSRE.2017.2766063
4. Mazzola, C., Rea, F., Sciutti, A.: Shared perception is different from individual perception: a new look on context dependency. IEEE Trans. Cogn. Develop. Syst. **15**(3), 1020–1032 (2022). https://doi.org/10.1109/TCDS.2022.3185403
5. Antonj, M., Zonca, J., Rea, F., Sciutti, A.: A controllable and repeatable method to study perceptual and motor adaptation in human-robot interaction. In: ACM/IEEE International Conference on Human-Robot Interaction, pp. 188–192 (2023). https://doi.org/10.1145/3568294.3580069
6. Miller, D.P., Nourbakhsh, I.: Robotics for education. In: Siciliano, B., Khatib, O. (eds.) Springer Handbook of Robotics, 2nd edn., pp. 2115–2134. Springer, Cham (2016). https://doi.org/10.1007/978-3-319-32552-1_79
7. Denavit, J., Hartenberg, R.S.: A kinematic notation for lower-pair mechanisms based on matrices. ASME J. Appl. Mech. **22**, 215–221 (1955)
8. Spong, M.W., Hutchinson, S., Vidyasagar, M.: Robot Modeling and Control. Wiley (2006)
9. Haddadin, S., Croft, E.: Erratum to: physical human–robot interaction. In: Siciliano, B., Khatib, O. (eds.) Springer Handbook of Robotics, pp. E1–E1. Springer, Cham (2016). https://doi.org/10.1007/978-3-319-32552-1_81

10. Aristidou, A., Lasenby, J.: FABRIK: a fast, iterative solver for the inverse kinematics problem. Graph. Models **73**(5), 243–260 (2011). https://doi.org/10.1016/j.gmod.2011.05.003
11. Tenneti, R.A., Sarkar, A.: Implementation of modified FABRIK for robot manipulators. In: Proceedings of the Advances in Robotics, pp. 1–6. ACM (2019). https://doi.org/10.1145/3352593.3352605
12. Bongard, J., Kormushev, P.: Learning inverse kinematics with a deep neural network. In: IEEE International Conference on Robotics and Automation, pp. 1094–1101 (2018). https://doi.org/10.1109/ICRA.2018.8462560
13. Rad, S., Dorrity, M.: Solving inverse kinematics with deep neural networks. Robot. Auton. Syst. **138**, 103713 (2021). https://doi.org/10.1016/j.robot.2020.103713
14. Habekost, J.G., Gäde, C., Allgeuer, P., Wermter, S.: Inverse kinematics for neurorobotic grasping with humanoid embodied agents (2024). arXiv. https://doi.org/10.48550/arXiv.2404.08825
15. Kerzel, M., Strahl, E., Magg, S., Navarro-Guerrero, N., Heinrich, S., Wermter, S.: NICO – neuro-inspired companion: a developmental humanoid robot platform for multimodal interaction. In: Proceedings of the IEEE International Symposium on Robot and Human Interactive Communication (RO-MAN), pp. 113–120 (2017). https://doi.org/10.1109/ROMAN.2017.8172289
16. Craig, J.J.: Introduction to Robotics: Mechanics and Control, 3rd ed. Pearson (2004)
17. Parmiggiani, A., et al.: The design of the iCub humanoid robot. Int. J. Hum. Robot. **9**(4) (2012). https://doi.org/10.1142/S0219843612500272
18. Farkaš, I., Lúčny, A., Vavrečka, M.: Approaches to generating arm movements in humanoid robot NICO. In: Cognition and Artificial Life, pp. 57–58 (2024)

Robotic Calibration Based on Haptic Feedback Improves Sim-to-Real Transfer

Juraj Gavura[1], Michal Vavrečka[1], Igor Farkaš[1]^(✉), and Connor Gäde[2]

[1] Department of Applied Informatics, Comenius University Bratislava, Bratislava, Slovakia
gavura4@uniba.sk, michal.vavrecka@cvut.cz, farkas@fmph.uniba.sk
[2] Department of Informatics, University of Hamburg, Hamburg, Germany
connor.gaede@uni-hamburg.de

Abstract. When inverse kinematics (IK) is adopted to control robotic arms in manipulation tasks, there is often a discrepancy between the end effector (EE) position of the robot model in the simulator and the physical EE in reality. In most robotic scenarios with sim-to-real transfer, we have information about joint positions in both simulation and reality, but the EE position is only available in simulation. We developed a novel method to overcome this difficulty based on haptic feedback calibration, using a touchscreen in front of the robot that provides information on the EE position in the real environment. During the calibration procedure, the robot touches specific points on the screen, and the information is stored. In the next stage, we build a transformation function from the data based on linear transformation and neural networks that is capable of outputting all missing variables from any partial input (simulated/real joint/EE position). Our results demonstrate that a fully nonlinear neural network model performs best, significantly reducing positioning errors.

Keywords: Calibration · Humanoid robot · Inverse kinematics · Haptic feedback

1 Introduction

Recent advances in robotics have significantly improved the capabilities of industrial and humanoid robots, enabling them to perform complex manipulation and interaction tasks with increasing autonomy and dexterity. Modern robotic systems integrate advanced perception techniques, such as deep learning-based vision [9], tactile sensing [6], and proprioception [4], allowing for more adaptive and precise control. However, to fully utilize their capabilities, robots must precisely control their actuators within their workspace to ensure accurate positioning of the end effector (EE). Small errors in joint actuation can lead to significant deviations in the EE position, affecting performance in tasks such as grasping objects or using tools. This need for precision highlights the importance of robust calibration and compensation techniques.

A significant challenge in robotic manipulation arises when using inverse kinematics (IK) solvers, as the model used in the simulator often fails to precisely match the real-world structure of the robot. In particular, the predicted position of the EE in the simulator may not align with its actual position in the real environment. This discrepancy is typically caused by inaccuracies in the robot's model, such as imperfections in the actuators, sensors, or the simulated physical properties that do not account for real-world dynamics. As a result, even when the IK solver calculates the correct joint angles for a desired EE position, the actual EE may not reach the target location. To address this issue, several compensation techniques have been proposed, including model calibration, sensor fusion, and machine learning-based methods.

In this paper, we propose a novel method to address the discrepancy between simulated and real-world EE positions in robotic systems. Our approach is based on a calibration procedure in which the robot touches specific points on a touchscreen, allowing us to gather data that map the simulated coordinates to real-world coordinates. Using this technique, a transformation function is calculated to bridge the gap between the two coordinate systems. Compared to other techniques, our method offers a low-cost, highly precise solution that does not require specialized hardware. This makes it adaptable to other robotic systems.

2 Related Work

Several studies have explored approaches to mitigate the sim-to-real gap in robotics, highlighting the effectiveness of integrating simulated data with additional sensory feedback to reduce discrepancies between model predictions and real-world outcomes [1]. Methods for compensating EE errors can be categorized based on how the real EE is measured, ranging from the absence of direct measurements to the use of motion capture, cameras, haptic feedback, or sensor fusion, and the type of compensation algorithm employed, such as conventional analytical methods or neural networks. Previous work combines these strategies to enhance accuracy. In [10], a two-stage framework was introduced that integrates an enhanced Newton-Raphson method with a ResNet model to refine the mapping of simulated joint angles to real-world EE positions. In [13], an online kinematic adaptation method for humanoid robot arms was proposed, utilizing both visual and proprioceptive sensors. The approach employs stereovision-based hand pose estimation, followed by a particle-based optimization to correct kinematic calibration errors. In addition, Bayesian methods have been applied for hand-eye kinematics calibration in humanoid robots, optimizing Denavit-Hartenberg parameters and joint gear reductions to improve accuracy [5].

Deep neural networks have been used to facilitate sim-to-real transfer by estimating arm joint configurations from stereo images, allowing precise reach without manual fine-tuning [12]. This approach was tested in the iCub robot, where a visuomotor predictor provided accurate joint estimates to quantify systematic errors in the robot joint measurements. In the subsequent stage, an automatic calibrator was implemented to compensate for these errors, with the potential to integrate both predictor and calibrator into a unified system. More recently, Gde et al. [3] proposed an end-to-end visuomotor architecture that incorporates domain adaptation and inherent IK. By embedding domain adaptation within their model, they enabled continuous calibration, which was validated through sim-to-real grasping experiments with the NICO humanoid robot. Their approach significantly improved accuracy, achieving an 80.30 % success rate.

If visual feedback lacks sufficient precision, a secondary robot or motion tracking system can be used to provide ground truth data for the EE position. An industrial Kuka manipulator was employed to calibrate the leg joints of the AR601M humanoid robot [8]. Using the precise EE positioning of the Kuka arm, they achieved a highly accurate joint offset calibration for humanoid robots. When ground truth data on EE position is available, calibration can also be extended to robots with elastic components and joints. Advanced kinematic models were introduced to account for joint and transverse elasticities, reducing absolute position errors in humanoid upper bodies from 21 to 3 mm [16].

If a robot is equipped with artificial skin, calibration can be performed using tactile feedback. Inspired by infant behavior, self-touch calibration has been implemented in humanoid robots, leveraging tactile arrays to refine kinematic representations without requiring external measurement systems [14]. Self-calibration approaches utilizing multiple kinematic chains have demonstrated superior performance in optimizing robot parameters [18]. The authors used a simulated humanoid robot iCub with a stereo camera system and EE contact emulation to perform self-touch-based calibration, achieving an EE accuracy of 2 mm after 100 calibration poses. More recently, a multisensory calibration framework was developed, combining conventional techniques with self-contained calibration strategies tailored for humanoid robots, facilitated by an open source toolbox for implementation and evaluation [15].

We can summarize that recent visuomotor coordination-based calibration methods often suffer from imprecision due to limitations in visual perception, such as occlusions, lighting conditions, and camera calibration errors. However, methods that rely on external calibration tools, such as motion capture systems or high-precision external sensors, are costly and require additional hardware, making them impractical for many applications. Another approach, self-touch calibration, provides direct feedback by using the robots own EE to interact with its body; however, this method requires robotic skin or tactile sensors, which can be expensive and not available on all robots.

To address these limitations, we propose a novel method that utilizes tactile feedback from a touchscreen as a calibration tool. This approach is more precise than vision-based methods, as it provides direct contact information without relying on external cameras. Additionally, it is significantly cheaper than motion capture systems and does not require robotic skin, making it a cost-effective and widely applicable solution for various robotic platforms.

3 Materials and Methods

Our aim was to ensure that when the robot was directed to a specific target point in Cartesian space, its EE would accurately reach the designated location with minimal deviation. To achieve this, we established relationships between the real world, with the robot and the touchscreen, and a simulated world.[1] Creating a perfect match between the Cartesian positions in the two worlds remains a challenge. The overall scheme is shown in Fig. 1.

Both domains use two coordinate systems: joint space and Cartesian space. In real space, we denote the joint angles by J_R, and in simulation J_S. There, we use (x, y, z) coordinates denoted as C_S, which are known at each step. In the real world, the touchscreen provides only 2D feedback, which means that we only have access to (x, y) coordinates denoted as C_R. Given that the touchscreen lies in a fixed plane, we can assume that the z-coordinate in reality is always 0 on the touchscreen.

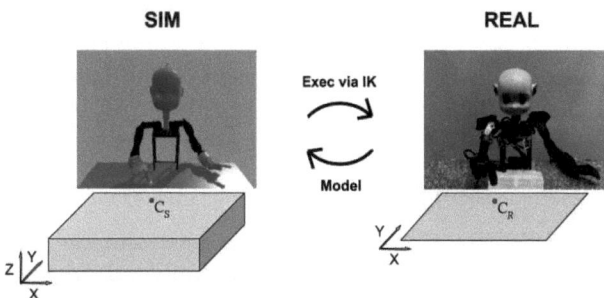

Fig. 1. Calibration schema of the sim-to-real transfer based on haptic feedback. For any target point on the touchscreen, a model is used to calculate the corresponding 3D position in the simulator. It is used by the IK module to enable the required move

3.1 Robot and Touchscreen

We conducted all experiments using the humanoid robot NICO, designed for multimodal interaction [11]. We used the robot's right arm equipped with 6 motors to control joints and a four-finger child hand with 4 motors. We controlled 7 DoF during the experiment, as touching requires only the index finger. We used a 1920×1080 px touchscreen fixed in front of the robot as a tactile feedback interface for the calibration procedure. To enable interaction with the screen, the robot's index finger was wrapped in a tactile conductive material, allowing it to make contact and receive feedback on its actual position. The screen with

---

[1] This approach may seem contradictory for sim-to-real transfer assuming we start with perfect simulation, which is then transferred to real world. But actually, we need perfect behavior in *real* world, so we calibrate the simulation to enable that.

54×33 cm covers approx. 60% of the robot's working area on the table. It is fixed at the height of the table, ensuring a stable reference frame and allowing a precise mapping of each pixel to a corresponding position C_R. Before working with NICO, we assessed the physical limitations of its arm and identified a specific screen region that NICO's right hand could reliably reach. Afterwards, the robot was ready for movement and calibration.

3.2 NicoIK

The first part of our calibration is the publicly available software NicoIK[2] that can be adapted with modifications for other robots. The software consists of several components. The simulation module is built on the PyBullet physics engine [2] and uses its IK solver and some functions from myGym [17]. It can calculate IK for any robot with a proper body model. We fine-tuned the NICO URDF file to better match the actual hardware, ensuring precise alignment between the simulated and real robot, which helps reduce final calibration errors. The robot control module is based on the NicoMotion library, which is part of [7] and can be exchanged with other control libraries to adopt a different robot. The NicoIK orchestrates these components and records calibration data. The results were then used as input for the error correction algorithms (see below).

3.3 Sim-to-Real Alignment

The first step of our calibration process was to determine the exact position of the touchscreen within the simulation, ensuring proper alignment of the virtual environment. To achieve this, we manually guided the robot's end-effector to three reachable edge points of the touchscreen in the real world and recorded the corresponding joint angle values of the robot's arm. Using forward kinematics, we then mapped these recorded joint angles to their respective positions in the simulated environment, allowing us to accurately establish the touchscreen's placement in the simulation.

However, three reference points differed not only in their x and y-coordinates, but also in the z coordinate (height), resulting in a slightly tilted touchscreen in the simulation. By applying linear interpolation between these points, we could determine any position on the simulated screen. To test the initial transition from simulation to reality, we generated multiple points on the simulated screen, computed the corresponding joint angles using IK, and executed these movements on the real robot. To assess accuracy, we relied on the touchscreen as the only ground truth by having the robot physically touch it. However, this approach did not guarantee precise alignment, revealing nonlinear discrepancies in the z-coordinate between the touchscreen positions in simulation and real world.

The simplest approach to address this nonlinearity issue was to empirically determine the z-coordinate for a set of regularly spaced points across the utilized portion of the touchscreen and then apply linear interpolation using four nearest

---
[2] https://github.com/Robotics-DAI-FMFI-UK/NicoIK

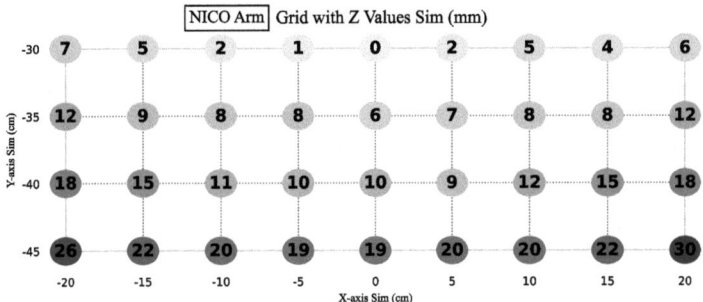

Fig. 2. Visualisation of manually measured z values (height) of touchscreen in grid-based points in simulation. Real NICO will touch the screen at point (x, y) from the grid if we set the goal z based on the corresponding z value in this grid. We can see that the differences are roughly symmetrical with respect to x axis

points (on the grid). To achieve this, we generated a grid of 36 points on the simulated screen. The EE of the robotic arm was then guided to each of these points, gradually decreasing the z-coordinate until the robot's fingertip reached contact with the real touchscreen. At the moment of contact, we record the corresponding z-coordinate. This process provided us with the measured heights of 36 uniformly distributed points on the touchscreen (see Fig. 2). With this dataset, we could now estimate the height of any point in the simulation by linearly interpolating between its nearest measured grid points.

3.4 Calibration Models

Piecewise Linear Model (M1). M1 takes a point C_R as input, linearly interpolates its coordinates in simulation using the edge points gathered when locating the touchscreen, and then interpolates the z-coordinate using the measured heights in the grid. This yields C_S, linearly mapping the real data to the simulation. This model served as a baseline for testing more advanced models. For sim-to-real transfer, we used IK to compute J_S corresponding to C_S. Once the real robot executed the movements, we recorded the EE touch positions on the real screen (C_R) and corresponding J_R after each motion. Based on previous experience, we tested three movement durations: one, two, and three seconds. For each duration, we collected data from 250 points, randomly distributed, or in specific patterns, and compared them to the simulated values. To achieve the most natural movement, we prioritized motions with a 2-sec duration.

Partially-Nonlinear Neural Network Model (M2). Data gathered using M1 was used to develop two more complex nonlinear models. Specifically, the data provided insight into where a real EE would move when given a corresponding point in the simulator. This relationship can also be viewed in reverse: To guide the robot's index finger to a specific point C_R, we must supply the appropriate point C_S. As a result, for 250 real-world points $C_R(x, y, 0)$, we identified 250 corresponding points in the simulation $C_S(x, y, z)$. Since the mapping between these points is nonlinear, we required adequate methods to enhance accuracy. We trained a partially nonlinear model M2, based on a multilayer perceptron with 16 hidden neurons and the ReLU activation function, which takes $C_R(x, y)$ as input and outputs the corresponding $C_S(x, y)$. The z-coordinate is estimated using the same linear interpolation method as in M1. The M2 was trained for 200 epochs with the Adam algorithm using the learning rate of 0.001, $\beta_1 = 0.9, \beta_2 = 0.999, \epsilon = 10^{-7}$.

Nonlinear Neural Network Model (M3). M3 was chosen to be a fully nonlinear approach that, unlike previous models, approximates a 3D point $C_S(x, y, z)$ from a 2D real point $C_R(x, y)$, hence eliminating the need for linear interpolation. M3 also has one hidden layer with ReLU, but with 64 neurons. Both neural networks were trained using the Adam optimizer minimizing the MSE with all data derived from the baseline M1 model. Then we tested both models M2 and M3, applying the same procedure as M1 but only on 250 randomly distributed points, and compared the results against the simulated values. The hyperparameters of M3 were the same as in M2.

3.5 Calibration Procedure

In summary, our calibration procedure includes 6 steps to obtain a model that minimizes the error in the sim-to-real transfer.

1. Find the operational space of the robot and align it with the haptic space of the touchscreen.
2. Locate the touchscreen in the simulated space.
3. Generate interpolated grid-based targets that lie on the simulated touchscreen and measure the value z for each of these points.
4. Create a data set of 2D interpolated targets covering the entire touchscreen and interpolate the z value for each target using the data from step 3.
5. Navigate a real robot to these targets using inverse kinematics and save the resulting positions of the hits.
6. Use data collected in the previous step to train the neural network that predicts the simulated position $C_S(x, y, z)$ for any real point $C_R(x, y)$.

4 Results

4.1 Model M1 Baseline

The model M1 serves as the baseline for our research. We applied M1 with a 1-sec. movement to grid-based points, and plotted the contact points on the screen relative to the intended targets. The results in the upper half of Fig. 3 reveal that the direction of each deviation rotates depending on the target position

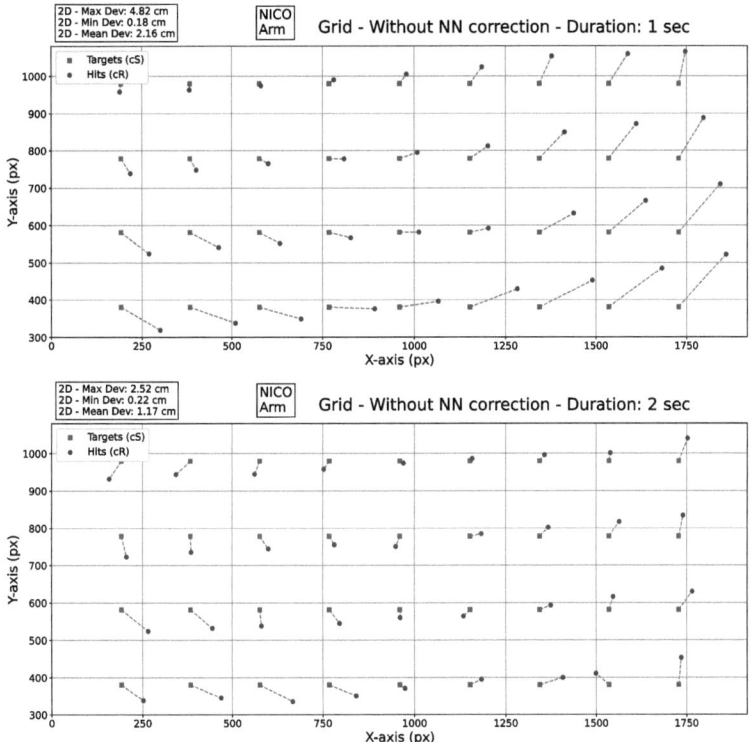

Fig. 3. Plot of deviations of hits (blue) from grid-based targets (red) in the physical space (on the touchscreen). We used the model M1 and NICO arm movement of 1-sec (top) and 2-sec (bottom) duration. The box "NICO Arm" denotes the base position (Color figure online)

relative to the arm base. In addition, the magnitude of the deviation increases considerably with the target distance from the base (i.e. for more stretched arm).

A similar relationship can be observed in lower half of Fig. 3, showing 2-sec movements. By comparison, we see that the average deviation decreased from 2.16 cm (for 1-sec) to 1.17 cm (for 2-sec), demonstrating that slower movements of NICO produce smaller errors. Further, we can see that the rotation trend is not as visible here at a 1-sec duration. Despite the slower and more precise movements, the direction of deviation from the target is less regular. 3-sec movements had very similar results to 2-sec movements.

Next, we measured 2D deviations from the target on the touchscreen at three different movement durations for each quadrant, as shown in Fig. 4. We can see that 1-sec movements are on average twice as inaccurate as slower movements, which may be due to overshooting the target. Movements of 2 and 3 s reveal similar behavior. We can also see that targets in Q1 and Q2, being closer to the robot base, yield a smaller error compared to more distant Q3 and Q4.

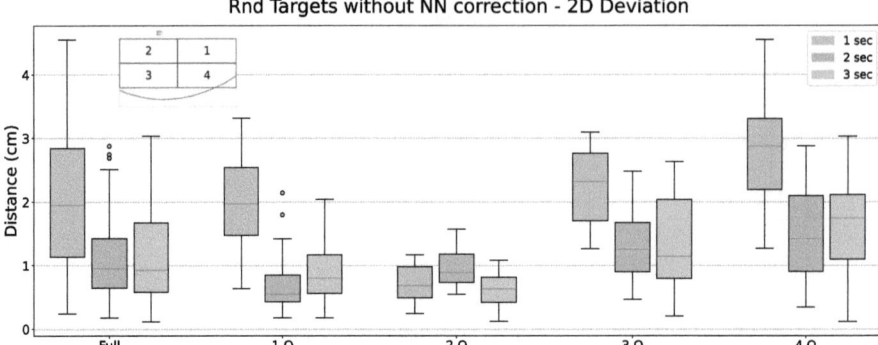

Fig. 4. Comparison of 2D deviations of hits from random targets within four quadrants for three durations of movement. Targets were calculated using M1. Small inset image top left shows the NICO reach limit (red line) and partitioning of the testing area. (Color figure online)

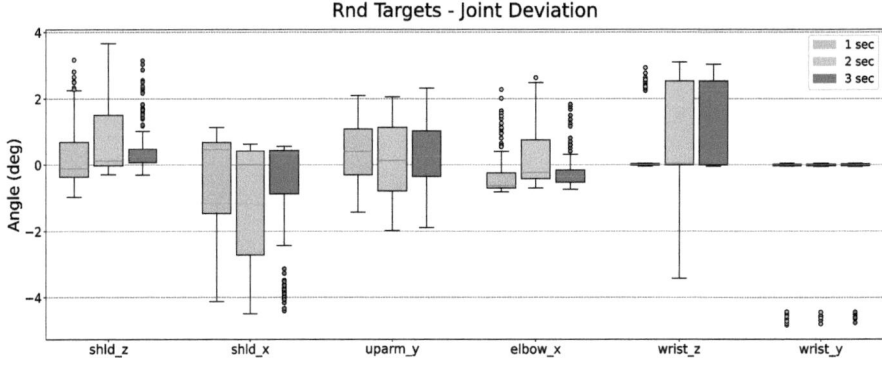

Fig. 5. Comparison of joint angle deviations for three different durations of movement. Joint deviation is calculated as a difference of joint angles returned from inverse kinematics (angles sent to robot) and joint angles read from the robot after the end of movement (using M1).

Figure 5 shows how the joint values of the robotic arm vary from the target positions after execution of the movement and compares similarly three different movement durations. The differences between the movement durations are not large. The deviation of the joint wrist_z, which moves the robot's palm, changes the most as the duration of the movement increases. For 3-sec movements, the median of the measured deviations for this joint reaches more than 2°C. In general, the largest deviations are for the joints shld_z and shld_x, which control the shoulder and move and rotate with the whole arm. This is probably due to the fact that the greatest force is applied to these joints.

4.2 Nonlinear Models

We implemented nonlinear models (M2 and M3) based on neural networks to solve the sim-to-real transfer and compared them with a linear baseline M1. The neural networks were tested by cross-validation five times, and achieved high accuracy with MSE < 0.001. With the data obtained from M2 and M3, we compared their performance against M1. As shown in Fig. 6, both nonlinear models significantly improve accuracy compared to M1, with M3 performing the best. This indicates that predicting x, y, and z simultaneously produces better results than first determining x, y and then interpolating z linearly. It suggests that z depends not only on x and y, but also vice versa. M3 achieves a median error less than half that of the linear model, which highlights its effectiveness.

Table 1. Accuracy of NICO robot 2-sec movement in 4 quadrants using our three models. Each cell contains the mean error and the standard deviation in centimeters

Model	Q1	Q2	Q3	Q4	Mean
M1	0.78 ± 0.45	1.00 ± 0.27	1.46 ± 0.53	1.34 ± 0.66	1.15 ± 0.58
M2	0.76 ± 0.45	1.18 ± 0.88	0.62 ± 0.29	0.80 ± 0.39	0.88 ± 0.65
M3	**0.56 ± 0.42**	**0.61 ± 0.53**	**0.46 ± 0.29**	**0.70 ± 0.53**	**0.58 ± 0.46**

However, we also observe that M2 and M3 produce more outliers than M1. In some cases, the error of M2 exceeds even the largest error of M1. This is likely due to the differing target distributions between the linear and nonlinear models. The neural networks in M2 and M3 were trained on data from M1, which did not include edge points. However, the target points for M2 and M3 do include edge cases, which requires extrapolation beyond the training data, resulting in larger errors.

We identified the quadrants where our nonlinear model produces the highest errors, but we were also interested in pinpointing the exact locations of the outliers seen in Fig. 6. For this, we visualized the accuracy of the model in the entire touchscreen testing area (Fig. 7). The visualization confirms that the largest errors occur in Q4, where the EE requires the longest trajectory. Furthermore, smaller regions in Q2 also exhibit high errors, particularly at extreme points that require extrapolation. In contrast, Q3 consistently shows the best results.

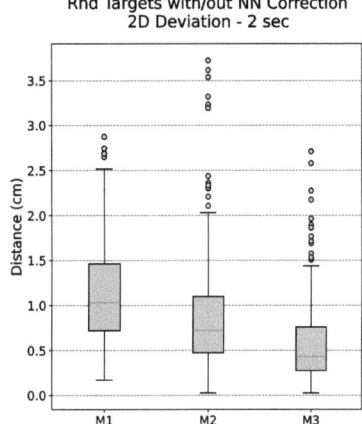

Fig. 6. Comparison of 2D deviations (Euclidean distances) of individual model predictions for random targets

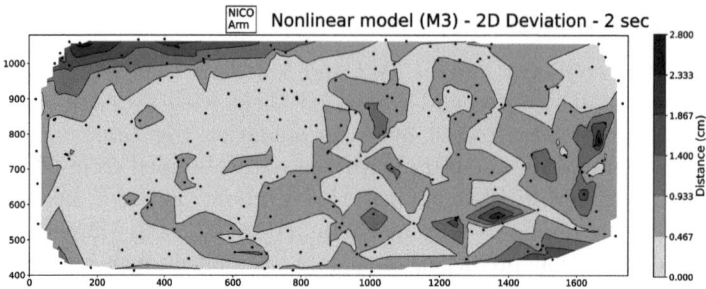

Fig. 7. Accuracy of NICO robot after the neural network based correction, trained to predict 3D points in the simulator space from target 2D points on the touchscreen. Accuracy is calculated as a deviation in 2D space

Table 1 presents the accuracy of our models in all four quadrants, plus the mean accuracy. The data set for M1 contains 130 regularly distributed points in certain patterns (e.g., grid) to visualise the direction of deviations and 120 randomly distributed points over the testing area of the touchscreen. The data set for M2 and M3 contains 250 random points, including points near the edge of the touchscreen. The data set for M1 does not include edge points because for many of them, NICO would hit outside the screen, making them unusable. In most cases, the error decreases as the complexity of the model increases. However, in Q2, M2 showed a slight increase in error from 1 cm to 1.18 cm, and also a significant increase in standard deviation, from 0.27 to 0.88 cm. This correlates with M2 having the most outliers in Fig. 6. For M3, Q3 showed the lowest average error, while Q4, being farthest from the base, showed the opposite. Overall, when considering all quadrants together, the mean error was reduced from 1.15 cm in the linear model to 0.58 cm in M3. Furthermore, the standard deviation decreased, indicating greater stability in our solution.

5 Discussion

Robotic tasks are highly specialized, and each study uses different testing methodologies, making direct comparisons challenging. In the work most comparable to ours, the same NICO robot was used to grasp objects [3]. Their best-performing model achieved an 80.3% grasp success rate with an accuracy of 0.93 cm. This was accomplished through a combination of full domain randomization, introducing variability in camera angles and visual features, and random-to-canonical adaptation, which enhanced sim-to-real transfer and outperformed a real-world-trained model that used six times more data. In contrast, our model, without relying on any visual input and using only a touchscreen and a neural network, achieved a higher accuracy of 0.58 cm, although the task was different. Roncone et al. [14], mentioned in Sect. 2, achieved a positional accuracy of 0.21 cm with the iCub humanoid robot using an automated self-touch calibration method. Although they report lower errors than ours, they use expensive visual systems and artificial skin, whereas our approach relies solely on a touchscreen and a simple neural network. And more importantly, iCub is an order of magnitude more expensive robot than NICO, which entails hardware properties.

This work focuses on haptic feedback in the 2D horizontal plane (touchpad), which may be seen as a limitation. However, even the 2D case turned out to be rather complex because of its nonlinearity. Extension to 3D is a natural next step, posing its own challenges (e.g. how to provide 3D haptic feedback).

In summary, we presented a novel calibration method to improve sim-to-real transfer in robotic manipulation using haptic feedback. Using a touchscreen to obtain the robot's end-effector positions, we developed transformation models to effectively bridge the discrepancy between simulation and reality. Our results demonstrate that a fully nonlinear neural network model significantly reduces positioning errors, outperforming traditional linear approaches. This low-cost and adaptable method can be applied to various robotic systems.

Acknowledgments. This research was supported by the Horizon Europe TERAIS project, no. 101079338 and, partially, by the national project VEGA 1/0373/23 (IF).

References

1. Al-Qurashi, Z.: Robot-human mapping model learning for robotic imitation using deep learning and virtual reality. Ph.D. thesis, Univ. of Illinois at Chicago (2020)
2. Coumans, E., Bai, Y.: PyBullet, a python module for physics simulation for games, robotics and machine learning (2016–2021). http://pybullet.org
3. Gäde, C., Habekost, J.G., Wermter, S.: Domain adaption as auxiliary task for sim-to-real transfer in vision-based neuro-robotic control. In: IJCNN. IEEE (2024)
4. Hogan, F., Carlo, J.D., Kim, S.: Proprioceptive control for dynamic quadrupedal locomotion. Sci. Robot. **7**(62), eabk2822 (2022)
5. Hubert, U., Stückler, J., Behnke, S.: Bayesian calibration of the hand-eye kinematics of an anthropomorphic robot. In: International Conference on Humanoid Robots (2012)
6. Kappassov, Z., Hostettler, J.B., Billard, A.: Tactile sensing in dexterous robot hands – review. Robot. Auton. Syst. **74**, 195–220 (2015)
7. Kerzel, M., Strahl, E., Magg, S., Navarro-Guerrero, N., Heinrich, S., Wermter, S.: NICO - Neuro-Inspired COmpanion: a developmental humanoid robot platform for multimodal interaction. In: IEEE RO-MAN. pp. 113–120 (2017)
8. Khusainov, R., Klimchik, A., Magid, E.: Humanoid robot kinematic calibration using industrial manipulator. In: ICMSC, pp. 184–189. IEEE (2017)
9. Levine, S., Abbeel, P., Finn, C., Darrell, T.: Learning hand-eye coordination for robotic grasping with deep learning and large-scale data collection. Inter. J. Robot. Res. **37**(4–5), 421–436 (2018)
10. Liu, W., Zhao, C., Liu, Y., Wang, H., Zhao, W., Zhang, H.: Sim2real kinematics modeling of industrial robots based on FPGA-acceleration. Robotics Comput.-Integrated Manufact. **77** (2022)
11. Ng, H.G., et al.: Hey robot, why don't you talk to me? In: IEEE International Symposium on Robot and Human Interactive Communication (RO-MAN) (2017)

12. Nguyen, P.D., Fischer, T., Chang, H.J., Pattacini, U., Metta, G., Demiris, Y.: Transferring visuomotor learning from simulation to the real world for robotics manipulation tasks. In: IEEE IROS, pp. 6667–6674 (2018)
13. Pedro, V.: Real time graphical simulation for visual based pose estimation and self-calibrating of a humanoid robotic arm. Master's thesis, Instituto Superior Técnico, Lisbon (2014)
14. Roncone, A., Hoffmann, M., Pattacini, U., Metta, G.: Automatic kinematic chain calibration using artificial skin: self-touch in the iCub humanoid robot. In: ICRA, pp. 2305–2312. IEEE (2014)
15. Rozlivek, J., Rustler, L., Štepánová, K., Hoffmann, M.: Multisensorial robot calibration framework and toolbox. In: International Conference on Humanoid Robots. IEEE (2021)
16. Tenhumberg, J., Bäuml, B.: Calibration of an elastic humanoid upper body and efficient compensation for motion planning. In: International Conference on Humanoid Robots. IEEE (2021)
17. Vavrečka, M., Sokovnin, N., Mejdrechová, M., Šejnová, G.: MyGym: modular toolkit for visuomotor robotic tasks. In: ICTAI, pp. 279–283 (2021)
18. Štepánová, K., Pajdla, T., Hoffmann, M.: Robot self-calibration using multiple kinematic chains—a simulation study on the iCub humanoid robot. IEEE Robot. Autom. Lett. **4**(2), 1900–1907 (2019)

Towards Bio-inspired Robotic Trajectory Planning via Self-supervised RNN

Miroslav Cibula[1(✉)], Kristína Malinovská[1], and Matthias Kerzel[2]

[1] Faculty of Mathematics, Physics and Informatics, Comenius University Bratislava, Bratislava, Slovakia
cibula25@uniba.sk, kristina.malinovska@fmph.uniba.sk
[2] Department of Informatics, University of Hamburg, Hamburg, Germany
matthias.kerzel@uni-hamburg.de

Abstract. Trajectory planning in robotics is understood as generating a sequence of joint configurations that will lead a robotic agent, or its manipulator, from an initial state to the desired final state, thus completing a manipulation task while considering constraints like robot kinematics and the environment. Typically, this is achieved via sampling-based planners, which are computationally intensive. Recent advances demonstrate that trajectory planning can also be performed by supervised sequence learning of trajectories, often requiring only a single or fixed number of passes through a neural architecture, thus ensuring a bounded computation time. Such fully supervised approaches, however, perform imitation learning; they do not learn based on whether the trajectories can successfully reach a goal, but try to reproduce observed trajectories. In our work, we build on this approach and propose a cognitively inspired self-supervised learning scheme based on a recurrent architecture for building a trajectory model. We evaluate the feasibility of the proposed method on a task of kinematic planning for a robotic arm. The results suggest that the model is able to learn to generate trajectories only using given paired forward and inverse kinematics models, and indicate that this novel method could facilitate planning for more complex manipulation tasks requiring adaptive solutions.

Keywords: self-supervised learning · forward model · inverse model · trajectory planning

1 Introduction

Robotic trajectory planning is vital for robots acting in real-world environments. The robot's planning machinery needs to estimate a viable trajectory for the end effector to reach the goal. Typically, sampling-based methods are used: random samples are drawn from the robot's configuration space and connected using a local planner. Provided the task goal is specified in Cartesian space, once a trajectory is found, an inverse kinematics (IK) solver computes the corresponding sequence of joint configurations. More advanced approaches refine the trajectory further, aiming for smoothness and compatibility with low-level motor control [7].

These methods rely on an accurate model of the robots kinematics, which is not always available, especially with custom-built or modified actuators. Moreover, sampling-based methods are generally non-optimal, can have unpredictable planning times, or result in jerky or unnatural movements. This is especially relevant for humanoid robots, where unpredictable or abrupt motions can pose safety risks and hinder human-robot collaboration. Therefore, existing approaches cannot solve all challenges for robots with complex or heavily constrained kinematics, such as humanoids with highly complex hand-like manipulators.

Developmental robotics [19] draws inspiration from biology and cognitive neuroscience: Robots are supposed to learn increasingly complex skills through self-exploration and interaction with the environment in a self-supervised manner, similar to how humans and animals develop motor control [23]. To follow this paradigm, bio-inspired and neuro-cognitively plausible models for sensory-motor learning are required.

In this proof-of-concept study, we propose a bio-inspired, self-supervised learning scheme for neural trajectory planning in robotics. Our approach proceeds in two stages: first, the robot performs motor babbling to train a forward model (FM) and an inverse model (IM) [26], both implemented as multilayer perceptrons (MLP) [6]. In the second stage, these trained models are embedded within a recurrent neural architecture based on gated recurrent units (GRU) [4] to reproduce trajectory shapes. By avoiding fully supervised training, which requires large datasets and tends to produce trajectories biased toward the training distribution (even when they fail to reach a goal), we enable the agent to generate novel movements grounded in its interaction with the environment. Although the components are standard neural networks, the overall scheme functionally resembles aspects of human cognition. Thus, our contribution is a bio-inspired architecture that enables a robot to acquire not only kinematics but also movement trajectories from experience, allowing it to generate increasingly complex actions by reusing prior knowledge. Our results are still preliminary and do not yet provide the full functionality of a trajectory planner; however, they can be a stepping stone towards a biologically plausible and adaptive trajectory planner.

2 Related Work

There are several different popular approaches to planning reach and grasp actions. While sampling-based trajectory planners like Probabilistic Roadmap [15] and Rapidly-Exploring Random Tree [17] are the de facto standard in applied robotics, these planners are not based on biological mechanisms, like learning. Furthermore, if the goal is specified in task space (e.g., Cartesian end-effector space), these approaches require a functioning and fast inverse kinematics solver – in short, a mathematical model that computes the robot's joint configuration(s) that bring the end-effector into a desired pose (position and rotation). The main challenge for inverse modeling remains the cumulative error in the approximated joint position and how to compensate for it [22], as well as the flexibility in trajectory planning to account for obstacles and environmental changes. One of the recent solutions to this problem in the field of humanoid robotics is the universal neuro-inspired inverse kinematics method, CycleIK, utilizing an MLP with custom L^1-based metrics and an additional generative adversarial network for obstacle avoidance [10].

Inverse models are complemented by forward models [26], that predict the sensorimotor consequences from a joint configuration sequence, i.e., the next state of the joints and the changes in the observed world. Both of these models are usually modeled using various versions of feedforward networks. The interconnected forward and inverse models can explain causal learning and mental simulation [6]. Another major approach is the use of reinforcement learning (RL), which learns an action policy without a kinematic model or IK-solver. For the review of the RL approaches in the context of this problem, refer to [9]. In this work, however, we are focusing on alternative methods that rely on neural network-based sequence modeling task solutions.

Alternatively to the inverse kinematics problem formulation and solutions, planning a trajectory (and related effector action) can be approached with sequence modeling. Sequence modeling in its autoregressive form is a problem considering the inference of a sequence of consecutive states by modeling the state sequence as conditioned on the final desired state. Typically, this task is solved using recurrent neural networks (RNN) or, more recently, Transformers [2,14]. Gated RNNs, such as long short-term memory (LSTM) [13] or gated recurrent units (GRU) [4], have been utilized for robot arm control applications [3,20]. Similarly, echo state networks have also been proposed as a solution for movement trajectory prediction [11], and have recently been enhanced to learn motor primitives for shared control tasks [1].

3 Methods

In our current work, we build on the paired FM and IM as defined in [6]. While the FM and IM operate only with time-adjacent states and actions, they cannot be directly used for long-term, multi-step planning. Hence, our proposed approach is to generate trajectories using a sequence model as

$$\text{TM}: [s(0), s(T)] \mapsto \hat{\tau}_s, \tag{1}$$

where $s(0)$ and $s(T)$ denote the initial and goal state in which the task is complete, respectively. The trajectory model (TM) infers an output trajectory of intermediate states $\hat{\tau}_s = [\hat{s}(1), \hat{s}(2), \ldots, \hat{s}(T-1)]$. Subsequently, it is possible to translate such a trajectory to an action sequence:

$$\hat{\tau}_a = \big[\,\text{IM}\,[\hat{s}(t), \hat{s}(t+1)] \mid 0 \leq t \leq T-1\,\big], \tag{2}$$

with $\hat{s}(t), \hat{s}(t+1) \in \hat{\tau}_s$, and $\hat{s}(0) \equiv s(0)$, $\hat{s}(T) \equiv s(T)$.

As a sequence model, the TM was implemented as a recurrent decoder architecture [4] (Fig. 1) using n_r GRU layers [4]. Our extensive experimentation [5] has shown that GRU networks have a slight advantage in this context over computationally heavier LSTMs [13]. In the general architecture, the recurrent layers feed a time-distributed prediction module, which is topologically equivalent to the FM architecture introduced in [6]. The module consists of one common fully-connected tanh-activated hidden layer connecting to k output heads, each separately predicting qualitatively different state subvectors $\hat{\boldsymbol{y}}_i \subseteq \hat{\boldsymbol{s}}(t)$ (e.g., end-effector position, joint configuration, object properties, etc.). Although we use only one output head in our experiment to predict $\boldsymbol{ef}(t)$, the architecture should be able to accommodate more complex state vector prediction using multiple prediction heads. In our implementation, the TM does not support generating variable-length trajectories. However, it should be possible for the TM to learn to compress the ends of the generated trajectories by producing almost identical states $\hat{\boldsymbol{s}}(t)$ if no more steps are needed.

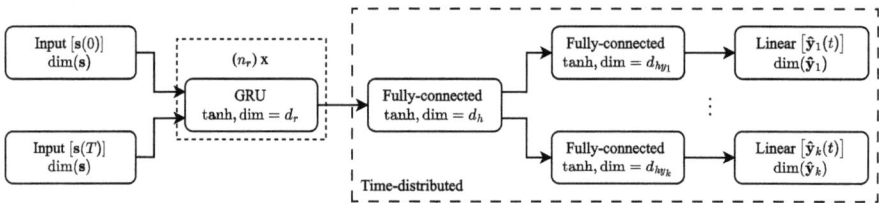

Fig. 1. TM architecture implemented as a GRU decoder with n_r tanh-activated GRU layers of d_r units. Input is the initial state $\boldsymbol{s}(0)$ and a target state $\boldsymbol{s}(T)$. Time-distributed module predicts the sequence of intermediate states' feature components $\hat{\boldsymbol{y}}_i(t) \in \hat{\boldsymbol{s}}(t)$ for discrete time points $1 < t < T$. Note that the dimensionalities of the hidden layers are task-specific; thus, we do not list them here

To train the TM, we propose a self-supervised scheme that traverses each generated trajectory and evaluates its states $\hat{\boldsymbol{s}}(t) \in \hat{\tau}_s$ in multiple steps (Fig. 2). The process starts with pairing the first intermediate state $\hat{\boldsymbol{s}}(1)$ with the ground-truth initial state $\boldsymbol{s}(0)$ and inputting them into the IM inferring action $\hat{\boldsymbol{a}}(0)$ responsible for the transition between $\boldsymbol{s}(0)$ and $\hat{\boldsymbol{s}}(1)$. Using the FM, we then predict the consequence of the execution of $\hat{\boldsymbol{a}}(0)$ in $\boldsymbol{s}(0)$. This step has the purpose of producing a rectified state $\tilde{\boldsymbol{s}}(1)$ with respect to the ground-truth initial state $\boldsymbol{s}(0)$. Assuming optimal IM and FM, the FM in this step essentially verifies whether the predicted $\hat{\boldsymbol{s}}(1)$ is achievable by the action $\hat{\boldsymbol{a}}(0)$ estimated on the basis of $\boldsymbol{s}(0)$. If $\hat{\boldsymbol{s}}(1)$ is predicted accurately by the TM, discrepancy of $\tilde{\boldsymbol{s}}(1)$ against it should be minimal. Thus, we can measure the prediction error of $\hat{\boldsymbol{s}}(1)$ as $\mathcal{L}[\hat{\boldsymbol{s}}(1), \tilde{\boldsymbol{s}}(1)]$ where

$$\mathcal{L}[\hat{\boldsymbol{s}}(t+1), \boldsymbol{s}(t+1)] \triangleq \frac{1}{k} \sum_{\substack{\hat{\boldsymbol{y}}_i \subseteq \hat{\boldsymbol{s}}(t+1) \\ \boldsymbol{y}_i \subseteq \boldsymbol{s}(t+1)}} \mathrm{MSE}\left(\hat{\boldsymbol{y}}_i, \boldsymbol{y}_i\right), \tag{3}$$

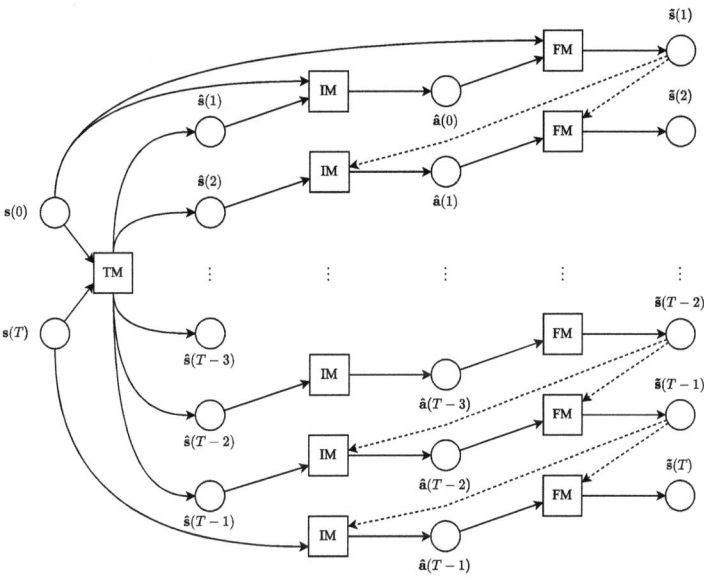

Fig. 2. FM/IM-aided generation of the intermediate state trajectory, acting as a partial target for the self-supervised learning of the TM. A *dashed line* designates the flow of the information from the previous timestep contributing to the rectification of the current state

with MSE denoting a mean square error and k being the total number of state feature subvectors.

For the next state $\hat{s}(t) \in \hat{\tau}_s$, the process is similar. However, instead of using $s(0)$ as the IM and FM input, we utilize the previous rectified state $\tilde{s}(t-1)$. This way, we can propagate the correcting signal in the form of more accurate rectified states originating in the ground-truth $s(0)$ throughout the whole $\hat{\tau}_s$. This rectified state trajectory generation procedure is formally described in Algorithm 1.

With the generated rectified trajectory $\tilde{\tau}_s$, we then compute the prediction error of $\hat{\tau}_s$ as

$$\mathcal{L}_{\text{TM}}\left[\hat{\tau}_s, \tilde{\tau}_s, s(0), s(T)\right] \triangleq \frac{1}{|\hat{\tau}_s|} \sum_{i=1}^{|\hat{\tau}_s|} \mathcal{L}\left[\hat{\tau}_s(i), \tilde{\tau}_s(i)\right] \quad (4)$$
$$+ \mathcal{L}\left[\hat{s}(1), s(0)\right] + \mathcal{L}\left[\hat{s}(T-1), s(T)\right].$$

The first term of $\mathcal{L}_{\text{TM}}$ measures the average magnitude of discrepancy of predicted trajectory state $\hat{\tau}_s(i)$ against the hypothetically more accurate corresponding rectified state $\tilde{\tau}_s(i)$, while the subsequent terms compute the distance of the $\hat{\tau}_s$ endpoints to the ground-truth endpoints to position the generated trajectory in space correctly. $\mathcal{L}_{\text{TM}}$ is then propagated by standard truncated backpropagation through time [25], optimizing the TM.

Algorithm 1: Generation of the rectified state trajectory $\tilde{\tau}_s$. $\hat{s}'(t)$ denotes $\hat{s}(t)$ without its joint configuration subvector $\hat{\theta}(t)$ as per the implementation of the IM.

Input: Ground-truth initial state $s(0)$ and goal state $s(T)$
Output: Trajectory of rectified intermediate states $\tilde{\tau}_s$ and the last rectified state $\tilde{s}(T)$

1    $\hat{\tau}_s \leftarrow \text{TM}\,[s(0), s(T)]$
2    $\tilde{s}(0) \leftarrow s(0)$
3   **for** $t = 1, \dots, T$ **do**
4       $\hat{s}'(t) \leftarrow \hat{\tau}_s(t)$
5       $\hat{a}(t-1) \leftarrow \text{IM}\,[\tilde{s}(t-1), \hat{s}'(t)]$
6       $\tilde{s}(t) \leftarrow \text{FM}\,[\tilde{s}(t-1), \hat{a}(t-1)]$
7   **if** $t < T$ **then**
8          $\tilde{\tau}_s(t) \leftarrow \tilde{s}(t)$

Table 1. Tested optimizer configurations of the TM training for the kinematics experiment. Each configuration was trained over 50 epochs in 10 trials. η denotes an initial learning rate of the Adam [16], RMSprop [12], and stochastic gradient descent (SGD) optimizers. γ represents the smoothing constant of RMSprop. Final $\mathcal{L}_{\text{TM}}$ is the measurement of $\mathcal{L}_{\text{TM}}$ (Eq. 4) from the last epoch of the training

Config.	Optimizer	Final $\mathcal{L}_{\text{TM}}$
#1	Adam($\eta = 10^{-3}$)	0.084
#2	Adam($\eta = 10^{-4}$)	0.170
#3	RMSprop($\eta = 10^{-2}, \gamma = 0.99$)	0.040
#4	RMSprop($\eta = 10^{-3}, \gamma = 0.99$)	**0.017**
#5	SGD($\eta = 0.5$)	0.034
#6	SGD($\eta = 1.0$)	0.048

4 Experiments

The feasibility of the proposed method was tested on the task of navigating an end-effector of a 7-DoF robotic arm, KUKA LBR iiwa, from a point in a fixed initial neighborhood in Cartesian space to a random final position, thereby performing trajectory planning. The experiments were performed in a simulated environment using the myGym framework [24]. A state space consisted of a Cartesian end-effector position $ef(t) \in \mathbb{R}^3$ and the arm's joint configuration $\theta(t) \in \mathbb{R}^7$, thus $s(t) = [\theta(t), ef(t)]$. The action vectors were defined as $a(t) = \theta(t+1) - \theta(t)$, representing change in the joint configuration. During the simulation, 12,000 trajectories with $T = 11$ (i.e., with 10 intermediate states) were recorded and their endpoints $[s^{(i)}(0), s^{(i)}(T)]$ isolated for the training. As is standard in trajectory planning, the goal joint configuration $\boldsymbol{\theta}^{(i)}(t)$ was specified at planning time.

Additionally, supplementary FM and IM for this task were separately trained using motor babbling, employing the same architectures and procedures described in Sect. 4.1 of [6]. The FM was trained for 60 epochs using the Adam optimizer [16] with an initial learning rate $\eta = 10^{-3}$, resulting in the average mean absolute error (MAE) of the end-effector position and joint configuration prediction of 1.1 mm and 6.3×10^{-4} rad. For the IM, the monolithic architecture [6] was chosen, and trained for 100 epochs using the AdamW optimizer [18] with an initial learning rate $\eta = 10^{-3}$ and weight decay $\lambda = 4 \times 10^{-3}$. Its average MAE of action prediction was 1.7×10^{-3} rad.

With the trained FM and IM and the collected set of endpoints, we constructed the TM. For this experiment, the architecture of the TM consisted of $n_r = 1$ GRU layer of $d_r = 20$ tanh-activated units feeding the fully-connected common layer of $d_h = d_r$ units. In this instance, there is only one output head predicting *ef* while $\boldsymbol{\theta}$ is computed by the FM. The exclusion of the joint configuration prediction by the TM here is biologically plausible – when humans perform motor planning, they primarily optimize with respect to task-relevant variables (in this case, the end-effector position) while leaving other variables (such as joint configuration) uncontrolled and conformable to variables of higher priority [21]. Topologically, the prediction head in this instance consists of an intermediate hidden layer of $d_{hy} = 10$ neurons and outputs to three linearly activated output neurons.

The TM was trained by numerous optimizer configurations with a focus on the Adam [16], RMSprop [12], and stochastic gradient descent (SGD) optimizers (best-performing configurations for each optimizer can be found in Table 1). The training was conducted for 50 epochs on the full dataset of 12,000 endpoints. Afterwards, the TM inferred a trajectory for each pair of endpoints in the dataset.

Table 2. Evaluated properties of 12,000 generated trajectories by each TM configuration in Table 1. Init. and final dist. refer to the Euclidean distances between the ground-truth endpoints and the first and last states of generated trajectories, formally $\|s(0) - \hat{s}(1)\|_2$ and $\|s(T) - \hat{s}(T-1)\|_2$, respectively. Max. sp. dev. represents maximum spacing deviation between the waypoints. All measurements were conducted on whole trajectories, including the initial and final ground-truth states

#	Init. dist. (m)	Final dist. (m)	Avg. spacing (m)	Max. sp. dev. (m)	Avg. angle (°)
1	0.429 ± 0.064	0.247 ± 0.066	0.078 ± 0.014	0.352 ± 0.054	153.4 ± 7.4
2	0.632 ± 0.129	0.296 ± 0.083	0.110 ± 0.027	0.522 ± 0.104	150.3 ± 4.3
3	0.265 ± 0.039	0.202 ± 0.081	0.064 ± 0.013	0.214 ± 0.037	142.3 ± 8.3
4	**0.134 ± 0.108**	**0.139 ± 0.051**	0.061 ± 0.014	**0.127 ± 0.083**	153.0 ± 8.8
5	0.183 ± 0.071	0.239 ± 0.084	0.063 ± 0.012	0.194 ± 0.075	157.5 ± 9.3
6	0.311 ± 0.052	0.197 ± 0.062	0.069 ± 0.012	0.244 ± 0.051	156.2 ± 8.3

To evaluate the quality of the generated trajectories, we measured several properties. First, we investigated how well trajectories adhere to the ground-truth endpoints. Optimally, for each generated trajectory $\hat{\tau}_s$, its first waypoint $\hat{s}(1) \equiv \hat{\tau}_s(1)$ must be close enough to the initial point $s(0)$ and its last waypoint $\hat{s}(10) = \hat{s}(T-1)$ to the final point $s(11) = s(T)$. These criteria are evaluated by computing the Euclidean distance between the given points – formally, $\|s(0) - \hat{s}(1)\|_2$ and $\|s(T) - \hat{s}(T-1)\|_2$, respectively, where $\|\cdot\|_2$ denotes the L^2-norm. Furthermore, it is desirable for the TM to produce waypoints as uniformly spaced as possible to achieve movement with a near-constant velocity. For each trajectory, this criterion is evaluated by the average Euclidean distance between every pair of succeeding points and the maximum deviation from this average. Note that the ground-truth endpoints are included in the measurement as well. For optimal waypoint placement, the maximum deviation should be minimal.

Finally, we measured the angles inside each trajectory to evaluate its smoothness. In the optimal case, we aim to avoid sharp turns within trajectories, as they negatively affect the arm dynamics during execution [8]. For each triplet of succeeding waypoints (including the ground-truth endpoints), we measured the angle formed at the middle point. Averaging these measurements across the whole trajectory, the value close to 180° indicates an almost linear trajectory, while the lower value suggests that the trajectory is curved. A low minimum angle in the trajectory indicates a sharp turn.

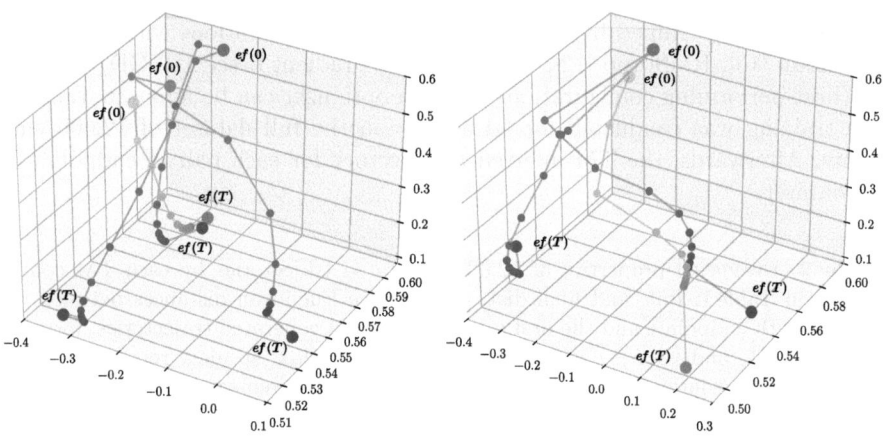

Fig. 3. Sample of generated trajectories guiding the arm's end-effector from an initial position ($ef(0)$) to a final position ($ef(T)$). Left: roughly optimal trajectories in reaching target effector positions $ef(T)$. Right: problems with generated trajectories – uneven spacing between the waypoints; large distances between extreme waypoints

The results of the quantitative evaluation of the configurations listed in Table 1 can be seen in Table 2. Among the optimizers, any configuration using the Adam optimizer failed to optimize the TM to produce viable trajectories.

The most problematic aspect is the distance between the endpoints and the extremes of the trajectories, which reaches, on average, in the best case (config. #1), 42.9 ± 6.4 cm for the initial endpoint and 24.7 ± 6.6 cm for the final one. Although such a model is capable of producing more or less smooth trajectories, they are significantly dissociated from the endpoints and thus do not adhere to the task at all. This is in line with the high final $\mathcal{L}_{\text{TM}}$ of the Adam models (Table 1).

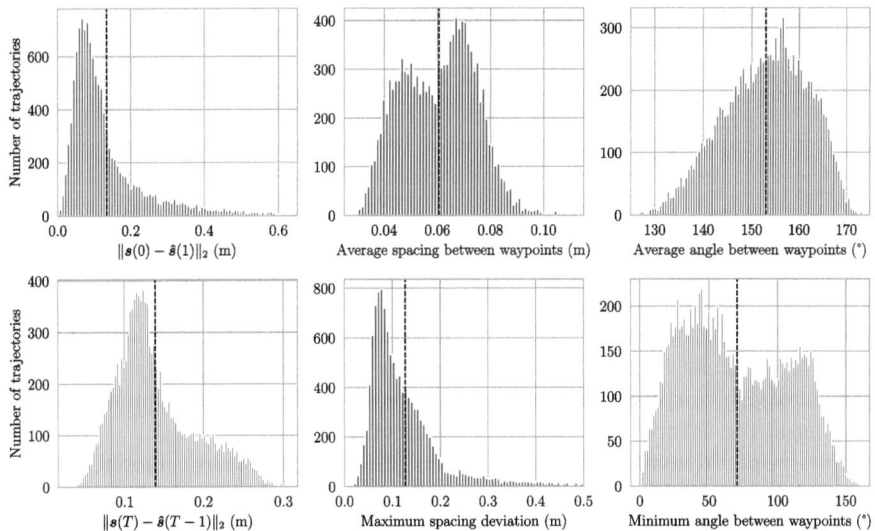

Fig. 4. Distributions of measurements over 12,000 trajectories. The first column depicts the distribution of distances between the ground-truth endpoints and the first and last states of generated trajectories. The measurements in the second and third columns were conducted on whole trajectories, including the initial and final ground-truth states. The *dashed lines* represent the expected value of each distribution

A similar behavior can be observed in the case of the SGD and RMSprop models with a higher learning rate (configs. #3 and #6). Interestingly, still, the TM training seems to require an unusually high learning rate for SGD. Initially, we hypothesized that the TM would prefer an optimizer with a fixed learning rate (e.g., SGD) over adaptive ones (e.g., RMSprop, Adam). However, results confirmed that the adaptive nature does not pose a problem, as RMSprop generally surpasses SGD in terms of trajectory quality.

The best configuration, both in terms of trajectory properties and the final $\mathcal{L}_{\text{TM}}$, we were able to find was #4 with the RMSprop optimizer set to a slower learning rate of $\eta = 10^{-3}$. An example of good trajectories produced by this TM can be seen in the left panel of Fig. 3. As shown in Table 2 and Fig. 4, on average, the TM was able to position the trajectories with a relatively low distance to the task endpoints; however, these distances still significantly deviate from the average spacing (more than twice on average), which indicates that the trajectory waypoints are usually not well uniformly spread between the endpoints. This property can also be seen in the right panel of Fig. 3. Although the TM in this configuration generates relatively smooth trajectories with mild curvature (avg. angle 153°), the left mode of the distribution in the bottom rightmost panel of Fig. 4 suggests that 6477 (54%) generated trajectories contain sharp turns of less than the mean (69.9° ± 1.3°). Finally, the TM after training in this configuration was able to generate a 10-step trajectory in 993 μs ± 277 μs (averaged over 12,000 trajectories in 5 trials) running on an Nvidia RTX 4080 SUPER.

5 Discussion and Future Work

We present preliminary work towards a biologically inspired neural trajectory planner that is trained in two stages: first, a neural inverse and forward model is trained in a supervised manner via motor babbling. Our evaluation shows that both the FM and the IM are sufficiently accurate (Sect. 4). In the next step, a recurrent neural architecture utilizing the frozen forward and inverse models is used to generate preliminary trajectories and correct them. We can demonstrate that the approach yields well-positioned trajectories that reach the goal end-effector position on average within a distance of 13.9 cm, while preserving a relatively smooth curve form (Figs. 3, 4). In comparison with more trivial methods such as linear interpolation between the endpoints, our approach is able to produce arbitrarily curved trajectories necessary to facilitate more complex planning in the future, for example, for object avoidance.

The proposed model does not require an accurate robotic model (usually provided as a URDF); the required training data can be gained from random movements, both in the form of motor babbling and random trajectories. Moreover, the model incrementally learns more complex tasks that build upon each other, progressing from forward and inverse models to complete trajectories. The model, therefore, fulfills the idea of developmental robotics: learning incrementally more complex abilities from interaction with the environment and the robot's own body.

While our approach could help to gain insight into the development of complex motor-sensory abilities in biological agents, a fully neural trajectory planner is also useful for robotics. In contrast to sampling-based planners, which have unpredictable runtime, our approach produces results within a fixed time. However, we do acknowledge that for application in robotics, some future work must be addressed. First, the trajectory model only learns the robot's kinematics and focuses on the Cartesian end-effector position; it does not account for environmental obstacles and does not directly model joint configurations to verify the kinematic feasibility of the actions produced. In future work, we will evaluate integrating these as an additional input to the neural network. Furthermore, our approach is evaluated on trajectories of comparable length and outputs trajectories with a fixed number of intermediate poses. For more complex and varied trajectories, we will alter the approach to produce trajectories of variable length. We acknowledge that the smoothness and accuracy of the produced trajectories are not competitive with those of optimized trajectory planners. This could be improved by further modifying the loss function of the TM (Eq. 4). For example, by reweighting the last two terms, $\mathcal{L}\left[\hat{s}(1), s(0)\right]$ and $\mathcal{L}\left[\hat{s}(T-1), s(T)\right]$, we suppose the TM could position the extremes of the generated trajectories closer to the ground-truth endpoints, thus increasing accuracy. Finally, in this proof-of-concept study, the proposed approach is tested only on a single task in a simple setting. To further verify the generality of our method, it will be tested on a more diverse and complex set of tasks and environments. An experimental comparison with other related planning methods will also be conducted.

In summary, we contribute a bio-inspired trajectory planner that does not rely on external knowledge about an agent's kinematics and can thus serve as a model for, e.g., early sensorimotor learning in humans.

Acknowledgements. The authors would like to thank Igor Farkaš for his advice and feedback. This research was supported by the Horizon Europe project TERAIS, GA no. 101079338, and in part by the Slovak Grant Agency for Science (VEGA), project 1/0373/23. Research results were partially obtained using the computational resources procured in the national EU-funded project 311070AKF2, National Competence Centre for High Performance Computing.

References

1. Amirshirzad, N., Eren, M.A., Oztop, E.: Context-based echo state networks with prediction confidence for human-robot shared control arXiv: 2412.00541 (2024) [cs.RO]
2. Chen, L., et al.: Decision transformer: reinforcement learning via sequence modeling. In: Advances in Neural Information Processing Systems, vol. 34, pp. 15084–15097. Curran Associates, Inc. (2021)
3. Chen, Z., Walters, J., Xiao, G., Li, S.: An enhanced GRU model with application to manipulator trajectory tracking. EAI Endorsed Trans. AI Robot. **1**, 1–11 (2022). https://doi.org/10.4108/airo.v1i.7
4. Cho, K., et al.: Learning phrase representations using RNN encoder–decoder for statistical machine translation. In: Proceedings of the 2014 Conference on Empirical Methods in Natural Language Processing (EMNLP), pp. 1724–1734. Association for Computational Linguistics (2014). https://doi.org/10.3115/v1/D14-1179
5. Cibula, M.: Cognitively-inspired learning of causal relations in a simulated robotic environment. Bachelor's thesis, Comenius University Bratislava (2024)
6. Cibula, M., Kerzel, M., Farkaš, I.: Learning low-level causal relations using a simulated robotic arm. In: Artificial Neural Networks and Machine Learning – ICANN 2024. pp. 285–298. Springer Nature Switzerland, Cham (2024). https://doi.org/10.1007/978-3-031-72359-9_21
7. Coleman, D., Sucan, I., Chitta, S., Correll, N.: Reducing the barrier to entry of complex robotic software: A Moveit! case study. arXiv preprint arXiv:1404.3785 (2014)
8. Dobiš, M., Dekan, M., Beňo, P., Duchoň, F., Babinec, A.: Evaluation criteria for trajectories of robotic arms. Robotics **11**(1) (2022). https://doi.org/10.3390/robotics11010029
9. Elguea-Aguinaco, Í., Inziarte-Hidalgo, I., Bøgh, S., Arana-Arexolaleiba, N.: A review on reinforcement learning for motion planning of robotic manipulators. Inter. J. Intell. Syst. **2024**(1) (2024). https://doi.org/10.1155/int/1636497
10. Habekost, J.G., Gäde, C., Allgeuer, P., Wermter, S.: Inverse kinematics for neuro-robotic grasping with humanoid embodied agents. In: 2024 IEEE/RSJ International Conference on Intelligent Robots and Systems (IROS), pp. 7315–7322. IEEE (2024). https://doi.org/10.1109/iros58592.2024.10802010

11. Hellbach, S., Strauss, S., Eggert, J.P., Körner, E., Gross, H.M.: Echo state networks for online prediction of movement data – comparing investigations. In: Artificial Neural Networks - ICANN 2008. pp. 710–719. Springer Berlin Heidelberg, Berlin (2008). https://doi.org/10.1007/978-3-540-87536-9_73
12. Hinton, G., Srivastava, N., Swersky, K.: Lecture 6a: Overview of mini-batch gradient descent (2012). https://www.cs.toronto.edu/~tijmen/csc321/slides/lecture_slides_lec6.pdf, lecture notes
13. Hochreiter, S., Schmidhuber, J.: Long short-term memory. Neural Comput. **9**(8), 1735–1780 (1997). https://doi.org/10.1162/neco.1997.9.8.1735
14. Janner, M., Li, Q., Levine, S.: Offline reinforcement learning as one big sequence modeling problem. In: Advances in Neural Information Processing Systems, vol. 34, pp. 1273–1286. Curran Associates, Inc. (2021)
15. Kavraki, L.E., Svestka, P., Latombe, J.C., Overmars, M.H.: Probabilistic roadmaps for path planning in high-dimensional configuration spaces. IEEE Trans. Robot. Autom. **12**(4), 566–580 (1996). https://doi.org/10.1109/70.508439
16. Kingma, D.P., Ba, J.: Adam: A method for stochastic optimization. arxiv preprint arXiv:1412.6980 (2014)
17. LaValle, S.M., Kuffner, J.J.: Randomized kinodynamic planning. Inter. J. Robot. Res. **20**(5), 378–400 (2001). https://doi.org/10.1177/02783640122067453
18. Loshchilov, I., Hutter, F.: Decoupled weight decay regularization. arxiv preprint arXiv:1711.05101 (2017)
19. Lungarella, M., Metta, G., Pfeifer, R., Sandini, G.: Developmental robotics: a survey. Connect. Sci. **15**(4), 151–190 (2003). https://doi.org/10.1080/09540090310001655110
20. Otte, S., Zwiener, A., Hanten, R., Zell, A.: Inverse recurrent models – an application scenario for many-joint robot arm control. In: Artificial Neural Networks and Machine Learning – ICANN 2016, pp. 149–157. Springer International Publishing. https://doi.org/10.1007/978-3-319-44778-0_18
21. Scholz, J.P., Schöner, G.: The uncontrolled manifold concept: identifying control variables for a functional task. Exp. Brain Res. **126**(3), 289–306 (1999). https://doi.org/10.1007/s002210050738
22. Sinha, A., Chakraborty, N.: Computing robust inverse kinematics under uncertainty. In: Volume 5A: 43rd Mechanisms and Robotics Conference. IDETC-CIE2019, American Society of Mechanical Engineers (2019). https://doi.org/10.1115/detc2019-97945
23. Smith, L., Gasser, M.: The development of embodied cognition: six lessons from babies. Artif. Life **11**(1–2), 13–29 (2005). https://doi.org/10.1162/1064546053278973
24. Vavrečka, M., Sokovnin, N., Mejdrechová, M., Šejnová, G.: MyGym: modular toolkit for visuomotor robotic tasks. In: 2021 IEEE 33rd International Conference on Tools with Artificial Intelligence (ICTAI), pp. 279–283. IEEE (2021). https://doi.org/10.1109/ictai52525.2021.00046
25. Williams, R.J., Peng, J.: An efficient gradient-based algorithm for on-line training of recurrent network trajectories. Neural Comput. **2**(4), 490–501 (1990). https://doi.org/10.1162/neco.1990.2.4.490
26. Wolpert, D.M., Kawato, M.: Multiple paired forward and inverse models for motor control. Neural Netw. **11**(7–8), 1317–1329 (1998). https://doi.org/10.1016/s0893-6080(98)00066-5

3rd International Workshop on Reservoir Computing

3rd International Workshop on Reservoir Computing

Reservoir Computing (RC) denotes a class of recurrent neural models whose dynamics are left unadapted after initialization. The approach is appealing for several reasons, among which are fast training, neuromorphic hardware implementations, and a natural propensity to edge computing.

In the wake of the recent success of the past editions, the 3rd International Workshop on Reservoir Computing (RC 2025) intends to once more bring together researchers to discuss the state-of-the-art and open challenges in the field of RC, in all its declinations. These include, among others, new models of Echo State Networks and Liquid State Machines, theoretical and empirical analysis of RC models, applications to problems of AI size with human-level performance (including natural language processing), emerging paradigms (e.g. RC for trustworthy AI), RC for structured data such as graph reservoirs and RC models for network data, deep RC, hybrid RC/fully trained RNN models, RC applied to neuroscience, and many more. The workshop provides an open forum for researchers to meet and present recent contributions and ideas in a fervent and highly interdisciplinary environment. In addition, a hands-on tutorial will offer a useful and practical introduction for young researchers interested in developing and applying RC models.

Organizers

Alessio Micheli	University of Pisa, Italy
Gouhei Tanaka	Nagoya Institute of Technology, Japan
Domenico Tortorella	University of Pisa, Italy
Benjamin Paaßen	University of Bielefeld, Germany
Claudio Gallicchio	University of Pisa, Italy
Xavier Hinaut	Inria, France
Andrea Ceni	University of Pisa, Italy

Impact of Plasticity-Based Reservoir Adaptation on Spectral Radius and Performance of ESNs

Franziska Weber[1]($\boxtimes$), Lluís Belanche-Muñoz[2], and Andreas Maier[1]

[1] Friedrich-Alexander University Erlangen-Nuremberg, Erlangen, Germany
franziska.fw.weber@fau.de
[2] Polytechnic University of Catalonia, Barcelona, Spain

Abstract. Echo state networks (ESNs) are recurrent neural networks belonging to the reservoir computing framework. While ESNs are conceptually simple, their successful application can be challenging. For instance, there are no generally applicable methods for optimally setting important hyperparameters like the reservoir spectral radius. Therefore, the development of strategies for appropriately initializing ESNs is an active field of research. Plasticity-based pretraining is a bio-inspired reservoir optimization approach. We analyze if this approach is able to improve the results of a non-optimized ESN and if the pretraining effects can be explained by the influence on the spectral radius. In our experiments, we evaluate the effects of four synaptic plasticity rules (SP), namely anti-Ojas, normalized anti-Hebbian, BCM, and dual-threshold BCM, and of intrinsic plasticity (IP) on the Mackey-Glass, NARMA, and Lorenz series. IP significantly improves the ESNs performance across all three benchmarks whereas this is not the case for any of the considered SP rules. Overall, the influence of plasticity on the spectral radius is not sufficient for explaining the pretraining effects. The cases, in which plasticity significantly worsens the results, however, can be explained by the spectral radius having been moved to a disadvantageous value.

Keywords: Echo state network · Plasticity rules · Spectral radius

1 Introduction

Recurrent neural networks (RNNs) are designed to process sequential data. Most types of RNNs are trained based on an error minimization approach which can be performed via backpropagation through time. This approach, however, is computationally expensive and tends to suffer from fading or exploding gradients.

The ESN was proposed by H. Jaeger in 2001 [9] as an alternative RNN architecture to circumvent these difficulties. It consists of a large randomly connected recurrent network of neurons called reservoir followed by a linear readout layer. Hence, ESNs map the low-dimensional input to a high-dimensional space from which it is then read out via basic methods. As only the readout weights are adapted while the remaining weights are random and fixed, ESNs can be trained with a simple linear regression. The ESN and similar models were later unified in the reservoir computing (RC) framework by Verstraeten et al. [22].

Despite their conceptual simplicity, the successful application of ESNs can be challenging. They often work excellently but sometimes poorly and it is not well understood why [11]. Therefore, the development of strategies for optimizing the hyperparameters and the reservoir topology of ESNs is an active field of research. The recent systematic literature review [20] gives an overview of such methods.

Some suggested approaches are expensive optimization algorithms which contradict the original idea of ESNs being easy to use alternatives to computationally expensive gradient-based RNNs. Plasticity-based pretraining, on the other hand, is an efficient and conceptually simple bio-inspired reservoir optimization approach. Furthermore, it is purely input driven and thus unsupervised.

In this paper, we will explore the effects of plasticity-based pretraining on the performance of ESNs. Our goals are to evaluate whether this pretraining is able to improve the results of a non-optimized network and whether the pretraining effects can be explained by the influence on the spectral radius.

2 Preliminaries

2.1 Echo State Networks

ESNs are RNNs composed of an input layer, a randomly generated recurrent layer called reservoir, and a linear readout layer. In this paper, we work with the basic version of ESNs originally introduced by H. Jaeger in [9].

Assuming K input, N internal reservoir and L output units, we denote the input at time t as $\boldsymbol{x}[t] \in \mathbb{R}^K$, the internal reservoir state as $\boldsymbol{s}[t] \in \mathbb{R}^N$, and the output as $\boldsymbol{y}[t] \in \mathbb{R}^L$. The weights of the input-to-reservoir, the internal reservoir, and the reservoir-to-output connections are stored in $\boldsymbol{W}^{\text{in}} = \left(w_{ij}^{\text{in}}\right) \in \mathbb{R}^{N \times K}$, $\boldsymbol{W}^{\text{res}} = \left(w_{ij}^{\text{res}}\right) \in \mathbb{R}^{N \times N}$, and $\boldsymbol{W}^{\text{out}} = \left(w_{ij}^{\text{out}}\right) \in \mathbb{R}^{L \times N}$, respectively.

At each discrete time step t, the internal state is updated according to

$$\boldsymbol{s}[t] = \tanh\left(\boldsymbol{W}^{\text{in}} \boldsymbol{x}[t] + \boldsymbol{W}^{\text{res}} \boldsymbol{s}[t-1]\right). \tag{1}$$

The output is obtained via a simple linear readout of this internal state:

$$\boldsymbol{y}[t] = \boldsymbol{W}^{\text{out}} \boldsymbol{s}[t]. \tag{2}$$

It is common to also include a bias in equations (1) and (2). This can be done by appending 1 to the input $\boldsymbol{x}[t]$ and the reservoir state $\boldsymbol{s}[t]$.

The distinctive feature of ESNs is that only their readout weights $\boldsymbol{W}^{\text{out}}$ are adjusted while the remaining weights $\boldsymbol{W}^{\text{in}}$ and $\boldsymbol{W}^{\text{res}}$ are random and fixed. This reduces their training to a linear regression, which can be performed very efficiently. The regression method of choice is usually ridge regression, as it offers a way to counter overfitting by regularizing the readout weights [13]. A detailed description of the training algorithm is given in [9].

Before an ESN can be trained, $\boldsymbol{W}^{\mathrm{in}}$ and $\boldsymbol{W}^{\mathrm{res}}$ need to be suitably initialized. Typically, the reservoir $\boldsymbol{W}^{\mathrm{res}}$ is connected sparsely with non-zero weights w_{ij}^{res} drawn from a zero-centered probability distribution [10]. Subsequently, $\boldsymbol{W}^{\mathrm{res}}$ is rescaled to set its spectral radius, i.e., the largest absolute value of its eigenvalues, to a specified value ρ. This rescaling effectively corresponds to modifying the variance of the non-zero weight distribution while leaving its mean unchanged. The elements w_{ij}^{in} of $\boldsymbol{W}^{\mathrm{in}}$ are usually drawn from the same probability distribution as the non-zero entries of $\boldsymbol{W}^{\mathrm{res}}$. Subsequently, $\boldsymbol{W}^{\mathrm{in}}$ is also rescaled [13].

The spectral radius ρ determines if an ESN has the echo state property (ESP). The ESP indicates that the influence of the initial reservoir state fades over time. As a result, the reservoir state is eventually fully determined by the input history and becomes an echo of prior input. This is essential for successfully training ESNs [10]. A mathematical definition of the ESP is given in [9].

The ESP is usually obtained in practice if the spectral radius ρ is below 1. Consequently, $\rho < 1$ being equivalent to obtaining the ESP is a widespread misconception in the RC literature. In reality, however, this condition is neither necessary nor sufficient for the ESP [28].

Additionally, the ESP on its own does not guarantee good performance, since the spectral radius is related to the intrinsic timescale of an ESN and therefore needs to be chosen according to the memory requirements of a specific task. There are no generally applicable strategies for optimally setting ρ [28] except for the rule of thumb that ρ should be closer to 1, the longer the memory of the input that a task requires. Overall, ρ is one of the most important hyperparameters of an ESN and typically needs to be fine-tuned manually.

2.2 Plasticity Rules

In very simplified terms, neural plasticity is the ability of networks in the brain to adapt and reorganize themselves. There is increasing evidence that this ability forms the basis of continual learning in adult brains [5]. We focus on the two most important types of plasticity, namely synaptic plasticity (SP) and intrinsic plasticity (IP). While SP changes the strength of synapses between pairs of neurons, IP modifies the internal excitability of individual neurons. Our mathematical definitions of the plasticity rules are taken from [5] if not stated otherwise.

The Hebbian rule [7] is an influential early SP model stating that connections between neurons that are active at the same time become stronger. Hence, transient experiences are incorporated into persistent memory traces, reflecting the idea of associative learning. Coincident neural activity is translated into associated activity and the correlation between neurons is increased.

The anti-Hebbian rule [2] arises if the connections between coincident neurons are weakened instead. It models dissociative learning and decorrelates the hidden neurons to maximize the information content in the network. Whether increasing the correlation of the output values through Hebbian-type or decreasing it through anti-Hebbian-type learning is more favorable for the performance of a neural network is a contradictory area in the theoretical role of plasticity. For pretraining ESNs, however, anti-Hebbian learning is preferred in the literature.

The basic anti-Hebbian rule is unsuitable in practice as it decreases the strength of synapses without limits. Therefore, we work with regulated versions of this rule. The anti-Oja's (AO) rule [17], which was developed by E. Oja by adding a counterweight term to the anti-Hebbian rule, is such a regulated version. Mathematically, it can be expressed as

$$w_{ij}^{\text{res}}[t+1] = w_{ij}^{\text{res}}[t] - \eta \left(s_j[t]s_i[t+1] - s_i[t+1]^2 w_{ij}^{\text{res}}[t] \right), \tag{3}$$

where η is the learning rate. As detailed in [16], Oja originally derived his rule as a local approximation of the normalized anti-Hebbian (NAH) rule:

$$w_{ij}^{\text{res}}[t+1] = \frac{w_{ij}^{\text{res}}[t] - \eta s_j[t]s_i[t+1]}{\sqrt{\sum_{k=1}^{N} \left(w_{ik}^{\text{res}}[t] - \eta s_k[t]s_i[t+1] \right)^2}}. \tag{4}$$

The Bienenstock-Cooper-Munro (BCM) rule [3] is another form of regulated Hebbian learning proposed at the same time as Oja's rule. It incorporates a sliding long-term potentiation (LTP) threshold to determine the direction of the weight update. Hence, this rule strikes a balance between connection strengthening and weakening. Like [29], we formulate the rule as suggested in [4]:

$$w_{ij}^{\text{res}}[t+1] = w_{ij}^{\text{res}}[t] + \eta \left(s_i[t+1] - \theta_{\text{LTP}_i} \right) s_j[t]s_i[t+1],$$

$$\theta_{\text{LTP}_i} = \frac{1}{h} \sum_{k=0}^{h} s_i[t+1-k]^2, \tag{5}$$

where θ_{LTP_i} is the LTP threshold of neuron i and h a specified time interval. This threshold marks the transition from long-term depression (LTD) to LTP.

In the BCM rule, synaptic LTD also affects non-active synapses which could cause an information loss for infrequent neuron activity patterns [23]. To reduce this loss, [23] extended the BCM rule with a second threshold for the activity of a postsynaptic neuron, below which the strength of its incoming connections remains unchanged. This yields the dual-threshold BCM (DT-BCM) rule:

$$w_{ij}^{\text{res}}[t+1] = \begin{cases} w_{ij}^{\text{res}}[t] + \eta \left(s_i[t+1] - \theta_{\text{LTP}_i} \right) s_j[t]s_i[t+1] & \text{if } s_i[t+1] > \theta_{\text{LTD}_i}, \\ w_{ij}^{\text{res}}[t] & \text{else,} \end{cases}$$

$$\theta_{\text{LTD}_i} = \alpha \sum_{k=0}^{h} s_i[t+1-k], \tag{6}$$

where α is a scaling factor and θ_{LTP_i} is calculated as in the BCM rule (5).

Contrary to SP, the investigation of IP was neglected for a long time. This was changed by the work of J. Triesch [21]. He derived gradient rules for the activation function of a neuron such that its output distribution becomes approximately exponential. It is assumed that the exponential distribution allows the neurons to transmit the maximum amount of information given fixed metabolic costs as it has the highest entropy of all non-negative distributions with a fixed mean.

J. Triesch used a parameterized sigmoid as activation function. Schrauwen et al. [19] transferred the gradient rules to neurons with hyperbolic tangent activation functions as commonly used in ESNs. They followed Triesch's original approach of maximizing the information contained in a neuron's output by maximizing the entropy of its output distribution while keeping certain moments of the distribution fixed. More specifically, they not only fixed the mean μ but also the standard deviation σ. This led to the Gaussian as target distribution.

To enable the transformation of a neuron's output distribution into a Gaussian, the state update Eq. (1) is extended by a gain $\boldsymbol{a}$ and a bias $\boldsymbol{b}$:

$$z[t] = \boldsymbol{W}^{\text{in}}\boldsymbol{x}[t] + \boldsymbol{W}^{\text{res}}\boldsymbol{s}[t-1], \quad \boldsymbol{s}[t] = \tanh\left(\boldsymbol{a}\boldsymbol{z}[t] + \boldsymbol{b}\right). \tag{7}$$

The gradient rules that [19] obtained for $\boldsymbol{a}$ and $\boldsymbol{b}$ are

$$\Delta b_k = -\eta \left(-\frac{\mu}{\sigma^2} + \frac{s_k[t]}{\sigma^2} \left(2\sigma^2 + 1 - s_k[t]^2 + \mu s_k[t] \right) \right), \quad \Delta a_k = \frac{\eta}{a_k} + \Delta b_k z_k[t]. \tag{8}$$

Contrary to SP, IP not only modifies $\boldsymbol{W}^{\text{res}}$ but also $\boldsymbol{W}^{\text{in}}$ and additionally introduces a bias $\boldsymbol{b}$ into the state update Eq. (1). This becomes evident by rewriting equation (7) as in Sect. 3.1 of [19].

3 Related Work

Pretraining an ESN with plasticity is supposed to make the network learn information embedded into the input data based on the activations created in the reservoir [29]. It is hoped that this prepares an ESN for learning how to generate predictions for the presented input and thereby leads to better results than a purely random reservoir. Hence, plasticity-based pretraining can be seen as a "learning-to-learn" [15] phase taking place before the actual learning step.

H. Jaeger mentioned the idea of pretraining the reservoir with plasticity in [11] soon after he had introduced the ESN. Although his attempts to decorrelate the reservoir activations with anti-Hebbian learning were unsuccessful, other researchers continued to work on this approach and reported promising results.

[1] enhanced the performance of an ESN on various time series prediction tasks through AO learning. [29] compared the effects of the AO and the BCM rule on multiple time series prediction and classification tasks. While both rules improved the results, this effect was more pronounced for the BCM rule. [23] introduced the DT-BCM rule, which caused a greater performance improvement than the regular BCM rule in multiple prediction tasks. [19] built on the work of [21] and used IP to maximize the information contained in the reservoir neuron states. This improved the results in multiple prediction tasks. [16,26] combined SP and IP into a synergistic learning rule which enhanced the performance more than either of these mechanisms on its own.

[23–25] introduced local versions of different plasticity rules, in which the parameters are learned individually for each of the reservoir neurons. These local versions led to better results than their global counterparts but made the pretraining substantially more computationally expensive.

There are also various more complex approaches for integrating plasticity into ESNs, e.g., [8] which introduced a delay-sensitive version of the BCM rule.

4 Methodology

Most of the works presented in Sect. 3 intended to improve the performance of an ESN with already optimized hyperparameters even further by applying plasticity-based pretraining. Our goal, however, is to evaluate whether this kind of pretraining can improve the performance of an ESN that is not already optimized for the given task. Additionally, we want to better understand how the pretraining modifies the network by analyzing its effect on the spectral radius.

4.1 Implementation

We implemented our experiments in Python using the library ReservoirPy[1], version 0.3.12. Our code is publicly available in our GitHub repository[2].

The considered ESN has a reservoir $\boldsymbol{W}^{\text{res}}$ of size $N = 100$ with a connectivity of 10%, normally distributed non-zero weights, and spectral radius $\rho = 0.5$. The input weights $\boldsymbol{W}^{\text{in}}$ also have a connectivity of 10%, which is the default value in ReservoirPy, and non-zero weights drawn from a standard Gaussian.

The task of the ESN is to predict the next value $\boldsymbol{x}[t+1]$ from the current input value $\boldsymbol{x}[t]$. We work with training and test series of lengths 4000 and 6000 respectively and normalize the training data to zero mean and unit variance, as this turned out to be beneficial in our experiments. For normalizing the test data, we use the mean and the variance of the training series. During the training, we dismiss an initial transient of length 500 after which we expect the reservoir state to be determined by the history of the preceding input up to a negligible error.

Before computing the readout weights $\boldsymbol{W}^{\text{out}}$ in the usual supervised way via ridge regression, where the regularization coefficient λ is chosen via generalized cross-validation (GCV) [6], we pretrain the reservoir with plasticity. As plasticity rules, we consider the AO, the NAH, the BCM, the DT-BCM rule, and IP, cf. Section 2.2. Note that the plasticity-based reservoir adaptation only takes place before the computation of $\boldsymbol{W}^{\text{out}}$, but no longer during the prediction phase.

Guided by [16,23], we set $\eta = 10^{-5}$ in the SP rules and $\eta = 10^{-6}$ in IP, $h = 10$ in BCM and DT-BCM, $\alpha = 0.1$ in DT-BCM, and $\mu = 0, \sigma = 1$ in IP. The plasticity rules are applied over a specified number of iterations, namely 10 iterations for the SP rules and 50 for IP, over the training series. At each discrete time step t, the weight updates are performed for all neurons in parallel.

---

[1] https://reservoirpy.readthedocs.io/.
[2] https://github.com/franziskaweber/impact_of_plasticity.

We assess the results with the normalized root mean squared error (NRMSE):

$$\text{NRMSE} = \frac{1}{\sigma(\boldsymbol{y})}\sqrt{\frac{1}{n}\sum_{t=1}^{n}(\boldsymbol{y}[t]-\hat{\boldsymbol{y}}[t])^2}, \tag{9}$$

where $\boldsymbol{y}$ is the target outcome, $\sigma(\boldsymbol{y})$ its standard deviation, and $\hat{\boldsymbol{y}}$ the prediction of the model. Because the performance of an ESN depends on the random initialization of $\boldsymbol{W}^{\text{in}}$ and $\boldsymbol{W}^{\text{res}}$, we report the average NRMSE and its standard deviation over 20 independent runs to get a more meaningful performance measure. For multi-dimensional series, we average these values across all dimensions.

To check if the influence of the pretraining on the performance of the network was statistically significant, we apply the Mann-Whitney U test at a significance level of 5%. We chose this test because it neither requires normality of the data nor equal variance of the two compared groups.

To better understand the effects of the different plasticity rules on the performance of an ESN, we first analyze the dependency of the performance on the spectral radius ρ by increasing ρ from 0.05 to 1.1 in steps of 0.05 and determining the NRMSE corresponding to each considered value of ρ. The remaining network parameters are left unchanged. Subsequently, we investigate how ρ changes through the application of the different pretraining methods by measuring its average and its standard deviation across the 20 independent runs.

4.2 Benchmark Datasets

In our experiments, we use three common RC benchmarks: the Mackey-Glass (MG), normalized auto-regressive moving average (NARMA), and Lorenz series.

The MG series was introduced in [14] to model certain physiological systems. It is described by the delay differential equation

$$\dot{x} = \frac{\beta x[t-\tau]}{1+x[t-\tau]^n} - \gamma x[t]. \tag{10}$$

We set $\beta = 0.2, n = 10, \gamma = 0.1$ which are the usual parameter values in the context of ESNs [27]. With these values, the system is chaotic for $\tau > 16.8$, meaning that small deviations in the current state can cause substantially different behavior. We use $\tau = 17$ which yields mildly chaotic behavior.

Our second benchmark is the NARMA series. Its underlying dynamics are described by a deterministic recurrent relation and randomness comes into play in the form of a uniformly distributed noise. The NARMA system of order n was formulated in [18] as

$$x[t+1] = \alpha x[t] + \beta x[t]\left(\sum_{i=0}^{n-1} x[t-i]\right) + \gamma u[t-n+1]u[t] + \delta, \tag{11}$$

where u is an external input drawn from the uniform distribution $\mathcal{U}(0, 0.5)$. The NARMA systems used for benchmarking ESNs are typically of order $n = 10$ or

$n = 30$ [27]. We work with a system of order $n = 10$ and use the same parameter values as [18], namely $\alpha = 0.3, \beta = 0.05, \gamma = 1.5, \delta = 0.1$.

Our third benchmark is the Lorenz system, which was initially derived in [12] to model certain weather-based dynamical systems. It is described by the following system of three coupled ordinary differential equations:

$$\dot{x}_1 = \sigma(x_1 - x_2), \quad \dot{x}_2 = x_1(\rho - x_3) - x_2, \quad \dot{x}_3 = x_1 x_2 - \beta x_3. \quad (12)$$

We adopt the parameter values which are typically used for benchmarking ESNs: $\sigma = 10, \rho = 28, \beta = 8/3$ [27].

5 Results

The effects of the different pretraining methods are presented in Table 1.

Table 1. Results achieved on our three benchmarks in terms of the average NRMSE and its standard deviation over 20 independent runs. Row 1 contains the results without pretraining and the following rows the results obtained with the different pretraining methods. Methods that significantly improved or worsened these results are marked with ($\uparrow$) and ($\downarrow$), respectively. Methods marked with ($-$) had no significant effect

	MG	NARMA	Lorenz
ESN	0.00257 ± 0.00031	0.73395 ± 0.00629	0.00236 ± 0.00044
AO	0.00209 ± 0.00023 ($\uparrow$)	0.73124 ± 0.00812 ($\uparrow$)	0.00368 ± 0.00196 ($\downarrow$)
NAH	0.00352 ± 0.00204 ($-$)	0.72141 ± 0.00653 ($\uparrow$)	0.01312 ± 0.00490 ($\downarrow$)
BCM	0.00225 ± 0.00018 ($\uparrow$)	0.73166 ± 0.00522 ($-$)	0.00178 ± 0.00027 ($\uparrow$)
DT-BCM	0.00258 ± 0.00032 ($-$)	0.73565 ± 0.00701 ($-$)	0.00247 ± 0.00056 ($-$)
IP	0.00213 ± 0.00030 ($\uparrow$)	0.73022 ± 0.00372 ($\uparrow$)	0.00198 ± 0.00028 ($\uparrow$)

To explain these effects, we first analyzed the dependency of the ESN's performance on its spectral radius. The resulting plots are provided in our GitHub repository[3]. Our observations can be summarized as follows:

- **MG:** The optimal spectral radius is $\rho = 0.75$ with a corresponding average NRMSE of about 0.00208. More generally speaking, $\rho \in [0.45, 0.95]$ leads to very good results, namely to an average NRMSE below 0.003.
- **NARMA:** The optimal spectral radius is $\rho = 0.6$ with a corresponding average NRMSE of about 0.732. Overall, the values $\rho \in [0.45, 1.05]$ all lead to a similar average NRMSE between 0.73 and 0.74.
- **Lorenz:** The optimal spectral radius is $\rho = 0.4$ with a corresponding average NRMSE of about 0.00223. More generally speaking, $\rho \in [0.2, 0.6]$ leads to very good results, namely to an average NRMSE below 0.003.

Subsequently, we investigated how ρ changed through the application of the different plasticity rules. The result is displayed in Fig. 1. We observe that the influence of each rule on ρ is similar across all three benchmarks:

---
[3] https://github.com/franziskaweber/impact_of_plasticity.

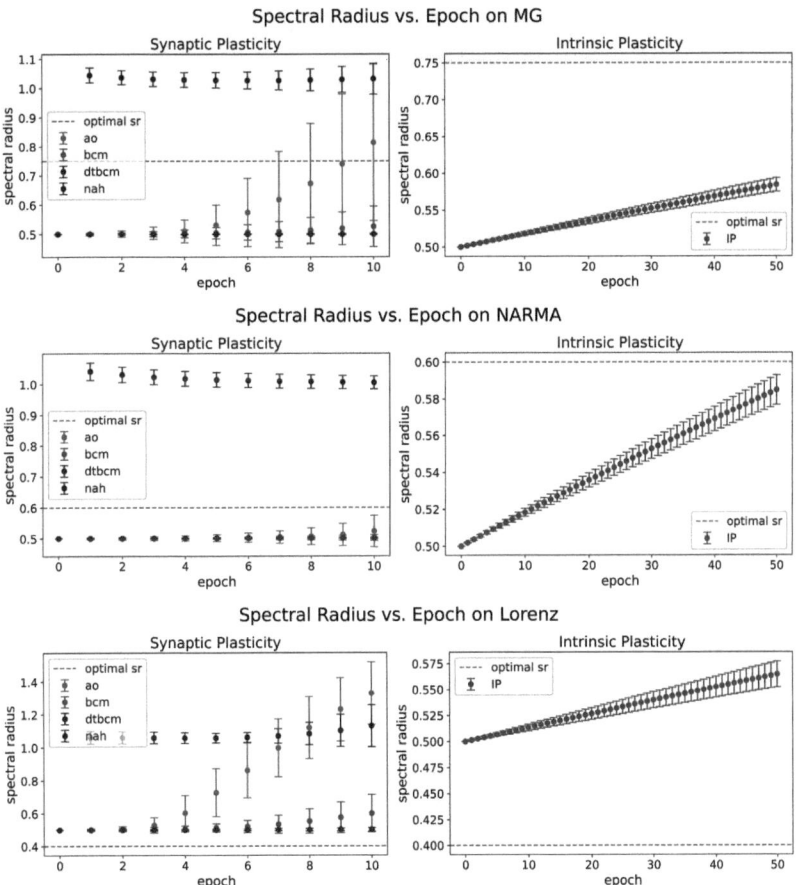

Fig. 1. Average value and standard deviation of ρ over the epochs of the different plasticity rules across the 20 independent runs

- **AO:** ρ increases, namely from 0.5 to 0.81 ± 0.27 in the MG, from 0.5 to 0.52 ± 0.05 in the NARMA, and from 0.5 to 1.33 ± 0.19 in the Lorenz task.
- **NAH:** ρ jumps from 0.5 to above 1 in the first epoch, namely to 1.04 in the MG and the NARMA task and to 1.06 in the Lorenz task. Afterwards, ρ remains mostly unchanged in the MG task, decreases slightly in the NARMA task, and increases in the Lorenz task. Hence, in the last epoch, ρ has values of 1.03 ± 0.05, 1 ± 0.02, and 1.13 ± 0.13, respectively.
- **BCM:** In the MG and the Lorenz task, ρ increases from 0.5 to 0.53 ± 0.07 and from 0.5 to 0.6 ± 0.11, respectively. In the NARMA task, ρ remains relatively unaffected and arrives at a value of 0.502 ± 0.01 in the last epoch.
- **DT-BCM:** ρ does not really change. Its value after the last epoch is 0.5 ± 0.002 in the MG and NARMA and 0.5 ± 0.01 in the Lorenz task.

- **IP:** ρ grows from 0.5 to 0.58 ± 0.01 in the MG and the NARMA task and from 0.5 to 0.56 ± 0.01 in the Lorenz task.

6 Discussion

While pretraining with IP significantly improved the ESN's performance across all benchmarks, this was not the case for any of the considered SP rules. Hence, based on our experiments, IP appears promising for improving the performance of a non-optimized ESN, whereas SP does not seem to be generally advantageous.

Of course, pretraining with SP rules might have worked better had we invested more effort into optimizing their hyperparameters. In particular, our LTD threshold in the DT-BCM rule seems to be unsuitable as this plasticity rule had very little effect on the network's performance across all three benchmarks. However, one would hope that the plasticity rules perform reasonably well for a wide range of hyperparameter values. Otherwise, their successful application would be similarly difficult as the original problem of appropriately initializing ESNs.

Regarding the effects of plasticity on the spectral radius ρ, it turned out that ρ was driven into regions of bad performance when the pretraining significantly worsened the results of the network. When the pretraining had no significant effect, ρ remained mostly unchanged or was moved into regions of similar performance. The relation of significant performance improvement to the change in the value of ρ, on the other hand, was not that clear. In this case, ρ generally stayed inside the region of well-performing values. However, ρ was sometimes moved into regions of slightly worse rather than better performance.

We intended to compare our findings about the effect of plasticity on the spectral radius ρ to the literature. Unfortunately, not a lot of works about plasticity-based pretraining analyzed this effect. To the best of our knowledge, the only works with analyses comparable to ours are [15, 16] which performed their investigations on the same mildly chaotic MG system as us. In [16], the application of the NAH rule also made ρ jump above 1 in the first epoch after which it remained roughly constant until it continued to grow further around epoch 10. In [15], it was observed that the application of the AO rule increased ρ. Hence, the results from [15, 16] are consistent with our findings.

Overall, this shows that the effect of plasticity on ρ is not sufficient for explaining why a pretraining method works in some cases but not in others. Further analysis is needed to fully understand how plasticity modifies the network. Investigations performed in [15, 16], for example, indicate that the beneficial effect of IP might be due to a widening of the activity range of at least a part of the reservoir neurons. Additionally, it would be interesting to analyze the effects of the modified input scaling and the additional bias, which are also caused by IP.

7 Conclusion

In this paper, we analyzed the effects of pretraining the reservoir with four different SP rules and with IP. Our goals were to evaluate whether such pretraining is able to improve the performance of an ESN that is not optimized for the task at hand. Additionally, we intended to better understand the influence of the plasticity rules on the network by analyzing their effect on the spectral radius ρ.

IP significantly improved the ESN's performance across all three benchmarks while this was not the case for any of the four considered SP rules. Overall, the effect of plasticity on the spectral radius ρ was not sufficient for explaining why a pretraining method worked in some cases but not in others. However, we could explain the cases where pretraining significantly worsened the results of the network by ρ having been moved into regions of bad performance.

In the future, our theoretical investigations about the influence of the different plasticity rules on an ESN should be extended. For example, in addition to the spectral radius, other important ESN hyperparameters such as the size of the reservoir or the leakage rate should be taken into account. This could help to obtain more generally valid conclusions about the potential of these rules as an unsupervised reservoir adaptation method.

References

1. Babinec, Š, Pospíchal, J.: Improving the prediction accuracy of echo state neural networks by anti-oja's learning. In: de Sá, J.M., Alexandre, L.A., Duch, W., Mandic, D. (eds.) ICANN 2007. LNCS, vol. 4668, pp. 19–28. Springer, Heidelberg (2007). https://doi.org/10.1007/978-3-540-74690-4_3
2. Barlow, H.B., Földiák, P.: Adaptation and Decorrelation in the Cortex. In: Comput. Neuron, pp. 54–72. Addison-Wesley, Wokingham (1989). https://doi.org/10.5555/103938.103942
3. Bienenstock, E.L., Cooper, L.N., Munro, P.W.: Theory for the development of neuron selectivity: orientation specificity and binocular interaction in visual cortex. J. Neurosci. **2**(1), 32–48 (1982). https://doi.org/10.1523/JNEUROSCI.02-01-00032.1982
4. Castellani, G.C., Intrator, N., Shouval, H., Cooper, L.N.: Solutions of the BCM learning rule in a network of lateral interacting nonlinear neurons. Netw. **10**(2), 111–121 (1999). https://pubmed.ncbi.nlm.nih.gov/10378187/
5. Chrol-Cannon, J., Jin, Y.: Computational modeling of neural plasticity for self-organization of neural networks. Biosyst. **125**, 43–54 (2014). https://doi.org/10.1016/J.BIOSYSTEMS.2014.04.003
6. Golub, G.H., Heath, M., Wahba, G.: Generalized cross-validation as a method for choosing a good ridge parameter. Technometr. **21**(2), 215–223 (1979). https://doi.org/10.2307/1268518
7. Hebb, D.O.: The Organization of Behavior: A Neuropsychological Theory. Wiley, New York (1949). https://doi.org/10.1002/sce.37303405110
8. Iacob, S., Chavlis, S., Poirazi, P., Dambre, J.: Delay-sensitive local plasticity in echo state networks. In: IJCNN 2023, pp. 1–8. IEEE (2023). https://doi.org/10.1109/IJCNN54540.2023.10191901

9. Jaeger, H.: The "Echo State" Approach to Analysing and Training Recurrent Neural Networks. GMD Report 148, GMD (2001). https://doi.org/10.24406/publica-fhg-291111
10. Jaeger, H.: Tutorial on Training Recurrent Neural Networks, covering BPPT, RTRL, EKF and the "Echo State Network" Approach. GMD Report 159, GMD (2002), https://publica.fraunhofer.de/entities/publication/483214eb-2e22-4b69-a5d8-5d8d198166e4
11. Jaeger, H.: Reservoir riddles: suggestions for echo state network research. In: Proceedings. IJCNN 2005, vol. 3, pp. 1460–1462. IEEE (2005). https://doi.org/10.1109/IJCNN.2005.1556090
12. Lorenz, E.N.: Deterministic Nonperiodic Flow. J. Atmos. Sci. **20**(2), 130–141 (1963). 10.1175/1520-0469(1963)020<0130:DNF>2.0.CO;2
13. Lukoševičius, M.: A practical guide to applying echo state networks. In: Montavon, G., Orr, G.B., Müller, K.-R. (eds.) Neural Networks: Tricks of the Trade. LNCS, vol. 7700, pp. 659–686. Springer, Heidelberg (2012). https://doi.org/10.1007/978-3-642-35289-8_36
14. Mackey, M.C., Glass, L.: Oscillation and chaos in physiological control systems. Sci. **197**(4300), 287–289 (1977). https://doi.org/10.1126/science.267326
15. Morales, G.B.: The Dynamics of Neural Codes in Biological and Artificial Neural Networks: From Criticality to Machine Learning and Drifting Representations. Ph.D. thesis, Universidad de Granada (2024), https://hdl.handle.net/10481/89202
16. Morales, G.B., Mirasso, C.R., Soriano, M.C.: Unveiling the role of plasticity rules in reservoir computing. Neurocomput. **461**, 705–715 (2021). https://doi.org/10.1016/J.NEUCOM.2020.05.127
17. Oja, E.: Simplified neuron model as a principal component analyzer. J. Math. Biol. **15**(3), 267–273 (1982). https://doi.org/10.1007/BF00275687
18. Rodan, A., Tiño, P.: Minimum Complexity Echo State Network. IEEE Trans. Neural Netw. **22**(1), 131–144 (2011). https://doi.org/10.1109/TNN.2010.2089641
19. Schrauwen, B., Wardermann, M., Verstraeten, D., Steil, J.J., Stroobandt, D.: Improving reservoirs using intrinsic plasticity. Neurocomput. **71**(7–9), 1159–1171 (2008). https://doi.org/10.1016/J.NEUCOM.2007.12.020
20. Soltani, R., Benmohamed, E., Ltifi, H.: Echo state network optimization: a systematic literature review. Neural Process. Lett. **55**(8), 10251–10285 (2023). https://doi.org/10.1007/S11063-023-11326-W
21. Triesch, J.: A gradient rule for the plasticity of a neuron's intrinsic excitability. In: Duch, W., Kacprzyk, J., Oja, E., Zadrożny, S. (eds.) ICANN 2005. LNCS, vol. 3696, pp. 65–70. Springer, Heidelberg (2005). https://doi.org/10.1007/11550822_11
22. Verstraeten, D., Schrauwen, B., D'Haene, M., Stroobandt, D.: An experimental unification of reservoir computing methods. Neural Netw. **20**(3), 391–403 (2007). https://doi.org/10.1016/J.NEUNET.2007.04.003
23. Wang, X., Jin, Y., Du, W., Wang, J.: Evolving dual-threshold bienenstock-cooper-munro learning rules in echo state networks. IEEE Trans. Neural Netw. Learn. Syst. **35**(2), 1572–1583 (2024). https://doi.org/10.1109/TNNLS.2022.3184004
24. Wang, X., Jin, Y., Hao, K.: Echo state networks regulated by local intrinsic plasticity rules for regression. Neurocomput. **351**, 111–122 (2019). https://doi.org/10.1016/J.NEUCOM.2019.03.032
25. Wang, X., Jin, Y., Hao, K.: Evolving local plasticity rules for synergistic learning in echo state networks. IEEE Trans. Neural Netw. Learn. Syst. **31**(4), 1363–1374 (2020). https://doi.org/10.1109/TNNLS.2019.2919903

26. Wang, X., Jin, Y., Hao, K.: Synergies between synaptic and intrinsic plasticity in echo state networks. Neurocomput. **432**, 32–43 (2021). https://doi.org/10.1016/J.NEUCOM.2020.12.007
27. Wringe, C., Trefzer, M., Stepney, S.: Reservoir Computing Benchmarks: A Review, a Taxonomy, Some Best Practices. arXiv preprint arXiv:2405.06561 (2024), arXiv:2405.06561
28. Yildiz, I.B., Jaeger, H., Kiebel, S.J.: Re-visiting the echo state property. Neural Netw. **35**, 1–9 (2012). https://doi.org/10.1016/J.NEUNET.2012.07.005
29. Yusoff, M., Chrol-Cannon, J., Jin, Y.: Modeling neural plasticity in echo state networks for classification and regression. Inf. Sci. **364–365**, 184–196 (2016). https://doi.org/10.1016/J.INS.2015.11.017

Benchmarking Nonlinear Readouts in Linear Reservoir Networks

Giacomo Lagomarsini[(✉)], Andrea Ceni, and Claudio Gallicchio

Department of Computer Science, University of Pisa, Largo Bruno Pontecorvo, 3, 56127 Pisa, Italy
g.lagomarsini@studenti.unipi.it,
{andrea.ceni,claudio.gallicchio}@unipi.it

Abstract. Recent theoretical advances have demonstrated the universality of linear Reservoir Computing (RC) models equipped with nonlinear readouts, showing their potential to approximate arbitrary input-output mappings. However, practical insights into the selection and performance of nonlinear readouts are limited. This paper addresses this gap by systematically benchmarking a spectrum of nonlinear readouts within linear RC frameworks. Our results reveal the practical trade-offs in accuracy and efficiency across tasks, offering insights on how to train performant RC systems with linear recurrence. These findings provide valuable guidelines for designing efficient recurrent architectures that combine theoretical guarantees with state-of-the-art performance in sequential data processing.

Keywords: Reservoir Computing · Echo State Networks · Linearity

1 Introduction

Recurrent neural networks (RNNs) are fundamental tools for modeling sequential and temporal data, offering powerful capabilities for tasks such as speech processing, time-series prediction, and control systems [6]. However, training RNNs effectively remains a challenge due to issues like vanishing gradients and high computational complexity, particularly when optimizing recurrent connections [10]. To address these challenges, Reservoir Computing (RC) emerged in the years as an alternative training approach for RNNs, where the recurrent dynamics are fixed, and the learning capacity resides in an external readout function [7,8,12,13]. Recently, a growing body of theoretical work has established the universality of linear RC models equipped with nonlinear readouts, demonstrating their ability to approximate arbitrary input-output mappings under certain conditions. These results provide a strong theoretical foundation for the potential of such systems in solving complex computational tasks. However, despite these universality theorems, the choice of nonlinear readout function is far from trivial, as the practical performance of different approaches can vary significantly. Understanding which nonlinear readouts are most effective remains an open question, motivating further empirical investigation.

Parallel to these theoretical advances, recent developments in deep learning have highlighted the practical power of linear recurrent systems, particularly in the context of linear State-Space Models (SSMs). Architectures like Structured State Space Model (S4) [4] and Linear Recurrent Unit (LRU) [9] have demonstrated exceptional performance across sequential learning tasks, achieving state-of-the-art results by leveraging linear recurrence for efficient sequence modeling while relegating nonlinear processing to specialized layers or blocks. These exceptional results suggest that shifting nonlinear operations outside the recurrence dynamics may not only preserve theoretical universality, but also improve computational efficiency and generalization in real-world applications.

Building on these theoretical insights and empirical breakthroughs, this paper investigates the effectiveness of various nonlinear readouts appended to linear RC models. Specifically, we conduct a systematic empirical evaluation of different trainable nonlinear functions, aiming to identify promising approaches that can harness the universal approximation power predicted by theory while achieving robust performance in practice. By bridging the theoretical underpinnings of RC with the experimental progress in deep learning, our work provides critical insights into the design of efficient and expressive models for sequential data.

The remainder of this paper is organized as follows. Section 2 introduces the required fundamental concepts on RC. Section 3 introduces the concept of linear reservoirs with nonlinear readouts, exploring their theoretical foundations and practical implementations. Section 4 presents our experimental analysis. Finally, Sect. 5 concludes the paper with a summary of our findings and potential avenues for future research.

2 Reservoir Computing

RC is a computational framework for efficiently training RNNs to process sequential and time-series data. The key idea of RC is to leverage the high-dimensional dynamics of a randomly initialised, fixed recurrent layer, called the reservoir, and train only a lightweight dense layer, called the readout.

The Echo State Network (ESN) model is the most prominent form of reservoir computer. This model consists of a nonlinear reservoir function, that defines the state dynamic of the model, $\mathbf{h}_t = \tanh(\mathbf{A}\mathbf{h}_{t-1} + \mathbf{B}\mathbf{x}_t + \mathbf{b})$, where $\mathbf{x}_t \in \mathbb{R}^{N_x}$ is the input vector at time t, $\mathbf{h}_t \in \mathbb{R}^{N_h}$ is the state space vector at time t, $\mathbf{A} \in \mathbb{R}^{N_h \times N_h}$, and $\mathbf{B} \in \mathbb{R}^{N_h \times N_x}$ are the hidden-to-hidden and input-to-hidden reservoir matrices, and $\mathbf{b}$ is the bias. The components of $\mathbf{A}$ and $\mathbf{B}$ are randomly drawn. We call $\mathbf{A}$ the *reservoir matrix*, and $\mathbf{B}$ the *input matrix* of the ESN. The readout function is simply a linear transformation, trained using least-squares regression. Usually, the ESN also comprises a leakage term, making the state equation

$$\mathbf{h}_t = \alpha \tanh(\mathbf{A}\mathbf{h}_{t-1} + \mathbf{B}\mathbf{x}_t + \mathbf{b}) + (1-\alpha)\mathbf{h}_{t-1}, \tag{1}$$

where $\alpha \in (0,1]$ is the leak rate. A reservoir computer with state transition function (1) is called a Leaky ESN.

A foundational concept in the theory of RC is the Echo State Property (ESP), which ensures the ability of the RC to process and store information in a stable and reliable manner. The ESP requires that the influence of initial conditions on the reservoir state vanishes over time, allowing the reservoir dynamics to develop a high-dimensional representation uniquely determined by the input signal driving the dynamics [14]. Precisely, we refer to the following definition of the ESP.

Definition 1. *Let $F(\mathbf{h}, \mathbf{x})$ be a function from $\mathbb{R}^{N_h} \times \mathbb{R}^{N_x}$ to $\mathbb{R}^{N_h}$. We say that F satisfies the Echo State Property (ESP) if, given any sequence $(\mathbf{x}_i)_i$, and any pair of initial conditions $\mathbf{h}_0, \mathbf{h}'_0 \in \mathbb{R}^{N_h}$, then*

$$\lim_{t \to \infty} \|\mathbf{h}_t - \mathbf{h}'_t\| = 0, \tag{2}$$

where, for each $t \in \mathbb{N}$, $\mathbf{h}_t = F(\mathbf{h}_{t-1}, \mathbf{x}_t)$ and $\mathbf{h}'_t = F(\mathbf{h}'_{t-1}, \mathbf{x}_t)$

A simple sufficient condition assuring the ESP for ESN models is $\|\mathbf{A}\| < 1$, where $\|\mathbf{A}\|$ denotes the spectral norm of the reservoir matrix $\mathbf{A}$. However, this condition constrains the reservoir dynamics to be strictly contracting at each time step. A widespread rule of thumb is to set the spectral radius $\rho(\mathbf{A})$ to be around 1. This results in a necessary condition for the ESP for the particular case of zero input.

3 Linear Reservoirs with Nonlinear Readout

Classically ESNs are provided with a nonlinear reservoir and a linear readout. Here we move the nonlinearity at the readout level keeping the reservoir dynamics linear. Specifically, we define a (leaky) Linear Reservoir Network (LRN) as the RC model with state-update function

$$\mathbf{h}_t = \alpha(\mathbf{A}\mathbf{h}_{t-1} + \mathbf{B}\mathbf{x}_t + \mathbf{b}) + (1-\alpha)\mathbf{h}_{t-1}, \tag{3}$$

and readout function $\mathbf{y}_t = f(\mathbf{h}_t)$, where f is a nonlinear function. Because the reservoir is linear, f should be nonlinear, or else the system should be able to only approximate linear systems. Our objective is validating possible readout functions, and finding the best trade-off between expressivity and computational complexity. Moreover, we want to verify if the linear reservoir is, in practice, expressive enough, when compared with a nonlinear leaky ESN. In the remainder of this section, in Subsect. 3.1, we briefly recall results on expressivity of linear reservoirs, and draw parallelism to linear reservoir models, in particular State Space Models (SSMs). Next, in Subsect. 3.2 we analyze the ESP of LRN, providing sufficient and necessary conditions. Finally, we introduce a range of possible readout functions, discussing theoretical expressivity and complexity.

3.1 Related Work

Universality of Linear Reservoirs. Expressivity of linear reservoir has been studied in various settings. Grygoreva et al. [3] states that linear reservoir with universal readout are universal in the class of time-invariant, fading memory filter with deterministic inputs, i.e. they can approximate arbitrarily well any filter in such class. This expressivity result is the very same proved for ESNs in [2]. For both ESN and linear reservoirs, the results have also been extended for stochastic inputs [1] (Proposition III.1).

State Space Models. Linear recurrence has been popularized in the context of deep learning as a possible alternative to classic RNN processing by structured SSMs like S4 [4] and LRU [9]. These innovative recurrent architectures are designed to maximize the memory capacity of the network, by dropping the nonlinearity between the recurrence steps, and smart initialization of the recurrence matrix. In SSMs, the dynamic of the hidden state $\mathbf{h}(t)$ is viewed as a continuous time dynamical system that is then integrated in a discrete time model. Then, SSMs focused on trying to find recurrence matrices that guarantee both efficiency in the matrix-vector multiplication, and long memory. Linear Recurrent Unit (LRU) showed that it is not necessary to view the dynamic as a discrete version of a continuous time system. They instead focused on initializing the transition matrix diagonally. The initialization allows to directly control the eigenvalues of the reservoir matrix. This approach is closer to that used in initializing the matrix in ESN theory, where the main concern is controlling the dynamic of the state transition function. The approach of LRU, though, moves the dynamic in the complex field. Instead, in this work we use a dense real matrix.

3.2 ESP of Linear Reservoirs

For LRNs, the ESP can be investigated through an exact analysis, due to the lack of the nonlinearity in the recurrence.

Theorem 1. *An LRN of Eq. (3) satisfies the ESP (2) if and only if* $\rho(\alpha \mathbf{A} + (1-\alpha)\mathbf{I}) < 1$.

Proof. The effective transition matrix of Eq. (3) is $\tilde{\mathbf{A}} = \alpha \mathbf{A} + (1-\alpha)\mathbf{I}$ Consider any vector $\mathbf{h}_0 \in \mathbb{R}^{N_h}$. Let $\mathbf{h}_{t+1}$ be the state vector obtained at time $t+1$ from the initial condition $\mathbf{h}_0$. Since the recursion is linear, we can unroll it to make the dependency of $\mathbf{h}_{t+1}$ from $\mathbf{h}_0$ explicit:

$$\mathbf{h}_{t+1} = \tilde{\mathbf{A}}\mathbf{h}_t + \mathbf{B}\mathbf{x}_{t+1} \tag{4}$$

$$= \tilde{\mathbf{A}}^2 \mathbf{h}_{t-1} + \tilde{\mathbf{A}}\mathbf{B}\mathbf{x}_t + \mathbf{B}\mathbf{x}_{t+1} \tag{5}$$

$$= \underbrace{\tilde{\mathbf{A}}^{t+1}\mathbf{h}_0}_{i.c.\ dependence} + \sum_{i=0}^{t} \tilde{\mathbf{A}}^i \mathbf{B}\mathbf{x}_{t-i} \tag{6}$$

If $\rho(\tilde{\mathbf{A}}) < 1$ then $\tilde{\mathbf{A}}^{t+1}$ converges to null matrix, as $t \to \infty$. Since $\tilde{\mathbf{A}}^{t+1}\mathbf{h}_0$ is the only dependence on the initial state, the ESP holds. This proves the sufficient condition for the ESP.

Otherwise, if $\rho(\tilde{\mathbf{A}}) > 1$, take $\mathbf{h}_0$ as the eigenvector associated to an eigenvalue λ of $\tilde{\mathbf{A}}$, such that $|\lambda| > 1$, and $\mathbf{h}'_0 = \mathbf{0}$. Then, from (4)-(6), $\|\mathbf{h}_{t+1} - \mathbf{h}'_{t+1}\|_2 = \|\tilde{\mathbf{A}}^{t+1}\mathbf{h}_0\|_2 = |\lambda^{t+1}| \cdot \|\mathbf{h}_0\|$ diverges. Therefore, if $\rho(\tilde{\mathbf{A}}) > 1$, the ESP does not hold. This proves the necessary condition.

We can see from Eq. (6) that the term involving the initial condition vanishes with the power of the reservoir matrix, if and only if the spectral radius $\rho(\mathbf{A}) < 1$. Therefore, the rule of thumb used in traditional ESNs turns out a necessary and sufficient condition for the ESP in an LRN model. Moreover, a sufficient condition for the ESP holds for LRN similar to standard nonlinear ESNs, as stated in the proposition below.

Proposition 1. *Let us call $\tilde{\mathbf{A}} = \alpha \mathbf{A} + (1-\alpha)\mathbf{I}$. An LRN of Equation (3) satisfies the ESP (2) if $\|\tilde{\mathbf{A}}\|_2 < 1$.*

Proof. Let $\mathbf{h}_0$ $\mathbf{h}'_0$ be two vectors in $\mathbb{R}^{N_h}$, and $(\mathbf{x}_i)_i$ be any sequence of inputs. By hypothesis, $\|\tilde{\mathbf{A}}\|_2 < 1$, therefore there exists an $\epsilon > 0$ such that $\|\tilde{\mathbf{A}}\|_2 = (1-\epsilon) < 1$. Then, for any $t \in \mathbb{N}$, by a recursive argument we get:

$$\begin{aligned}
\|\mathbf{h}_t - \mathbf{h}'_t\|_2 &= \|\tilde{\mathbf{A}}\mathbf{h}_{t-1} + \mathbf{B}\mathbf{x}_t - (\tilde{\mathbf{A}}\mathbf{h}'_{t-1} + \mathbf{B}\mathbf{x}_t)\|_2 \\
&= \|\tilde{\mathbf{A}}(\mathbf{h}_{t-1} - \mathbf{h}'_{t-1})\|_2 \\
&\leq \|\tilde{\mathbf{A}}\|_2 \cdot \|(\mathbf{h}_{t-1} - \mathbf{h}'_{t-1})\|_2 \\
&= (1-\epsilon) \cdot \|(\mathbf{h}_{t-1} - \mathbf{h}'_{t-1})\|_2 \leq \ldots \\
&\leq (1-\epsilon)^t \cdot \|\mathbf{h}_0 - \mathbf{h}'_0\| \xrightarrow{t \to \infty} 0.
\end{aligned}$$

Clearly, the sufficient condition for the ESP of Proposition 1 is much stronger than Theorem 1, since the former implies contraction at each time step, while the latter is an asymptotic condition of stability.

3.3 Nonlinear Readout Functions

In traditional ESNs, the system exhibits nonlinearity in its recurrent dynamics, while the readout layer is typically a simple linear model, often trained in closed form. When using a linear reservoir model, a nonlinearity must necessarily be in the readout, otherwise we lose guarantees of universality. There are several choices for this nonlinearity, and now we will analyze those that we will benchmark in the next section.

tanh *Readout.* The most straightforward option is moving the tanh nonlinearity after the recursion, obtaining a readout of the form

$$\mathbf{y}_t = \mathbf{W}\tanh(\mathbf{h}_t), \tag{7}$$

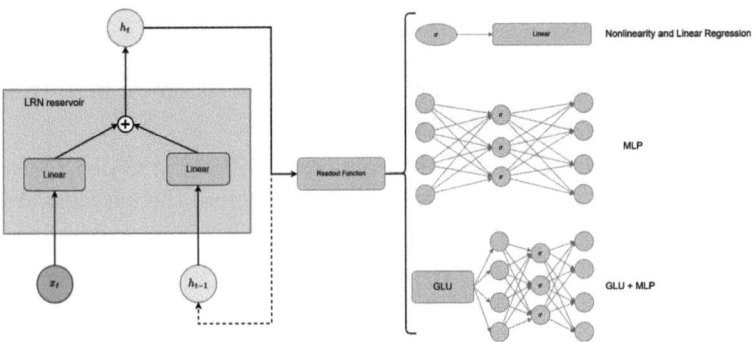

Fig. 1. Left: LRN reservoir; the only distinction from a standard ESN is the absence of a nonlinear transformation after combining the input and recurrent components, represented by a + symbol. **Right:** possible readout functions considered: any nonlinearity followed by a linear layer, an MLP, and a GLU-MLP. Notice that in the case given by *nonlinearity+Linear Readout*, in the paper we consider as σ nonlinearity either the hyperbolic tangent tanh or a degree 2 polynomial. See details in the text (Sect. 3.3).

where $\mathbf{W}$ is the trainable readout matrix. We call this readout function a tanh readout.

Polynomial Readout Linear reservoir computers with polynomial readouts

$$\mathbf{y}_t = p(\mathbf{h}_t) \tag{8}$$

have been shown to be universal approximators of fading memory filters in [3]. This readout can simply be trained by creating the polynomial features and fitting the coefficients of the polynomial. For example, suppose we are training a polynomial readout p of degree 2, and denote by $(\mathbf{h}_t)_i$ the i-th component of the vector $\mathbf{h}_t$. In this case,

$$p(\mathbf{h}_t) = \sum_{i,j=0, i \geq j}^{N_h} p_{i,j}^{(2)} \cdot (\mathbf{h}_t)_i \cdot (\mathbf{h}_t)_j + \sum_{k=0}^{N_h} p_k^{(1)} \cdot (\mathbf{h}_t)_k + p^{(0)},$$

where $p_{i,j}^{(2)}$ are the polynomial coefficients relative to the degree 2 part, $p_i^{(1)}$ are the coefficient relative to the linear part, and $p^{(0)}$ is the constant. Concretely, first we create the polynomial variables, multiplying $(\mathbf{h}_t)_i \cdot (\mathbf{h}_t)_j$ for each pair of reservoir variables i and j. Calling $\mathbf{z}_t$ the vector obtained by concatenating the second degree and the first degree variables, we can train the readout using least square regression on $\mathbf{z}_1, \ldots, \mathbf{z}_t$. Notice that, in general, the dimensionality of $\mathbf{z}_t$ will be much larger than $\mathbf{h}_t$. As a result, despite the polynomial readout being also trainable in closed form, the training could be more expensive than that of a tanh readout.

MLP Readout. Another possible class of readouts is that of one hidden layer MLP readouts,

$$\mathbf{y}_t = \mathbf{W}_1 \sigma \left(\mathbf{W}_2 \mathbf{h}_t \right) = \text{MLP}(\mathbf{h}_t), \tag{9}$$

where σ is a nonlinearity.

MLP readouts are a family of functions that approximate arbitrarily well any continuous function in a compact space, therefore as shown in [1] (Corollary III.6), the resulting reservoir model is universal.

GLU-MLP Readout. In many state space models [4,9,11], a Gated Linear Unit (GLU) is used between each recurrence layer and before the feed-forward readout. A GLU layer is defined by

$$\mathbf{z}_t = \mathbf{W}\mathbf{h_t} * \sigma(\mathbf{W}_g \mathbf{h}_t), \tag{10}$$

where $\mathbf{W}, \mathbf{W}_g \in \mathbb{R}^{N_z \times N_h}$ are trainable matrices, σ is the sigmoid function, and $*$ is a component-wise product. Therefore, we also benchmarked a GLU-MLP readout, that is composed by a GLU layer and one hidden layer MLP.

Figure 1 illustrates the LRN model, with the benchmarked nonlinear readouts. Table 1 shows the number of trainable parameters for each readout type, assuming the same reservoir size N_h and number of outputs N_y. For MLP-based models, we tied the size of the hidden layer to the reservoir size. Moreover, we only reported the leading coefficients (e.g. we omitted the biases from the count).

Table 1. Number of trainable parameters for each readout type, in function of the reservoir size N_h, and the output size N_y.

readout	trainable parameters	trainable in closed form
tanh	$N_h \cdot N_y$	Yes
poly (degree p)	$\frac{(N_h+p)\cdot\ldots\cdot(N_h+1)}{p!} \cdot N_y$	Yes
MLP	$N_h^2 + N_h \cdot N_y$	No
GLU-MLP	$3N_h^2 + N_h \cdot N_y$	No

4 Experiments

In this section, we present a comparative analysis of the different readouts introduced in Sect. 3. Section 4.1 lists the explored variants for the experimental analysis, as well as the model selection for each model. In Sect. 4.2, we describe the tasks used for benchmarking the different models. Finally, Sect. 4.3 presents the results and a discussion of the model performances.

4.1 Experimental Setting

Variants Explored. We study the performance of the different readouts on various tasks concerning time-series regression and sequence classification. For sequence classification tasks, we use the last states produced from each sequence as inputs to the readout. The readout we have chosen to consider following Sect. 3.3 are:

- A tanh readout, followed by a linear matrix, trained using ridge regression, labeled *LRN*-tanh
- a polynomial readout, also trained using ridge regression, labeled *LRN-poly*. We fixed the degree of the polynomial to 2.
- a one-hidden-layer MLP readout, labeled *LRN-MLP*.
- a GLU layer, followed by a one-hidden-layer MLP readout, labeled *LRN-GLU*.

Regarding the MLPs of the last two readouts, we simplified the setup and improved training efficiency by setting the hidden size equal to the reservoir size of the models. We also report, as baselines, the results of a standard leaky ESN and a linear reservoir with linear readout, trained through ridge regression, labeled LRN-linear.

Model Selection. For the time series regression tasks (NARMA and MG), the models selection was performed using grid-search for LRN-tanh and LRN-poly. We instead performed a Bayesian Search for LRN-MLP and LRN-GLU, due to the larger number of hyper-parameters, and the more computationally expensive training. The search was stopped after 300 configurations. For the classification tasks (sMNIST and psMNIST), we performed a Bayesian Search for all the models, stopped after 300 configurations. For time-series regression tasks, the normalized root mean squared error (NRMSE) is used as the evaluation metric. It is calculated by dividing the root mean squared error by the root mean square of the target values, ensuring normalization. For classification tasks, we measured the accuracy score. For all models and tasks, we explored key hyperparameters of the Echo State Network (ESN), including the spectral radius, bias and input matrix scaling, and the leak rate. For the neural network readouts, we used Adam optimizer, and investigated a range of values for learning rate, batch size and weight decay. Table 2 shows the search ranges in detail. In LRN, we constrain the spectral radius ρ to be at most 1 in order to prevent the states from exploding.

4.2 Tasks

We now describe the tasks considered, with the train-validation-test splits. For the time series regression tasks (NARMA and MG) in the training phase we discarded the first 100 steps as warm-up. For the classification task (MNIST), we used the last hidden state for each example to train the readouts.

NARMA. We tested the models on the Nonlinear Autoregressive Moving Average (NARMA) task. The task consists in predicting the state at time t of the time-series $y(t) = 0.3y(t-1) + 0.05y(t-1)\sum_{i=1}^{k} y(t-i) + 1.5x(t-k)x(t-1) + 0.1$, where $x(t)$ is randomly drawn in $[0, 0.5]$ for each t, and k is a positive whole number, that is the order of the task. We tested the orders $k = 10$ (NARMA10) and $k = 30$ (NARMA30). The first 4000 steps of the time series are used to train the models, then 1000 steps are used for validating, and the last 5000 steps for testing the model.

Mackey-Glass. Mackey-Glass dynamical system is defined by the differential equation $\frac{df(t)}{dt} = \frac{0.2f(t-17)}{1+f(t-17)^{10}} - 0.1f(t)$. The task is predicting n−steps ahead a numerical integration of the equation, i.e. the target at time t is $y(t) = x(t + n)$. We considered next step prediction, i.e. $n = 1$ (MG), and also $n = 84$ (84-MG), as in [5], for a more challenging task, that requires considering long-range interactions. The entire time series has a length of 10000 steps, with the first 5000 used for training, the following 1000 for validation, and the last 4000 for testing.

Pixel-by-Pixel Image Classification. We also tested the models in two tasks of time series classifications, specifically focusing on pixel-by-pixel image classification. The MNIST datasets consists in gray-scale images of handwritten digits. The resolution of each image is 28 × 28 pixels. Sequential-MNIST (sMNIST) task consists in predicting the digits of the MNIST dataset, fed pixel-by-pixel to the models. Permuted sequential-MNIST (psMNIST) is a variant of sMNIST, in which a random permutation is applied to the pixels of the images. To perform validation, we split the provided training set of 60000 examples in 48000 for training, and 12000 for validation.

4.3 Results

Table 3 shows the results of the various models in both the regression and classification tasks.

For regression tasks, we used the same reservoir size of 100 for all the models. We notice that the simplest LRN-tanh achieves surprisingly robust results across the majority of the tasks. In particular, LRN-tanh outperforms or does as well as the leaky ESN on 3 out of 4 of the regression tasks, and it is close in the 84-MG. We emphasize once again that this model is the only one with

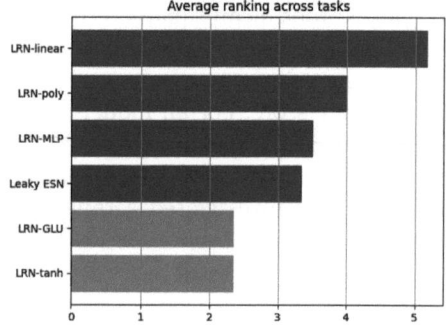

Fig. 2. Average ranking of the models (the lower the better), for equal reservoir sizes.

a parameter count comparable to that of the leaky ESN, when the reservoir sizes are equal. We also notice how the addition of a GLU layer enhances the performance of the MLP readout in 3 out of 4 tasks, and obtained the overall best result in 84-MG.

For the case of classification tasks, i.e. sMNIST and psMNIST, we used reservoirs of 500 units. For the polynomial readout (poly), we were not able to perform the training, since it required storing a large number of vectors of more than 250000 units each, after applying the polynomial to the reservoir states. Overall, LRN-GLU was the best performing model on the pixel-by-pixel classification, and all LRN models did better or equally well as the Leaky ESN.

We determined an overall best score by ranking models in each task, assigning 1 point to the best-performing model, 2 points to the second-best, and so on. The final average rank was then computed by summing these ranks across all tasks and dividing by the number of tasks. The lower the rank is, the best the model performed. Figure 2 shows the results, highlighting LRN-tanh and LRN-GLU as the two best performing models.

Table 2. Hyperparameters searched. Values of the spectral radius ρ greater than 1 only searched for the ESN.

Reservoir	$\rho \in \{0.1, 0.3, 0.5, 0.7, 0.9, 0.99, 1, 1.1, 2\}$ Values of $\rho > 1$ searched only for Leaky ESN
	$\alpha \in \{0.1, 0.3, 0.5, 0.7, 0.9, 1\}$
	bias scaling $\in \{0., 0.001, 0.01, 0.1, 1, 10\}$
	input scaling $\in \{0.001, 0.01, 0.1, 1, 5\}$
LRN-tanh and LRN-poly readouts	regularization $\in \{10^{-3}, 10^{-4}, 10^{-5}, 10^{-6}, 10^{-7}, 10^{-8}\}$
LRN-MLP and LRN-GLU readouts	batch size $\in \{64, 128, 256, 512, 1024, 2048\}$ for MNIST, $\{16, 32, 64, 128\}$ for NARMA and MG
	learning rate $\in \{10^{-2}, 10^{-3}, 10^{-4}, 10^{-5}, 10^{-6}\}$
	weight decay $\in \{10^{-3}, 10^{-4}, 10^{-5}, 10^{-6}, 10^{-7}, 10^{-8}\}$

Table 3. Results on time-series regression (MG and NARMA) and classification (MNIST) tasks. Number of reservoir units is 100 for regression tasks and 500 for classification tasks. Best model in bold, second best model underlined.

Task	Leaky ESN	LRN-linear	LRN-tanh	LRN-poly	LRN-MLP	LRN-GLU
MG ($\times 10^{-2}$) ↓	**0.039 ± 0.005**	0.091 ± 0.0049	**0.039 ± 0.002**	0.14 ± 0.028	0.45 ± 0.0007	0.43 ± 0.07
84-MG ↓	0.15 ± 0.03	0.19 ± 0.02	0.17 ± 0.03	0.24 ± 0.02	0.19 ± 0.08	**0.08 ± 0.02**
NARMA10 ↓	0.073 ± 0.006	0.11 ± 0.00003	0.058 ± 0.007	**0.0063 ± 0.004**	0.023 ± 0.009	0.037 ± 0.008
NARMA30 ↓	0.19 ± 0.01	0.20 ± 0.003	**0.12 ± 0.004**	0.15 ± 0.04	0.19 ± 0.025	0.17 ± 0.018
sMNIST ↑	76.4 ± 1.1	63.1 ± 0.1	77.5 ± 0.3	–	77.5 ± 1.7	**78.2 ± 0.3**
psMNIST ↑	82.3 ± 3.0	79.6±	82.3 ± 3.0	–	86.6 ± 6.1	**88.7 ± 3.2**

Additionally, we analyzed the computational cost of training the models[1] Table 5 shows the emissions for MG and sMNIST task, for the same reservoir sizes used in the experiments. We can see how LRN-tanh is the only one that has similar emissions and training time to a standard ESN, while all the other models are computationally more expensive. For the sMNIST task, due to the relative large dataset size, the batch size makes a significant difference in training time. The best LRN-MLP model turned out having a smaller batch size than the best LRN-GLU, therefore training LRN-MLP readout resulted to be slower.

We also conducted a comparison of the models by fixing the number of trainable parameters instead of the reservoir size. Specifically, we selected an Echo State Network (ESN) with 1000 reservoir units. Given that the MNIST dataset comprises 10 output variables, the total number of trainable parameters amounts to 10000 (excluding the bias term). The LRN-tanh model was configured to have the same number of units, since the number of trainable parameters remains the same. In contrast, the LRN-poly model has only 64 units, while the LRN-MLP

---
[1] Emissions were calculated using CodeCarbon 2.8.2.

and LRN-GLU models have 96 and 57, respectively. The results of the experiment are presented in Table 4. In this case, LRN-tanh performs better than all the other models, and it is the only one achieving better performances than the Leaky ESN. This result highlights the importance of a large and rich reservoir: for the complex readouts, fixing the total number of trainable parameters results in smaller reservoirs for these models, limiting their expressivity.

Table 4. results on MNIST classification tasks. Number of trainable parameters is approximately 10.000 for every model. Best model in bold, second best model underlined.

Tasks	Leaky ESN	LRN-tanh	LRN-poly	LRN-MLP	LRN-GLU
sMNIST ↑	75.5 ± 1.0	**79.1 ± 1.0**	61.8 ± 1.7	64.8 ± 3.3	66.8 ± 1.8
psMNIST ↑	83.3 ± 0.6	**85.0 ± 0.7**	73.6 ± 0.4	72.3 ± 4.3	52.5 ± 0.3

Table 5. Emissions and execution time for different readouts, for MG and sMNIST tasks. Reservoir size is respectively 100 and 500. Best model (lower time or emissions) in bold, second best model underlined.

Metric	Leaky ESN	LRN-linear	LRN-tanh	LRN-poly	LRN-MLP	LRN-GLU
MG Emissions (gCO$_2$) ↓	0.02446	0.02492	**0.02341**	0.04459	1.21025	3.39883
MG Time (s) ↓	0.55	0.56	**0.53**	0.99	26.98	75.76
sMNIST Emissions (gCO$_2$) ↓	0.95603	0.95791	**0.82342**	–	4.49792	3.36130
sMNIST Time (s) ↓	20.46	20.51	**17.53**	–	98.77	73.52

5 Conclusions

In this work, we have analyzed and benchmarked linear reservoir computers, and investigated the trade-off in terms of accuracy and computational efficiency of various types of readout functions.

Our findings revealed that the simplest LRN-tanh model delivers robust performance, surpassing more complex alternatives in several tasks, while maintaining a computational cost comparable to that of a standard Leaky ESN. Our experiments also indicate that implementing a GLU layer can enhance the performance, but at the cost of a larger number of parameters, and often slower training.

These results reinforce the idea, drawn from SSM literature, that relocating the nonlinearity outside the recurrence can be highly effective in practice, even when applied in the RC domain, and open for further research. One promising direction for future research is the use of structured or diagonal transition matrices, as done in LRU, to enable parallelization of the recurrence. Exploring these structured initializations could lead to models that keep the simplicity and efficiency of LRNs, while further improving their scalability and applicability to more complex sequential tasks. Overall, this work provides valuable insights into the practical aspect of designing linear reservoir computing models, opening the way for future research on structured linear recurrent architectures that balance expressivity, efficiency, and scalability.

Acknowledgments. The work has been partially supported by EU-EIC EMERGE (Grant No. 101070918), and by NEURONE, a project funded by the European Union - Next Generation EU, M4C1 CUP I53D23003600006, under program PRIN 2022 (prj code 20229JRTZA).

References

1. Gonon, L., Ortega, J.-P.: Reservoir computing universality with stochastic inputs. IEEE Trans. Neural Netw. Learn. Syst. **31**(1), 100–112 (2020)
2. Grigoryeva, L., Ortega, J.-P.: Echo state networks are universal. Neural Netw. **108**, 495–508 (2018)
3. Grigoryeva, L., Ortega, J.-P.: Universal discrete-time reservoir computers with stochastic inputs and linear readouts using non-homogeneous state-affine systems. J. Mach. Learn. Res. **19**, 1–40 (2018)
4. Gu, A., Goel, K., Ré, C.: Efficiently modeling long sequences with structured state spaces. arXiv preprint arXiv:2111.00396 (2021)
5. Jaeger, H., Haas, H.: Harnessing nonlinearity: predicting chaotic systems and saving energy in wireless communication. Science **304**(5667), 78–80 (2004)
6. Kolen, J.F., Kremer, S.C.: A field guide to dynamical recurrent networks. John Wiley & Sons (2001)
7. Lukoševičius, M., Jaeger, H.: Reservoir computing approaches to recurrent neural network training. Comput. Sci. Rev. **3**(3), 127–149 (2009)
8. Nakajima, K., Fischer, I.: Reservoir computing. Springer (2021)
9. Orvieto, A., et al.: Resurrecting recurrent neural networks for long sequences. In: International Conference on Machine Learning, pp. 26670–26698. PMLR (2023)
10. Pascanu, R., Mikolov, T., Bengio, Y.: On the difficulty of training recurrent neural networks. In: Dasgupta, S., McAllester, D. (eds.) Proceedings of the 30th International Conference on Machine Learning, vol. 28 of Proceedings of Machine Learning Research, pp. 1310–1318, Atlanta, Georgia, USA, 17–19 Jun 2013. PMLR
11. Smith, J.T., Warrington, A., Linderman, S.W.: Simplified state space layers for sequence modeling. arXiv preprint arXiv:2208.04933 (2022)
12. Tanaka, G., et al.: Recent advances in physical reservoir computing: a review. Neural Netw. **115**, 100–123 (2019)
13. Yan, M., Huang, C., Bienstman, P., Tino, P., Lin, W., Sun, J.: Emerging opportunities and challenges for the future of reservoir computing. Nat. Commun. **15**(1), 2056 (2024)
14. Yildiz, I.B., Jaeger, H., Kiebel, S.J.: Re-visiting the echo state property. Neural Netw. **35**, 1–9 (2012)

Investigating Time-Scales in Deep Echo State Networks for Natural Language Processing

Corrado Baccheschi[1], Alessandro Bondielli[1], Alessandro Lenci[2], Alessio Micheli[1], Lucia Passaro[1], Marco Podda[1], and Domenico Tortorella[1](✉)

[1] Department of Computer Science, University of Pisa, Largo B. Pontecorvo, 3, 56127 Pisa, Italy
c.baccheschi@studenti.unipi.it,
{abondielli,alenci,amicheli,lpassaro,mpodda,dtortorella}@unipi.it
[2] Department of Philology, Literature, and Linguistics, University of Pisa, Piazza E. Torricelli, 2, 56126 Pisa, Italy

Abstract. Reservoir Computing (RC) enables efficiently-trained deep Recurrent Neural Networks (RNNs) by removing the need to train the hierarchy of representations of the input sequences. In this paper, we analyze the performance and the dynamical behavior of RC models, specifically Deep Bidirectional Echo State Networks (Deep-BiESNs), applied to Natural Language Processing (NLP) tasks. We compare the performance of Deep-BiESNs against fully-trained NLP baseline models on six common NLP tasks: three sequence-to-vector tasks for sequence-level classification and three sequence-to-sequence tasks for token-level labeling. Experimental results demonstrate that Deep-BiESNs achieve comparable or superior performance to these baseline models. We then adapt the class activation mapping technique for explainability to analyze the dynamical properties of these deep RC models, highlighting how the hierarchy of representations in Deep-BiESNs layers contributes to forming the class prediction in the different NLP tasks. Investigating time scales in deep RNN layers is highly relevant for NLP because language inherently involves dependencies that occur over various temporal horizons. The findings not only underscore the potential of Deep ESNs as a competitive and efficient alternative for NLP applications, but also contribute to a deeper understanding of how to effectively model such architectures for addressing other NLP challenges.

Keywords: Echo State Networks · Reservoir Computing · Recurrent Neural Networks · Natural Language Processing · Computational Linguistics

1 Introduction

Recurrent Neural Networks (RNNs) [7] have certainly represented a key step forward in natural language processing (NLP), as the sequential nature of language demands models capable of capturing contextual dependencies over time. Despite this, traditional RNNs face well-documented challenges—such as vanishing and exploding gradients—which limit their ability to capture long-term dependencies [1]. In this context, Reservoir Computing (RC) [21,35] has emerged as a state-of-the-art paradigm for designing efficiently trainable RNNs, offering an alternative that emphasizes computational simplicity without compromising predictive performance. The most well-known model within the Reservoir Computing paradigm is the Echo State Network (ESN) [17,18], a form of RNN in which only the final readout layer is trained, while the recurrent part—referred to as the *reservoir*—remains untrained. On one hand, by eliminating the need for training, ESNs avoid the typical challenges faced by traditional RNNs. On the other hand, training is significantly faster and more efficient, as it is limited to the readout layer. The NLP literature has advanced to focusing mostly on Transformer-based architectures, both for discriminative [5] and generative [24,30] tasks. While these models have shown groundbreaking capabilities in modeling text and generalization, they come with the burden of a very high computational cost, even for small-sized ones. Thus, in this work, we ask ourselves whether the key advantages of the RC paradigm, namely efficiency and the advantages of deep reservoir in representing different time-scales [11,12,32], can be effectively leveraged in the context of NLP tasks. We pose the following research questions:

RQ1 What are the performances of a Deep ESN on NLP classification tasks?
RQ2 Does the model's dynamical behavior give any indication of effective text modeling?

To answer RQ1, we look at a subset of the classification tasks proposed in [26]. Specifically, we focus on sequence-level classification (e.g., Sentiment Analysis), modeling it as a sequence-to-vector task, and on token-level classification (e.g., POS-tagging), modeling it as a sequence-to-sequence task. We evaluate the performance of a Bidirectional Deep ESN [2] (Deep-BiESN) on three tasks for each category. We restrict our attention to the bidirectional case since, being able to model the context in both directions, it is inherently more expressive; in fact, it is the *de facto* architecture for recurrent models applied to NLP [20]. To answer RQ2, we resort to: (i) analyzing which hyperparameters (in the considered tasks) lead to dynamics that enable best performance; (ii) leveraging Class Activation Mapping (CAM) Scores to understand the importance of each layer in the network for the final classification.

2 Related Works

Reservoir Computing (RC) in NLP spans multiple research directions, including speech recognition [12], language modeling, and text classification [27], with additional implications in psycholinguistics and cognitive science. Research in this area typically emphasizes the neurobiological plausibility of RC—particularly Echo State Networks (ESNs) for sentence processing [14,37]—especially when compared to architectures such as RNNs and Transformers. The possibility of using an ESN as a language model is explored in [15], where the authors propose a classical ESN architecture enhanced with additional working memories [22]. Similarly, in [23], an enhanced ESN with a pre-recurrent feature layer and a nonlinear readout is proposed, demonstrating strong performance in next-word prediction. Bidirectional ESN architectures (Deep-BiESNs) have been explored in [28,29], showing accuracy comparable to Bi-LSTMs on the Word Sense Disambiguation (WSD) task, and confirming the ability of Deep-BiESNs to capture richer contextual information. A related study [25] applies both bidirectional and unidirectional ESNs to Named Entity Recognition (NER), finding that Bi-ESNs outperform their unidirectional counterparts—indicating that NER benefits from bidirectional context. Furthermore, in [9] and [10], ESNs are analyzed from a cognitive science perspective. The authors demonstrate that ESNs not only perform well on next-word prediction tasks but also exhibit strong systematicity–i.e., the human ability to use and understand language in a structured and coherent way, generalizing syntactic and semantic rules to novel word combinations [8]. A comparison between an ESN and a fully trained RNN for next-word prediction is presented in [31], where findings confirm that ESNs are sensitive to grammatical patterns, even without explicit training. Recently, given the success of the Transformer architecture, especially the attention mechanism [34], research has moved in two directions: enhancing ESN performance with self-attention mechanisms, and comparing Transformers and ESNs in terms of both performance and training time. For example, in [4], an ESN equipped with a frozen attention mechanism is used for sentiment analysis on the IMDB dataset, achieving accuracy comparable to Bi-LSTM while requiring less training time. In [6], two bidirectional ESN models (Bi-ESNs) are evaluated on the TREC question classification benchmark. Their models demonstrate competitive performance compared to state-of-the-art approaches, especially in terms of training efficiency and number of trainable parameters. Finally, in [33], authors show that ESNs match or even surpass the performance of Transformers (trained from scratch) in capturing syntactic structure.

3 Deep Echo State Networks

Deep Echo State Network (DeepESN) [11] is an RC model designed within the deep learning framework. Its reservoir architecture is constructed by stacking multiple ESN layers sequentially, where the output of each layer serves as the input for the next. This approach allows DeepESN to encode the input sequence $\mathbf{x}(t) \in \mathbb{R}^{N_X}$ as a hierarchy of representations $\mathbf{h}^{(l)}(t) \in \mathbb{R}^{N_R}$, $l = 1, \ldots, L$, where each layer focuses on a different time scale [32]. The state transition function of a DeepESN layer is

$$\mathbf{h}^{(l)}(t) = (1-a)\,\mathbf{h}^{(l)}(t-1) + a \tanh\left(\mathbf{W_h}^{(l)}\mathbf{h}^{(l)}(t-1) + \mathbf{W_x}^{(l)}\mathbf{x}^{(l)}(t) + \mathbf{b}^{(l)}\right) \quad (1)$$

where $0 < a \leq 1$ is the leakage constant [16]. The recurrent weights $\mathbf{W_h}^{(l)} \in \mathbb{R}^{N_R \times N_R}$ are randomly initialized and rescaled to satisfy the echo state property

[17], while the input weights $\mathbf{W_x}^{(l)} \in \mathbb{R}^{N_R \times N_X}$ and bias $\mathbf{b}^{(l)} \in \mathbb{R}^{N_R}$ are randomly initialized taking into account the input range.

In this work, we focus on a DeepESN [11,12] variant where the layers are made bidirectional (as in [2]) by encoding the input sequence in both forward and backward temporal directions with two different ESNs. Hereafter, this variant is termed Deep-BiESN. More precisely, the forward and backward directions are encoded as $\overrightarrow{\mathbf{h}}^{(l)}(t), \overleftarrow{\mathbf{h}}^{(l)}(t)$, with their concatenation $\bar{\mathbf{h}}^{(l)}(t) = [\overrightarrow{\mathbf{h}}^{(l)}(t)\ \overleftarrow{\mathbf{h}}^{(l)}(t)]$ serving as the overall embedding of time-step t in layer l. In this case, the input to layer $l > 1$ is $\mathbf{x}^{(l)}(t) = \bar{\mathbf{h}}^{(l-1)}(t)$. In sequence-to-vector tasks, we encode the whole sequence via mean-state mapping $\mathbf{H}^{(l)} = \frac{1}{T}\sum_{t=1}^{T} \bar{\mathbf{h}}^{(l)}(t)$. For downstream tasks, we train a linear readout $\hat{\mathbf{y}} = \mathbf{W_o}\mathbf{h} + \mathbf{b_o}$ by closed-form ridge regression [38], either on the concatenation of all layer embeddings or on the last layer representation.

4 Experiments

In this Section, we detail our experimental setup to answer RQ1 and present the results comparing Deep-BiESN with fully-trained NLP baseline models.

4.1 Experimental Setup

Our experiments involve applying a Deep-BiESN to several NLP classification tasks. As our source of data, we follow [19] and consider a subset of the tasks and dataset proposed in [26]. Specifically, we focus on three sequence-level classification tasks, namely *Sentence Sentiment*, *Subjectivity*, and *Document Sentiment Classification*, and three token-level classification tasks, namely *Part-of-Speech (POS) Tagging*, *Named Entity Recognition (NER)*, and *Chunking*. We chose these tasks as they are relatively common in the NLP literature, and encompass a relatively wide array of characteristics, from the number of output classes to the linguistic features typically learned to solve the tasks, that make our experiments more robust. For the three sequence-level tasks, we evaluated our models using accuracy, whereas for token-level POS, NER, and Chunking, we used the weighted F1-score as the evaluation metric.

As inputs to the Deep-BiESN, we feed each data point as a sequence of token embeddings. As embedding model we use 300-dimensional pre-trained FastText word embeddings [3]. We chose to use FastText embeddings rather than other methods to maintain continuity with results presented in [19], that serve as our baseline. In the case of sequence-level classification tasks, mean-state mapping is applied to obtain the global sequence embedding. For token-level classification tasks, the output sequence from the model (excluding the padding) is reshaped to be suitable for the readout. Following [38], a closed-form, efficient ridge regression is used as the final readout, enabling batch processing for computationally intensive tasks. As for the model selection, we applied the *hold-out* method, reserving between 10% and 25% of the data for validation and following the split in [26]. We employed an exhaustive grid search, allowing us to explore

Table 1. Comparison of fully-trained NLP baselines [19] and Deep-BiESN

Task	Baseline model	Baseline score	Deep-BiESN score
Document Sentiment	LSTM	0.761 ± 0.008	0.841 ± 0.002
Sentence Sentiment	CNN	0.782 ± 0.004	0.774 ± 0.002
Subjectivity	Mean Embedding LR	0.910 ± 0.002	0.932 ± 0.001
POS Tagging	Sliding Window LR	0.904 ± 0.001	0.894 ± 0.001
NER	Sliding Window LR	0.942 ± 0.001	0.939 ± 0.001
Chunking	Sliding Window LR	0.905 ± 0.001	0.916 ± 0.001

every possible combination of hyper-parameters. To obtain the desired spectral radius ρ and rescale the recurrent matrix $\mathbf{W_h}$, we use the fast initialization approach introduced in [13]. Other hyperparameters selected include number of reservoir units N_R (from the set $\{1000, 3000, 5000, 10000\}$, number of layers L (from the set $\{1, 2, 3, 4, 5\}$, leakage rate a (from the set $\{0.05, 0.1, 0.5, 0.9, 1\}$), whether to use only the last layer or the concatenation of all layers' states, and the L2 ridge regularization (within the logarithmic range $[10^{-8}, 10^{-5}]$). Results are averaged over 10 random initializations of reservoir weights.

4.2 Results

We report the average and standard deviation of test scores in Table 1 for Deep-BiESN and fully-trained NLP baseline models from [19], which include an LSTM recurrent neural network, a convolutional neural network (CNN), a logistic regression (LR) on mean word embeddings, and LRs on sliding windows of the input sequence. All of them have been trained on the same FastText300 word embeddings for a fair comparison. We observe that Deep-BiESN scores are generally comparable to or better than the baseline results. Deep-BiESNs exhibit also a high stability in performance, as reflected by small standard deviations. For document sentiment classification, we outperform the baseline accuracy of LSTM. Conversely, we achieve comparable performance in sentence sentiment classification, albeit with a marginal decline in accuracy of 0.01. For subjectivity, Deep-BiESN again outperforms the baseline in terms of accuracy. For POS and NER we obtain comparable results to the baseline, while also outperforming the performance for Chunking.

Table 2 reports the hyperparameters obtained via model selection for Deep-BiESN in sequence-level and token-level classification tasks. An initial insight into the memory requirements of different tasks can be obtained by analyzing the values of the leakage parameter a, where smaller values denote longer-lasting influence of previous time-steps. In the sentence sentiment classification task, the optimal leakage is $a = 0.05$. This confirms that this task involves more diffuse and long-range temporal dependencies, as the meaning of a sentence often relies on the accumulation of subtle cues distributed across the input. Surprisingly, document-level sentiment classification, which is arguably a more complex task, does not seem to require such a long-term memory, as indicated by the high optimal leakage value ($a = 0.9$). However, the model selection also favored a three layers architecture, suggesting that the model may rely on hierarchical abstraction across layers to obtain the required information. Similarly, token-level tasks such as POS tagging, Chunking, and NER favored high leakage values ($a = 0.9$), while at the same time benefiting from deeper architectures with five layers.

5 Analysis

To answer RQ2, we look into the dynamical behavior and information retention of the Deep-BiESN models selected for each NLP task. We do so by characterizing the time-scales of each layer via the respective temporal constants (Sect. 5.1), and by measuring the contribution of each layer to the class prediction (Sect. 5.2).

5.1 Temporal Scales

We study the dynamical behavior of the Deep-BiESN architectures selected for each NLP task to investigate the temporal scales of the sequence representations required to address the respective learning tasks. We characterize the properties of these models as dynamical systems by measuring their impulse response as done in [32], i.e. how embeddings $\tilde{\mathbf{h}}(t)$ evolve after the input sequence has been perturbed at time-step t_0 compared to the unperturbed embeddings $\mathbf{h}(t)$. Specifically, we measure the *decay time* τ as the time-steps required for the perturbation $\|\mathbf{h}(t) - \tilde{\mathbf{h}}(t)\|$ to decay below 1% of the peak value after t_0. We report in Table 3 the average temporal constants measured over 10 random input sequences and Deep-BiESN weights initializations, both for the global state that is fed to the readout classifier, as well as for each of the architecture layers individually. As a general trend, we observe that τ increases from the shallowest to the deeper layers. This is in agreement with the results of [32]: temporal responses become more delayed as information has to propagate through the layers, while state perturbations are more lasting in deeper layers compared to shallower layers.

Table 2. Hyperparameters from the Deep-BiESN model selection. When present, "last" denotes that only the last layer was used as input to the readout.

Task	Selected hyper-parameters
Document Sentiment	N_R=5,000, $a = 0.9$, $L = 3$
Subjectivity	N_R=10,000, $a = 0.9$, $L = 2$, last
Sentence Sentiment	N_R=10,000, $a = 0.05$, $L = 1$
POS Tagging	N_R =5,000, $a = 0.9$, $L = 5$
NER	N_R =5,000, $a = 0.9$, $L = 5$
Chunking	N_R =5,000, $a = 0.9$, $L = 5$

Table 3. Average values of temporal constants τ computed across 10 random inputs and weight initializations.

Task	Setting	Layer	Decay time τ
Sentence Sentiment	L=1, a=0.05	(global)	79.85 ± 0.35
Subjectivity	L=2, a=0.9	global	4.00 ± 0.00
		layer 1	4.50 ± 0.00
		layer 2	4.50 ± 0.00
Document Sentiment	L=3, a=0.9	global	3.00 ± 0.00
		layer 1	2.00 ± 0.00
		layer 2	3.00 ± 0.00
		layer 3	3.95 ± 0.15
POS Tagging	L=5, a=0.9	global	10.15 ± 0.35
		layer 1	5.00 ± 0.00
		layer 2	5.00 ± 0.00
		layer 3	7.00 ± 0.00
		layer 4	9.55 ± 0.49
		layer 5	12.00 ± 0.00
NER	L=5, a=0.9	global	6.00 ± 0.00
		layer 1	3.00 ± 0.00
		layer 2	4.00 ± 0.00
		layer 3	5.00 ± 0.00
		layer 4	6.00 ± 0.00
		layer 5	7.00 ± 0.00
Chunking	L=5, a=0.9	global	5.00 ± 0.00
		layer 1	3.00 ± 0.00
		layer 2	3.00 ± 0.00
		layer 3	4.00 ± 0.00
		layer 4	5.00 ± 0.00
		layer 5	6.00 ± 0.00

In the sentence sentiment task, the extremely large temporal constant $\tau \approx 80$ is a consequence of the small leakage value $a = 0.05$. As already observed in Sect. 4.2, this is an indication that long-range temporal dependencies are required. Regarding other sequence-level tasks, the models for document sentiment and subjectivity classification primarily rely on short-term information, effectively acting like a sliding window over time, while information on the whole sequence is supplied by mean-state mapping. This behavior is evidenced by significantly smaller τ values around 3-4 and shallower architectures. For token-level labeling tasks such as NER and Chunking, the values of τ are similarly low notwithstanding the deeper architectures, a hint of similar temporal dynamics. In contrast, for POS tagging, the influence of the input persists further in time, as evidenced by τ values that are noticeably higher than those observed in the other token-level tasks. From a linguistic perspective, we highlight an interesting aspect. We observe that the τ values for the best configuration for each task actually closely match the span of tokens needed to solve them. For example, Named Entities and Chunks are generally composed of a few tokens; to understand the sentiment of an entire sentence the whole content is typically needed; subjectivity cues often revolve around first person pronouns and construction such as "I think", "I believe", etc. We however identify two notable exceptions. First, for POS tagging, most traditional systems leverage local, i.e., word level, features, and a small context window, e.g. the preceding and subsequent tokens, while our best configuration for the task has a slightly larger memory. Second, for Document Sentiment Classification, the best performing configuration has actually a very small memory with respect to how the task is typically handled. We leave analysis of this phenomenon to future works.

5.2 Layer Importance

As observed by the temporal constants, each layer in a Deep-BiESN model encodes information on the input sequence on different time-scales. To estimate the contribution of each layer to the final prediction, we apply the Class Activation Mapping (CAM) [36] method to assign importance scores to layers. CAM scores are computed by exploiting the linearity of the readout, decomposing the classifier output $\hat{y}^{(k)}$ of class k into the individual contribution of each layer:

$$\hat{y}^{(k)} = \mathbf{W_o}^{(k)} \mathbf{h} + b_o^{(k)} = \sum_{l=1}^{L} \underbrace{\mathbf{w_o}^{(k,l)} \mathbf{h}^{(l)}}_{\text{importance score}} + b_o \qquad (2)$$

The larger is the value $\left|\mathbf{w_o}^{(k,l)} \mathbf{h}^{(l)}\right|$, the more relevant is layer l for the prediction of class k.

In Fig. 1 we report the average relative importance computed by CAM for the tasks that exploit more than one layer in the readout classifier, namely: document classification, POS, NER and Chunking. Overall, relevant linguistic information tends to concentrate within the first two layers of the Deep-BiESN. From a linguistic perspective, this effect may be partially attributed to the local nature of tasks such as POS tagging, chunking, and NER. It is reasonable to expect that the readout receives sufficient information for accurate predictions, relying only on the layers closer to the input. In particular, for POS, we observe that classes corresponding to singular and plural common nouns (NN, NNS), proper singular nouns (NNP), cardinal numbers (CD), and adverbs (RB) are especially influenced by layer 2. For chunking, we observe a similar trend, with layer 1 also emerging as particularly relevant for classes corresponding to the beginning of a noun phrase (B-NP), the inside of a noun phrase (I-NP), and tokens outside of syntactic structures, such as punctuation (O). Additionally, for NER task classes like B-MISC and B-PER seem to be strongly influenced

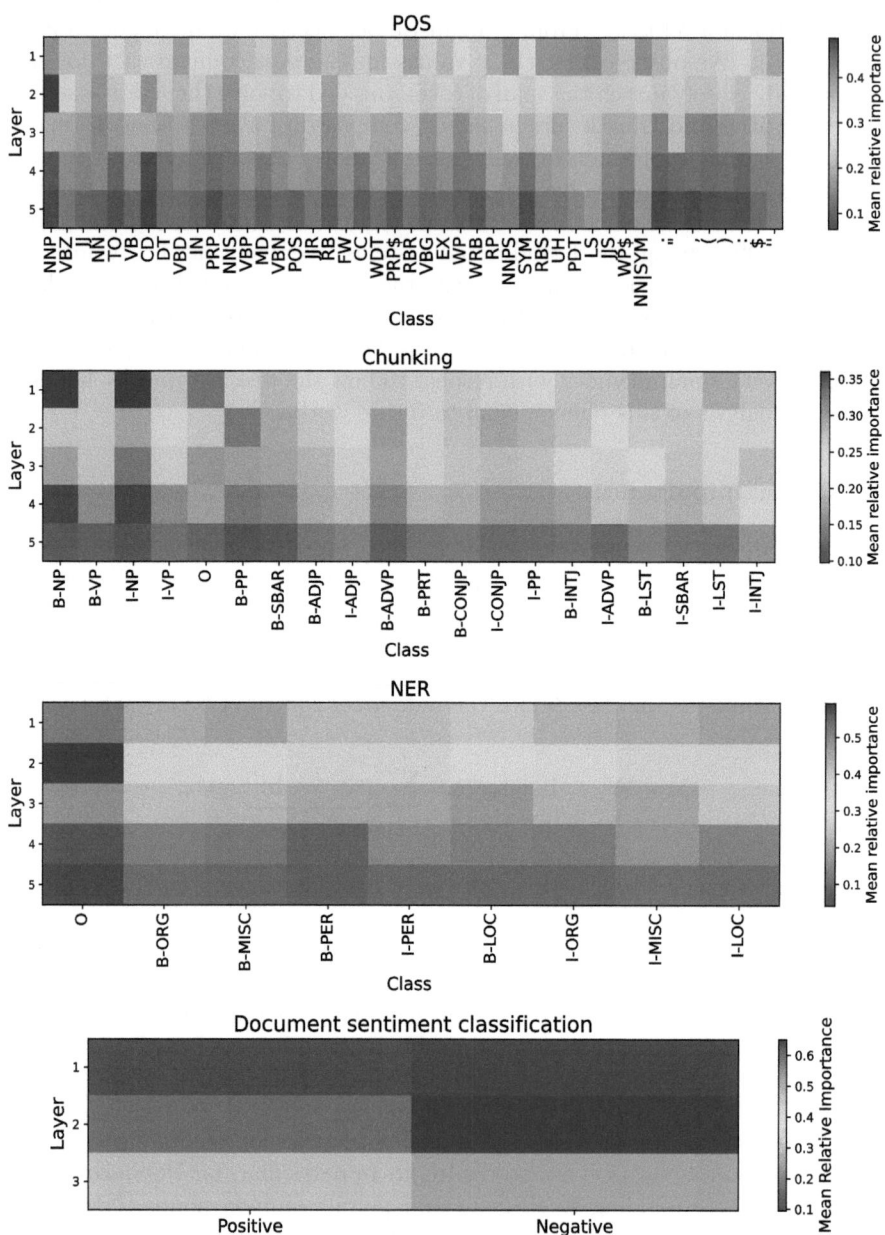

Fig. 1. Layer importance analysis with CAM-Score for POS, Chunking, NER and document sentiment classification.

by layer 2; the former indicates a named entity (NE) related to a person (such as "Harry") while the latter regards NE that don't fit into the other categories. All of these mentioned classes for POS, NER and Chunking reflect surface-level grammatical features, which are typically easier to detect and require less hierarchical abstraction, thus supporting the idea that early layers are sufficient to capture the necessary information for these predictions. Interestingly, a marginal yet non-negligible role of layer 3 can be observed in chunking in classes such as I-ADVP (Inside of Adverbial Phrase) and I-LST (Inside of List Marker). A possible linguistic explanation is unlike noun or verb phrases, the internal tokens of adverbial or list chunks typically require more contextual integration to be correctly identified. Thus, the third layer may act as a refinement stage, aggregating temporal patterns and supporting the resolution of ambiguities that are not fully captured by the lower layers.

6 Conclusions

In this work, we applied bidirectional Deep Echo State Networks (Deep-BiESNs) to six widely adopted NLP benchmarks. The experimental results demonstrate that our models consistently achieved strong performance both on sequence-level and token-level tasks, generally matching or surpassing the results of the fully-trained baseline models proposed in [19]. We have performed an analysis of the dynamical properties of Deep-BiESNs to characterize the temporal scales in the hierarchy of layer representations, revealing how these models encode information over different time horizons. This has enabled us to provide insights into the short- and long-term dependencies required by different NLP tasks, investigating the contribution of each layer to the final prediction via Class Activation Mapping (CAM). The analysis revealed that the depth of the network is related to the linguistic traits of the tasks, with layers close to the input encoding surface-level grammatical features, and deeper layers acting as a refinement over local contextual information. Overall, our research has contributed to a better understanding of how to tailor reservoir configurations for specific NLP tasks, with potential applications also to the improvement of fully-trained deep recurrent models. In future works, we plan to extend the scope of our analysis to more comprehensive and complex NLP tasks, applying the same tools of this work to investigate the dynamical properties of end-to-end trained RNNs.

Acknowledgments. Research partly supported by PNRR - M4C2 - Investimento 1.3, Partenariato Esteso PE0000013-"FAIR - Future Artificial Intelligence Research" - Spoke 1 "Human-centered AI", funded by the European Commission under the NextGeneration EU programme, and the EU EIC project EMERGE (Grant No. 101070918).

References

1. Bengio, Y., Frasconi, P., Schmidhuber, J.: Gradient flow in recurrent nets: the difficulty of learning long-term dependencies. A Field Guide to Dynamical Recurrent Neural Networks (03 2003)
2. Bianchi, F.M., Scardapane, S., Løkse, S., Jenssen, R.: Bidirectional deep-readout echo state networks. In: ESANN 2018 proceedings, pp. 425–430 (2018)
3. Bojanowski, P., Grave, E., Joulin, A., Mikolov, T.: Enriching word vectors with subword information. Trans. Assoc. Comput. Linguist. **5**, 135–146 (2017). https://doi.org/10.1162/tacl_a_00051
4. Cabessa, J., Hernault, H., Kim, H., Lamonato, Y., Levy, Y.Z.: Efficient text classification with echo state networks. In: 2021 International Joint Conference on Neural Networks (IJCNN) (2021)
5. Devlin, J., Chang, M.W., Lee, K., Toutanova, K.: BERT: pre-training of deep bidirectional transformers for language understanding. In: Burstein, J., Doran, C., Solorio, T. (eds.) Proceedings of the 2019 Conference of the North American Chapter of the Association for Computational Linguistics: Human Language Technologies, Volume 1 (Long and Short Papers), Minneapolis, Minnesota, pp. 4171–4186. Association for Computational Linguistics (2019). https://doi.org/10.18653/v1/N19-1423
6. Di Sarli, D., Gallicchio, C., Micheli, A.: Question classification with untrained recurrent embeddings. In: Alviano, M., Greco, G., Scarcello, F. (eds.) AI*IA 2019. LNCS (LNAI), vol. 11946, pp. 362–375. Springer, Cham (2019). https://doi.org/10.1007/978-3-030-35166-3_26
7. Elman, J.L.: Finding structure in time. Cogn. Sci. **14**(2), 179–211 (1990). https://doi.org/10.1207/s15516709cog1402_1
8. Fodor, J.A., Pylyshyn, Z.W.: Connectionism and cognitive architecture: a critical analysis. Cognition **28**(1–2), 3–71 (1988)
9. Frank, S.L.: Strong systematicity in sentence processing by an echo state network. In: Kollias, S.D., Stafylopatis, A., Duch, W., Oja, E. (eds.) ICANN 2006. LNCS, vol. 4131, pp. 505–514. Springer, Heidelberg (2006). https://doi.org/10.1007/11840817_53
10. Frank, S.L., Haselager, W.F.G.: Robust semantic systematicity and distributed representations in a connectionist model of sentence comprehension. In: Miyake, N., Sun, R. (eds.) Proceedings of the 28th Annual Conference of the Cognitive Science Society, Erlbaum, Mahwah, NJ (2006, in press)
11. Gallicchio, C., Micheli, A., Pedrelli, L.: Deep reservoir computing: a critical experimental analysis. Neurocomputing **268**, 87–99 (2017)
12. Gallicchio, C., Micheli, A., Pedrelli, L.: Design of deep echo state networks. Neural Networks **108**, 33–47 (2018). https://doi.org/10.1016/j.neunet.2018.08.002
13. Gallicchio, C., Micheli, A., Pedrelli, L.: Fast spectral radius initialization for recurrent neural networks. In: Oneto, L., Navarin, N., Sperduti, A., Anguita, D. (eds.) INNSBDDL 2019. PINNS, vol. 1, pp. 380–390. Springer, Cham (2020). https://doi.org/10.1007/978-3-030-16841-4_39
14. Hinaut, X., Dominey, P.F.: Real-time parallel processing of grammatical structure in the fronto-striatal system: A recurrent network simulation study using reservoir computing. PLoS ONE **8**(2), e52946 (2013). epub 2013 Feb 1
15. Homma, Y., Hagiwara, M.: An echo state network with working memories for probabilistic language modeling. In: Mladenov, V., Koprinkova-Hristova, P., Palm, G., Villa, A.E.P., Appollini, B., Kasabov, N. (eds.) ICANN 2013. LNCS, vol. 8131, pp.

595–602. Springer, Heidelberg (2013). https://doi.org/10.1007/978-3-642-40728-4_74
16. Jaeger, H., Lukoševičius, M., Popovici, D., Siewert, U.: Optimization and applications of echo state networks with leaky-integrator neurons. Neural Netw. **20**(3), 335–352 (2007)
17. Jaeger, H.: The "echo state" approach to analysing and training recurrent neural networks–with an erratum note. Technical report 148, German National Research Institute for Computer Science (2001)
18. Jaeger, H., Haas, H.: Harnessing nonlinearity: predicting chaotic systems and saving energy in wireless communication. Science **304**(5667), 78–80 (2004)
19. Lenci, A., Sahlgren, M., Jeuniaux, P., et al.: A comparative evaluation and analysis of three generations of distributional semantic models. Lang. Resour. Eval. **56**, 1269–1313 (2022). https://doi.org/10.1007/s10579-021-09575-z
20. Li, Q., et al.: A survey on text classification: From traditional to deep learning. ACM Trans. Intell. Syst. Technol. **13**(2) (2022). https://doi.org/10.1145/3495162
21. Lukoševičius, M., Jaeger, H.: Reservoir computing approaches to recurrent neural network training. Comput. Sci. Rev. **3**(3), 127–149 (2009)
22. Pascanu, R., Jaeger, H.: A neurodynamical model for working memory. Neural Netw. **24**(2), 199–207 (2011)
23. Rachez, A., Hagiwara, M.: Augmented echo state networks with a feature layer and a nonlinear readout. In: The 2012 International Joint Conference on Neural Networks (IJCNN). pp. 1–8 (2012). https://doi.org/10.1109/IJCNN.2012.6252505
24. Radford, A., Narasimhan, K.: Improving language understanding by generative pre-training (2018). https://api.semanticscholar.org/CorpusID:49313245
25. Ramamurthy, R., Stenzel, R., Sifa, R., Ladi, A., Bauckhage, C.: Echo state networks for named entity recognition. In: Tetko, I.V., Kůrková, V., Karpov, P., Theis, F. (eds.) ICANN 2019. LNCS, vol. 11731, pp. 110–120. Springer, Cham (2019). https://doi.org/10.1007/978-3-030-30493-5_11
26. Rogers, A., Hosur Ananthakrishna, S., Rumshisky, A.: What's in your embedding, and how it predicts task performance. In: Bender, E.M., Derczynski, L., Isabelle, P. (eds.) Proceedings of the 27th International Conference on Computational Linguistics, Santa Fe, New Mexico, USA, pp. 2690–2703. Association for Computational Linguistics (2018)
27. Schaetti, N.: Behaviors of reservoir computing models for textual documents classification. In: The 2019 International Joint Conference on Neural Networks (2019)
28. Simov, K., Koprinkova-Hristova, P., Popov, A., Osenova, P.: Word embeddings improvement via echo state networks. In: 2019 IEEE International Symposium on INnovations in Intelligent SysTems and Applications (INISTA) (2019)
29. Simov, K., Koprinkova-Hristova, P., Popov, A., et al.: A reservoir computing approach to word sense disambiguation. Cogn. Comput. **15**, 1409–1418 (2023)
30. Team, G., Anil, R., Borgeaud, S., Alayrac, J.B., et al.: Gemini: a family of highly capable multimodal models (2025), https://arxiv.org/abs/2312.11805
31. Tong, M.H., Bickett, A.D., Christiansen, E.M., Cottrell, G.W.: Learning grammatical structure with echo state networks. Neural Networks **20**(3), 424–432 (2007). echo State Networks and Liquid State Machines
32. Tortorella, D., Gallicchio, C., Micheli, A.: Hierarchical dynamics in deep echo state networks. In: Pimenidis, E., Angelov, P., Jayne, C., Papaleonidas, A., Aydin, M. (eds.) ICANN 2022. LNCS, vol. 13531 pp. 668–679. Springer, Cham (2022). https://doi.org/10.1007/978-3-031-15934-3_55
33. Ueda, R., Kuribayashi, T., Kando, S., Inui, K.: Syntactic learnability of echo state neural language models at scale (2025). https://arxiv.org/abs/2503.01724

34. Vaswani, A., et al.: Attention is all you need. In: NeurIPS 2017 (2027)
35. Verstraeten, D., Schrauwen, B., d'Haene, M., Stroobandt, D.: An experimental unification of reservoir computing methods. Neural Netw. **20**(3), 391–403 (2007)
36. Wang, H., et al.: Score-cam: score-weighted visual explanations for convolutional neural networks (2020). https://arxiv.org/abs/1910.01279
37. Yeruva, M., Reddy, J., Atmakuri, U., Marreddy, M.: Brain encoding using randomized recurrent networks. In: Proceedings of the 45th Annual Meeting of the Cognitive Science Society, vol. 45. Cognitive Science Society (2023)
38. Zhang, T., Yang, B.: An exact approach to ridge regression for big data. Comput. Stat. **32**(3), 909–928 (2017). https://doi.org/10.1007/s00180-017-0731-5

A Spectral Interpretation of Redundancy in a Graph Reservoir

Anna Bison and Alessandro Sperduti

Department of Mathematics "Tullio Levi-Civita", University of Padova, Padova, Italy
anna.bison@studenti.unipd.it, alessandro.sperduti@unipd.it

Abstract. Reservoir computing has been successfully applied to graphs as a preprocessing method to improve the training efficiency of Graph Neural Networks (GNNs). However, a common issue that arises when repeatedly applying layer operators on graphs is over-smoothing, which consists in the convergence of graph signals toward low-frequency components of the graph Laplacian. This work revisits the definition of the reservoir in the Multiresolution Reservoir Graph Neural Network (MRGNN), a spectral reservoir model, and proposes a variant based on a Fairing algorithm originally introduced in the field of surface design in computer graphics. This algorithm provides a pass-band spectral filter that allows smoothing without shrinkage, and it can be adapted to the graph setting through the Laplacian operator. Given its spectral formulation, this method naturally connects to GNN architectures for tasks where smoothing, when properly controlled, can be beneficial, such as graph classification. The core contribution of the paper lies in the theoretical analysis of the algorithm from a random walks perspective. In particular, it shows how tuning the spectral coefficients can be interpreted as modulating the contribution of redundant random walks. Exploratory experiments based on the MRGNN architecture illustrate the potential of this approach and suggest promising directions for future research.

Keywords: Reservoir Computing · Fairing algorithm · GNN

1 Introduction

In recent years, Reservoir Computing (RC) has been successfully applied to learning in graph domains in order to reduce the training computational burden while maintaining excellent performances (see, for example, [1,2,10]). In almost all the proposed RC models, the reservoir is based on convolution operators for graphs (e.g., the ones defined in [9] for Graph Convolutional Neural Networks) that inevitably lead to a smoothing effect on the embeddings of the nodes of the processed graphs. The smoothing effect can be a desirable property in tasks such as graph classification, since it filters node signals that have high local variation, often encoding local information, and selects low-frequency components, which are more likely to encode global information that is more important for this kind of task. For this reason, it could make sense to implement an algorithm that optimizes smoothing in a model that performs graph classification. Indeed, the main risk when dealing with smoothing filters for GNNs is the over-smoothing problem, extensively discussed in [12], which consists in the exponential convergence of the node embeddings of a graph to the same vector, or to embeddings whose differences only depend on the node-degree distribution. In recent literature, some methods have been proposed to manage over-smoothing by acting on the input expression without altering the model definition, as in [11]. These kinds of methods may not solve the problem in cases where GNN layers are defined as low-pass filters, since they will behave like that independently of the input shape.

In this work, we explore, mainly from a theoretical point of view, how the Fairing algorithm introduced in [5] relates to spectral-based GNNs, and in particular to the *Multiresolution Reservoir Graph Neural Network* (MRGNN), introduced in [10]. The main motivation for considering the Fairing algorithm hinges on the fact that it proposes a procedure to define a filter that selects not only the desired frequencies to dampen or amplify, but also the number of iterations needed to reach the desired result. Even though it was proposed almost twenty years before the definition of Graph Convolutional Networks (GCN) [9], it effectively explains how to perform the equivalent of a convolution of degree-n, obtained by iterating n times a layer that is a degree-one polynomial of a spectral operator (which, in the case of graphs, can be chosen to be the symmetric Laplacian). The difference is that in the case of the Fairing algorithm, the parameters are tuned by the user, who, being familiar with spectral methods for signal processing, knows what is needed. In this work, these parameters will be presented from the perspective of random walks, as equivalent to controlling the weight with which specific walks contribute to the diffusion of signals through graph nodes. Based on this theoretical analysis, we propose a novel Fairing-based reservoir that we preliminary experiment within the MRGNN architecture, obtaining encouraging results.

2 Background

Here we concisely present the definitions of the two conceptual assets that form the basis of our analysis. The MRGNN model [10], focusing on reservoir computing, and the Fairing algorithm [5]. Despite their differences, they can be linked via a spectral perspective.

Notation. Uppercase letters will refer to matrices, and the elements of a matrix X are indicated as $[X]_{ij} = x_{ij}$. Let $G(V, E, (X, A))$ be a graph, where V denotes the set of nodes, E denotes the set of edges. Nodes are referred to by their indices, i.e., $i \in V$ denotes the i-th node, and $(i,j) \in E$ indicates that there is an edge connecting node i and node j. X denotes the embedding matrix: its i-th row denotes features vector (embedding) of node i, and the j-th column denotes the graph scalar signal associated to the j-th feature. A denotes the adjacency matrix, whose elements $a_{ij} = 1 \iff (i,j) \in E$. D denotes the diagonal degree matrix. Let $\Delta_{\text{sym}} = I - D^{-1/2} A D^{-1/2}$ be the symmetric normalized Laplacian. The set of first neighbours of node i is denoted with $\mathcal{N}_i$.

Multiresolution Reservoir Graph Neural Network. The MRGNN is a supervised graph neural network model based on a variant of a reservoir computing model, a k-hop reservoir that is mathematically equivalent to evolve the input embedding matrix with a pass-band filter. In a typical RC model, recursive neurons are run until a precise condition is satisfied (either convergence or maximum number of iterations). In MRGNN instead, the reservoir consists in a forward non-linear model that extracts graph features up to the k-hop neighbourhood, called *multiresolution features*. Then, intermediate features extracted for all the neighbourhoods of intermediate levels up to the k-th are considered simultaneously, and linearly combined with a method that presents some analogies with a spectral approach. Specifically, the formal definition of the transformation implemented by the reservoir consists in k iterations of a convolution:

$$H^{k,\mathcal{T}} = \left[X, \sigma(\tilde{A} X), \sigma(\tilde{A}\sigma(\tilde{A} X)), \ldots \right] = \left[H_{(0)}^{k,\mathcal{T}}, H_{(1)}^{k,\mathcal{T}}, H_{(2)}^{k,\mathcal{T}}, \ldots, H_{(k)}^{k,\mathcal{T}} \right]$$

where σ is the tanh activation function, $\tilde{A} = \mathcal{T}(A)$ is a function of the adjacency matrix and $H_{(i)}^{k,\mathcal{T}}$ represents the embedding matrix of node representations where the j-th one is obtained by convolving signals from nodes connected through a path of length i from the j-th node.

Finally, a readout function is implemented taking in input these multiresolution features and performing the final classification or regression task. In the paper, different definitions of the readout function, spanning from linear model to neural network are analyzed.

In the experimental evaluations presented in this work, we considered only the readout architecture with two fully connected layers, which corresponds to the case $q = 2$ as defined in the original MRGNN paper.

For further theoretical details on other components of the original model that are not essential for understanding the next sections, refer to the original paper.

Fairing Algorithm. The Fairing algorithm, introduced in [4,5], was proposed within the graph signal processing field. It aims to smooth graph signals without causing shrinkage and it is straightforward to see that it can be implemented in a GNN-like structure, as depicted in Fig. 1, where the symmetric operator K defined in the paper acts as the signal propagator. The subsequent paragraphs will present an analysis of the algorithm using random walks to connect it with the reservoir computing framework discussed in [10] and to give a spatial viewpoint on the spectral approaches. As shown in Fig. 1, the core of the algorithm involves mathematically applying a degree-$2N$ polynomial of an operator K to the initial embedding through iterative application of a degree-one polynomial of K. Parameters λ and μ are tuned statically to ensure the transformation acts as a pass-band filter w.r.t. the frequencies of K, a symmetric operator with a spectrum bounded in $[0, 2]$. This is achieved by alternating a shrinking layer, obtained with the positive-valued parameter λ, with an unshrinking layer, obtained with the negative-valued parameter μ. For further theoretical background refer to [4,5].

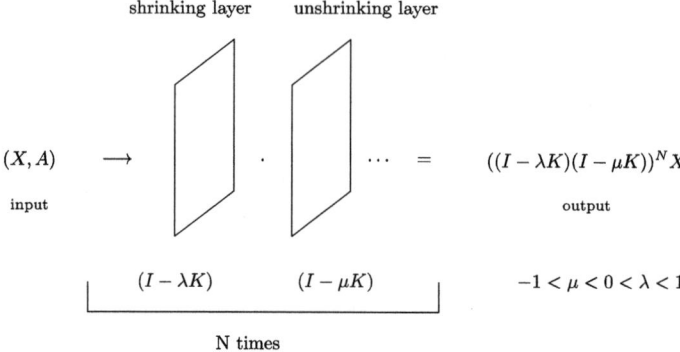

Fig. 1. Scheme of the implementation of the Fairing algorithm introduced in [5] with a GNN-like structure.

3 Linking the Fairing Algorithm with Spectral GNN

In this section, we give our first contribution. We show how the Fairing algorithm can be linked with spectral GNN (MRGNN belongs to this class of architectures) via the Dirichlet energy induced by the symmetric Laplacian matrix Δ_{sym}, defined as

$$\mathcal{E}^{\Delta_{\text{sym}}}(X) = \text{tr}(X^\top \Delta_{\text{sym}} X),$$

where $\text{tr}()$ is the trace operator. Consider now the gradient of $\mathcal{E}^{\Delta_{\text{sym}}}$, for simplicity in a graph scalar signal $\boldsymbol{x} \in \mathbb{R}^n$:

$$\nabla_{\boldsymbol{x}} \mathcal{E}^{\Delta_{\text{sym}}}(\boldsymbol{x}) = \nabla_{\boldsymbol{x}} \text{tr}(\boldsymbol{x}^\top \Delta_{\text{sym}} \boldsymbol{x}) = \nabla_{\boldsymbol{x}}(\boldsymbol{x}^\top \Delta_{\text{sym}} \boldsymbol{x}) = (\Delta_{\text{sym}}^\top + \Delta_{\text{sym}}) \boldsymbol{x} = 2\Delta_{\text{sym}} \boldsymbol{x},$$

i.e., $\mathcal{E}^{\Delta_{\text{sym}}}$ is a quadratic form induced by the symmetric Laplacian. In particular, it holds that its Hessian matrix is $2\Delta_{\text{sym}}$, that is positive semi-definite, so $\mathcal{E}^{\Delta_{\text{sym}}}$ is convex. This means that the following equality holds:

$$\boldsymbol{x}' = (I + \eta \Delta_{\text{sym}})\boldsymbol{x} = \boldsymbol{x} + \frac{\eta}{2} \nabla_{\boldsymbol{x}} \mathcal{E}^{\Delta_{\text{sym}}}(\boldsymbol{x})$$

i.e., a general Fairing layer can be interpreted as evolving graph signals along the gradient of $\mathcal{E}^{\Delta_{\text{sym}}}$, with direction determined by the sign of the hyperparameter η. This allows to link the Fairing algorithm with a spectral GNNs perspective: it is like to define a GNN that alternates gradient descent with gradient ascent using $\mathcal{E}^{\Delta_{\text{sym}}}$ as a loss function. The direction of the steps is defined by the sign of the coefficients, in analogy with the learning rate. If the steps in the negative direction of the gradient of $\nabla \mathcal{E}^{\Delta_{\text{sym}}}$ are enough, then the composition will reduce $\mathcal{E}$.

4 Tottering in MRGNN

The main definition of the reservoir layer proposed in MRGNN [10] is $X' = \tanh(\Delta_{\text{sym}} X)$, where the activation function tanh is introduced to mitigate the problem of *tottering*. This phenomenon arises when random walks repeatedly traverse the same edge back and forth between two neighboring nodes, leading to redundant or uninformative paths. The effect of the tanh function is to compress the signal values within the range $(-1, 1)$ through a smooth non-linearity. However, this operation uniformly shrinks all feature dimensions, without distinction. Moreover, since the reservoir layer is not subject to training, the inclusion of a non-linearity is not motivated by the usual aim of enlarging the hypothesis space toward non-linear functions. To more precisely address redundancy while preserving the spectral nature of the original formulation, we propose an alternative method that allows for a more targeted influence on the tottering effect. A formal analysis of the redundancies induced by the Δ_{sym} propagator will follow. Consider the k-th power of the symmetric Laplacian:

$$\Delta_{\text{sym}}^k = (I - D^{-1/2} A D^{-1/2})^k = (I - D^{-1/2}(AD^{-1})D^{1/2})^k$$

$$= \sum_{t=0}^{k} \binom{k}{t}(-1)^t D^{-1/2} P^t D^{1/2} = D^{-1/2}\left(\sum_{t=0}^{k}\binom{k}{t}(-1)^t P^t\right)D^{1/2}$$

where $P = AD^{-1}$ is called *transition matrix*:

$$[P]_{ij} = \sum_r [A]_{ir}[D^{-1}]_{rj} = \sum_r a_{ir}\frac{1}{d_r}\delta_{rj} = \frac{a_{ij}}{d_j} = p(i|j) = \begin{cases} \frac{1}{d_j} & \text{if } i \in \mathcal{N}_j, \\ 0 & \text{otherwise.} \end{cases}$$

i.e., $[P]_{ij}$ is the probability of reaching node i with a path of length 1 starting from node j when the probability to reach any first neighbour is uniform. Let's see what happens for $t = 2$:

$$[P^2]_{ij} = \sum_r [P]_{ir}[P]_{rj} = \begin{cases} \sum_r p(i|r)p(r|j) \neq 0 & \text{if } \exists r \in \mathcal{N}_i \cap \mathcal{N}_j, \\ 0 & \text{otherwise.} \end{cases}$$

This means that the matrix elements of P^2 represents the probability of reaching node i with a path of length 2 starting from node j.

By repeated application, it's straightforward to see that in general $[P^{t+1}]_{ij} = \sum_r [P]_{ir}[P^t]_{rj} = \sum_r p(i|r)p_t(r|j)$ represents the probability to reach any node r starting from node j with a path of length t, multiplied by the probability to end in i with one additional step.

The problem of tottering consists in the fact that random walks can travel edges going back and forth between two neighbors nodes indefinitely. For example, going from a node j to node i then come back to j and finally going to node i, constitutes a path of length 3 from j to i.

Considering $[P^3]_{ij}$, this specific cases contribute with the following terms:

$$\sum_r \sum_l [P]_{ir}[P]_{rl}[P]_{lj}\delta_{il}\delta_{rj} = \sum_r \sum_l p(i|r)p(r|l)p(l|j)\delta_{il}\delta_{rj} = p(i|j)p(j|i)p(i|j).$$

Let's now analyze the binomial coefficients. One possible interpretation is to consider a random walk of length *at most* k as a walk of length exactly k if vacuous steps are allowed: at each step it can be decided to walk from a node to one of its first neighbors, or to stay still.

There are the following possibilities to reach i-th node with at most k steps of which t non-vacuous steps:

- $t = 0 \rightarrow P^0 = I$: there is just one way, i.e., to stand in i-th node;
- $t = 1 \rightarrow P$: to reach node i when j-th node is a first neighbor, there are k ways to chose when to do the single non-vacuous step;
- $1 < t \leq k \rightarrow P^t$: there exist $\binom{k}{t}$ possibilities to select the t necessary steps to reach the i-th node, provided it is reachable, and in the remaining $(k-t)$ steps it will be sufficient to stay still.

The sign, i.e., the factor $(-1)^t$, can be seen as an analogue of a phase to the contributions of the walks to the final signal on the i-th node after k iterations, since Δ_{sym} propagates differences, then the contributions coming from first neighbours have opposite sign. And propagating *differences of differences* preserves the sign, and therefore signals that reach i-th node with even non vacuous steps give a positive contribution, while for odd number of steps the phase is opposite, giving a negative contribution. Recall the expression:

$$\Delta_{\text{sym}}^k = \sum_{t=0}^{k} \binom{k}{t}(-1)^t D^{-1/2} P^t D^{1/2} = D^{-1/2} \sum_{t=0}^{k} \binom{k}{t}(-1)^t P^t D^{1/2}$$

Consider the operator in the middle (without considering the symmetrization applied by $D^{\pm 1/2}$): for k iterations, if this operator would be applied to a signal $X^{(0)}$, the resulting signal component $[X^{(k)}]_{ij}$ would be

$$[X^{(k)}]_{ij} = [(I-P)^k X^{(0)}]_{ij} = \sum_r [(I-P)^k]_{ir} x_{rj}^{(0)}$$

where

$$[(I-P)^k]_{ir} = \delta_{ir} + \sum_{t=1}^{k} \binom{k}{t}(-1)^t p_t(i|r)$$

and then

$$[X^{(k)}]_{ij} = x_{ij}^{(0)} +$$

$$+ \sum_{r \in V} \left(-\binom{k}{1} p(i|r) + \binom{k}{2} p_2(i|r) + \cdots + (-1)^k \binom{k}{k} p_k(i|r) \right) x_{rj}^{(0)}.$$

This formally shows that the j-th component of the signal on the i-th node after k applications of Δ_{sym} results in a weighted average of the j-th component of the signal of the k-hop neighbours, where the weight assigned to the contribution from the r-th node depends on the total number of *signed* random walks of length at most k that exist between r-th node and i-th node.

Tottering occurs whenever a reflection between two nodes takes place. As a result, paths of length t can be counted multiple times, depending on how many such back-and-forth steps (i.e., reflections) can be inserted. Since reflections preserve the parity of the path length, tottering amplifies the contributions of many paths. However, it does not affect paths that reach nodes whose minimum distance from the source is k or $k-1$, as such paths cannot admit reflections without exceeding the length constraint.

The earlier expression shows that the signal from the r-th node is influenced by all possible random walks. Redundancies arise first from tottering walks, represented mathematically by powers of the P matrix, and second from counting each walk with a multiplicity reflecting vacuous steps that leave the path unchanged, given by the I matrix. Suppose now to tune the weights with which this two redundant contributions are considered. One way to do that is to introduce a weighting parameter α to balance them, obtaining the following variant of the layer definition:

$$X^{(k+1)} = D^{-1/2}(\alpha I + (1-\alpha)P)^k D^{1/2} X^{(0)}$$

the term $(\alpha I + (1-\alpha)P)^k$ consists in the following transformation for $x_{ij}^{(t)}$

$$[X^{(t)}]_{ij} = \alpha^k x_{ij}^{(0)} +$$

$$+ \sum_{r \in \mathcal{V}} \left(\binom{k}{1} \alpha^{k-1}(1-\alpha)p(i|r) + \binom{k}{2} \alpha^{k-2}(1-\alpha)^2 p_2(i|r) + \cdots + \right.$$

$$\left. + \binom{k}{t} \alpha^{k-t}(1-\alpha)^t \alpha p_t(i|r) + \cdots + \binom{k}{k}(1-\alpha)^k p_k(i|r) \right) x_{rj}^{(0)}.$$

Rearranging the expression of the variant of the layer just analyzed:

$$L = \alpha I + (1-\alpha)D^{-1/2}PD^{1/2} = I - (1-\alpha)\Delta_{\text{sym}}$$

that for $0 < \alpha < 1$ coincides with the expression of an iteration of a Fairing layer as in [5] where $\lambda = 1-\alpha$, i.e., a shrinking step. Therefore, a way to interpret the shrinking step from the point of view of random walks, is to read λ as a tunable parameter that balances the redundancies, and since in this case $1-\alpha > 0$, it does not account for the parity of walks. The case of negative coefficients (that is, the unshrinking step) in the range $-1 < \mu < 0 < \lambda < 1$ can be expressed by considering $1 < \alpha < 2$ and recognizing $1 - \alpha = \mu$, that instead accounts for the walks' parity.

Hence, tuning the Fairing parameters is equivalent to controlling the influence of random walks in an interpretable manner, in contrast to the effect of the tanh function, which instead shrinks all entries indiscriminately. Based on this conclusions, it may be worthwhile to evaluate the impact of the Fairing algorithm on the reservoir component of MRGNN.

5 Reservoir Based on the Fairing Algorithm

In spatial terms, the Fairing algorithm allows for controlling the contribution of different random walks. Suppose we perform a static tuning of the parameter α, meaning that its value is chosen analytically by the user (i.e., not learned empirically) to achieve a desired behavior. The effect of such tuning becomes immediately clear. If we set $\alpha \sim \varepsilon$, with $0 < \varepsilon \ll 1$, we suppress the contributions of random walks that contain any vacuous steps. In practice, this dampens all walks whose effective length is shorter than the maximum walk length k, leaving only the paths of length exactly k to dominate the dynamics. However, among these, tottering walks have an high contribution, leading to the removal of one form of redundancy while leaving the other unchanged. Conversely, if we choose $\alpha \sim 1-\varepsilon$, the contribution of all random walks is practically eliminated, and the propagator collapses to the identity function. This results in a model with limited expressivity. A more balanced setting, such as $\alpha \sim 0.5$, mitigates both types of redundancy more equally. This observation may offer an explanation for why values of α in this range are also those empirically recommended in [5] both for the shrinking and the unshrinking steps, as yielding fair smoothing without shrinkage.

The introduction of the Fairing algorithm is particularly suited for the basic definition of MRGNN, since Δ_{sym} has a limited spectrum $\sigma_{\Delta_{\text{sym}}} \subset [0, 2]$ exactly like the K operator presented in [5]. This suggests to exploit values of the constants λ, μ recommended in the paper to obtain an effect of smoothing without shrinkage. The reservoir is now defined alternating a shrinking layer $X' = (I - \lambda\Delta_{\text{sym}})X$ with an unshrinking layer $X' = (I - \mu\Delta_{\text{sym}})X$, obtaining after k iterations the following embedding matrix for a graph:

$$X^{(k)} = (I - \lambda\Delta_{\text{sym}})^n (I - \mu\Delta_{\text{sym}})^m X^{(0)}$$

where $n + m = k$, since there are several combinations possible that allow to filter the signal in a different way.

The corresponding Dirichlet energy induced by Δ_{sym} can be written as

$$\mathcal{E}^{\Delta_{\text{sym}}}(X^{(k)}) = \sum_{\omega \in \sigma_{\Delta_{\text{sym}}}} (1 - \lambda\omega)^{2n}(1 - \mu\omega)^{2m} \mathcal{E}_\omega^{\Delta_{\text{sym}}}(X^{(0)})$$

that constitutes the filter reported in [4]. Depending on the values of the hyperparameters λ and μ, the filter selects a pass-band.

In figures Fig. 2-3 we report examples of plots of the Dirichlet energy for different values of λ and μ for some of the graphs in the Enzymes dataset.

In Fig. 2 it's clear the effect of the shrinking step, when the energy decreases, and the unshrinking step, when it increases. This perfectly represents the mathematical expectations, indeed, indicating a general step with $(I - \alpha\Delta_{\text{sym}})$:

$$\mathcal{E}^{\Delta_{\text{sym}}}(X^{(t+1)}) = \sum_{\omega \in \sigma_{\Delta_{\text{sym}}}} (1 - \alpha\omega)^2 \mathcal{E}_\omega^{\Delta_{\text{sym}}}(X^{(t)})$$

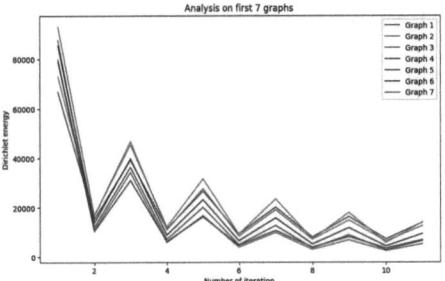

Fig. 2. Plot of $\mathcal{E}^{\Delta_{\text{sym}}}$ for a Fairing reservoir $\lambda = 0.5$, $\mu = -0.66667$ of seven graphs of the dataset Enzymes after each iteration of the layer.

$$= \mathcal{E}^{\Delta_{\text{sym}}}(X^{(t)}) + \sum_{\omega \in \sigma_{\Delta_{\text{sym}}}} (\alpha\omega - 2)\alpha\omega \mathcal{E}_\omega^{\Delta^{\text{sym}}}(X^{(t)})$$

that for a shrinking step, i.e. $0 < \alpha = \lambda < 1$ results in $(\alpha\omega - 2)\alpha\omega < 0$, i.e., a decrease of the energy, while for $\alpha = \mu < 0$ results in $(\alpha\omega - 2)\alpha\omega > 0$, that is, an increase of the energy, reflecting the effect of unshrinking.

Acting on the hyperparameters λ and μ allows to tune the frequencies that are filtered: decreasing λ to 0.25 and μ to -0.5 causes a shift of the pass-band treshold $k_{PB} = \frac{1}{\lambda} + \frac{1}{\mu}$ to 2, making the resulting filter passing the complete band, with the resulting effect of amplification after many iterations (see Fig. 3).

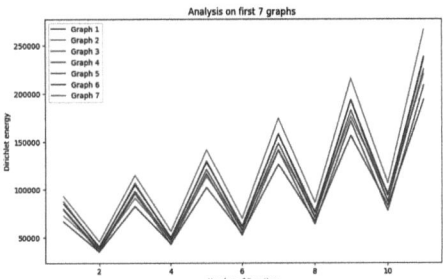

Fig. 3. Plot of $\mathcal{E}^{\Delta_{\text{sym}}}$ for a Fairing reservoir $\lambda = 0.25$, $\mu = -0.5$ of seven graphs of the dataset Enzymes after each iteration of the layer.

This methodology allows to control the signal's energy by adjusting the hyperparameters of the filter. It is particularly interesting because it is based on the same mathematical principles as GCNs, even though it was published in 1995, slightly before the widespread research on GNNs. This highlights that the side effects of smoothing were already understood and managed before the rise of GNNs.

6 Exploratory Experiments

A limited experimental campaign was conducted to preliminarily assess the potential of the proposed approach, with no aim to perform a fair comparison versus the MRGNN model. Specifically, we reused the hyperparameters already optimized on the MRGNN model, observing encouraging results. This suggests that the modified reservoir architecture is promising, and that a more thorough hyperparameter tuning could further enhance its competitiveness.

Datasets

Experiments on the proposed reservoir were conducted on four molecular graph classification benchmarks: PTC [6], NCI1 [8], PROTEINS [7], and ENZYMES [7]. These datasets were selected to ensure comparability with the original MRGNN model, which was tested on the same benchmarks.

As described in [10], PTC and NCI1 consist of molecular graphs representing chemical compounds, where nodes correspond to atoms and edges to chemical bonds. The classification task in PTC aims to determine the carcinogenicity of compounds in male rats, while in NCI1 the goal is to classify compounds based on their activity in anticancer screens. PROTEINS and ENZYMES are datasets in which graphs represent proteins, with nodes denoting amino acids and edges connecting amino acids that lie within a 6Å distance in the 3D structure. ENZYMES involves a six-class classification task, whereas the others are binary (Table 1).

Table 1. Molecular graph datasets statistics.

Dataset	#Graphs	#Nodes	#Edges	Avg #Nodes per Graph	Avg #Edges per Graph
PTC	344	4915	10108	14.29	14.69
NCI1	4110	122747	265506	29.87	32.30
PROTEINS	1113	43471	162088	39.06	72.82
ENZYMES	600	19580	74564	32.63	124.27

Implementation Details

The implementation of the Fairing variant of the reservoir was implemented modifying the original code of MRGNN publicly available on GitHub[1]. In particular, a variant of the reservoir was defined with a new reservoir version that, depending on the parity of the reservoir layer iteration, applies either a shrinking step ($\lambda = 0.5$) or an unshrinking step ($\mu = -0.66667$).

6.1 Results

In order to test the impact of the Fairing algorithm on the reservoir definition, experiments were conducted for each dataset using the "optimal" values

---
[1] https://github.com/lpasa/MRGNN.

Table 2. Hyperparameters used in the experimental setup for each dataset.

Dataset	epochs	LR	Dropout	Weight Decay	Batch Size	# Hidden	k
PTC	400	0.0005	0.6	0.005	32	15	4
NCI1	500	0.001	0.5	0.0005	32	100	4
PROTEINS	200	0.001	0.5	0.0005	32	50	5
ENZYMES	200	0.001	0.5	0.0005	32	100	6

Table 3. Mean test accuracies for MRGNN (Table III- [10]) and the Fairing approach. Results for the Fairing approach are: *i)* obtained by using the optimal hyperparameters's values of MRGNN (**no model selection performed**); *ii)* computed over five runs of 10-folds cross-validation, with sample standard deviation defined as $s = \sqrt{s^2}$, where $s^2 = \frac{1}{n-1}\sum_{i=1}^{n}(x_i - \bar{x})^2$, $\bar{x}$ is the sample mean, and n denotes the number of runs.

Dataset	MRGNN Test Accuracy (%)	Fairing Test Accuracy (%)
PTC	57.60 ± 10.01	59.58 ± 1.73
NCI1	80.58 ± 1.88	79.02 ± 0.27
PROTEINS	75.84 ± 3.51	74.39 ± 0.83
ENZYMES	68.20 ± 6.86	68.37 ± 1.89

of the hyperparameters documented in the MRGNN original paper (reported in Table 2). Then, a 10-fold cross-validation was done for 5 runs. For each split of the 10-fold cross-validation, the highest value of the validation accuracy was selected, and it was selected the test accuracy of the epoch nearest to the last one to which the highest value of the validation accuracy was associated. In this way, for each run expectation values of the test accuracies were calculated, and finally, the expectation of this expectations was calculated with respect to the five runs. The obtained results are reported in Table 3, jointly with the ones obtained by MRGNN so to provide an idea of the performance of the original architecture. These very preliminary Fairing-based reservoir results exhibit values that are comparable to those obtained by MRGNN after a complete model selection, suggesting that a comparable model selection procedure for the proposed approach could lead to SOTA results.

7 Conclusions

This work introduced a theoretical analysis of the impact of Fairing algorithms when applied to reservoir computing architectures. In particular, it derived and demonstrated the connection between the smoothing behavior induced by Taubin Fairing and the dynamics of random walks on graphs, showing how such Fairing acts on the structural and spectral properties of the underlying reservoir. This theoretical contribution offers a perspective on the role of graph-based smoothing in reservoir dynamics and lays the groundwork for further extensions.

For what concerns the exploratory experiments proposed, while no formal comparison was performed, the observed similarity in performance suggests that a more rigorous evaluation between the original and Fairing-based models could be an interesting direction for future research.

References

1. Wang, S., et al.: Echo state graph neural networks with analogue random resistive memory arrays. Nat. Mac. Intell. **5**(2), 104–113 (2023)
2. Bianchi, F.M., Gallicchio, C., Micheli, A.: Pyramidal reservoir graph neural network. Neurocomputing **470**, 389–404 (2022)
3. Lindeberg, T.: Scale-space for discrete signals. IEEE Trans. Pattern Anal. Mach. Intell. **12**(3), 234–254 (1990). https://doi.org/10.1109/34.49051
4. Taubin, G.: A signal processing approach to fair surface design. In: Proceedings of the 22nd Annual Conference on Computer Graphics and Interactive Techniques, pp. 351–358. ACM, New York (1995). https://doi.org/10.1145/218380.218473
5. Taubin, G.: Curve and surface smoothing without shrinkage. In: Proceedings of the Fifth IEEE International Conference on Computer Vision (ICCV), pp. 852–857. IEEE, Washington (1995). https://doi.org/10.1109/ICCV.1995.466848
6. Helma, C., King, R.D., Kramer, S., Srinivasan, A.: The predictive toxicology challenge 2000–2001. Bioinformatics **17**(1), 107–108 (2001)
7. Borgwardt, K.M., Ong, C.S., Schönauer, S., Vishwanathan, S.V.N., Smola, A.J., Kriegel, H.-P.: Protein function prediction via graph kernels. Bioinformatics **21**(Suppl. 1), i47–i56 (2005)
8. Wale, N., Watson, I.A., Karypis, G.: Comparison of descriptor spaces for chemical compound retrieval and classification. Knowl. Inf. Syst. **14**(3), 347–375 (2008)
9. Kipf, T.N., Welling, M.: Semi-supervised classification with graph convolutional networks. In: Proceedings of the 5th International Conference on Learning Representations (ICLR), Toulon, France, April 24–26 2017 (2017)
10. Pasa, L., Navarin, N., Sperduti, A.: Multiresolution reservoir graph neural network. IEEE Trans. Neural Netw. Learn. Syst. (2021). https://doi.org/10.1109/TNNLS.2021.3061412
11. Zhao, L., Akoglu, L.: PairNorm: Tackling oversmoothing in GNNs. *arXiv* preprint arXiv:1909.12223 (2020). https://arxiv.org/abs/1909.12223
12. Rusch, T.K., Bronstein, M.M., Mishra, S.: A survey on oversmoothing in graph neural networks. arXiv:abs/2303.10993 (2023). https://api.semanticscholar.org/CorpusID:257632346

Shaping Attractor Landscapes in Boolean Liquid State Machines via STDP and Global Plasticity

Jérémie Cabessa[1](✉) and Alessandro E. P. Villa[2]

[1] DAVID Lab, University of Versailles (UVSQ) – Paris-Saclay,
78035 Versailles, France
`jeremie.cabessa@uvsq.fr`
[2] NeuroHeuristic Research Group, DESI – HEC, University of Lausanne (UNIL),
1015 Lausanne, Switzerland
`alessandro.villa@unil.ch`

Abstract. Small Boolean Liquid State Machines (B-LSMs) offer a simplified yet expressive biologically inspired model of recurrent computation, in which network attractor dynamics can be systematically analyzed. In their untrained form, B-LSMs exhibit complex, often chaotic dynamics with short-lived memory traces. This study investigates how local synaptic plasticity (STDP) and a global plasticity (GP) mechanism jointly shape the attractor landscapes of these networks. Specifically, we show that synaptic modifications can drive B-LSMs to exhibit exponentially many attractors, each corresponding to a potential memory. Such high attractor regimes are attainable through global synaptic crafting. Under noisy background conditions, STDP tends to drive the networks back to low attractor regimes; however, when receiving carefully designed inputs, STDP maintains the networks' rich attractor dynamics. Overall, our findings highlight the theoretical potential for storing an impressive number of memories in recurrent neural networks, with significant implications for theoretical neuroscience and neuromorphic computing.

Keywords: Reservoir computing · Liquid state machines · Boolean networks · Synaptic plasticity · STDP · Global plasticity · Attractors · finite state automata

1 Introduction

Attractor dynamics constitute a core framework in computational neuroscience and machine learning. In neuroscience, attractors refer to stable firing patterns in the cerebral cortex and have been critically linked to long-term and short-term memory, attention, decision-making, and mental disorders [18]. The mechanisms underlying attractor formation, their roles in representation and memory, and the empirical evidence supporting their existence in the brain have been thoroughly studied [10] (and references therein).

In machine learning, attractor states are used to model associative memory, wherein a system evolves toward stable configurations that represent stored patterns–typically corresponding to local or global minima of an energy function [6,19]. Hopfield networks provide a classical model of fixed-point attractors, employing symmetric connectivity to ensure convergence to stable states [6]. Subsequent developments have extended this framework to accommodate asymmetric interactions [19], higher-order synaptic terms [12], and dense memory representations [3]. More recent innovations introduce continuous energy landscapes and update rules inspired by attention mechanisms, significantly enhancing both memory capacity and convergence speed [17]. Boltzmann machines–and their restricted variants–generalize this paradigm by incorporating stochastic dynamics, enabling the modeling of richer probability distributions and laying the groundwork for modern generative models [4,5].

Reservoir Computing (RC) frameworks [13], such as Echo State Networks (ESNs) [8] and Liquid State Machines (LSMs) [14], leverage fixed recurrent network topologies with rich, dynamic internal states to project input streams into high-dimensional temporal representations. In particular, LSMs were introduced as a biologically inspired model of computation based on spiking neural networks with fading memory, offering a principled alternative to traditional rate-based neural networks [14]. Here, we consider Boolean Liquid State Machines (B-LSMs), a biologically inspired instantiation in which units operate in binary states, enabling a systematic analysis of the network's attractor dynamics [1].

The mechanisms and computational implications of spike-timing-dependent plasticity (STDP) have been extensively studied [2]. Notably, the emergence of cell assemblies – underlying attractor dynamics – can be promoted by stimulus-driven synaptic pruning in conjunction with STDP in large neural networks operating amid background noise [7]. Furthermore, the interaction between excitatory and inhibitory couplings has been shown to give rise to new attractor states, characterized by stable, synchronous activity patterns [21]. The combined action of STDP and homeostatic plasticity mechanisms also enhances both the storage and maintenance of time-varying attractor dynamics [20].

In this work, we investigate the attractor landscapes of small Boolean Liquid State Machines (B-LSMs) subject to the combined effects of spike-timing-dependent plasticity (STDP) and global synaptic plasticity. This simplified yet expressive framework enables a systematic analysis of the networks' attractor dynamics. We demonstrate that global plasticity can drive the network into rich attractor regimes, which can be sustained over time through carefully designed input patterns. Our findings highlight the theoretical potential for storing an exponential number of memories in recurrent neural networks, with implications for both theoretical neuroscience and the development of neuromorphic hardware.

2 Model

2.1 Boolean Liquid State Machines (B-LSMs)

Boolean Liquid State Machines (B-LSMs) are recurrent neural networks composed of binary-valued inputs and reservoir units [15]. Formally, a B-LSM is defined as a tuple

$$\mathcal{N} = \left(U, X, \{W^{[res]}(t)\}_{t \geq 0}, \{W^{[in]}(t)\}_{t \geq 0}, \{b(t)\}_{t \geq 0}\right)$$

where $U = \{1, \ldots, M\}$ denotes the indices of the M input units, and $X = \{1, \ldots, N\}$ the indices of the N reservoir units. At any time t, the input-to-reservoir weight matrix is $W^{[in]}(t) \in \mathbb{R}^{N \times M}$, the recurrent reservoir weight matrix is $W^{[res]}(t) \in \mathbb{R}^{N \times N}$, and $b(t) \in \mathbb{R}^N$ is the bias vector of the reservoir cells. The network $\mathcal{N}$ is said to be *static* if the weights and biases $W^{[in]}(t)$, $W^{[res]}(t)$ and $b(t)$ remain constant over time t; it is called *evolving* otherwise. A B-LSM is illustrated in Fig. 1 (left). The dynamics of a B-LSM is governed by the following equation

$$x(t+1) = \theta\left(W^{[res]}(t) \cdot x(t) + W^{[in]}(t) \cdot u(t) + b(t)\right) \quad (1)$$

where $u(t) \in \mathbb{B}^M$ is the binary input vector, $x(t) \in \mathbb{B}^N$ and $x(t+1) \in \mathbb{B}^N$ the reservoir state at time t and $t+1$, respectively, and θ the element-wise hard threshold function:

$$\theta(x) = \begin{cases} 0 & \text{if } x < 0 \\ 1 & \text{otherwise} \end{cases}$$

Given an infinite input stream

$$\bar{u} = \left(u(0), u(1), u(2), \ldots\right) \in \left(\mathbb{B}^M\right)^\infty,$$

the system evolves to generate a corresponding state trajectory

$$\mathcal{N}(\bar{u}) = \left(x(0), x(1), x(2), \ldots\right) \in \left(\mathbb{B}^N\right)^\infty,$$

where each state $x(t)$ is determined by Eq. (1), for all $t > 0$. The sequence $\mathcal{N}(\bar{u})$ is called the *dynamics* of $\mathcal{N}$ for the input stream $\bar{u}$.

2.2 Attractors

Attractors in a B-LSM are state configurations toward which the network dynamics evolve and stabilize into fixed-point, cyclic, or chaotic behavior. Formally, a finite set of states $A = \{x_0, x_1, \ldots, x_k\} \subseteq \mathbb{B}^N$ is said to be an *attractor* of a B-LSM if there exist some input stream $\bar{u} = (u(0), u(1), u(2), \ldots)$ and time step t_0 such that the induced network dynamics $\mathcal{N}(\bar{u}) = (x(0), x(1), x(2), \ldots)$ satisfies $x(t) \in A$ for all $t \geq t_0$.

Boolean recurrent neural networks, and consequently B-LSMs, are computationally equivalent to finite-state automata (FSA) [11,15,16]. More precisely,

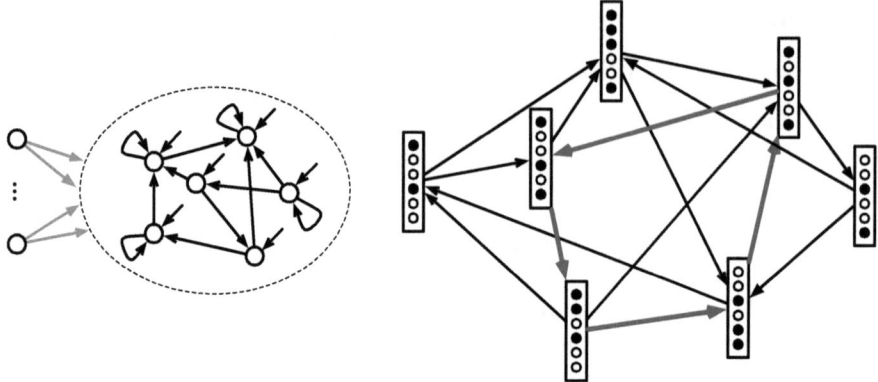

Fig. 1. A Boolean liquid state machine (left) and its corresponding automaton (right). The different dynamics of the network correspond to the different paths in the automaton. The attractors of the network correspond to the cycles in the automaton.

for any B-LSM $\mathcal{N}$ of size N (i.e., with N reservoir cells), one can construct a corresponding FSA $\mathcal{A}$ of size $O(2^N)$. The nodes of $\mathcal{A}$ are the Boolean states of $\mathcal{N}$, and there is a transition from node x to node x' labeled by input u in $\mathcal{A}$ if and only if $\mathcal{N}$ transitions from state x to x' upon receiving input u. According to this construction, the *dynamics* of $\mathcal{N}$ correspond to *paths* in the automaton $\mathcal{A}$, and, in particular, the *attractors* of the network $\mathcal{N}$ correspond to *(simple) cycles* in $\mathcal{A}$ [1]. The reverse translation from a given automaton $\mathcal{A}$ to its corresponding network $\mathcal{N}$ is of no interest for our purposes [16]. This correspondance from B-LSM to FSA is illustrated in Fig. 1 (right).

Based on these considerations, the number of attractors of a B-LSM corresponds to the number of elementary circuits in its corresponding FSA:

Fact 1. *The number of attractors of a B-LSM with N reservoir cells is in $\Theta(2^N!)$.*

The attractors of $\mathcal{N}$ can therefore be systematically enumerated using the following procedure:

1. Construct the FSA $\mathcal{A}$ associated to $\mathcal{N}$;
2. Enumerate all simple cycles (or elementary circuits) of $\mathcal{A}$ using Johnson's algorithm [9].

Note that the number of attractors in a B-LSM fluctuates in response to synaptic modifications. As the network adjusts its synaptic configuration, the structure of the associated automaton changes accordingly, revealing a new set of cycles that define the updated attractor regime of the network. Overall, the combinatorial explosion in the number of attractors (Fact 1) underscores the substantial memory capacity of B-LSMs and motivates a tractable analysis framework focused on small networks ($N \leq 8$).

2.3 Synaptic Plasticity

We consider two forms of synaptic plasticity that govern learning in the B-LSM framework:

(i) Spike-Timing-Dependent Plasticity (STDP): While receiving random background inputs, the network undergoes synaptic modifications governed by an STDP rule, which updates the reservoir weights $w_{ij}^{\text{res}}(t)$ at each time step based on local pre- and post-synaptic activity, as follows:

$$\Delta w_{ij}^{\text{res}}(t+1) = \eta_{ij} \cdot (x_j(t) \cdot x_i(t+1) - x_j(t+1) \cdot x_i(t))$$
$$w_{ij}^{\text{res}}(t+1) = \texttt{clip}\left[w_{ij}^{\text{res}}(t) + \Delta w_{ij}^{\text{res}}(t+1)\right].$$

Here, $\eta_{ij} = \eta \cdot \epsilon$ is a noisy learning rate, with $\epsilon \sim \mathcal{U}([0.95, 1.05])$ and $\eta \in \mathbb{R}$, and weights are bounded via the $\texttt{clip}$ function to the interval $[w_{-}^{\text{res}}, w_{+}^{\text{res}}]$, with $w_{-}^{\text{res}}, w_{+}^{\text{res}} \in \mathbb{R}$.

(i) Global Plasticity (GP): Upon receiving a predefined trigger input pattern, the entire reservoir undergoes a *global plasticity (GP)* rule modeled as a simulated annealing process that adjusts the reservoir synapses for the duration of the pattern as follows:

$$\begin{cases} \boldsymbol{W}^{[res]}(t+1) = \boldsymbol{W}^{[res]}(t) + \boldsymbol{\epsilon}, \text{ with } \boldsymbol{\epsilon} \sim \mathcal{U}\left([-\epsilon, +\epsilon]^{M \times N}\right) \\ \Delta E(t+1) = \text{attr}\left(\boldsymbol{W}^{[res]}(t)\right) - \text{attr}\left(\boldsymbol{W}^{[res]}(t+1)\right) \\ P_{\text{accept}}(t+1) = \exp\left(-\frac{\Delta E(t+1)}{T_t}\right) \\ T_{t+1} = T_t \cdot \alpha, \text{ with } T_0 \in \mathbb{R} \text{ and } 0 < \alpha < 1 \end{cases}$$

where $\boldsymbol{W}^{[res]}(t+1)$ is a noisy update of $\boldsymbol{W}^{[res]}(t)$, which is accepted if it results in more attractors than $\boldsymbol{W}^{[res]}(t)$ (computed using the attr function) or with a probability $P_{\text{accept}}(t+1)$, which depends on the decreasing temperature T_{t+1}. The objective is to explore synaptic configurations in order to maximize the number of attractors, balancing stochastic exploration (through noise addition) with convergence (through a cooling mechanism).

3 Results

3.1 Experimental Setup

We consider Boolean Liquid State Machines (B-LSMs) with one input cell and $N \in \{5, 6, 7, 8\}$ reservoir cells. The reservoir weights are drawn from a normal distribution, i.e., $\boldsymbol{W}^{[res]} \sim \mathcal{N}(\boldsymbol{0}, \boldsymbol{1})$, and the input weights and biases are set to $\boldsymbol{W}^{[in]} = \boldsymbol{1}$ and $\boldsymbol{b} = \boldsymbol{0}$, respectively.

These networks are submitted to background input streams and trigger patterns. For the background activity, we generate a random binary input stream $\bar{u} = \big(u(0), u(1), u(2), \dots\big)$ of length 1000, where each inter-spike interval satisfies $\text{ISI}_i \sim \text{Pois}(\lambda = 2)$. For the trigger patterns, we generate a random binary sequence $\bar{p} = \big(p(0), p(1), p(2), \dots\big) \sim \text{Binomial}(n = 50, p = 0.5)$, and then insert it at P non-overlapping random positions inside the input stream $\bar{u}$, where $P \in \{0, 1, 3, 5, 7, 9, 11\}$ (blue regions in Fig. 3).

A simulation involves the random generation of a Boolean network $\mathcal{N}$ (reservoir weights) and a background binary input stream $\bar{u}$ interspersed with P trigger patterns. The network processes this input and undergoes STDP or GP, depending on whether it receives background activity or a trigger pattern (white and blue regions in Fig. 3). At each time step, these plasticity mechanisms modify the network's synaptic weights, thereby modifying its corresponding automaton, and thus altering its number of attractors, referred to as the *attractor regime* (cf. Sect. 2.2). The successive attractor regimes are computed at every time step, and their evolution over time is analyzed (see Fig. 3). Each simulation was repeated 10 times with different random seeds.

3.2 Attractor Regimes

Figure 2 presents the distribution of the number of attractors observed in B-LSMs composed of N reservoir nodes ($N \in \{5, 6, 7, 8\}$) and driven by 11 trigger patterns (a configuration giving rise to the largest number of attractors). As the network size increases from 5 to 8 internal nodes, the maximum number of attractors rises sharply from 32 to 23042. The average number of attractors also grows with the network size, indicating that larger networks can settle into higher attractor regimes. These results underscore the capacity of B-LSMs to support a large number of attractors, each corresponding to a potential memory state, as formally stated in Fact 1.

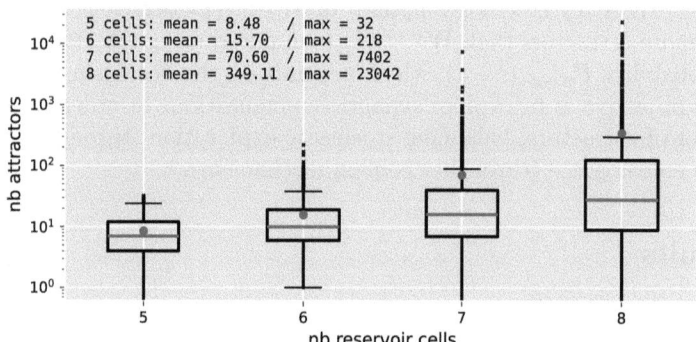

Fig. 2. Distribution of the number of attractors achieved by B-LSMs composed of $N \in \{5, 6, 7, 8\}$ reservoir nodes and driven by input streams of length 1000 containing 11 trigger patterns. Each box plot summarizes results from 10 simulations, with the median indicated by a blue line and the mean by a blue circle. The y-axis is shown on a logarithmic scale.

3.3 Effect of Global Plasticity (GP)

Every time the network encounters a trigger pattern, it undergoes the global plasticity (GP) process for the duration of the pattern (see Sect. 2.3). GP is a network-level mechanism designed to amplify the number of attractors, implemented as a simulated annealing process. The network adjusts all its reservoir synaptic weights and, with high probability, transitions into successive configurations that increase the number of attractors.

As expected, the GP mechanism significantly enhances the attractor regime of the network. This effect is clearly illustrated in Fig. 3, where the trigger periods (indicated by blue bands) correspond to pronounced increases in the attractor regime. These substantial rises in attractor numbers are generally accompanied by large synaptic changes, quantified as the sum of absolute differences between synaptic weights at successive time steps ($t-1$ and t). The GP mechanism is essential for achieving large attractor regimes, as disabling this process leads to stagnation within very low regimes. In this context, the GP mechanism can be viewed as a form of *learning*.

To quantify this phenomenon on a larger scale, we analyzed all simulations involving B-LSMs subjected to 11 trigger patterns. For each pattern, we computed the difference between the number of attractors two time steps prior to the pattern's onset and at the pattern's termination. The average of these differences, referred to as the *rise in the attractor regime*, are reported in Table 1. We see that the expansion of the attractor regime induced by trigger patterns grows significantly with network size, indicating greater responsiveness and dynamical complexity in larger reservoirs.

Table 1. Rises and drops in attractor regimes induced by the onsets and terminations of trigger patterns, respectively. Each pair in the form x/y represents the average decrease ("drop") and increase ("rise") in attractor count associated with the terminations and onsets of triggers pattern, respectively.

Nb nodes	5 nodes	6 nodes	7 nodes	8 nodes
drop/rise	−5.5/5.4	−15.6/16.9	−142.0/141.6	−1015.8/1012.1

3.4 Effect of Spike-Timing-Dependent Plasticity (STDP)

Between trigger patterns, the network undergoes spike-timing-dependent plasticity (STDP) driven by random background inputs (see Sect. 2.3). STDP is a local mechanism that adjusts synaptic strengths by reinforcing or weakening connections based on the timing of pre- and post-synaptic spikes. This mechanism is commonly associated with learning, as it refines neural circuits to encode salient input patterns.

The STDP mechanism drives the network abruptly into low attractor regimes. This effect is illustrated in Fig. 3, where the terminations of trigger

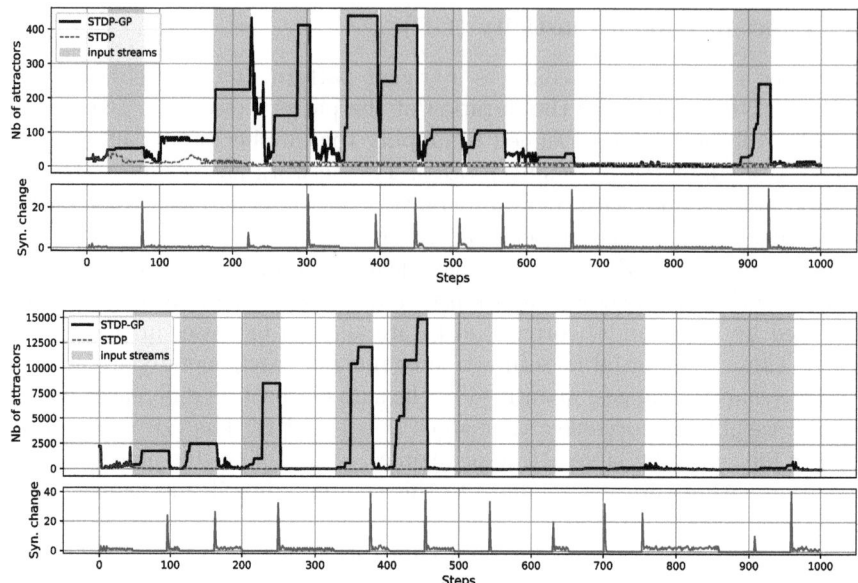

Fig. 3. Simulations of Boolean networks subject to random background activity and trigger patterns (indicated by blue bands). Top: a B-LSMs with 7 reservoir nodes. Bottom: a B-LSM with 8 reservoir nodes. The networks undergo STDP during background activity and GP during trigger patterns. At each time step, the number of attractors is computed, and the evolution of the attractor regime is displayed (black trace). For comparison, the attractor regime evolution without GP is shown (dotted trace). The synaptic change induced by the STDP and GP plasticity mechanisms are also shown (red trace). (Color figure online)

periods – marked by the reactivation of STDP – coincide with sudden drops in the attractor regime. STDP typically induces small but targeted synaptic changes that can disrupt the attractor structure of the network. We hypothesize that maintaining a high-dimensional attractor regime incurs an energetic cost that STDP alone, when driven by random background input, is unable to support. In this context, STDP can be interpreted as a form of *memory recalibration*, enabling the network to adapt and support new learning. It is important to emphasize that the behavior of STDP differs markedly when applied to structured input streams, as opposed to random ones, as detailed in Sect. 3.5.

To better understand this phenomenon, we analyzed simulations involving networks with 11 trigger patterns. For each pattern, we measured the difference between the number of attractors attained during the pattern and two time steps after its termination. The averages of these differences, referred to as the *drop in the attractor regime*, is reported in Table 1. The results reveal that the magnitude of the drops mirrors that of the rises, both showing a significant correlation with network size.

3.5 Stability of Attractor Regimes

Consider a network operating in a high attractor regime. If its synaptic weights were frozen, the network would necessarily preserve this regime over time, as its associated automaton (and the cycles it contains) would remain unchanged (see Sect. 2.2). However, in biological neural networks, synaptic weights are not abruptly frozen after learning; rather, they are continuously shaped by ongoing network activity. Furthermore, STDP induced by background activity tends to significantly reduce the attractor regime, as shown in Sect. 3.4. This raises a natural question: Can neural networks maintain high attractor regimes over time despite the continuous influence of activity-dependent plasticity?

We demonstrate that a network exposed to specific input streams – rather than random background activity – can effectively maintain high attractor regimes over extended periods, even in the presence of STDP. More precisely, we consider a synaptic configuration of a B-LSM associated with a regime R of 878 attractors. We then compute a specific input stream that drives the network through attractors of R, as long as no STDP is enabled. Afterward, we re-enable the STDP mechanism and track the evolution of the attractor regime in response to this specific input stream.

The results of this simulation, presented in Fig. 4, demonstrate that the network is capable of maintaining its attractor regime over time, depending on the learning rate η. For a very small learning rate ($\eta = 0.0001$), the network retains its high attractor regime indefinitely. In this case, the synaptic changes induced by this minimal learning rate are too small to alter the dynamical automaton associated with the network, thereby preserving its attractor regime. At an intermediate learning rate ($\eta = 0.001$), the network initially sustains its high attractor regime but gradually transitions to lower regimes, displaying plateauing effects. In contrast, for larger learning rates ($\eta = 0.01$ and $\eta = 0.1$), the network rapidly collapses into low attractor regimes.

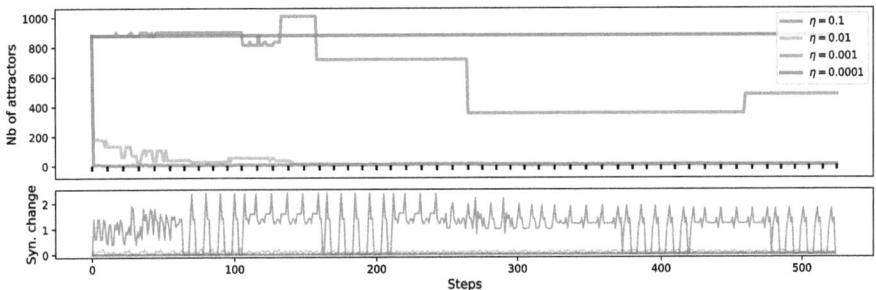

Fig. 4. Evolution of the attractor regime in the a B-LSM composed of 7 nodes, under a specific input stream and different STDP learning rates. (Top) The network begins in a high attractor regime of 878 attractors and receives a crafted inputs (black ticks) that would confine it to this regime in the absence of STDP. The evolution of the attractor regime is shown for three STDP learning rates ($\eta = 0.0001$, $\eta = 0.001$, $\eta = 0.01$). (Bottom) Magnitude of synaptic changes induced by STDP over time.

These observations suggest that the magnitude of synaptic changes directly influences the stability of the dynamical automaton underlying the network. Small synaptic changes are associated with stability and preservation of the attractor regime, while large changes lead to its disruption. Overall, this mechanism may be interpreted as a form of *progressive memory loss* in the absence of memory reactivation.

4 Conclusion

This study investigates the attractor dynamics of small Boolean Liquid State Machines (B-LSMs) subjected to both local and global synaptic plasticity mechanisms: spike-timing-dependent plasticity (STDP) and global plasticity (GP). This bio-inspired model offers the key advantage of enabling precise enumeration of attractors. Our theoretical and experimental results demonstrate that B-LSMs can exhibit remarkably rich attractor landscapes.

Our findings demonstrate that STDP alone is insufficient to drive a substantial expansion of a network's attractor regime. In most cases, local synaptic adjustments induced by unstructured inputs result in a collapse of the attractor dynamics. In contrast, global synaptic modifications enable a marked expansion of the attractor landscape of the networks. The association between global synaptic changes and specific trigger patterns can be interpreted as a form of learning or memory retrieval, whereby additional attractor states are (re)incorporated into the network's dynamics. Our results also indicate that networks can sustain high-dimensional attractor regimes, provided their inputs consistently guide them into specific attractor patterns rather than subjecting them to random, unstructured input.

This study is limited to small networks, as the sheer number of attractors in larger systems renders direct computation impractical. A promising direction for future research involves identifying computable networks' metrics capable of predicting their attractor regime, thereby enabling the systematic study of attractor dynamics in larger networks.

References

1. Cabessa, J., Villa, A.E.P.: An attractor-based complexity measurement for Boolean recurrent neural networks. PLoS ONE **9**(4), e94204+ (2014)
2. Caporale, N., Dan, Y.: Spike timing-dependent plasticity: a Hebbian learning rule. Annu. Rev. Neurosci. **31**, 25–46 (2008)
3. Demircigil, M., Heusel, J., Löwe, M., Upgang, S., Vermet, F.: On a model of associative memory with huge storage capacity. J. Stat. Phys. **168**(2), 288–299 (2017)
4. Fischer, A., Igel, C.: Training restricted Boltzmann machines: an introduction. Pattern Recogn. **47**(1), 25–39 (2014). https://doi.org/10.1016/j.patcog.2013.05.025,. https://www.sciencedirect.com/science/article/pii/S0031320313002495
5. Hinton, G.E., Sejnowski, T.J.: Optimal perceptual inference. In: Proceedings of the IEEE Conference on Computer Vision (1983)

6. Hopfield, J.J.: Neural networks and physical systems with emergent collective computational abilities. Proc. Natl. Acad. Sci. **79**(8), 2554–2558 (1982)
7. Iglesias, J., Eriksson, J., Pardo, B., Tomassini, M., Villa, A.E.P.: Stimulus-driven unsupervised synaptic pruning in large neural networks. In: De Gregorio, M., Di Maio, V., Frucci, M., Musio, C. (eds.) BVAI 2005. LNCS, vol. 3704, pp. 59–68. Springer, Heidelberg (2005). https://doi.org/10.1007/11565123_6
8. Jaeger, H.: The 'echo state' approach to analysing and training recurrent neural networks. Technical report, German National Research Center for Information Technology GMD Technical Report (2001)
9. Johnson, D.B.: Finding all the elementary circuits of a directed graph. SIAM J. Comput. **4**(1), 77–84 (1975). https://doi.org/10.1137/0204007
10. Khona, M., Fiete, I.R.: Attractor and integrator networks in the brain. Nat. Rev. Neurosci. **23**, 744–766 (2022). https://doi.org/10.1038/s41583-022-00642-0
11. Kleene, S.C.: Representation of events in nerve nets and finite automata. In: Shannon, C., McCarthy, J. (eds.) Automata Studies, pp. 3–41. Princeton University Press, Princeton (1956)
12. Krotov, D., Sompolinsky, H.: Dense associative memory for pattern recognition. In: Advances in Neural Information Processing Systems (NeurIPS 2016), pp. 1172–1180 (2016)
13. Lukosevicius, M., Jaeger, H.: Reservoir computing approaches to recurrent neural network training. Comput. Sci. Rev. **3**(3), 127–149 (2009). https://doi.org/10.1016/J.COSREV.2009.03.005
14. Maass, W., Natschläger, T., Markram, H.: Real-time computing without stable states: a new framework for neural computation based on perturbations. Neural Comput. **14**(11), 2531–2560 (2002)
15. McCulloch, W.S., Pitts, W.: A logical calculus of the ideas immanent in nervous activity. Bull. Math. Biophys. **5**, 115–133 (1943)
16. Minsky, M.L.: Computation: Finite and Infinite Machines. Prentice-Hall Inc., Englewood Cliffs (1967)
17. Ramsauer, H., et al.: Hopfield networks is all you need. arXiv preprint arXiv:2008.02217 (2020). https://arxiv.org/abs/2008.02217
18. Rolls, E.T.: Attractor networks. Wiley Interdiscip. Rev. Cogn. Sci. **1**(1), 119–134 (2010). https://doi.org/10.1002/wcs.3
19. Sompolinsky, H., Kanter, I.: Temporal association in asymmetric neural networks. Phys. Rev. Lett. **57**, 2861–2864 (1986). https://doi.org/10.1103/PhysRevLett.57.2861, https://link.aps.org/doi/10.1103/PhysRevLett.57.2861
20. Susman, L., Brenner, N., Barak, O.: Stable memory with unstable synapses. Nat. Commun. **10**(1), 4441 (2019). https://doi.org/10.1038/s41467-019-12306-2
21. Yazdanbakhsh, A., Babadi, B., Rouhani, S., Arabzadeh, E., Abbassian, A.: New attractor states for synchronous activity in synfire chains with excitatory and inhibitory coupling. Biol. Cybern. **86**(5), 367–78 (2002). https://doi.org/10.1007/s00422-001-0293-y

Correction to: ADMETrix: ADMET-Driven De Novo Molecular Generation

Nikolaos Mourdoukoutas, Aigli Korfiati, and Vassilis Pitsikalis

Correction to:
Chapter 3 in: W. Senn et al. (Eds.): *Artificial Neural Networks and Machine Learning*, **LNCS 16072, https://doi.org/10.1007/978-3-032-04552-2_3**

The book was published with a typo in Chapter 3. Specifically, the first name of the third co-author was misspelled; it was subsequently corrected from Vasilis to Vassilis.

The updated version of this chapter can be found at
https://doi.org/10.1007/978-3-032-04552-2_3

© The Author(s), under exclusive license to Springer Nature Switzerland AG 2026
W. Senn et al. (Eds.): ICANN 2025, LNCS 16072, p. C1, 2026.
https://doi.org/10.1007/978-3-032-04552-2_21

Abstracts from Workshops and Special Sessions

A Cost-Effective Deep-Learning Method for Extraction of Single and Multi-stage Organic Synthesis Procedures

Mantas Vaškevičius(✉) and Jurgita Kapočiūtė-Dzikienė

Vytautas Magnus University, Kaunas, Lithuania
mantas.vaskevicius@vdu.lt

Keywords: organic chemistry · deep learning · large language model · neural networks · data extraction

Vaškevičius One of the richest sources of chemical reactions is the US and European patent databases. M. D. Lowe pioneered the extraction of various organic chemical reactions from the USPTO database and produced one of the first open-source reaction procedure datasets in 2016 [1]. Such data is especially relevant to chemists, data analysts, and computer scientists working on chemical modeling [2]. In recent years, our research groups effort has led to the development of novel methods for extraction and standardization of even larger collections of chemical reaction procedure data. However, despite the formal structure of patents, the challenge of recognizing and denoting the boundaries of each individual reaction is still open. The main difficulties are as follows: (1) The boundaries of individual reaction descriptions are arbitrary, with only a small portion following consistent rules or templates. (2) Reaction lengths vary widely, ranging from a single sentence to multiple paragraphs and even pages in multi-stage reactions. As a result, traditional named entity recognition (NER) is not suitable, as it requires an extensive context window, leading to increased computational demand (3) While modern LLMs may be leveraged for extraction, the sheer volume of USTPO and EPO patents, approximately 766,000 documents with an average of 75 pages each, makes their application impractical.

The goal of this research is to overcome all these challenges by developing a highly efficient, scalable, and accurate deep-learning-based extraction methodology that can process massive patent databases at a fraction of the computational cost of conventional LLMs.
Our research presents the following contributions:

Cost-Effective and Scalable Deep-Learning-Based Extraction. We have developed a novel deep-learning-based methodology that effectively overcomes existing challenges, enabling efficient and affordable extraction of chemical patent data. Our approach achieves state-of-the-art performance through custom vectorization and multi-stage model fine-tuning techniques. The developed methods support both single and multi-stage reaction extraction, by employing two different models that classify headers and paragraphs into one of four groups: irrelevant, start, continuation, or end of reaction description.

High-Accuracy Classification for Reaction Extraction. We have tested classic methods, such as XGB embedding classifiers, a series of neural network architectures, such as simple LSTM and BiLSTM neural networks, BART, T5, FLAN-T5, and Llama 3.2 LORA [3, 4]. The top-performing models are based on the T5 architecture and have achieved accuracy scores of 97.1% (single reactions) and 97.5% (multi-stage).

Custom Vectorization for Improved Reaction Detection. One of the most significant findings is a vectorization technique that addresses the need for sufficient textual context around the paragraph being classified by including only small portions of text from previous and following paragraphs. The input text also includes a set number of previous predictions, enhancing the continuity of data extraction which enables the achievement of near-perfect scores.

Two-Stage Training with Knowledge Distillation. The models were trained in two stages, first, using large models on a small number of manually created datasets, and then fine-tuned on small models using a larger dataset generated by the large model (knowledge distillation technique). The smaller models achieve identical results and improve the runtime significantly, enabling the processing of reaction detection in a reasonable timeframe. On a single thread, top-performing models can process around 350 patents per hour, and when multiprocessing, around 1200 patents can be processed on a single consumer-grade GPU.

Open-Source Datasets and Models. We plan to share our findings with the research community by making datasets and models open-source along with the entire processed data from UPSTO and EPO for single and multi-stage reactions. This will enable researchers to use the largest open-source reaction procedure dataset for their studies, while the multi-stage reaction procedure description data will be the first-ever dataset released with no analogs.

In conclusion, our study introduces a highly efficient, scalable, and cost-effective deep-learning methodology for extracting single and multi-stage organic synthesis procedures from chemical patents, achieving state-of-the-art accuracy while significantly reducing computational costs. In the future, we plan to extend the methodology to enable extraction from scanned documents, such as old patents or chemical research papers. In addition, we hope that the insights in our study will be applicable to other areas of data extraction for chemical, genomic, or medical data.

Disclosure of Interests. The authors have no competing interests to declare that are relevant to the content of this article.

References

1. Vaucher, A.C., Zipoli, F., Geluykens, J., Nair, V.H., Schwaller, P., Laino, T.: Automated extraction of chemical synthesis actions from experimental procedures. Nat. Commun. **11**, 3601 (2020). https://doi.org/10.1038/s41467-020-17266-6
2. Kononova, O., He, T., Huo, H., Trewartha, A., Olivetti, E.A., Ceder, G.: Opportunities and challenges of text mining in materials research. iScience **24**, 3, 102155 (2021). https://doi.org/10.1016/j.isci.2021.102155
3. Raffel, C., et al.: Exploring the Limits of Transfer Learning with a Unified Text-to-Text Transformer. arXiv (2019). https://doi.org/10.48550/ARXIV.1910.10683
4. Grattafiori, A., et al.: The Llama 3 Herd of Models. arXiv (2024). https://doi.org/10.48550/ARXIV.2407.21783

MARCUS: A Multimodal AI Platform for Chemical Structure Extraction and Analysis from Scientific Literature

Kohulan Rajan[1], Viktor Weißenborn[1], Laurin Lederer[1], Achim Zielesny[2], and Christoph Steinbeck[1(✉)]

[1] Institute for Inorganic and Analytical Chemistry, Friedrich Schiller University Jena, Lessingstr. 8, 07743 Jena, Germany
christoph.steinbeck@uni-jena.de
[2] Institute for Bioinformatics and Chemoinformatics, Westphalian University of Applied Sciences, August-Schmidt-Ring 10, 45665 Recklinghausen, Germany

Keywords: Chemical structure extraction · Natural products · Optical chemical structure recognition · Machine learning · Cheminformatics · Drug discovery

Natural Products or secondary metabolites are essential in defence, regulation and communication in organisms and ecosystems. They are also crucial as leads for novel drug candidates. The time-consuming process of extracting and analysing chemical structures from scientific literature significantly hinders the documentation of existing natural products in open-access databases. Automating this process is, therefore, vital for accelerating drug discovery and unlocking the full potential of natural product research. Despite the large amount of information about chemical structures available in published papers as images and text metadata, most remains untapped due to the challenges in automatically recognising, extracting, and processing molecular structure information from PDF documents. This work introduces MARCUS (Molecular Annotation and Recognition for Curating Unravelled Structures). This platform processes both text and images of chemical structures from scientific documents using natural language processing, computer vision, and cheminformatics techniques.

MARCUS implements a modular architecture incorporating multiple open-source optical chemical structure recognition (OCSR) engines, including DECIMER [1], MolNexTR [2] and MolScribe [3]. This ensemble approach allows for cross-validation of extracted structures, significantly improving accuracy and reliability. The system facilitates the automated extraction of both textual information and chemical structures from PDF documents, converting visual representations into machine-readable formats such as SMILES and molfiles.

Text extraction in MARCUS is performed using Docling [4], after which the extracted content is formatted to suit our specific requirements. We manually annotated 100 articles from the Journal of Natural Products using the open-source Doccano [5] software, focusing on key entities such as compound trivial names, compound groups, compound classes, organism names, organism parts, IUPAC names, geographical locations, and abbreviations. This manually curated dataset was then used to fine-tune a GPT-4 model, which now automatically annotates these entities in a given paragraph.

Chemical structures are extracted from PDFs using the DECIMER segmentation algorithm. Users can select which segments to process using OCSR engines. The selected segments are processed, and the predicted structures are immediately visualised. If there are uncertainties, users can compare predictions across multiple OCSR engines to ensure accuracy.

A key improvement in MARCUS is its comparison framework for structure recognition results. By incorporating similarity analysis and maximum common substructure [6] identification, the system enables researchers to visualise agreements and differences between predictions from different engines. This is crucial for establishing confidence in extracted structures, especially for complex or degraded images common in scientific literature. Preliminary results show that the ensemble approach significantly improves structure recognition accuracy compared to single-engine methods, particularly for challenging cases with poor image quality or complex molecular structures.

By making MARCUS completely open source, we contribute to the field of chemical data extraction by automating the process of knowledge extraction from scientific literature and generating machine-readable representations suitable for further research. By making the vast chemical knowledge in published literature more accessible, MARCUS accelerates the drug discovery pipeline and supports data-driven decision-making in pharmaceutical research.

Future development efforts are currently focused on fine-tuning a local large language model (LLM) to improve the accuracy of text annotation, automatically identify and exclude non-chemical structure segments, and optimise model performance to reduce processing times significantly.

References

1. Rajan, K., Brinkhaus, H.O., Agea, M.I., Zielesny, A., Steinbeck, C.: DECIMER.ai: an open platform for automated optical chemical structure identification, segmentation and recognition in scientific publications. Nat. Commun. **14**, 5045 (2023)
2. Chen, Y., Leung, C.T., Huang, Y., Sun, J., Chen, H., Gao, H.: MolNexTR: a generalized deep learning model for molecular image recognition. J. Cheminform. **16**, 141 (2024). https://doi.org/10.1186/s13321-024-00926-w
3. Qian, Y., Guo, J., Tu, Z., Li, Z., Coley, C.W., Barzilay, R.: MolScribe: robust molecular structure recognition with image-to-graph generation. J. Chem. Inf. Model. **63**, 1925–1934 (2023)
4. Auer, C., Lysak, M., Nassar, A., et al.: Docling Technical Report (2024)
5. GitHub - doccano/doccano: Open source annotation tool for machine learning practitioners. https://github.com/doccano/doccano. Accessed 15 Apr 2025
6. Dalke, A., Hastings, J.: FMCS: a novel algorithm for the multiple MCS problem. J. Cheminform. **5**, 1 (2013)

Interpreting Graph Neural Networks with Myerson Values for Cheminformatics Approaches

Samuel K. R. Homberg[1], Malte L. Modlich[2], Marlon Becker[2], Janosch Menke[1], Garrett M. Morris[3], Benjamin Risse[2], and Oliver Koch[1(✉)]

[1] Institute of Medicinal and Pharmaceutical Chemistry, University of Münster, Münster, Germany
{samuel.homberg,janosch.menke,oliver.koch}@uni-muenster.de
[2] Institute for Geoinformatics and Faculty of Mathematics and Computer Science, University of Münster, Münster, Germany
{malte.modlich,marlon.becker,benjamin.risse}@uni-muenster.de
[3] Department of Statistics, University of Oxford, Oxford, UK
garrett.morris@stats.ox.ac.uk

Keywords: Explainable AI · Graph Neural Networks

Graph neural networks (GNNs) are a natural choice to process chemical data, due to their inherent ability to handle arbitrary input topologies. They avoid the need to convert molecules into molecular fingerprints with a fixed vector length by directly processing the molecular graph. However, like most deep learning models, GNNs are not intrinsically interpretable and common explainability methods fail because of the variable input size. We introduce a novel method to interpret the predictions of GNNs based on Myerson values from cooperative game theory [1].

By using Myerson values as explanations for GNNs, a numerical contribution to the network prediction is obtained for each node in the input graph, which can be easily mapped to the corresponding molecular structure as a node heatmap (see Fig. 1).

Myerson values are closely related to Shapley values [2] but instead of every player being able to interact with every other player, the players interactions are restricted by a graph structure. Shapley values have been adapted into SHAP values [3], an agnostic and popular method of explaining machine learning models. However, simply applying SHAP to GNNs has proven to be challenging because of their varying graph size. In addition we can operate directly on the graphs node features and thus do not need SHAPs local approximation step. Our approach treats a GNN as a coalition game and the nodes of the input graph as the game's players. The Myerson value of a node then determines the contribution to the prediction of the model, with only connected nodes contributing to coalitions. The values of all nodes add up to the predicted value of the model,

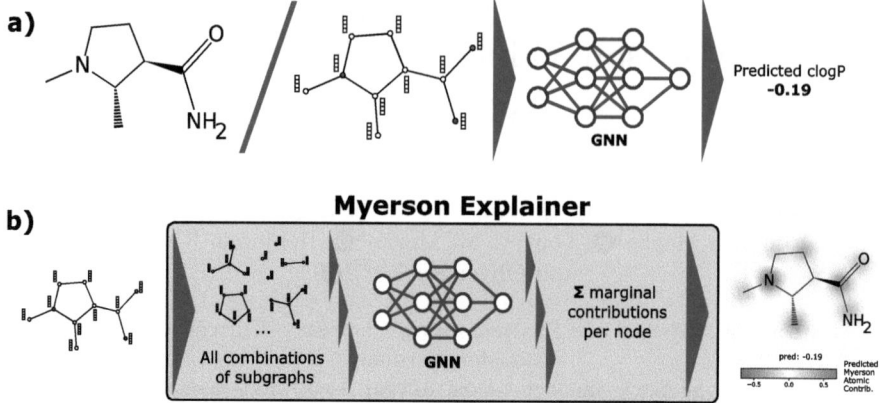

Fig. 1. **a)** Predicting clogP (computed logarithmic octanol-water coefficient) from the molecular graph. **b)** Explaining the prediction using Myerson values. For each node in the graph, the marginal contributions each node makes to the prediction on each possible subgraph are calculated.

allowing for a simple and intuitive interpretation of the prediction, especially in the case of regression tasks.

However, due to the evaluation of the contribution of each node to all possible combinations of $N \in \mathbb{N}$ nodes, the computational demand grows exponentially with the graph size with time complexity in $\mathcal{O}(2^N)$, increased to $\mathcal{O}(N \cdot 2^N)$ if calculating for all nodes. Thus, a naive calculation of the Myerson values becomes computationally infeasible for large graphs. We circumvent this problem by implementing an efficient and accurate approximation technique using Monte Carlo sampling to uniformly and unbiasedly sample permutations of subgraphs. We developed our proposed explanation technique for applications in cheminformatics and drug discovery, but it can also be used in any application that uses GNNs for graph prediction tasks.

The effectiveness of our approach is validated through successful applications to two proof-of-concept datasets (logP and molecular weight) and a real-world dataset featuring kinase inhibitors, highlighting its broad applicability and promise in explaining graph-based cheminformatic models. We also compare our method with a variety of other graph explainers featured in the GraphXAI package [4] such as GNNExplainer [5].

References

1. Myerson, R.B.: Graphs and cooperation in games. Math. Oper. Res. **2**(3), 225–229 (1977)
2. Shapley, L.S.: A value for n-person games. In: Annals of Mathematics Studies, pp. 307–318. Princeton University Press, Princeton (1953)
3. Lundberg, S.M., Lee, S.-I.: A unified approach to interpreting model predictions. In: Advances in Neural Information Processing Systems (2017)

4. Agarwal, C., Queen, O., Lakkaraju, H., Zitnik, M.: Evaluating explainability for graph neural networks. Sci. Data **10**, 144 (2023)
5. Ying, R., Bourgeois, D., You, J., Zitnik, M., Leskovec, J.: GNNExplainer: generating explanations for graph neural networks. In: Advances in Neural Information Processing Systems (2019)

Protein Content-Based Microbial Representations Improve Predictions of Antimicrobial Activity

Roberto Olayo-Alarcon[1,2(✉)], Daniele Pugno[1,2], and Christian L. Müller[1,2,3]

[1] Department of Statistics, Ludwig-Maximilians-Universität München, Munich, Germany
roberto.olayo@lmu.de
[2] Institute of Computational Biology, Helmholtz Zentrum München, Munich, Germany
[3] Center for Computational Mathematics, Flatiron Institute, New York, USA

Abstract. Deep learning-assisted strategies have enabled the identification of novel antimicrobial compounds with broad-spectrum activity. While these discoveries hold great value, targeted therapies that are effective against specific pathogens and have minimal impact on commensal microbes remain a key objective in the fight against antibiotic resistance. Here, we address this challenge by developing and evaluating proteome-based representations of bacterial species. We find that these representations enable species-resolved predictions of a compound's growth-inhibiting activity. In particular, microbial representations based on the presence of homologous protein groups enable generalizable predictions for unseen compound-microbe pairs. These microbe-specific predictions more accurately recapitulate findings from large-scale chemical screens involving compounds and bacterial pathogens not encountered during model training. We envision that this framework can facilitate the development of targeted therapies.

Keywords: Microbe representations · Antimicrobials · Proteome

1 Proteome-Based Representations of Bacterial Species

In order to predict the growth-inhibitory activity of a compound against any microbe of interest, a representation that captures key biological features and that can be created for a large number of species is needed. To provide such a representation, we developed two general frameworks that leverage the information contained in a microbe's proteome and do not require any prior functional annotations. Specifically, we construct representations for the 40 bacterial strains present in [4]:

1. Representations based on protein clusters: The amino acid sequences of all 40 bacterial species are grouped into distinct protein clusters either by

MMSeqs2's linclust algorithm [8] or by applying strict alignment quality cutoffs typical of **homology** searches [6]. Each microbe is represented as a binary vector, indicating the presence or absence of a protein in a given cluster.
2. Representations based on pre-trained embeddings of protein sequences: We gathered the pre-trained ESM2 [3] representation for all protein sequences encoded by an individual microbe. The resulting matrix is decomposed via SVD, with the first SVD component representing the microbe. We employ the **ESM2-650M** and **ESM2-3B** models.

To evaluate their utility for microbe-specific predictions of antimicrobial activity, we concatenated the microbe representation with one of three possible molecular representations: 1) ECFP4 [7], 2) tabular Chemical Descriptors [1], or 3) MolE [5]. This concatenated input is fed to an XGBoost model that predicts the probability that a given compound will inhibit the growth of the specified microbe. We evaluated three scenarios to create training, validation, and testing sets: 1) New compounds: the data is split based on molecular scaffolds, 2) New microbes: each split contains strains from different phyla, and 3) New interactions: where a combination of scaffold and phyla splitting is used. Models are evaluated based on the area under the precision-recall curve (PRC-AUC).

2 Microbe-Specific Predictions of Antimicrobial Activity

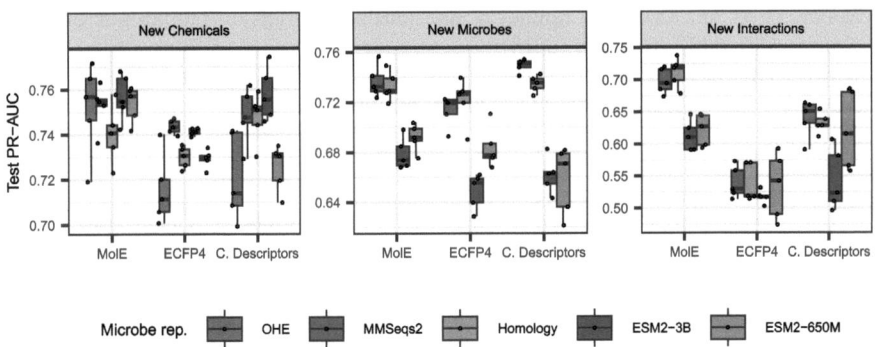

Fig. 1. Test set PRC-AUC, from models using different combinations of molecular and microbe representations.

We observed that incorporating our described microbial representations improved the predictions of growth inhibition compared to the baseline one-hot-encoding (OHE) of microbial species (Fig. 1, New chemicals). Moreover, representations based on protein clustering led to the greatest performance when making predictions for unseen microbes (Fig. 1, New Microbes). Finally, the MolE

+ `Homology` performed best when predicting the outcome for unseen compound-microbe pairs (Fig. 1, New Interactions).

We further assessed the ability of this strategy by evaluating its ability to recapitulate the findings from an orthogonal dataset [2], where an unseen microbe (*Salmonella enterica*) is screened against unseen compounds. We found that the microbe-specific scores from `MolE + Homology` lead to improved predictive performance (PRC-AUC: 0.45) compared to the Gram-negative-specific (PRC-AUC: 0.41) and general (PRC-AUC: 0.38) Antimicrobial Potential scores as described in [5]. Taken together, these results indicate that incorporating microbial information improves the accuracy of predictions of a compound's antimicrobial activity. Such species-resolved predictions can increase the rate at which targeted therapies are developed.

Disclosure of Interests. The authors have no competing interests to declare that are relevant to the content of this article.

References

1. Algavi, Y.M., Borenstein, E.: A data-driven approach for predicting the impact of drugs on the human microbiome. Nat. Commun. **14**(1), 3614 (2023). https://doi.org/10.1038/s41467-023-39264-0
2. Feldl, M., et al.: Statistical end-to-end analysis of large-scale microbial growth data with DGrowthR. bioRxiv, pp. 2025–03 (2025)
3. Lin, Z., et al.: Evolutionary-scale prediction of atomic-level protein structure with a language model. Science **379**(6637), 1123–1130 (2023)
4. Maier, L., et al.: Extensive impact of non-antibiotic drugs on human gut bacteria. Nature **555**(7698), 623–628 (2018)
5. Olayo-Alarcon, R., et al.: Pre-trained molecular representations enable antimicrobial discovery. Nat. Commun. **16**(1), 3420 (2025). https://doi.org/10.1038/s41467-025-58804-4
6. Pearson, W.R.: An introduction to sequence similarity ("homology") searching. Curr. Protoc. Bioinform. **42**(1), 1–3 (2013)
7. Rogers, D., Hahn, M.: Extended-connectivity fingerprints. J. Chem. Inf. Model. **50**(5), 742–754 (2010)
8. Steinegger, M., Söding, J.: MMseqs2 enables sensitive protein sequence searching for the analysis of massive data sets. Nat. Biotechnol. **35**(11), 1026–1028 (2017). https://doi.org/10.1038/nbt.3988

Guided Molecular Generation Through Logical Constraints

Emma Meneghini, Paolo Frazzetto$^{(\boxtimes)}$, and Nicolò Navarin

Department of Mathematics "Tullio Levi-Civita", University of Padua, Via Trieste 63, 35121 Padua, Italy
emma.meneghini@studenti.unipd.it,
{paolo.frazzetto,nicolo.navarin}@unipd.it

Motivation. Score-based diffusion models are top-performing for generating complex graphs such as molecules. However, existing conditional methods support only simple conjunctions, limiting the range of enforceable constraints. Many real-world rules—such as Lipinski's Rule of Five—are more complex, involving cardinality conditions (e.g., "at least three of four properties"). We test whether diffusion models can satisfy constraints while preserving diversity and quality. As a case study, we use Lipinski's rule, given its prominence in drug discovery and its formulation based on physicochemical thresholds.

Method. Building on the discrete denoising diffusion model DiGress [1], parameterised by θ, and its classifier guidance mechanism, we cast rule satisfaction as a Bernoulli event defined by a formula in full Disjunctive Normal Form (DNF). For a generic cardinality constraint "at least k out of K properties hold", and under the conditional independence assumption, the satisfaction probability of a noisy graph G_t factorises as

$$p_{\text{rule}}(G_t) = \sum_{\substack{S \subseteq \{1,\ldots,K\} \\ |S| \geq k}} \left(\prod_{i \in S} p_i \right) \left(\prod_{j \notin S} (1 - p_j) \right), \quad (1)$$

where $p_i = \mathbb{P}(X_i = 1 \mid G_t)$ is estimated by a lightweight predictor parameterised by η. During sampling, we maximise a KL-regularised objective that exponentiates a utility function, yielding a closed-form adjusted kernel

$$G_{t-1} \sim p_\theta(G_{t-1} \mid G_t) \exp(\lambda \langle \nabla_{G_t} \log p_{\text{rule},\eta}, G_{t-1} \rangle)$$

seamlessly plugging into the reverse chain. Adopting a rigorous probabilistic approach enables precise guidance for each individual condition in the rule, rather than treating the overall constraint as a black box.

Results. On the GuacaMol benchmark [2], we compare the conditional DiGress baseline—a pure conjunction—to our guided sampler on 5 000 molecules, showing that our method boosts Lipinski's Rule of Five satisfaction while optimizing a simple, easy-to-tune objective that yields statistically different pharmacokinetic distributions—measured both as binary thresholds and continuous values via Chi-squared and MMD tests. Unlike the baseline, which sharply peaks at full rule satisfaction, our approach also preserves all 3-of-4 combinations among the top frequency modes. An ablation on the guidance strength λ confirms that validity remains high under constraint enforcement. Our approach remains closer to the training distribution than the baseline, as reflected by higher FCD and KL scores, while preserving Tanimoto diversity both within and relative to the training set. These results demonstrate that logical guidance preserves validity and structural diversity while enabling meaningful shifts in molecular properties.

Impact and Conclusion. Our method supports *de novo* drug discovery by generating molecules under complex pharmacokinetic constraints. More generally, it enables graph generation with logical constraints beyond biochemistry. Any DNF-expressible condition with a tractable approximation can guide sampling without retraining, making a single model adaptable across domains.

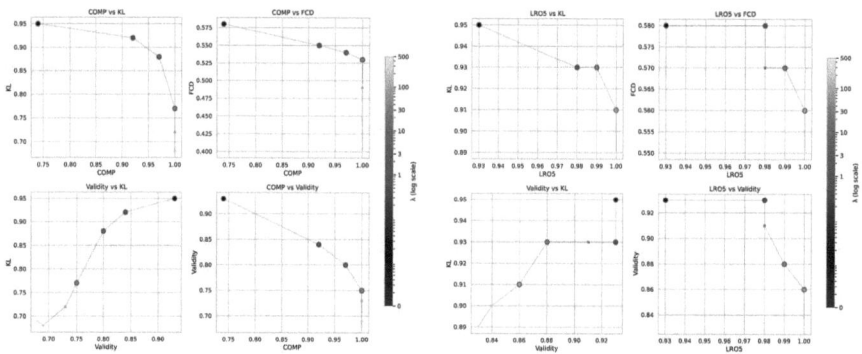

(a) A strict conjunction over all four properties.

(b) The Lipinski's Rule of Five (at least 3 of 4 rules satisfied).

Fig. 1. Trade-offs between compliance, distributional similarity (KL, FCD), and validity across guidance strengths λ (colour-coded, log scale). Red-circled points mark the Pareto frontier. (Color figure online)

Acknowledgments. We acknowledge the support of the project "Future AI Research (FAIR) - Spoke 2 Integrative AI - Symbolic conditioning of Graph Generative Models (SymboliG)" funded by the European Union under the National Recovery and Resilience Plan (NRRP), Mission 4 Component 2 Investment 1.3 - Call for tender No. 341 of March 15, 2022 of Italian Ministry of University and Research NextGenerationEU, Code PE0000013, Concession Decree No. 1555 of October 11, 2022 CUP C63C22000770006.

Disclosure of Interests. The authors have no competing interests to declare that are relevant to the content of this article.

References

1. Vignac, C., Brown, N., et al.: DiGress: discrete denoising diffusion for graph generation. In: Proceedings of the 11th International Conference on Learning Representations (ICLR), pp. 1–10 (2023)
2. Brown, N., et al.: GuacaMol: benchmarking models for de novo molecular design. J. Chem. Inf. Model. **59**(5), 1063–1077 (2019)

Towards an Investigation of Over-Squashing in Temporal Graph Neural Networks

Domenico Tortorella[(✉)] and Alessio Micheli

Department of Computer Science, University of Pisa, Largo B. Pontecorvo, 3, 56127 Pisa, Italy
{domenico.tortorella,alessio.micheli}@unipi.it

Abstract. Temporal Graph Neural Networks are models that address learning tasks on temporal graphs, that represent relationships between entities that evolve through time. This class of models is based on a temporal version of message-passing, carrying on as a consequence the same issues that non-temporal GNNs have to face. We outline the problem of over-squashing in TGNNs, pointing out directions of future investigation.

Keywords: Temporal Graphs · Spatio-Temporal Convolution · Graph Neural Networks

Temporal Graph Neural Networks (TGNNs) are specialized models designed to process dynamic graph data where both the structure of the graph and its node or edge features evolve over time. Common TGNNs follow a temporal version of message-passing [3], which obtains node representations by combining node input features $\mathbf{x}_t(v)$ and a convolution over temporal neighbors $\mathcal{N}_t(v)$:

$$\mathbf{h}_t(v) = \text{COMBINE}\left(\mathbf{x}_t(v), \mathbf{h}_{t-1}(v), \text{AGGREGATE}\left(\{\mathbf{h}_{t-1}(v') : v' \in \mathcal{N}_t(v)\}\right)\right) \quad (1)$$

Equation (1) can be interpreted as a state transition function $\mathbf{h}_t = F(\mathbf{x}_t, \mathbf{h}_{t-1})$ in the context of dynamical systems. In [4], it has been demonstrated that such function must be contractive (i.e., $\|\nabla_\mathbf{h} F\| < 1$). Indeed, this is a consequence of the *temporal* nature of TGNNs: this constraint ensures the Markovianity of the representation space, and that the $\mathbf{h}_t$ are useful to discriminate according to input suffixes [2].

Over-Squashing in the Temporal Setting. In purely spatial GNNs, repeated message-passing (MP) steps can lead to *over-squashing* [1], i.e. the inability to encode in node representation an increasingly large receptive field. This poses a limit on the number of MP layers that a GNN can have before leading to indistinguishable representations. However, TGNNs must necessarily perform as many temporal MPs as the number of time-steps T. Over-squashing can be quantified via the sensitivity $\left\|\frac{\partial \mathbf{h}_{t+\tau}(v)}{\partial \mathbf{x}_t(v)}\right\|$ of node representations to past inputs.

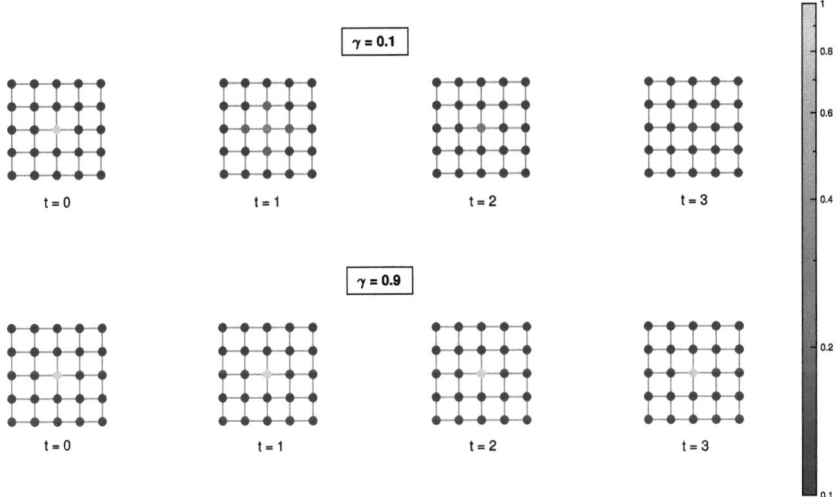

Fig. 1. Evolution of input sensitivity after 3 steps of spatio-temporal diffusion.

In Fig. 1, we analyze a simple linear version of the temporal MP of Eq. (1), which performs a form of spatio-temporal diffusion:

$$\mathbf{h}_t(v) = \mathbf{x}_t(v) + \gamma \, \mathbf{h}_{t-1}(v) + (1-\gamma)\frac{1}{|\mathcal{N}_t(v)|} \sum_{v' \in \mathcal{N}_t(v)} \mathbf{h}_{t-1}(v') \qquad (2)$$

Equation (2) is parameterized by $\gamma \in [0,1]$ and satisfies contractivity. The amount of spatial diffusion is regulated by γ: (a) for $\gamma \to 0$, the information is propagated to neighboring nodes, but input sensitivity is lost extremely fast through time; (b) for $\gamma \to 1$, no spatial diffusion is performed, the input sensitivity lasts longer through time but no information is passed to the neighbors.

Directions of Investigation. The example presented in Fig. 1 illustrates the trade-off that over-squashing forces TGNNs to face: it may be impossible to leverage both spatial and temporal long-range interactions. This is a strong hint to investigate the precise nature of the intrinsic limitations of TGNNs, and whether they can be overcome by going beyond message-passing altogether. We can leverage the tools developed in the over-squashing literature to help us in this endeavor.

Acknowledgements. Research partly supported by: PNRR, PE00000013, "FAIR - Future Artificial Intelligence Research", Spoke 1, funded by European Commission under NextGeneration EU programme; Project DEEP-GRAPH, funded by the Italian Ministry of University and Research, PRIN 2022 (project code: 2022YLRBTT, CUP: I53C24002440006); Project PAN-HUB, funded by the Italian Ministry of Health (POS 2014–2020, project ID: T4-AN-07, CUP: I53C22001300001).

References

1. Alon, U., Yahav, E.: On the bottleneck of graph neural networks and its practical implications. In: Proceedings of the 9th International Conference on Learning Representations (2021). https://openreview.net/forum?id=i80OPhOCVH2
2. Gallicchio, C., Micheli, A.: Architectural and Markovian factors of echo state networks. Neural Netw. **24**(5), 440–456 (2011). https://doi.org/10.1016/j.neunet.2011.02.002
3. Gravina, A., Bacciu, D.: Deep learning for dynamic graphs: models and benchmarks. IEEE Trans. Neural Netw. Learn. Syst. **35**(9), 11788–11801 (2024). https://doi.org/10.1109/tnnls.2024.3379735
4. Micheli, A., Tortorella, D.: Discrete-time dynamic graph echo state networks. Neurocomputing **496**, 85–95 (2022). https://doi.org/10.1016/j.neucom.2022.05.001

The Impact of Readout Strategies on the Memory Capacity of Reservoir Networks

Denis Kleyko[1,2(✉)] and Martin Nilsson[2]

[1] Örebro University, Örebro, Sweden
[2] RISE Research Institutes of Sweden, Kista, Sweden
denis.kleyko@ri.se

Deep reservoir networks have demonstrated superior short-term memory capacity (MC) compared to shallow ones [1]. This is shown using least squares (LS) to compute readout matrices. However, LS is not always feasible, e.g., in streaming scenarios or with large reservoirs. We, therefore, evaluate MC in shallow (Fig. 1**A**) and deep (Fig. 1**B**) reservoir networks using six alternative readout strategies. Our results show that stochastic gradient descent (SGD) matches LS performance in shallow networks, but underperforms in deep ones. Local readouts trained on subpopulations of reservoir neurons generally yield lower MC than LS or SGD readouts trained on the entire reservoir.

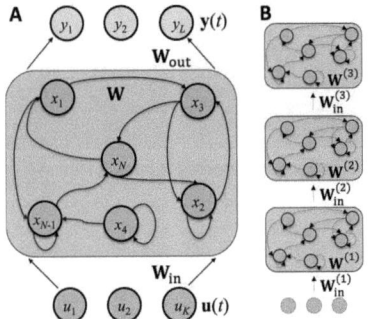

Fig. 1. Architectures of shallow (**A**) and deep (**B**) reservoir networks. Deep network stacks several reservoir layers together.

Though, performance of local readouts improves when trained on residuals of the training signal in a greedy, successive approximation manner.

MC is computed following the standard procedure from [2] using a univariate input signal $u(t)$ sampled uniformly from $[-0.8, 0.8]$. The signal spans $6,000$ time steps: $5,000$ for training and $1,000$ for testing. During testing, the task at each time step t is to reconstruct past inputs $k \in \mathbb{N} \mid k \geq 0$ steps ago: $y_k(t) = u(t-k)$. Network's MC is defined as: $\mathrm{MC} = \sum_{k=0}^{\infty} r^2\left(u(t-k), \hat{y}_k(t)\right)$, where $r^2(\cdot,\cdot)$ is the squared correlation coefficient. In our experiments, the maximum delay k was set to twice the number of reservoir neurons.

To isolate the impact of readout strategies, we investigate two reservoir network variants with distinct transition functions:

- shallow: $\mathbf{x}(t) = (1-\alpha)\mathbf{x}(t-1) + \alpha \tanh(\beta \mathbf{W}_{in}\mathbf{u}(t) + \gamma \mathbf{W}\mathbf{x}(t-1))$; and
- deep: $\mathbf{x}^{(l)}(t) = (1-\alpha)\mathbf{x}^{(l)}(t-1) + \alpha \tanh(\beta \mathbf{W}_{in}^{(l)}\mathbf{i}^{(l)}(t) + \gamma \mathbf{W}^{(l)}\mathbf{x}^{(l)}(t-1))$,

where α is the leaky integration parameter; β and γ scale input and recurrent feedback, respectively. $\mathbf{W}_{in}$ and $\mathbf{W}$ are the input and recurrent connectivity matrices. In deep networks, each layer l uses the same transition function. The input to layer l is $\mathbf{i}^{(l)}(t) = \mathbf{u}(t)$ for $l=1$ and $\mathbf{i}^{(l)}(t) = \mathbf{x}^{(l-1)}(t)$ for $l > 1$.

We evaluate six readout strategies in the MC experiments reported in Fig. 2, differing along two dimensions: learning algorithm (LS or SGD) and access to reservoir state information. In the baseline (global readout), a single readout (trained via LS or SGD) uses the full reservoir(s) state. Beyond this, we explore two local readout strategies with m non-overlapping subpopulations of reservoir(s) neurons ($m = l$ in the experiments). In the independent strategy, each of the m readouts is trained separately to predict a fraction of the training signal, i.e., $\frac{y(t)}{m}$. In the residual strategy, local readouts are trained sequentially: the first approximates the training signal while each subsequent readout approximates the residual error left unexplained by the previous ones.

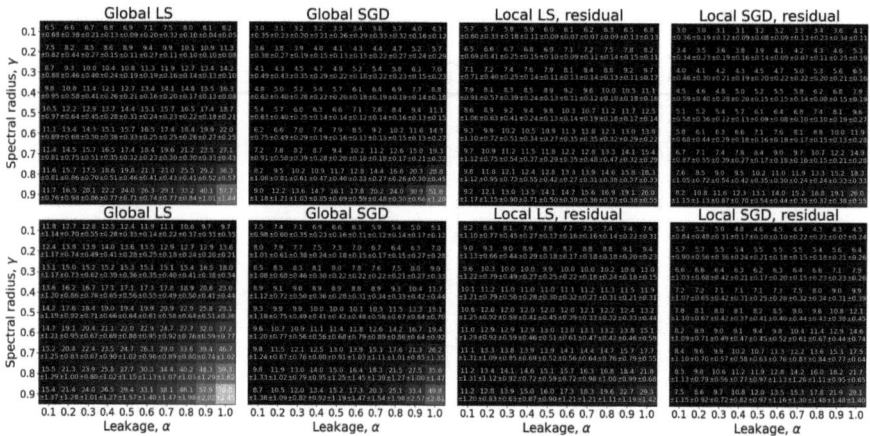

Fig. 2. Memory capacity of shallow (top row) and deep ($l = 10$, bottom row) networks across different α and γ values. Each column represents a distinct readout strategy. Results for independent local readouts are excluded due to space limitations. Cell values indicate the mean and standard deviation of MC over ten random network initializations.

The experiments in Fig. 2 follow the setup from [1] with shallow networks using $N = 100$ neurons and deep networks using $l = 10$ layers with 10 neurons each, (100 neurons in total); β is fixed at 0.1, while α and γ vary over $\{0.1, 0.2, \ldots, 1.0\}$ and $\{0.1, 0.2, \ldots, 0.9\}$, respectively. For SGD, we use scikit-learn's SGDRegressor with 200 epochs, default learning rate (0.01), and adaptive learning schedule.

The results in Fig. 2 confirm that deep reservoir networks exhibit higher MC when using the global LS readout (1st column). While the global SGD readouts (2nd column) still favor deep networks, the performance gap narrows noticeably. Local readouts cause a substantial drop in MC across all settings, though deep networks consistently maintain a slight advantage over shallow ones. In the local setting, LS and SGD yield comparable MC. The most notable observation is that the residual strategy (3rd & 4th columns) consistently outperforms independent local readouts (omitted from Fig. 2), highlighting the benefit of cooperative training via the greedy successive approximation of the training signal.

Acknowledgments. This work was supported by the AFOSR under award number FA8655-25-1-7007.

References

1. Gallicchio, C., Micheli, A., Pedrelli, L.: Deep reservoir computing: a critical experimental analysis. Neurocomputing **268**, 87–99 (2017)
2. Jaeger, H.: Short term memory in echo state networks. Technical report, GMD Forschungszentrum Informationstechnik (2001)

ResLens: A Visualisation, Optimisation and Descriptive Toolkit for Designing Deep Echo State Networks

Robert Clarke(✉)

University of Bath, Bath, UK
robertclarke813@yahoo.co.uk

Abstract. Reservoir Computing (RC) has emerged as a powerful paradigm for temporal information processing, with Echo State Networks (ESNs) emerging as a promising neuromorphic architecture. Given the proliferation of variants described in the literature (clustered, connectome-informed, cycle-based, community-structured, etc.) this creates implementation and optimisation of these networks daunting. ResLens bridges this gap by implementing a wide variety of reservoir connectivity types, while making their dynamics visible and actionable. It visualises network topologies and weight matrices, employs manifold learning to uncover essential low dimensional manifolds, and applies dynamical systems metrics, such as Lyapunov exponents, Procrustes and Trajectory tangling to provide quantitative insight into these networks and their differences. ResLens further integrates explainable AI to connect dynamics with prediction outcomes, and uses Bayesian optimisation to efficiently navigate the hyperparameter space of each of these networks. By putting all of these techniques in one package, ResLens empowers the development and exploration of novel deep and hierarchical ESN architectures.

Keywords: Echo State Networks · Reservoir Computing · Network Visualisation · Manifold Learning · Dynamical Systems · Bayesian Optimisation · Explainable AI · Deep ESN

1 Visualisation Components

ResLens provides comprehensive visualisation tools for examining network structure and dynamics. It renders neurons and their connections as graphs, displays connection strength distributions via weight matrix heat maps, and shows dynamic activity to reveal information flow and the temporal evolution of reservoir states.

2 Dimensionality Reduction

This software makes use of advanced manifold learning techniques (such as stepwise PCA and t-SNE) to uncover lower dimensional state spaces that govern reservoir behaviour. These reduced spaces make complex transformations interpretable and furnish meaningful features for downstream tasks. Interactive plots expose clusters, trajectories, and attractors, providing insight into how ESN architectures encode information.

3 Dynamical Systems Analysis

ResLens implements a variety of metrics to characterise reservoir behaviour. Lyapunov exponents quantify chaos at both layer and network levels, revealing how sensitivity to initial conditions affects processing. Beyond these chaos indicators, ResLens also measures a variety of other metrics, such as geometric alignment between layersusing principal-angle (Grassmann) distances and GromovWasserstein alongside fading-memory curves and Fisher information profiles. These allow users the ability to trace how each reservoir stage bends or straightens the low-dimensional manifolds that encode inputs quantify and track how long past inputs continue to influence current states, providing an empirical handle on short- and long-term dynamics.

4 Explainable AI Integration

The framework links reservoir states to predictions, allowing ESN behaviour to become more transparent. Visual tools illustrate how reservoirs transform inputs, highlighting influential components. For deep ESNs, ResLens shows the progressive abstraction across layers, supplying another descriptor for comparison.

5 Optimisation Capabilities

Given the array of ESNs which can be used, creating homogeneous or heterogeneous multi ESN networks creates a challenging parameter space. To this end, ResLens employs Bayesian optimization to explore this space efficiently, while benchmarking modules to objectively compare configurations on standard tasks such as chaotic timeseries prediction and signal reconstruction.

6 ESN Architectures

A novelty of ResLens is that it unifies a spectrum of ESN variants such traditional sparse, clustered, cycle-based and community structured reservoirs amongst many others into a single package. These can be used as modules or subunits to build deep or hierarchical echo state network chains, with user-defined input and output patterns. In doing so, this toolkit simplifies the creation and exploration of novel deep networks with ease.

Author Index

A
Achten, Sonny 55
Alcaide, Eric 34
Ali, Hassan 85
Allgeuer, Philipp 85, 98
Antonj, Matilde 124

B
Baccheschi, Corrado 188
Beketov, Maxim 29
Belanche-Muñoz, Lluís 163
Bison, Anna 201
Bondielli, Alessandro 188

C
Cabessa, Jérémie 213
Ceni, Andrea 176
Cevher, Volkan 55
Cibula, Miroslav 149
Clasmeier, Lennart 98

D
de Carvalho, Paulo Victor Rorigues 111

E
Engkvist, Ola 42

F
Farkaš, Igor 124, 136
Fetzel, Simon 69

G
Gäde, Connor 98, 136
Gajdošech, Lukáš 85
Gallicchio, Claudio 176
Gansterer, Wilfried N. 69
Gao, Zhifeng 34
Gavura, Juraj 136
Godin, Guillaume 45

H
Habekost, Jan-Gerrit 98
Hornáčková, Hana 124

J
Jablonka, Kevin M. 45

K
Kabeshov, Mikhail 42
Ke, Guolin 34
Kerzel, Matthias 149
Kireev, Dmitri 5
Korfiati, Aigli 17
Kriege, Nils M. 69
Krüger, Fabian P. 42
Kummer, Lorenz 69

L
Lagomarsini, Giacomo 176
Lenci, Alessandro 188
Li, Yaqi 34
Lúčny, Andrej 124

M
Maier, Andreas 163
Malinovská, Kristína 149
Mazzola, Carlo 124
Micheli, Alessio 188
Mirza, Adrian 45
Mourdoukoutas, Nikolaos 17
Moustafa, Samir 69
Müller, Luca 85

N
Nedjah, Nadia 111

O
Op de Beeck, Zander 55
Österbacka, Nicklas 42

P

Passaro, Lucia 188
Patiny, Luc 45
Pitsikalis, Vassilis 17
Podda, Marco 188

R

Rajan, Kohulan 8
Ramos, Joelmir 111

S

Smolyar, Ivan 29
Sperduti, Alessandro 201
Steinbeck, Christoph 8
Suykens, Johan A. K. 55
Sycheva, Tatiana 29

T

Tetko, Igor V. 45
Tetko, Igor 42
Tonin, Francesco 55
Tortorella, Domenico 188

V

Vavrečka, Michal 136
Villa, Alessandro E. P. 213

W

Weber, Franziska 163
Wermter, Stefan 85, 98

Z

Zhang, Linfeng 34
Zheng, Hang 34
Zhou, Gengmo 34
Zielesny, Achim 8

MIX
Papier aus verantwortungsvollen Quellen
Paper from responsible sources
FSC® C105338

If you have any concerns about our products,
you can contact us on
ProductSafety@springernature.com

In case Publisher is established outside the EU,
the EU authorized representative is:
**Springer Nature Customer Service Center GmbH
Europaplatz 3, 69115 Heidelberg, Germany**

Printed by Libri Plureos GmbH
in Hamburg, Germany